THE HARVARD CLASSICS

The Five-Foot Shelf of Books

Martin Luther at the Diet of Worms, 1521

THE HARVARD CLASSICS
EDITED BY CHARLES W. ELIOT, LL.D.

The Prince
By Niccolo Machiavelli

Utopia
By Sir Thomas More

Ninety-Five Theses
ADDRESS TO THE GERMAN NOBILITY
CONCERNING CHRISTIAN LIBERTY

By Martin Luther

With Introductions and Notes
Volume 36

P. F. Collier & Son Company
NEW YORK

CONTENTS

INTRODUCTORY NOTE

NICCOLO MACHIAVELLI, one of the most brilliant and versatile intellects of the Italian Renaissance, was born at Florence, May 3, 1469. He entered the public service as a young man, and between 1500 and 1512 he was employed in a number of diplomatic missions to the other Italian cities, to France, and to Germany. When the Medici returned to power in Florence in 1512, Machiavelli lost his positions, and suffered imprisonment and torture. On his release in the following year, he retired to the country and devoted himself to study and the composition of his most famous work, "The Prince." Other writings followed; and in the last year of his life we find him again in active life, this time as a soldier. He died June 21, 1527.

A more detailed account of Machiavelli, by Lord Macaulay, will be found in the volume of "English Essays" in the Harvard Classics.

Machiavelli's aim in "The Prince" has been very variously interpreted. His motive was probably mainly patriotic; but the exclusion of moral considerations in his treatment of politics led, even in his own century, to his name's becoming a synonym for all that is diabolical in public and private policy. Whatever may be the relation of the methods expounded in "The Prince" to his personal ideals, the book remains a most vivid and suggestive picture of political conditions in the Italy of the Renaissance.

Machiavelli's "Discourses on Livy's Decades" deals on a larger scale with many of the topics of "The Prince"; his "Art of War" elaborates his views on the military side; and his "History of Florence," his "Life of Castruccio Castracani," and his comedy, "Mandragola," are characteristic products of an accomplished man of letters who one time was diplomat and soldier, at another historian, poet, and dramatist. Few men represent so thoroughly the extraordinary versatility of that wonderful age.

"Of all Machiavelli's writings," says Garnett, " 'The Prince' is the most famous, and deservedly, for it is the most characteristic. Few subjects of literary discussion have occasioned more controversy than the purpose of this celebrated book. Some have beheld in it a manual for tyrants, like the memoirs of Tiberius, so diligently perused by Domitian; others have regarded it as a refined irony upon tyranny, on the sarcastic plan of Swift's Directions to Servants, if so humble an analogy be permissible. From various points of view it might alternately pass for either, but its purpose is accurately conveyed by neither interpretation. Machiavelli was a sincere though too supple a republican, and by no means desired the universal prevalence of tyranny throughout Italy. . . . His aim probably was to show how to build up a principality capable of expelling the foreigner and restoring the independence of Italy. But this intention could not be safely expressed, and hence his work seems repulsive, because the reason of state which he propounds as an apology for infringing the moral code appears not patriotic, but purely selfish. . . . With all his faults and oversights, nothing can deprive Machiavelli of the glory of having been the modern Aristotle in politics, the first, or at least the first considerable writer who derived a practical philosophy from history, and exalted statecraft into science."

DEDICATION

To the Magnificent Lorenzo Di Piero De' Medici

It is customary for such as seek a Prince's favour, to present themselves before him with those things of theirs which they themselves most value, or in which they perceive him chiefly to delight. Accordingly, we often see horses, armour, cloth of gold, precious stones, and the like costly gifts, offered to Princes as worthy of their greatness. Desiring in like manner to approach your Magnificence with some token of my devotion, I have found among my possessions none that I so much prize and esteem as a knowledge of the actions of great men, acquired in the course of a long experience of modern affairs and a continual study of antiquity. Which knowledge most carefully and patiently pondered over and sifted by me, and now reduced into this little book, I send to your Magnificence. And though I deem the work unworthy of your greatness, yet am I bold enough to hope that your courtesy will dispose you to accept it, considering that I can offer you no better gift than the means of mastering in a very brief time, all that in the course of so many years, and at the cost of so many hardships and dangers, I have learned, and know.

This work I have not adorned or amplified with rounded periods, swelling and high-flown language, or any other of those extrinsic attractions and allurements wherewith many authors are wont to set off and grace their writings; since it is my desire that it should either pass wholly unhonoured, or that the truth of its matter and the importance of its subject should alone recommend it.

Nor would I have it thought presumption that a person of very mean and humble station should venture to discourse and lay down rules concerning the government of Princes. For as those who make maps of countries place themselves low down in the plains to study the character of mountains and elevated lands, and place themselves high up on the mountains to get a better view of the plains, so in like manner to understand the People a man should be a Prince, and to have a clear notion of Princes he should belong to the People.

Let your Magnificence, then, accept this little gift in the spirit in which I offer it; wherein, if you diligently read and study it, you will recognize

5

my extreme desire that you should attain to that eminence which Fortune and your own merits promise you. Should you from the height of your greatness some time turn your eyes to these humble regions, you will become aware how undeservedly I have to endure the keen and unremitting malignity of Fortune.

NICCOLO MACHIAVELLI

CHAPTER I

Of the Various Kinds of Princedom,
and of the Ways In Which They Are Acquired

ALL the States and Governments by which men are or ever have been ruled, have been and are either Republics or Princedoms. Princedoms are either hereditary, in which the sovereignty is derived through an ancient line of ancestors, or they are new. New Princedoms are either wholly new, as that of Milan to Francesco Sforza; or they are like limbs joined on to the hereditary possessions of the Prince who acquires them, as the Kingdom of Naples to the dominions of the King of Spain. The States thus acquired have either been used to live under a Prince or have been free; and he who acquires them does so either by his own arms or by the arms of others, and either by good fortune or by merit.

CHAPTER II

Of Hereditary Princedoms

Of Republics I shall not now speak, having elsewhere spoken of them at length. Here I shall treat exclusively of Princedoms, and, filling in the outline above traced out, shall proceed to examine how such States are to be governed and maintained.

I say, then, that hereditary States, accustomed to the family of their Prince, are maintained with far less difficulty than new States, since all that is required is that the Prince shall not depart from the usages of his ancestors, trusting for the rest to deal with events as they arise. So that if an hereditary Prince be of average address, he will always maintain himself in his Princedom, unless deprived of it by some extraordinary and irresistible force; and even if so deprived will recover it, should any, even the least, mishap overtake the usurper. We have in Italy an example of this in the Duke of Ferrara, who never could have withstood the attacks of the Venetians in 1484, nor those of Pope Julius in 1510, had not his authority in that State been consolidated by time. For since a Prince by birth has fewer occasions and less need to give offence, he ought to be better loved, and will naturally be popular with his subjects unless outrageous vices make him odious. Moreover, the very antiquity and continuance of his rule will efface the memories and causes which lead to innovation. For one change always leaves a dovetail into which another will fit.

CHAPTER III

Of Mixed Princedoms

But in new Princedoms difficulties abound. And, first, if the Princedom be not wholly new, but joined on to the ancient dominions of the Prince, so as to form with them what may be termed a mixed Princedom, changes will come from a cause common to all new States, namely, that men, thinking to better their condition, are always ready to change masters, and in this expectation will take up arms against any ruler; wherein they deceive themselves, and find afterwards by experience that they are worse off than before. This again results naturally and necessarily from the circumstance that the Prince cannot avoid giving offence to his new subjects, either in respect of the troops he quarters on them, or of some other of the numberless vexations attendant on a new acquisition. And in this way you may find that you have enemies in all those whom you have injured in seizing the Princedom, yet cannot keep the friendship of those who helped you to gain it; since you can neither reward them as they expect, nor yet, being under obligations to them, use violent remedies against them. For however strong you may be in respect of your army, it is essential that in entering a new Province you should have the good will of its inhabitants.

Hence it happened that Louis XII of France, speedily gaining possession of Milan, as speedily lost it; and that on the occasion of its first capture, Lodovico Sforza was able with his own forces only to take it from him. For the very people who had opened the gates to the French King, when they found themselves deceived in their expectations and hopes of future benefits, could not put up with the insolence of their new ruler. True it is that when a State rebels and is again got under, it will not afterwards be lost so easily. For the Prince, using the rebellion as a pretext, will not scruple to secure himself by punishing the guilty, bringing the suspected to trial, and otherwise strengthening his position in the points where it was weak. So that if to recover Milan from the French it was enough on the first occasion that a Duke Lodovico should raise alarms on the frontiers to wrest it from them a second time the whole world had to be ranged against them, and their armies destroyed and driven out of Italy. And this for the reasons above assigned. And yet, for a second time, Milan was lost to the King. The general causes of its first loss have been shown. It remains to note the causes of the second, and to point out the remedies which the French King had, or which might have been used by another in like circumstances to maintain his conquest more successfully than he did.

I say, then, that those States which upon their acquisition are joined on to the ancient dominions of the Prince who acquires them, are either of the same Province and tongue as the people of these dominions, or they are not. When they are, there is a great ease in retaining them, especially when they have not been accustomed to live in freedom. To hold them securely it is enough to have rooted out the line of the reigning Prince; because if in other respects the old condition of things be continued, and there be no discordance in their customs, men live peaceably with one another, as we see to have been the case in Brittany, Burgundy, Gascony, and Normandy, which have so long been united to France. For although there be some slight difference in their languages, their customs are similar, and they can easily get on together. He, therefore, who acquires such a State, if he mean to keep it, must see to two things; first, that the blood of the ancient line of Princes be destroyed; second, that no change be made in respect of laws or taxes; for in this way the newly acquired State speedily becomes incorporated with the hereditary.

But when States are acquired in a country differing in language, usages, and laws, difficulties multiply, and great good fortune, as well as address, is needed to overcome them. One of the best and most efficacious methods for dealing with such a State, is for the Prince who acquires it to go and dwell there in person, since this will tend to make his tenure more secure and lasting. This course has been followed by the Turk with regard to Greece, who, had he not, in addition to all his other precautions for securing that Province, himself come to live in it, could never have kept his hold of it. For when you are on the spot, disorders are detected in their beginnings and remedies can be readily applied; but when you are at a distance, they are not heard of until they have gathered strength and the case is past cure. Moreover, the Province in which you take up your abode is not pillaged by your officers; the people are pleased to have a ready recourse to their Prince; and have all the more reason if they are well disposed, to love, if disaffected, to fear him. A foreign enemy desiring to attack that State would be cautious how he did so. In short, where the Prince resides in person, it will be extremely difficult to oust him.

Another excellent expedient is to send colonies into one or two places, so that these may become, as it were, the keys of the Province; for you must either do this, or else keep up a numerous force of men-at-arms and foot soldiers. A Prince need not spend much on colonies. He can send them out and support them at little or no charge to himself, and the only persons to whom he gives offence are those whom he deprives of their fields and houses to bestow them on the new inhabitants. Those who are thus injured form but a small part of the community, and remaining scattered and poor can never become dangerous. All others being left unmolested, are in consequence easily quieted, and at the same time are afraid to make a false move, lest they share the fate of those who have been deprived of their possessions. In few words, these colonies cost less than soldiers, are more faithful, and give less offence, while those who are offended, being, as I have said, poor and dispersed, cannot hurt. And let it here be noted that men are either to be kindly treated, or utterly crushed, since they can revenge lighter injuries, but not graver. Wherefore the injury we do to a man should be of a sort to leave no fear of reprisals.

But if instead of colonies you send troops, the cost is vastly greater, and the whole revenues of the country are spent in guarding it; so that the gain becomes a loss, and much deeper offence is given; since in shifting the quarters of your soldiers from place to place the whole country suffers hardship, which as all feel, all are made enemies; and enemies who remaining, although vanquished, in their own homes, have power to hurt. In every way, therefore, this mode of defence is as disadvantageous as that by colonizing is useful.

The Prince who establishes himself in a Province whose laws and language differ from those of his own people, ought also to make himself the head and protector of his feebler neighbours, and endeavour to weaken the stronger, and must see that by no accident shall any other stranger as powerful as himself find an entrance there. For it will always happen that some such person will be called in by those of the Province who are discontented either through ambition or fear; as we see of old the Romans brought into Greece by the Aetolians, and in every other country that they entered, invited there by its inhabitants. And the usual course of things is that so soon as a formidable stranger enters a Province, all the weaker powers side with him, moved thereto by the ill-will they bear towards him who has hitherto kept them in subjection. So that in respect of these lesser powers, no trouble is needed to gain them over, for at once, together, and of their own accord, they throw in their lot with the government of the stranger. The new Prince, therefore, has only to see that they do not increase too much in strength, and with his own forces, aided by their good will, can easily subdue any who are powerful, so as to remain supreme in the Province. He who does not manage this matter well, will soon lose whatever he has gained, and while he retains it will find in it endless troubles and annoyances.

In dealing with the countries of which they took possession the Romans diligently followed the methods I have described. They planted colonies, conciliated weaker powers without adding to their strength, humbled the great, and never suffered a formidable stranger to acquire influence. A single example will suffice to show this. In Greece the Romans took the Achaians and Aetolians into their pay; the Macedonian monarchy was humbled; Antiochus was driven out. But the services of the Achaians and Aetolians never obtained for them any addition to their power; no persuasions on the part of Philip could induce the Romans to be his friends on the condition of sparing him humiliation; nor could all the power of Antiochus bring them to consent to his exercising any authority within that Province. And in thus acting the Romans did as all wise rulers should, who have to consider not only present difficulties but also future, against which they must use all diligence to provide; for these, if they be foreseen while yet remote, admit of easy remedy, but if their approach be awaited, are already past cure, the disorder having become hopeless; realizing what the physicians tell us of hectic fever, that in its beginning it is easy to cure, but hard to recognize; whereas, after a time, not having been detected and treated at the first, it becomes easy to recognize but impossible to cure.

And so it is with State affairs. For the distempers of a State being discovered while yet inchoate, which can only be done by a sagacious ruler, may easily be dealt with; but when, from not being observed, they are suffered to grow until they are obvious to every one, there is no longer any remedy. The Romans, therefore, foreseeing evils while they were yet far off, always provided against them, and never suffered them to take their course for the sake of avoiding war; since they knew that war is not so to be avoided, but is only postponed to the advantage of the other side. They chose, therefore, to make war with Philip and Antiochus in Greece, that they might not have to make it with them in Italy, although for a while they might have escaped both. This they did not desire, nor did the maxim *leave it to Time,* which the wise men of our own day have always on their lips, ever recommend itself to them. What they looked to enjoy were the fruits of their own valour and foresight. For Time, driving all things before it, may bring with it evil as well as good.

But let us now go back to France and examine whether she has followed any of those methods of which I have made mention. I shall speak of Louis and not of Charles, because from the former having held longer possession of Italy, his manner of acting is more

plainly seen. You will find, then, that he has done the direct opposite of what he should have done in order to retain a foreign State.

King Louis was brought into Italy by the ambition of the Venetians, who hoped by his coming to gain for themselves a half of
the State of Lombardy. I will not blame this coming, nor the part
taken by the King, because, desiring to gain a footing in Italy, where
he had no friends, but on the contrary, owing to the conduct of
Charles, every door was shut against him, he was driven to accept
such friendships as he could get. And his designs might easily
have succeeded had he not made mistakes in other particulars of
conduct.

By the recovery of Lombardy, Louis at once regained the credit
which Charles had lost. Genoa made submission; the Florentines
came to terms; the Marquis of Mantua, the Duke of Ferrara, the
Bentivogli, the Countess of Forli, the Lords of Faenza, Pesaro,
Rimini, Camerino, and Piombino, the citizens of Lucca, Pisa, and
Siena, all came forward offering their friendship. The Venetians,
who to obtain possession of a couple of towns in Lombardy had
made the French King master of two-thirds of Italy, had now cause
to repent the rash game they had played.

Let any one, therefore, consider how easily King Louis might have
maintained his authority in Italy had he observed the rules which I
have noted above, and secured and protected all those friends of his,
who being weak, and fearful, some of the Church, some of the
Venetians, were of necessity obliged to attach themselves to him, and
with whose assistance, for they were many, he might readily have
made himself safe against any other powerful State. But no sooner
was he in Milan than he took a contrary course, in helping Pope
Alexander to occupy Romagna; not perceiving that in seconding
this enterprise he weakened himself by alienating friends and those
who had thrown themselves into his arms, while he strengthened
the Church by adding great temporal power to the spiritual power
which of itself confers so mighty an authority. Making this first mistake, he was forced to follow it up, until at last, in order to curb the
ambition of Pope Alexander, and prevent him becoming master of
Tuscany, he was obliged to come himself into Italy.

And as though it were not enough for him to have aggrandized the Church and stripped himself of friends, he must needs in his desire to possess the Kingdom of Naples, divide it with the King of Spain; thus bringing into Italy, where before he had been supreme, a rival to whom the ambitious and discontented in that Province might have recourse. And whereas he might have left in Naples a King willing to hold as his tributary, he displaced him to make way for another strong enough to effect his expulsion. The wish to acquire is no doubt a natural and common sentiment, and when men attempt things within their power, they will always be praised rather than blamed. But when they persist in attempts that are beyond their power, mishaps and blame ensue. If France, therefore, with her own forces could have attacked Naples, she should have done so. If she could not, she ought not to have divided it. And if her partition of Lombardy with the Venetians may be excused as the means whereby a footing was gained in Italy, this other partition is to be condemned as not justified by the like necessity.

Louis, then, had made these five blunders. He had destroyed weaker States, he had strengthened a Prince already strong, he had brought into the country a very powerful stranger, he had not come to reside, and he had not sent colonies. And yet all these blunders might not have proved disastrous to him while he lived, had he not added to them a sixth in depriving the Venetians of their dominions. For had he neither aggrandized the Church, nor brought Spain into Italy, it might have been at once reasonable and necessary to humble the Venetians; but after committing himself to these other courses, he should never have consented to the ruin of Venice. For while the Venetians were powerful they would always have kept others back from an attempt on Lombardy, as well because they never would have agreed to that enterprise on any terms save of themselves being made its masters, as because others would never have desired to take it from France in order to hand it over to them, nor would ever have ventured to defy both. And if it be said that King Louis ceded Romagna to Alexander, and Naples to Spain in order to avoid war, I answer that for the reasons already given, you ought never to suffer your designs to be crossed in order to avoid war, since war is not so to be avoided, but is only deferred to your disadvantage. And if others should allege the King's promise to the Pope to undertake that enterprise on his behalf, in return for the dissolution of his marriage, and for the Cardinal's hat conferred on d'Amboise, I answer by referring to what I say further on concerning the faith of Princes and how it is to be kept.

King Louis, therefore, lost Lombardy from not following any one of the methods pursued by others who have taken Provinces with the resolve to keep them. Nor is this anything strange, but only what might reasonably and naturally be looked for. And on this very subject I spoke to d'Amboise at Nantes, at the time when Duke Valentino, as Cesare Borgia, son to Pope Alexander, was vulgarly called, was occupying Romagna. For, on the Cardinal saying to me that the Italians did not understand war, I answered that the French did not understand statecraft, for had they done so, they never would have allowed the Church to grow so powerful. And the event shows that the aggrandizement of the Church and of Spain in Italy has been brought about by France, and that the ruin of France has been wrought by them. Whence we may draw the general axiom, which never or rarely errs, that *he who is the cause of another's greatness is himself undone,* since he must work either by address or force, each of which excites distrust in the person raised to power.

CHAPTER IV

WHY THE KINGDOM OF DARIUS, CONQUERED BY ALEXANDER, DID NOT, ON ALEXANDER'S DEATH, REBEL AGAINST HIS SUCCESSORS

ALEXANDER the Great having achieved the conquest of Asia in a few years, and dying before he had well entered on possession, it might have been expected, having regard to the difficulty of preserving newly acquired States, that on his death the whole country would rise in revolt. Nevertheless, his successors were able to keep their hold, and found in doing so no other difficulty than arose from their own ambition and mutual jealousies.

If any one think this strange and ask the cause, I answer, that all the Princedoms of which we have record have been governed in one or other of two ways, either by a sole Prince, all others being his servants permitted by his grace and favour to assist in governing the kingdom as his ministers; or else, by a Prince with his Barons who hold their rank, not by the favour of a superior Lord, but by antiquity of blood, and who have States and subjects of their own who recognize them as their rulers and entertain for them a natural affection. States governed by a sole Prince and by his servants vest in him a more complete authority; because throughout the land none but he is recognized as sovereign, and if obedience be yielded to any others, it is yielded as to his ministers and officers for whom personally no special love is felt.

Of these two forms of government we have examples in our own days in the Turk and the King of France. The whole Turkish empire is governed by a sole Prince, all others being his slaves. Dividing his kingdom into *sandjaks,* he sends thither different governors whom he shifts and changes at his pleasure. The King of France, on the other hand, is surrounded by a multitude of nobles of ancient descent, each acknowledged and loved by subjects of his own, and each asserting a precedence in rank of which the King can deprive him only at his peril.

He, therefore, who considers the different character of these two States, will perceive that it would be difficult to gain possession of that of the Turk, but that once won it might be easily held. The obstacles to its conquest are that the invader cannot be called in by a native nobility, nor expect his enterprise to be aided by the defection of those whom the sovereign has around him. And this for the various reasons already given, namely, that all being slaves and under obligations they are not easily corrupted, or if corrupted can render little assistance, being unable, as I have already explained, to carry the people with them. Whoever, therefore, attacks the Turk must reckon on finding a united people, and must trust rather to his own strength than to divisions on the other side. But were his adversary once overcome and defeated in the field, so that he could not repair his armies, no cause for anxiety would remain, except in the family of the Prince; which being extirpated, there would be none else to fear; for since all beside are without credit with the people, the invader, as before his victory he had nothing to hope from them, so after it has nothing to dread.

But the contrary is the case in kingdoms governed like that of

France, into which, because men who are discontented and desirous of change are always to be found, you may readily procure an entrance by gaining over some Baron of the Realm. Such persons, for the reasons already given, are able to open the way to you for the invasion of their country and to render its conquest easy. But afterwards the effort to hold your ground involves you in endless difficulties, as well in respect of those who have helped you, as of those whom you have overthrown. Nor will it be enough to have destroyed the family of the Prince, since all those other Lords remain to put themselves at the head of new movements; whom being unable either to content or to destroy, you lose the State whenever occasion serves them.

Now, if you examine the nature of the government of Darius, you will find that it resembled that of the Turk, and, consequently, that it was necessary for Alexander, first of all, to defeat him utterly and strip him of his dominions; after which defeat, Darius having died, the country, for the causes above explained, was permanently secured to Alexander. And had his successors continued united they might have enjoyed it undisturbed, since there arose no disorders in that kingdom save those of their own creating.

But kingdoms ordered like that of France cannot be retained with the same ease. Hence the repeated risings of Spain, Gaul, and Greece against the Romans, resulting from the number of small Princedoms of which these Provinces were made up. For while the memory of these lasted, the Romans could never think their tenure safe. But when that memory was worn out by the authority and long continuance of their rule, they gained a secure hold, and were able afterwards in their contests among themselves, each to carry with him some portion of these Provinces, according as each had acquired influence there; for these, on the extinction of the line of their old Princes, came to recognize no other Lords than the Romans.

Bearing all this in mind, no one need wonder at the ease wherewith Alexander was able to lay a firm hold on Asia, nor that Pyrrhus and many others found difficulty in preserving other acquisitions; since this arose, not from the less or greater merit of the conquerors, but from the different character of the States with which they had to deal.

CHAPTER V

How Cities or Provinces Which Before Their Acquisition Have Lived Under Their Own Laws Are To Be Governed

When a newly acquired State has been accustomed, as I have said, to live under its own laws and in freedom, there are three methods whereby it may be held. The first is to destroy it; the second, to go and reside there in person; the third, to suffer it to live on under its own laws, subjecting it to a tribute, and entrusting its government to a few of the inhabitants who will keep the rest your friends. Such a Government, since it is the creature of the new Prince, will see that it cannot stand without his protection and support, and must therefore do all it can to maintain him; and a city accustomed to live in freedom, if it is to be preserved at all, is more easily controlled through its own citizens than in any other way.

We have examples of all these methods in the histories of the Spartans and the Romans. The Spartans held Athens and Thebes by creating oligarchies in these cities, yet lost them in the end. The Romans, to retain Capua, Carthage, and Numantia, destroyed them and never lost them. On the other hand, when they thought to hold Greece as the Spartans had held it, leaving it its freedom and allowing it to be governed by its own laws, they failed, and had to destroy many cities of that Province before they could secure it. For, in truth, there is no sure way of holding other than by destroying, and whoever becomes master of a City accustomed to live in freedom and does not destroy it, may reckon on being destroyed by it. For if it should rebel, it can always screen itself under the name of liberty and its ancient laws, which no length of time, nor any benefits conferred will ever cause it to forget; and do what you will, and take what care you may, unless the inhabitants be scattered and dispersed, this name, and the old order of things, will never cease to be remembered, but will at once be turned against you whenever misfortune overtakes you, as when Pisa rose against the Florentines after a hundred years of servitude.

If, however, the newly acquired City or Province has been accustomed to live under a Prince, and his line is extinguished, it will be impossible for the citizens, used, on the one hand, to obey, and deprived, on the other, of their old ruler, to agree to choose a leader from among themselves; and as they know not how to live as freemen, and are therefore slow to take up arms, a stranger may readily gain them over and attach them to his cause. But in Republics there is a stronger vitality, a fiercer hatred, a keener thirst for revenge. The memory of their former freedom will not let them rest; so that the safest course is either to destroy them, or to go and live in them.

CHAPTER VI

Of New Princedoms Which a Prince Acquires With His Own Arms and by Merit

Let no man marvel if in what I am about to say concerning Princedoms wholly new, both as regards the Prince and the form of Government, I cite the highest examples. For since men for the most part follow in the footsteps and imitate the actions of others, and yet are unable to adhere exactly to those paths which others have taken, or attain to the virtues of those whom they would resemble, the wise man should always follow the roads that have been trodden by the great, and imitate those who have most excelled, so that if he cannot reach their perfection, he may at least acquire something of its savour. Acting in this like the skilful archer, who seeing that the object he would hit is distant, and knowing the range of his bow, takes aim much above the destined mark; not designing that his arrow should strike so high, but that flying high it may alight at the point intended.

I say, then, that in entirely new Princedoms where the Prince himself is new, the difficulty of maintaining possession varies with the greater or less ability of him who acquires possession. And, because the mere fact of a private person rising to be a Prince presupposes either merit or good fortune, it will be seen that the presence of one or other of these two conditions lessens, to some extent, many difficulties. And yet, he who is less beholden to Fortune has often in the end the better success; and it may be for the advantage of a Prince that, from his having no other territories, he is obliged to reside in person in the State which he has acquired.

Looking first to those who have become Princes by their merit and not by their good fortune, I say that the most excellent among them are Moses, Cyrus, Romulus, Theseus, and the like. And though perhaps I ought not to name Moses, he being merely an instrument for carrying out the Divine commands, he is still to be admired for those qualities which made him worthy to converse with God. But if we consider Cyrus and the others who have acquired or founded kingdoms, they will all be seen to be admirable. And if their actions and the particular institutions of which they were the authors be studied, they will be found not to differ from those of Moses, instructed though he was by so great a teacher. Moreover, on examining their lives and actions, we shall see that they were debtors to Fortune for nothing beyond the opportunity which enabled them to shape things as they pleased, without which the force of their spirit would have been spent in vain; as on the other hand, opportunity would have offered itself in vain, had the capacity for turning it to account been wanting. It was necessary, therefore, that Moses should find the children of Israel in bondage in Egypt, and oppressed by the Egyptians, in order that they might be disposed to follow him, and so escape from their servitude. It was fortunate for Romulus that he found no home in Alba, but was exposed at the time of his birth, to the end that he might become king and founder of the City of Rome. It was necessary that Cyrus should find the Persians discontented with the rule of the Medes, and the Medes enervated and effeminate from a prolonged peace. Nor could Theseus have displayed his great qualities had he not found the Athenians disunited and dispersed. But while it was their opportunities that made these men fortunate, it was their own merit that enabled them to recognize these opportunities and turn them to account, to the glory and prosperity of their country.

They who come to the Princedom, as these did, by virtuous paths, acquire with difficulty, but keep with ease. The difficulties which they have in acquiring arise mainly from the new laws and institutions which they are forced to introduce in founding and securing their government. And let it be noted that there is no more delicate matter to take in hand, nor more dangerous to conduct, nor more doubtful in its success, than to set up as a leader in the introduction of changes. For he who innovates will have for his enemies all those who are well off under the existing order of things, and only lukewarm supporters in those who might be better off under the new. This lukewarm temper arises partly from the fear of adversaries who have the laws on their side, and partly from the incredulity of mankind, who will never admit the merit of anything new, until they have seen it proved by the event. The result, however, is that whenever the enemies of change make an attack, they do so with all the zeal of partisans, while the others defend themselves so feebly as to endanger both themselves and their cause.

But to get a clearer understanding of this part of our subject, we must look whether these innovators can stand alone, or whether they depend for aid upon others; in other words, whether to carry out their ends they must resort to entreaty, or can prevail by force. In the former case they always fare badly and bring nothing to a successful issue; but when they depend upon their own resources and can employ force, they seldom fail. Hence it comes that all armed Prophets have been victorious, and all unarmed Prophets have been destroyed.

For, besides what has been said, it should be borne in mind that the temper of the multitude is fickle, and that while it is easy to persuade them of a thing, it is hard to fix them in that persuasion. Wherefore, matters should be so ordered that when men no longer believe of their own accord, they may be compelled to believe by force. Moses, Cyrus, Theseus, and Romulus could never have made their ordinances be observed for any length of time had they been unarmed, as was the case, in our own days, with the Friar Girolamo Savonarola, whose new institutions came to nothing so soon as the multitude began to waver in their faith; since he had not the means to keep those who had been believers steadfast in their belief, or to make unbelievers believe.

Such persons, therefore, have great difficulty in carrying out their designs; but all their difficulties are on the road, and may be overcome by courage. Having conquered these, and coming to be held in reverence, and having destroyed all who were jealous of their influence, they remain powerful, safe, honoured, and prosperous.

To the great examples cited above, I would add one other, of less note indeed, but assuredly bearing some proportion to them, and which may stand for all others of a like character. I mean the example of Hiero the Syracusan. He from a private station rose to be Prince of Syracuse, and he too was indebted to Fortune only for his opportunity. For the Syracusans being oppressed, chose him to be their Captain, which office he so discharged as deservedly to be made their King. For even while a private citizen his merit was so remarkable, that one who writes of him says, he lacked nothing that a King should have save the Kingdom. Doing away with the old army, he organized a new, abandoned existing alliances and assumed new allies, and with an army and allies of his own, was able on that foundation to build what superstructure he pleased; having trouble enough in acquiring, but none in preserving what he had acquired.

CHAPTER VII

OF NEW PRINCEDOMS ACQUIRED BY THE AID OF OTHERS AND BY GOOD FORTUNE

THEY who from a private station become Princes by mere good fortune, do so with little trouble, but have much trouble to maintain themselves. They meet with no hindrance on their way, being carried as it were on wings to their destination, but all their difficulties overtake them when they alight. Of this class are those on whom States are conferred either in return for money, or through the favour of him who confers them; as it happened to many in the Greek cities of Ionia and the Hellespont to be made Princes by Darius, that they might hold these cities for his security and glory; and as happened in the case of those Emperors who, from privacy, attained the Imperial dignity by corrupting the army. Such Princes are wholly dependent on the favour and fortunes of those who have made them great, than which supports none could be less stable or secure; and they lack both the knowledge and the power that would enable them to maintain their position. They lack the knowledge, because unless they have great parts and force of character, it is not to be expected that having always lived in a private station they should have learned how to command. They lack the power, since they cannot look for support from attached and faithful troops. Moreover, States suddenly acquired, like all else that is produced and that grows up rapidly, can never have such root or hold as that the first storm which strikes them shall not overthrow them; unless, indeed, as I have said already, they who thus suddenly become Princes have a capacity for learning quickly how to defend what Fortune has placed in their lap, and can lay those foundations after they rise which by others are laid before.

Of each of these methods of becoming a Prince, namely, by merit and by good fortune, I shall select an instance from times within my own recollection, and shall take the cases of Francesco Sforza and Cesare Borgia. By suitable measures and singular ability, Francesco Sforza rose from privacy to be Duke of Milan, preserving with little trouble what it cost him infinite efforts to gain. On the other hand, Cesare Borgia, vulgarly spoken of as Duke Valentino, obtained his Princedom through the favourable fortunes of his father, and with these lost it, although, so far as in him lay, he used every effort and practised every expedient that a prudent and able man should, who desires to strike root in a State given him by the arms and fortune of another. For, as I have already said, he who does not lay his foundations at first, may, if he be of great parts, succeed in laying them afterwards, though with inconvenience to the builder and risk to the building. And if we consider the various measures taken by Duke Valentino, we shall perceive how broad were the foundations he had laid whereon to rest his future power.

These I think it not superfluous to examine, since I know not what lessons I could teach a new Prince, more useful than the example of his actions. And if the measures taken by him did not profit him in the end, it was through no fault of his, but from the extraordinary and extreme malignity of Fortune.

In his efforts to aggrandize the Duke his son, Alexander VI had to face many difficulties, both immediate and remote. In the first place, he saw no way to make him Lord of any State which was not a State of the Church, while, if he sought to take for him a State belonging to the Church, he knew that the Duke of Milan and the Venetians would withhold their consent; Faenza and Rimini being already under the protection of the latter. Further, he saw that the arms of Italy, and those more especially of which he might have availed himself, were in the hands of men who had reason to fear his aggrandizement, that is, of the Orsini, the Colonnesi, and their followers. These therefore he could not trust. It was consequently necessary that the existing order of things should be changed, and the States of Italy thrown into confusion, in order that he might safely make himself master of some part of them; and this became easy for him when he found that the Venetians, moved by other causes, were plotting to bring the French once more into Italy. This design he accordingly did not oppose, but furthered by annulling the first marriage of the French King.

King Louis therefore came into Italy at the instance of the Venetians, and with the consent of Pope Alexander, and no sooner was he in Milan than the Pope got troops from him to aid him in his enterprise against Romagna, which Province, moved by the reputation of the French arms, at once submitted. After thus obtaining possession of Romagna, and after quelling the Colonnesi, Duke Valentino was desirous to follow up and extend his conquests. Two causes, however, held him back, namely, the doubtful fidelity of his own forces, and the waywardness of France. For he feared that the Orsini, of whose arms he had made use, might fail him, and not merely prove a hindrance to further acquisitions, but take from him what he had gained, and that the King might serve him the same turn. How little he could count on the Orsini was made plain when, after the capture of Faenza, he turned his arms against Bologna, and saw how reluctantly they took part in that enterprise. The King's mind he understood, when, after seizing on the Dukedom of Urbino, he was about to attack Tuscany; from which design Louis compelled him to desist. Whereupon the Duke resolved to depend no longer on the arms or fortune of others. His first step, therefore, was to weaken the factions of the Orsini and Colonnesi in Rome. Those of their following who were of good birth, he gained over by making them his own gentlemen, assigning them a liberal provision, and conferring upon them commands and appointments suited to their rank; so that in a few months their old partisan attachments died out, and the hopes of all rested on the Duke alone.

He then awaited an occasion to crush the chiefs of the Orsini, for those of the house of Colonna he had already scattered, and a good opportunity presenting itself, he turned it to the best account. For when the Orsini came at last to see that the greatness of the Duke and the Church involved their ruin, they assembled a council at Magione in the Perugian territory, whence resulted the revolt of Urbino, commotions in Romagna, and an infinity of dangers to the Duke, all of which he overcame with the help of France. His credit thus restored, the Duke trusting no longer either to the French or to any other foreign aid, that he might not have to confront them openly, resorted to stratagem, and was so well able to dissemble his designs, that the Orsini, through the mediation of Signor Paolo (whom he failed not to secure by every friendly attention, furnishing him with clothes, money, and horses), were so won over as to be drawn in their simplicity into his hands at Sinigaglia. When the leaders were thus disposed of, and their followers made his friends, the Duke had laid sufficiently good foundations for his future power, since he held all Romagna together with the Dukedom of Urbino, and had ingratiated himself with the entire population of these States, who now began to see that they were well off.

And since this part of his conduct merits both attention and imitation, I shall not pass it over in silence. After the Duke had taken Romagna, finding that it had been ruled by feeble Lords, who thought more of plundering than correcting their subjects, and gave them more cause for division than for union, so that the country was overrun with robbery, tumult, and every kind of outrage, he judged it necessary, with a view to render it peaceful and obedient to his authority, to provide it with a good government. Accordingly he set over it Messer Remiro d'Orco, a stern and prompt ruler, who being entrusted with the fullest powers, in a very short time, and with much credit to himself, restored it to tranquillity and order. But afterwards apprehending that such unlimited authority might become odious, the Duke decided that it was no longer needed, and established in the centre of the Province a civil Tribunal, with an excellent President, in which every town was represented by its advocate. And knowing that past severities had generated ill-feeling against himself, in order to purge the minds of the people and gain their good-will, he sought to show them that any cruelty which had been done had not originated with him, but in the harsh disposition of his minister. Availing himself of the pretext which this afforded, he one morning caused Remiro to be beheaded, and exposed in the market place of Cesena with a block and bloody axe by his side. The barbarity of which spectacle at once astounded and satisfied the populace.

But, returning to the point whence we diverged, I say that the Duke, finding himself fairly strong and in a measure secured against present dangers, being furnished with arms of his own choosing and having to a great extent got rid of those which, if left near him, might have caused him trouble, had to consider, if he desired to follow up his conquests, how he was to deal with France, since he saw he could expect no further support from King Louis, whose eyes were at last opened to his mistake. He therefore began to look about for new alliances, and to waver in his adherence to the French, then occupied with their expedition into the kingdom of Naples against the Spaniards, at that time laying siege to Gaeta; his object being to secure himself against France; and in this he would soon have succeeded had Alexander lived.

Such was the line he took to meet present exigencies. As regards the future, he had to apprehend that a new Head of the Church might not be his friend, and might even seek to deprive him of what Alexander had given. This he thought to provide against in four ways. First, by exterminating all who were of kin to those Lords whom he had despoiled of their possessions, that they might not become instruments in the hands of a new Pope. Second, by gaining over all the Roman nobles, so as to be able with their help to put a bridle, as the saying is, in the Pope's mouth. Third, by bringing the College of Cardinals, so far as he could, under his control. And fourth, by establishing his authority so firmly before his father's death, as to be able by himself to withstand the shock of a first onset.

Of these measures, at the time when Alexander died, he had already effected three, and had almost carried out the fourth. For of the Lords whose possessions he had usurped, he had put to death all whom he could reach, and very few had escaped. He had gained over the Roman nobility, and had the majority in the College of Cardinals on his side.

As to further acquisitions, his design was to make himself master of Tuscany. He was already in possession of Perugia and Piombino, and had assumed the protectorship of Pisa, on which city he was about to spring; taking no heed of France, as indeed he no longer had occasion, since the French had been deprived of the kingdom of Naples by the Spaniards under circumstances which made it necessary for both nations to buy his friendship. Pisa taken, Lucca and Siena would soon have yielded, partly through jealousy of Florence, partly through fear, and the position of the Florentines must then have been desperate.

Had he therefore succeeded in these designs, as he was succeeding in that very year in which Alexander died, he would have won such power and reputation that he might afterwards have stood alone, relying on his own strength and resources, without being beholden to the power and fortune of others. But Alexander died five years from the time he first unsheathed the sword, leaving his son with the State of Romagna alone consolidated, with all the rest unsettled, between two powerful hostile armies, and sick almost to death. And yet such were the fire and courage of the Duke, he knew so well how men must either be conciliated or crushed, and so solid were the foundations he had laid in that brief period, that had these armies not been upon his back, or had he been in sound health, he must have surmounted every difficulty.

How strong his foundations were may be seen from this, that Romagna waited for him for more than a month; and that although half dead, he remained in safety in Rome, where though the Baglioni, the Vitelli, and the Orsini came to attack him, they met with no success. Moreover, since he was able if not to make whom he liked Pope, at least to prevent the election of any whom he disliked, had he been in health at the time when Alexander died, all would have been easy for him. But he told me himself on the day on which Julius II was created, that he had foreseen and provided for everything else that could happen on his father's death, but had never anticipated that when his father died he too should be at death's-door.

Taking all these actions of the Duke together, I can find no fault with him; nay, it seems to me reasonable to put him forward, as I have done, as a pattern for all such as rise to power by good fortune and the help of others. For with his great spirit and high aims he could not act otherwise than he did, and nothing but the shortness of his father's life and his own illness prevented the success of his designs. Whoever, therefore, on entering a new Princedom, judges it necessary to rid himself of enemies, to conciliate friends, to prevail by force or fraud, to make himself feared yet not hated by his subjects, respected and obeyed by his soldiers, to crush those who can or ought to injure him, to introduce changes in the old order of things, to be at once severe and affable, magnanimous and liberal, to do away with a mutinous army and create a new one, to maintain relations with Kings and Princes on such a footing that they must see it for their interest to aid him, and dangerous to offend, can find no brighter example than in the actions of this Prince.

The one thing for which he may be blamed was the creation of Pope Julius II, in respect of whom he chose badly. Because, as I have said already, though he could not secure the election he desired, he could have prevented any other; and he ought never to have consented to the creation of any one of those Cardinals whom he had injured, or who on becoming Pope would have reason to fear him; for fear is as dangerous an enemy as resentment. Those whom he had offended were, among others, San Pietro ad Vincula, Colonna, San Giorgio, and Ascanio; all the rest, excepting d'Amboise and the Spanish Cardinals (the latter from their connexion and obligations, the former from the power he derived through his relations with the French Court), would on assuming the Pontificate have had reason to fear him. The Duke, therefore, ought, in the first place, to have laboured for the creation of a Spanish Pope; failing in which, he should have agreed to the election of d'Amboise, but never to that of San Pietro ad Vincula. And he deceives himself who believes that with the great, recent benefits cause old wrongs to be forgotten.

The Duke, therefore, erred in the part he took in this election; and his error was the cause of his ultimate downfall.

CHAPTER VIII

OF THOSE WHO BY THEIR CRIMES COME TO BE PRINCES

BUT since from privacy a man may also rise to be a Prince in one or other of two ways, neither of which can be referred wholly either to merit or to fortune, it is fit that I notice them here, though one of them may fall to be discussed more fully in treating of Republics.

The ways I speak of are, first, when the ascent to power is made by paths of wickedness and crime; and second, when a private person becomes ruler of his country by the favour of his fellow-citizens. The former method I shall make clear by two examples, one ancient, the other modern, without entering further into the merits of the matter, for these, I think, should be enough for any one who is driven to follow them.

Agathocles the Sicilian came, not merely from a private station, but from the very dregs of the people, to be King of Syracuse. Son of a potter, through all the stages of his fortunes he led a foul life. His vices, however, were conjoined with so great vigour both of mind and body, that becoming a soldier, he rose through the various grades of the service to be Praetor of Syracuse. Once established in that post, he resolved to make himself Prince, and to hold by violence and without obligation to others the authority which had been spontaneously entrusted to him. Accordingly, after imparting his design to Hamilcar, who with the Carthaginian armies was at that time waging war in Sicily, he one morning assembled the people and senate of Syracuse as though to consult with them on matters of public moment, and on a preconcerted signal caused his soldiers to put to death all the senators, and the wealthiest of the commons. These being thus got rid of, he assumed and retained possession of the sovereignty without opposition on the part of the people; and although twice defeated by the Carthaginians, and afterwards besieged, he was able not only to defend his city, but leaving a part of his forces for its protection, to invade Africa with the remainder, and so in a short time to raise the siege of Syracuse, reducing the Carthaginians to the utmost extremities, and compelling them to make terms whereby they abandoned Sicily to him and confined themselves to Africa.

Whoever examines this man's actions and achievements will discover little or nothing in them which can be ascribed to Fortune, seeing, as has already been said, that it was not through the favour of any, but by the regular steps of the military service, gained at the cost of a thousand hardships and hazards, he reached the princedom which he afterwards maintained by so many daring and dangerous enterprises. Still, to slaughter fellow-citizens, to betray friends, to be devoid of honour, pity, and religion, cannot be counted as merits, for these are means which may lead to power, but which confer no glory. Wherefore, if in respect of the valour with which he encountered and extricated himself from difficulties, and the constancy of his spirit in supporting and conquering adverse fortune, there seems no reason to judge him inferior to the greatest captains that have ever lived, his unbridled cruelty and inhumanity, together with his countless crimes, forbid us to number him with the greatest men; but, at any rate, we cannot attribute to Fortune or to merit what he accomplished without either.

In our own times, during the papacy of Alexander VI, Oliverotto of Fermo, who some years before had been left an orphan, and had been brought up by his maternal uncle Giovanni Fogliani, was sent while still a lad to serve under Paolo Vitelli, in the expectation that a thorough training under that commander might qualify him for high rank as a soldier. After the death of Paolo, he served under his brother Vitellozzo, and in a very short time, being of a quick wit, hardy and resolute, he became one of the first soldiers of his company. But thinking it beneath him to serve under others, with the countenance of the Vitelleschi and the connivance of certain citizens of Fermo who preferred the slavery to the freedom of their country, he formed the design to seize on that town.

He accordingly wrote to Giovanni Fogliani that after many years of absence from home, he desired to see him and his native city once more, and to look a little into the condition of his patrimony; and as his one endeavour had been to make himself a name, in order that his fellow-citizens might see that his time had not been mis-spent, he proposed to return honourably attended by a hundred horsemen from among his own friends and followers; and he begged Giovanni graciously to arrange for his reception by the citizens of Fermo with corresponding marks of distinction, as this would be creditable not only to himself, but also to the uncle who had brought him up.

Giovanni accordingly, did not fail in any proper attention to his nephew, but caused him to be splendidly received by his fellow-citizens, and lodged him in his house; where Oliverotto having passed some days, and made the necessary arrangements for carrying out his wickedness, gave a formal banquet, to which he invited his uncle and all the first men of Fermo. When the repast and the other entertainments proper to such an occasion had come to an end, Oliverotto artfully turned the conversation to matters of grave interest, by speaking of the greatness of Pope Alexander and Cesare his son, and of their enterprises; and when Giovanni and the others were replying to what he said, he suddenly rose up, observing that these were matters to be discussed in a more private place, and so withdrew to another chamber; whither his uncle and all the other citizens followed him, and where they had no sooner seated themselves, than soldiers rushing out from places of concealment put Giovanni and all the rest to death.

After this butchery, Oliverotto mounted his horse, rode through the streets, and besieged the chief magistrate in the palace, so that all were constrained by fear to yield obedience and accept a government of which he made himself the head. And all who from being disaffected were likely to stand in his way, he put to death, while he strengthened himself with new ordinances, civil and military, to such purpose, that for the space of a year during which he retained the Princedom, he not merely kept a firm hold of the city, but grew formidable to all his neighbours. And it would have been as impossible to unseat him as it was to unseat Agathocles, had he not let himself be overreached by Cesare Borgia on the occasion when, as has already been told, the Orsini and Vitelli were entrapped at Sinigaglia; where he too being taken, one year after the commission of his parricidal crime, was strangled along with Vitellozzo, whom he had assumed for his master in villany as in valour.

It may be asked how Agathocles and some like him, after num-

berless acts of treachery and cruelty, have been able to live long in
their own country in safety, and to defend themselves from foreign
enemies, without being plotted against by their fellow-citizens,
whereas, many others, by reason of their cruelty, have failed to
maintain their position even in peaceful times, not to speak of the
perilous times of war. I believe that this results from cruelty being
well or ill-employed. Those cruelties we may say are well employed,
if it be permitted to speak well of things evil, which are done once
for all under the necessity of self-preservation, and are not afterwards
persisted in, but so far as possible modified to the advantage of the
governed. Ill-employed cruelties, on the other hand, are those which
from small beginnings increase rather than diminish with time.
They who follow the first of these methods, may, by the grace of
God and man, find, as did Agathocles, that their condition is not
desperate; but by no possibility can the others maintain themselves.

Hence we may learn the lesson that on seizing a state, the usurper
should make haste to inflict what injuries he must, at a stroke, that
he may not have to renew them daily, but be enabled by their dis-
continuance to reassure men's minds, and afterwards win them over
by benefits. Whosoever, either through timidity or from following
bad counsels, adopts a contrary course, must keep the sword always
drawn, and can put no trust in his subjects, who suffering from continued and constantly renewed severities, will never yield him their
confidence. Injuries, therefore, should be inflicted all at once, that
their ill savour being less lasting may the less offend; whereas, benefits should be conferred little by little, that so they may be more
fully relished.

But, before all things, a Prince should so live with his subjects
that no vicissitude of good or evil fortune shall oblige him to alter
his behaviour; because, if a need to change come through adversity,
it is then too late to resort to severity; while any leniency you may
use will be thrown away, for it will be seen to be compulsory and
gain you no thanks.

CHAPTER IX

OF THE CIVIL PRINCEDOM

I COME now to the second case, namely, of the leading citizen who, not by crimes or violence, but by the favour of his fellow-citizens is made Prince of his country. This may be called a Civil Princedom, and its attainment depends not wholly on merit, nor wholly on good fortune, but rather on what may be termed a *fortunate astuteness*. I say then that the road to this Princedom lies either through the favour of the people or of the nobles. For in every city are to be found these two opposed humours having their origin in this, that the people desire not to be domineered over or oppressed by the nobles, while the nobles desire to oppress and domineer over the people. And from these two contrary appetites there arises in cities one of three results, a Princedom, or Liberty, or Licence. A Princedom is created either by the people or by the nobles, according as one or other of these factions has occasion for it. For when the nobles perceive that they cannot withstand the people, they set to work to magnify the reputation of one of their number, and make him their Prince, to the end that under his shadow they may be enabled to indulge their desires. The people, on the other hand, when they see that they cannot make head against the nobles, invest a single citizen with all their influence and make him Prince, that they may have the shelter of his authority.

He who is made Prince by the favour of the nobles, has greater difficulty to maintain himself than he who comes to the Princedom by aid of the people, since he finds many about him who think themselves as good as he, and whom, on that account, he cannot guide or govern as he would. But he who reaches the Princedom by the popular support, finds himself alone, with none, or but a very few about him who are not ready to obey. Moreover, the demands of the nobles cannot be satisfied with credit to the Prince, nor without injury to others, while those of the people well may, the aim of the people being more honourable than that of the nobles, the latter seeking to oppress, the former not to be oppressed. Add to this, that a Prince can never secure himself against a disaffected people, their number being too great, while he may against a disaffected nobility, since their number is small. The worst that a Prince need fear from a disaffected people is, that they may desert him, whereas when the nobles are his enemies he has to fear not only that they may desert him, but also that they may turn against him; because, as they have greater craft and foresight, they always choose their time to suit their safety, and seek favour with the side they think will win. Again, a Prince must always live with the same people, but need not always live with the same nobles, being able to make and unmake these from day to day, and give and take away their authority at his pleasure.

But to make this part of the matter clearer, I say that as regards the nobles there is this first distinction to be made. They either so govern their conduct as to bind themselves wholly to your fortunes, or they do not. Those who so bind themselves, and who are not grasping, should be loved and honoured. As to those who do not so bind themselves, there is this further distinction. For the most part they are held back by pusillanimity and a natural defect of courage, in which case you should make use of them, and of those among them more especially who are prudent, for they will do you honour in prosperity, and in adversity give you no cause for fear. But where they abstain from attaching themselves to you of set purpose and for ambitious ends, it is a sign that they are thinking more of themselves than of you, and against such men a Prince should be on his guard, and treat them as though they were declared enemies, for in his adversity they will always help to ruin him.

He who becomes a Prince through the favour of the people should always keep on good terms with them; which it is easy for him to do, since all they ask is not to be oppressed. But he who against the will of the people is made a Prince by the favour of the nobles, must, above all things, seek to conciliate the people, which he readily may by taking them under his protection. For since men who are well treated by one whom they expected to treat them ill, feel the more beholden to their benefactor, the people will at once become better disposed to such a Prince when he protects them, than if he owed his Princedom to them.

There are many ways in which a Prince may gain the good-will of the people, but, because these vary with circumstances, no certain rule can be laid down respecting them, and I shall, therefore, say no more about them. But this is the sum of the matter, that it is essential for a Prince to be on a friendly footing with his people, since, otherwise, he will have no resource in adversity. Nabis, Prince of Sparta, was attacked by the whole hosts of Greece, and by a Roman army flushed with victory, and defended his country and crown against them; and when danger approached, there were but few of his subjects against whom he needed to guard himself, whereas had the people been hostile, this would not have been enough.

And what I affirm let no one controvert by citing the old saw that *'he who builds on the people builds on mire,'* for that may be true of a private citizen who presumes on his favour with the people, and counts on being rescued by them when overpowered by his enemies or by the magistrates. In such cases a man may often find himself deceived, as happened to the Gracchi in Rome, and in Florence to Messer Giorgio Scali. But when he who builds on the people is a Prince capable of command, of a spirit not to be cast down by ill-fortune, who, while he animates the whole community by his courage and bearing, neglects no prudent precaution, he will not find himself betrayed by the people, but will be seen to have laid his foundations well.

The most critical juncture for Princedoms of this kind, is at the moment when they are about to pass from the popular to the absolute form of government: and as these Princes exercise their authority either directly or through the agency of the magistrates, in the latter case their position is weaker and more hazardous, since they are wholly in the power of those citizens to whom the magistracies are entrusted, who can, and especially in difficult times, with the greatest ease deprive them of their authority, either by opposing, or by not obeying them. And in times of peril it is too late for a Prince to assume to himself an absolute authority, for the citizens and subjects who are accustomed to take their orders from the magistrates, will not when dangers threaten take them from the Prince, so that at such seasons there will always be very few in whom he can trust. Such Princes, therefore, must not build on what they see in tranquil times when the citizens feel the need of the State. For then every one is ready to run, to promise, and, danger of death being remote, even to die for the State. But in troubled times, when the State has need of its citizens, few of them are to be found. And the risk of the experiment is the greater in that it can only be made once. Wherefore, a wise Prince should devise means whereby his subjects may at all times, whether favourable or adverse, feel the need of the State and of him, and then they will always be faithful to him.

CHAPTER X

How the Strength of All Princedoms Should Be Measured

In examining the character of these Princedoms, another circumstance has to be considered, namely, whether the Prince is strong enough, if occasion demands, to stand alone, or whether he needs continual help from others. To make the matter clearer, I pronounce those to be able to stand alone who, with the men and money at their disposal, can get together an army fit to take the field against any assailant; and, conversely, I judge those to be in constant need of help who cannot take the field against their enemies, but are obliged to retire behind their walls, and to defend themselves there. Of the former I have already spoken, and shall speak again as occasion may require. As to the latter there is nothing to be said, except to exhort such Princes to strengthen and fortify the towns in which they dwell, and take no heed of the country outside. For whoever has thoroughly fortified his town, and put himself on such a footing with his subjects as I have already indicated and shall hereafter speak of, will always be attacked with much circumspection; for men are always averse to enterprises that are attended with difficulty, and it is impossible not to foresee difficulties in attacking a Prince whose town is strongly fortified and who is not hated by his subjects.

The towns of Germany enjoy great freedom. Having little territory, they render obedience to the Emperor only when so disposed, fearing neither him nor any other neighbouring power. For they are so fortified that it is plain to every one that it would be a tedious and difficult task to reduce them, since all of them are protected by moats and suitable ramparts, are well supplied with artillery, and keep their public magazines constantly stored with victual, drink and fuel, enough to last them for a year. Besides which, in order to support the poorer class of citizens without public loss, they lay in a common stock of materials for these to work on for a year, in the handicrafts which are the life and sinews of such cities, and by which the common people live. Moreover, they esteem military exercises and have many regulations for their maintenance.

A Prince, therefore, who has a strong city, and who does not make himself hated, can not be attacked, or should he be so, his assailant will come badly off; since human affairs are so variable that it is almost impossible for any one to keep an army posted in leaguer for a whole year without interruption of some sort. Should it be objected that if the citizens have possessions outside the town, and see them burned, they will lose patience, and that self-interest, together with the hardships of a protracted siege, will cause them to forget their loyalty; I answer that a capable and courageous Prince will always overcome these difficulties, now, by holding out hopes to his subjects that the evil will not be of long continuance; now, by exciting their fears of the enemy's cruelty; and, again, by dexterously silencing those who seem to him too forward in their complaints. Moreover, it is to be expected that the enemy will burn and lay waste the country immediately on their arrival, at a time when men's minds are still heated and resolute for defence. And for this very reason the Prince ought the less to fear, because after a few days, when the first ardour has abated, the injury is already done and suffered, and cannot be undone; and the people will now, all the more readily, make common cause with their Prince from his seeming to be under obligations to them, their houses having been burned and their lands wasted in his defence. For it is the nature of men to incur obligation as much by the benefits they render as by those they receive.

Wherefore, if the whole matter be well considered, it ought not to be difficult for a prudent Prince, both at the outset and afterwards, to maintain the spirits of his subjects during a siege; provided always that victuals and other means of defence do not run short.

CHAPTER XI

OF ECCLESIASTICAL PRINCEDOMS

IT now only remains for me to treat of Ecclesiastical Princedoms, all the difficulties in respect of which precede their acquisition. For they are acquired by merit or good fortune, but are maintained without either; being upheld by the venerable ordinances of Religion, which are all of such a nature and efficacy that they secure the authority of their Princes in whatever way they may act or live. These Princes alone have territories which they do not defend, and subjects whom they do not govern; yet their territories are not taken from them through not being defended, nor are their subjects concerned at not being governed, or led to think of throwing off their allegiance; nor is it in their power to do so. Accordingly these Princedoms alone are secure and happy. But inasmuch as they are sustained by agencies of a higher nature than the mind of man can reach, I forbear to speak of them: for since they are set up and supported by God himself, he would be a rash and presumptuous man who should venture to discuss them.

Nevertheless, should any one ask me how it comes about that the temporal power of the Church, which before the time of Alexander was looked on with contempt by all the Potentates of Italy, and not only by those so styling themselves, but by every Baron and Lordling however insignificant, has now reached such a pitch of greatness that the King of France trembles before it, and that it has been able to drive him out of Italy and to crush the Venetians; though the causes be known, it seems to me not superfluous to call them in some measure to recollection.

Before Charles of France passed into Italy, that country was under the control of the Pope, the Venetians, the King of Naples, the Duke of Milan, and the Florentines. Two chief objects had to be kept in view by all these powers: first, that no armed foreigner should be allowed to invade Italy; second, that no one of their own number should be suffered to extend his territory. Those whom it was especially needed to guard against, were the Pope and the Venetians. To hold back the Venetians it was necessary that all the other

States should combine, as was done for the defence of Ferrara; while to restrain the Pope, use was made of the Roman Barons, who being divided into two factions, the Orsini and Colonnesi, had constant cause for feud with one another, and standing with arms in their hands under the very eyes of the Pontiff, kept the Popedom feeble and insecure.

And although there arose from time to time a courageous Pope like Sixtus, neither his prudence nor his good fortune could free him from these embarrassments. The cause whereof was the shortness of the lives of the Popes. For in the ten years, which was the average duration of a Pope's life, he could barely succeed in humbling one of these factions; so that if, for instance, one Pope had almost exterminated the Colonnesi, he was followed by another, who being the enemy of the Orsini had no time to rid himself of them, but so far from completing the destruction of the Colonnesi, restored them to life. This led to the temporal authority of the Popes being little esteemed in Italy.

Then came Alexander VI, who more than any of his predecessors showed what a Pope could effect with money and arms, achieving by the instrumentality of Duke Valentino, and by taking advantage of the coming of the French into Italy, all those successes which I have already noticed in speaking of the actions of the Duke. And although his object was to aggrandize, not the Church but the Duke, what he did turned to the advantage of the Church, which after his death, and after the Duke had been put out of the way, became the heir of his labours.

After him came Pope Julius, who found the Church strengthened by the possession of the whole of Romagna, and the Roman Barons exhausted and their factions shattered under the blows of Pope Alexander. He found also a way opened for the accumulation of wealth, which before the time of Alexander no one had followed. These advantages Julius not only used but added to. He undertook the conquest of Bologna, the overthrow of the Venetians, and the expulsion of the French from Italy; in all which enterprises he succeeded, and with the greater glory to himself in that whatever he did, was done to strengthen the Church and not to aggrandize any private person. He succeeded, moreover, in keeping the factions of the Orsini and Colonnesi within the same limits as he found them; and, though some seeds of insubordination may still have been left among them, two causes operated to hold them in check; first, the great power of the Church, which overawed them, and second, their being without Cardinals, who had been the cause of all their disorders. For these factions while they have Cardinals among them can never be at rest, since it is they who foment dissension both in Rome and out of it, in which the Barons are forced to take part, the ambition of the Prelates thus giving rise to tumult and discord among the Barons.

His Holiness, Pope Leo, has consequently found the Papacy most powerful; and from him we may hope, that as his predecessors made it great with arms, he will render it still greater and more venerable by his benignity and other countless virtues.

CHAPTER XII

How Many Different Kinds of Soldiers There Are, and of Mercenaries

Having spoken particularly of all the various kinds of Princedom whereof at the outset I proposed to treat, considered in some measure what are the causes of their strength and weakness, and pointed out the methods by which men commonly seek to acquire them, it now remains that I should discourse generally concerning the means for attack and defence of which each of these different kinds of Princedom may make use.

I have already said that a Prince must lay solid foundations, since otherwise he will inevitably be destroyed. Now the main foundations of all States, whether new, old, or mixed, are good laws and good arms. But since you cannot have the former without the latter, and where you have the latter, are likely to have the former, I shall here omit all discussion on the subject of laws, and speak only of arms.

I say then that the arms wherewith a Prince defends his State are either his own subjects, or they are mercenaries, or they are auxiliaries, or they are partly one and partly another. Mercenaries and auxiliaries are at once useless and dangerous, and he who holds his State by means of mercenary troops can never be solidly or securely seated. For such troops are disunited, ambitious, insubordinate, treacherous, insolent among friends, cowardly before foes, and without fear of God or faith with man. Whenever they are attacked defeat follows; so that in peace you are plundered by them, in war by your enemies. And this because they have no tie or motive to keep them in the field beyond their paltry pay, in return for which it would be too much to expect them to give their lives. They are ready enough, therefore, to be your soldiers while you are at peace, but when war is declared they make off and disappear. I ought to have little difficulty in getting this believed, for the present ruin of Italy is due to no other cause than her having for many years trusted to mercenaries, who though heretofore they may have helped the fortunes of some one man, and made a show of strength when matched with one another, have always revealed themselves in their true colours so soon as foreign enemies appeared. Hence it was that Charles of France was suffered to conquer Italy *with chalk;* and he who said our sins were the cause, said truly, though it was not the sins he meant, but those which I have noticed. And as these were the sins of Princes, they it is who have paid the penalty.

But I desire to demonstrate still more clearly the untoward character of these forces. Captains of mercenaries are either able men or they are not. If they are, you cannot trust them, since they will always seek their own aggrandizement, either by overthrowing you who are their master, or by the overthrow of others contrary to your desire. On the other hand, if your captain be not an able man the chances are you will be ruined. And if it be said that whoever has arms in his hands will act in the same way whether he be a mercenary or no, I answer that when arms have to be employed by a Prince or a Republic, the Prince ought to go in person to take command as captain, the Republic should send one of her citizens, and if he prove incapable should change him, but if he prove capable should by the force of the laws confine him within proper bounds. And we see from experience that both Princes and Republics when they depend on their own arms have the greatest success, whereas from employing mercenaries nothing but loss results. Moreover, a

Republic trusting to her own forces, is with greater difficulty than one which relies on foreign arms brought to yield obedience to a single citizen. Rome and Sparta remained for ages armed and free. The Swiss are at once the best armed and the freest people in the world.

Of mercenary arms in ancient times we have an example in the Carthaginians, who at the close of their first war with Rome, were well-nigh ruined by their hired troops, although these were commanded by Carthaginian citizens. So too, when, on the death of Epaminondas, the Thebans made Philip of Macedon captain of their army, after gaining a victory for them, he deprived them of their liberty. The Milanese, in like manner, when Duke Filippo died, took Francesco Sforza into their pay to conduct the war against the Venetians. But he, after defeating the enemy at Caravaggio, combined with them to overthrow the Milanese, his masters. His father too while in the pay of Giovanna, Queen of Naples, suddenly left her without troops, obliging her, in order to save her kingdom, to throw herself into the arms of the King of Aragon.

And if it be said that in times past the Venetians and the Florentines have extended their dominions by means of these arms, and that their captains have served them faithfully, without seeking to make themselves their masters, I answer that in this respect the Florentines have been fortunate, because among those valiant captains who might have given them cause for fear, some have not been victorious, some have had rivals, and some have turned their ambition in other directions.

Among those not victorious, was Giovanni Acuto, whose fidelity, since he was unsuccessful, was not put to the proof: but any one may see, that had he been victorious the Florentines must have been entirely in his hands. The Sforzas, again, had constant rivals in the Bracceschi, so that the one following was a check upon the other; moreover, the ambition of Francesco was directed against Milan, while that of Braccio was directed against the Church and the kingdom of Naples. Let us turn, however, to what took place lately. The Florentines chose for their captain Paolo Vitelli, a most prudent commander, who had raised himself from privacy to the highest renown in arms. Had he been successful in reducing Pisa, none can deny that the Florentines would have been completely in his power, for they would have been ruined had he gone over to their enemies, while if they retained him they must have submitted to his will.

Again, as to the Venetians, if we consider the growth of their power, it will be seen that they conducted their affairs with glory and safety so long as their subjects of all ranks, gentle and simple alike, valiantly bore arms in their wars; as they did before they directed their enterprises landwards. But when they took to making war by land, they forsook those methods in which they excelled and were content to follow the customs of Italy.

At first, indeed, in extending their possessions on the mainland, having as yet but little territory and being held in high repute, they had not much to fear from their captains; but when their territories increased, which they did under Carmagnola, they were taught their mistake. For as they had found him a most valiant and skilful leader when, under his command, they defeated the Duke of Milan, and, on the other hand, saw him slack in carrying on the war, they made up their minds that no further victories were to be had under him; and because, through fear of losing what they had gained, they could not discharge him, to secure themselves against him they were forced to put him to death. After him they have had for captains, Bartolommeo of Bergamo, Roberto of San Severino, the Count of Pitigliano, and the like, under whom their danger has not been from victories, but from defeats; as, for instance, at Vaila, where they lost in a single day what it had taken the efforts of eight hundred years to acquire. For the gains resulting from mercenary arms are slow, and late, and inconsiderable, but the losses sudden and astounding.

And since these examples have led me back to Italy, which for many years past has been defended by mercenary arms, I desire to go somewhat deeper into the matter, in order that the causes which led to the adoption of these arms being seen, they may the more readily be corrected. You are to understand, then, that when in these later times the Imperial control began to be rejected by Italy, and the temporal power of the Pope to be more thought of, Italy suddenly split up into a number of separate States. For many of the larger cities took up arms against their nobles, who, with the favour of the Emperor, had before kept them in subjection, and were supported by the Church with a view to add to her temporal authority: while in many others of these cities, private citizens became rulers. Hence Italy, having passed almost entirely into the hands of the Church and of certain Republics, the former made up of priests, the latter of citizens unfamiliar with arms, began to take foreigners into her pay.

The first who gave reputation to this service was Alberigo of Conio in Romagna, from whose school of warlike training descended, among others, Braccio and Sforza, who in their time were the arbiters of Italy; after whom came all those others who down to the present hour have held similar commands, and to whose merits we owe it that our country has been overrun by Charles, plundered by Louis, wasted by Ferdinand, and insulted by the Swiss.

The first object of these mercenaries was to bring foot soldiers into disrepute, in order to enhance the merit of their own followers; and this they did, because lacking territory of their own and depending on their profession for their support, a few foot soldiers gave them no importance, while for a large number they were unable to provide. For these reasons they had recourse to horsemen, a less retinue of whom was thought to confer distinction, and could be more easily maintained. And the matter went to such a length, that in an army of twenty thousand men, not two thousand foot soldiers were to be found. Moreover, they spared no endeavour to relieve themselves and their men from fatigue and danger, not killing one another in battle, but making prisoners who were afterwards released without ransom. They would attack no town by night; those in towns would make no sortie by night against a besieging army. Their camps were without rampart or trench. They had no winter campaigns. All which arrangements were sanctioned by their military rules, contrived by them, as I have said already, to escape fatigue and danger; but the result of which has been to bring Italy into servitude and contempt.

CHAPTER XIII

OF AUXILIARY, MIXED, AND NATIONAL ARMS

THE second sort of unprofitable arms are auxiliaries, by whom I mean, troops brought to help and protect you by a potentate whom you summon to your aid; as when in recent times, Pope Julius II observing the pitiful behaviour of his mercenaries at the enterprise of Ferrara, betook himself to auxiliaries, and arranged with Ferdinand of Spain to be supplied with horse and foot soldiers.

Auxiliaries may be excellent and useful soldiers for themselves, but are always hurtful to him who calls them in; for if they are defeated, he is undone, if victorious, he becomes their prisoner. Ancient histories abound with instances of this, but I shall not pass from the example of Pope Julius, which is still fresh in men's minds. It was the height of rashness for him, in his eagerness to gain Ferrara, to throw himself without reserve into the arms of a stranger. Nevertheless, his good fortune came to his rescue, and he had not to reap the fruits of his ill-considered conduct. For after his auxiliaries were defeated at Ravenna, the Swiss suddenly descended and, to their own surprise and that of every one else, swept the victors out of the country, so that, he neither remained a prisoner with his enemies, they being put to flight, nor with his auxiliaries, because victory was won by other arms than theirs. The Florentines, being wholly without soldiers of their own, brought ten thousand French men-at-arms to the siege of Pisa, thereby incurring greater peril than at any previous time of trouble. To protect himself from his neighbours, the Emperor of Constantinople summoned ten thousand Turkish soldiers into Greece, who, when the war was over, refused to leave, and this was the beginning of the servitude of Greece to the Infidel.

Let him, therefore, who would deprive himself of every chance of success, have recourse to auxiliaries, these being far more dangerous than mercenary arms, bringing ruin with them ready made. For they are united, and wholly under the control of their own officers; whereas, before mercenaries, even after gaining a victory, can do you hurt, longer time and better opportunities are needed; because, as they are made up of separate companies, raised and paid by you, he whom you place in command cannot at once acquire such authority over them as will be injurious to you. In short, with mercenaries your greatest danger is from their inertness and cowardice, with auxiliaries from their valour. Wise Princes, therefore, have always eschewed these arms, and trusted rather to their own, and have preferred defeat with the latter to victory with the former, counting that as no true victory which is gained by foreign aid.

I shall never hesitate to cite the example of Cesare Borgia and his actions. He entered Romagna with a force of auxiliaries, all of them French men-at-arms, with whom he took Imola and Forli. But it appearing to him afterwards that these troops were not to be trusted, he had recourse to mercenaries from whom he thought there would be less danger, and took the Orsini and Vitelli into his pay. But finding these likewise while under his command to be fickle, false, and treacherous, he got rid of them, and fell back on troops of his own raising. And we may readily discern the difference between these various kinds of arms, by observing the different degrees of reputation in which the Duke stood while he depended upon the French alone, when he took the Orsini and Vitelli into his pay, and when he fell back on his own troops and his own resources; for we find his reputation always increasing, and that he was never so well thought of as when every one perceived him to be sole master of his own forces.

I am unwilling to leave these examples, drawn from what has taken place in Italy and in recent times; and yet I must not omit to notice the case of Hiero of Syracuse, who is one of those whom I have already named. He, as I have before related, being made captain of their armies by the Syracusans, saw at once that a force of mercenary soldiers, supplied by men resembling our Italian *condottieri,* was not serviceable; and as he would not retain and could not disband them, he caused them all to be cut to pieces, and afterwards made war with native soldiers only, without other aid.

And here I would call to mind a passage in the Old Testament as bearing on this point. When David offered himself to Saul to go forth and fight Goliath the Philistine champion, Saul to encourage him armed him with his own armour, which David, so soon as he had put it on, rejected, saying that with these untried arms he could not prevail, and that he chose rather to meet his enemy with only his sling and his sword. In a word, the armour of others is too wide, or too strait for us; it falls off us, or it weighs us down.

Charles VII, the father of Louis XI, who by his good fortune and valour freed France from the English, saw this necessity of strengthening himself with a national army, and drew up ordinances regulating the service both of men-at-arms and of foot soldiers throughout his kingdom. But afterwards his son, King Louis, did away with the national infantry, and began to hire Swiss mercenaries. Which blunder having been followed by subsequent Princes, has been the cause, as the result shows, of the dangers into which the kingdom of France has fallen; for, by enhancing the reputation of the Swiss, the whole of the national troops of France have been deteriorated. For from their infantry being done away with, their men-at-arms are made wholly dependent on foreign assistance, and being accustomed to co-operate with the Swiss, have grown to think they can do nothing without them. Hence the French are no match for the Swiss, and without them cannot succeed against others.

The armies of France, then, are mixed, being partly national and partly mercenary. Armies thus composed are far superior to mere mercenaries or mere auxiliaries, but far inferior to forces purely national. And this example is in itself conclusive, for the realm of France would be invincible if the military ordinances of Charles VII had been retained and extended. But from want of foresight men make changes which relishing well at first do not betray their hidden venom, as I have already observed respecting hectic fever. Nevertheless, the ruler is not truly wise who cannot discern evils before they develop themselves, and this is a faculty given to few.

If we look for the causes which first led to the overthrow of the Roman Empire, they will be found to have had their source in the employment of Gothic mercenaries, for from that hour the strength of the Romans began to wane and all the virtue which went from them passed to the Goths. And, to be brief, I say that without national arms no Princedom is safe, but on the contrary is wholly dependent on Fortune, being without the strength that could defend it in adversity. And it has always been the deliberate opinion of the wise, that nothing is so infirm and fleeting as a reputation for power not founded upon a national army, by which I mean one composed of subjects, citizens, and dependents, all others being mercenary or auxiliary.

The methods to be followed for organizing a national army may readily be ascertained, if the rules above laid down by me, and by which I abide, be well considered, and attention be given to the manner in which Philip, father of Alexander the Great, and many other Princes and Republics have armed and disposed their forces.

CHAPTER XIV

OF THE DUTY OF A PRINCE IN RESPECT OF MILITARY AFFAIRS

A PRINCE, therefore, should have no care or thought but for war, and for the regulations and training it requires, and should apply himself exclusively to this as his peculiar province; for war is the sole art looked for in one who rules, and is of such efficacy that it not merely maintains those who are born Princes, but often enables men to rise to that eminence from a private station; while, on the other hand, we often see that when Princes devote themselves rather to pleasure than to arms, they lose their dominions. And as neglect of this art is the prime cause of such calamities, so to be a proficient in it is the surest way to acquire power. Francesco Sforza, from his renown in arms, rose from privacy to be Duke of Milan, while his descendants, seeking to avoid the hardships and fatigues of military life, from being Princes fell back into privacy. For among other causes of misfortune which your not being armed brings upon you, it makes you despised, and this is one of those reproaches against which, as shall presently be explained, a Prince ought most carefully to guard.

Between an armed and an unarmed man no proportion holds, and it is contrary to reason to expect that the armed man should voluntarily submit to him who is unarmed, or that the unarmed man should stand secure among armed retainers. For with contempt on one side, and distrust on the other, it is impossible that men should work well together. Wherefore, as has already been said, a Prince who is ignorant of military affairs, besides other disadvantages, can neither be respected by his soldiers, nor can he trust them. A Prince, therefore, ought never to allow his attention to be diverted from warlike pursuits, and should occupy himself with them even more in peace than in war. This he can do in two ways, by practice or by study.

As to the practice, he ought, besides keeping his soldiers well trained and disciplined, to be constantly engaged in the chase, that he may inure his body to hardships and fatigue, and gain at the same time a knowledge of places, by observing how the mountains slope, the valleys open, and the plains spread; acquainting himself with the characters of rivers and marshes, and giving the greatest attention to this subject. Such knowledge is useful to him in two ways; for first, he learns thereby to know his own country, and to understand better how it may be defended; and next, from his familiar acquaintance with its localities, he readily comprehends the character of other districts when obliged to observe them for the first time. For the hills, valleys, plains, rivers, and marshes of Tuscany, for example, have a certain resemblance to those elsewhere; so that from a knowledge of the natural features of that province, similar knowledge in respect of other provinces may readily be gained. The Prince who is wanting in this kind of knowledge, is wanting in the first qualification of a good captain, for by it he is taught how to surprise an enemy, how to choose an encampment, how to lead his army on a march, how to array it for battle, and how to post it to the best advantage for a siege.

Among the commendations which Philopoemon, Prince of the Achaians, has received from historians is this—that in times of peace he was always thinking of methods of warfare, so that when walking in the country with his friends he would often stop and talk with them on the subject. 'If the enemy,' he would say, 'were posted on that hill, and we found ourselves here with our army, which of us would have the better position? How could we most safely and in the best order advance to meet them? If we had to retreat, what direction should we take? If they retired, how should we pursue?' In this way he put to his friends, as he went along, all the contingencies that can befall an army. He listened to their opinions, stated his own, and supported them with reasons; and from his being constantly occupied with such meditations, it resulted, that when in actual command no complication could ever present itself with which he was not prepared to deal.

As to the mental training of which we have spoken, a Prince should read histories, and in these should note the actions of great men, observe how they conducted themselves in their wars, and examine the causes of their victories and defeats, so as to avoid the latter and imitate them in the former. And above all, he should, as many great men of past ages have done, assume for his models those persons who before his time have been renowned and celebrated, whose deeds and achievements he should constantly keep in mind, as it is related that Alexander the Great sought to resemble Achilles, Cæsar Alexander, and Scipio Cyrus. And any one who reads the life of this last-named hero, written by Xenophon, recognizes afterwards in the life of Scipio, how much this imitation was the source of his glory, and how nearly in his chastity, affability, kindliness, and generosity, he conformed to the character of Cyrus as Xenophon describes it.

A wise Prince, therefore, should pursue such methods as these, never resting idle in times of peace, but strenuously seeking to turn them to account, so that he may derive strength from them in the hour of danger, and find himself ready should Fortune turn against him, to resist her blows.

CHAPTER XV

OF THE QUALITIES IN RESPECT OF WHICH MEN, AND MOST OF ALL PRINCES, ARE PRAISED OR BLAMED

IT now remains for us to consider what ought to be the conduct and bearing of a Prince in relation to his subjects and friends. And since I know that many have written on this subject, I fear it may be thought presumptuous in me to write of it also; the more so, because in my treatment of it, I depart from the views that others have taken.

But since it is my object to write what shall be useful to whosoever understands it, it seems to me better to follow the real truth of things than an imaginary view of them. For many Republics and

Princedoms have been imagined that were never seen or known to exist in reality. And the manner in which we live, and that in which we ought to live, are things so wide asunder, that he who quits the one to betake himself to the other is more likely to destroy than to save himself; since any one who would act up to a perfect standard of goodness in everything, must be ruined among so many who are not good. It is essential, therefore, for a Prince who desires to maintain his position, to have learned how to be other than good, and to use or not to use his goodness as necessity requires.

Laying aside, therefore, all fanciful notions concerning a Prince, and considering those only that are true, I say that all men when they are spoken of, and Princes more than others from their being set so high, are characterized by some one of those qualities which attach either praise or blame. Thus one is accounted liberal, another miserly (which word I use, rather than *avaricious,* to denote the man who is too sparing of what is his own, *avarice* being the disposition to take wrongfully what is another's); one is generous, another greedy; one cruel, another tender-hearted; one is faithless, another true to his word; one effeminate and cowardly, another high-spirited and courageous; one is courteous, another haughty; one impure, another chaste; one simple, another crafty; one firm, another facile; one grave, another frivolous; one devout, another unbelieving; and the like. Every one, I know, will admit that it would be most laudable for a Prince to be endowed with all of the above qualities that are reckoned good; but since it is impossible for him to possess or constantly practise them all, the conditions of human nature not allowing it, he must be discreet enough to know how to avoid the infamy of those vices that would deprive him of his government, and, if possible, be on his guard also against those which might not deprive him of it; though if he cannot wholly restrain himself, he may with less scruple indulge in the latter. He need never hesitate, however, to incur the reproach of those vices without which his authority can hardly be preserved; for if he well consider the whole matter, he will find that there may be a line of conduct having the appearance of virtue, to follow which would be his ruin, and that there may be another course having the appearance of vice, by following which his safety and well-being are secured.

CHAPTER XVI

Of Liberality and Miserliness

Beginning, then, with the first of the qualities above noticed, I say that it may be a good thing to be reputed liberal, but, nevertheless, that liberality without the reputation of it is hurtful; because, though it be worthily and rightly used, still if it be not known, you escape not the reproach of its opposite vice. Hence, to have credit for liberality with the world at large, you must neglect no circumstance of sumptuous display; the result being, that a Prince of a liberal disposition will consume his whole substance in things of this sort, and, after all, be obliged, if he would maintain his reputation for liberality, to burden his subjects with extraordinary taxes, and to resort to confiscations and all the other shifts whereby money is raised. But in this way he becomes hateful to his subjects, and growing impoverished is held in little esteem by any. So that in the end, having by his liberality offended many and obliged few, he is worse off than when he began, and is exposed to all his original dangers. Recognizing this, and endeavouring to retrace his steps, he at once incurs the infamy of miserliness.

A Prince, therefore, since he cannot without injury to himself practise the virtue of liberality so that it may be known, will not, if he be wise, greatly concern himself though he be called miserly. Because in time he will come to be regarded as more and more liberal, when it is seen that through his parsimony his revenues are sufficient; that he is able to defend himself against any who make war on him; that he can engage in enterprises against others without burdening his subjects; and thus exercise liberality towards all from whom he does not take, whose number is infinite, while he is miserly in respect of those only to whom he does not give, whose number is few.

In our own days we have seen no Princes accomplish great results save those who have been accounted miserly. All others have been ruined. Pope Julius II, after availing himself of his reputation for liberality to arrive at the Papacy, made no effort to preserve that reputation when making war on the King of France, but carried on all his numerous campaigns without levying from his subjects a single extraordinary tax, providing for the increased expenditure out of his long-continued savings. Had the present King of Spain been accounted liberal, he never could have engaged or succeeded in so many enterprises.

A Prince, therefore, if he is enabled thereby to forbear from plundering his subjects, to defend himself, to escape poverty and contempt, and the necessity of becoming rapacious, ought to care little though he incur the reproach of miserliness, for this is one of those vices which enable him to reign.

And should any object that Cæsar by his liberality rose to power, and that many others have been advanced to the highest dignities from their having been liberal and so reputed, I reply, 'Either you are already a Prince or you seek to become one; in the former case liberality is hurtful, in the latter it is very necessary that you be thought liberal; Cæsar was one of those who sought the sovereignty of Rome; but if after obtaining it he had lived on without retrenching his expenditure, he must have ruined the Empire.' And if it be further urged that many Princes reputed to have been most liberal have achieved great things with their armies, I answer that a Prince spends either what belongs to himself and his subjects, or what belongs to others; and that in the former case he ought to be sparing, but in the latter ought not to refrain from any kind of liberality. Because for a Prince who leads his armies in person and maintains them by plunder, pillage, and forced contributions, dealing as he does with the property of others this liberality is necessary, since otherwise he would not be followed by his soldiers. Of what does not belong to you or to your subjects you should, therefore, be a lavish giver, as were Cyrus, Cæsar, and Alexander; for to be liberal with the property of others does not take from your reputation, but adds to it. What injures you is to give away what is your own. And there is no quality so self-destructive as liberality; for while you practise it you lose the means whereby it can be practised, and become poor and despised, or else, to avoid poverty, you become rapacious and hated. For liberality leads to one or other of these two results, against which, beyond all others, a Prince should guard. Wherefore it is wiser to put up with the name of being miserly, which breeds ignominy, but without hate, than to be obliged, from the desire to be reckoned liberal, to incur the reproach of rapacity, which breeds hate as well as ignominy.

CHAPTER XVII

OF CRUELTY AND CLEMENCY, AND WHETHER IT IS BETTER TO BE LOVED OR FEARED

PASSING to the other qualities above referred to, I say that every Prince should desire to be accounted merciful and not cruel. Nevertheless, he should be on his guard against the abuse of this quality of mercy. Cesare Borgia was reputed cruel, yet his cruelty restored Romagna, united it, and brought it to order and obedience; so that if we look at things in their true light, it will be seen that he was in reality far more merciful than the people of Florence, who, to avoid the imputation of cruelty, suffered Pistoja to be torn to pieces by factions.

A Prince should therefore disregard the reproach of being thought cruel where it enables him to keep his subjects united and obedient. For he who quells disorder by a very few signal examples will in the end be more merciful than he who from too great leniency permits things to take their course and so to result in rapine and bloodshed; for these hurt the whole State, whereas the severities of the Prince injure individuals only.

And for a new Prince, of all others, it is impossible to escape a name for cruelty, since new States are full of dangers. Wherefore Virgil, by the mouth of Dido, excuses the harshness of her reign on the plea that it was new, saying:—

'A fate unkind, and newness in my reign
Compel me thus to guard a wide domain.'

Nevertheless, the new Prince should not be too ready of belief, nor too easily set in motion; nor should he himself be the first to raise alarms; but should so temper prudence with kindliness that too great confidence in others shall not throw him off his guard, nor groundless distrust render him insupportable.

And here comes in the question whether it is better to be loved rather than feared, or feared rather than loved. It might perhaps be answered that we should wish to be both; but since love and fear can hardly exist together, if we must choose between them, it is far safer to be feared than loved. For of men it may generally be affirmed that they are thankless, fickle, false, studious to avoid danger, greedy of gain, devoted to you while you are able to confer benefits upon them, and ready, as I said before, while danger is distant, to shed their blood, and sacrifice their property, their lives, and their children for you; but in the hour of need they turn against you. The Prince, therefore, who without otherwise securing himself builds wholly on their professions is undone. For the friendships which we buy with a price, and do not gain by greatness and nobility of character, though they be fairly earned are not made good, but fail us when we have occasion to use them.

Moreover, men are less careful how they offend him who makes himself loved than him who makes himself feared. For love is held by the tie of obligation, which, because men are a sorry breed, is broken on every whisper of private interest; but fear is bound by the apprehension of punishment which never relaxes its grasp.

Nevertheless a Prince should inspire fear in such a fashion that if he do not win love he may escape hate. For a man may very well be feared and yet not hated, and this will be the case so long as he does not meddle with the property or with the women of his citizens and subjects. And if constrained to put any to death, he should do so only when there is manifest cause or reasonable justification. But, above all, he must abstain from the property of others. For men will sooner forget the death of their father than the loss of their patrimony. Moreover, pretexts for confiscation are never to seek, and he who has once begun to live by rapine always finds reasons for taking what is not his; whereas reasons for shedding blood are fewer, and sooner exhausted.

But when a Prince is with his army, and has many soldiers under his command, he must needs disregard the reproach of cruelty, for without such a reputation in its Captain, no army can be held together or kept under any kind of control. Among other things remarkable in Hannibal this has been noted, that having a very great army, made up of men of many different nations and brought to fight in a foreign country, no dissension ever arose among the soldiers themselves, nor any mutiny against their leader, either in his good or in his evil fortunes. This we can only ascribe to the transcendent cruelty, which, joined with numberless great qualities, rendered him at once venerable and terrible in the eyes of his soldiers; for without this reputation for cruelty these other virtues would not have produced the like results.

Unreflecting writers, indeed, while they praise his achievements, have condemned the chief cause of them; but that his other merits would not by themselves have been so efficacious we may see from the case of Scipio, one of the greatest Captains, not of his own time only but of all times of which we have record, whose armies rose against him in Spain from no other cause than his too great leniency in allowing them a freedom inconsistent with military strictness. With which weakness Fabius Maximus taxed him in the Senate House, calling him the corrupter of the Roman soldiery. Again, when the Locrians were shamefully outraged by one of his lieutenants, he neither avenged them, nor punished the insolence of his officer; and this from the natural easiness of his disposition. So that it was said in the Senate by one who sought to excuse him, that there were many who knew better how to refrain from doing wrong themselves than how to correct the wrong-doing of others. This temper, however, must in time have marred the name and fame even of Scipio, had he continued in it, and retained his command. But living as he did under the control of the Senate, this hurtful quality was not merely disguised, but came to be regarded as a glory.

Returning to the question of being loved or feared, I sum up by saying, that since his being loved depends upon his subjects, while his being feared depends upon himself, a wise Prince should build on what is his own, and not on what rests with others. Only, as I have said, he must do his utmost to escape hatred.

CHAPTER XVIII

How Princes Should Keep Faith

Every one understands how praiseworthy it is in a Prince to keep faith, and to live uprightly and not craftily. Nevertheless, we see from what has taken place in our own days that Princes who have set little store by their word, but have known how to overreach men by their cunning, have accomplished great things, and in the end got the better of those who trusted to honest dealing.

Be it known, then, that there are two ways of contending, one in accordance with the laws, the other by force; the first of which is proper to men, the second to beasts. But since the first method is often ineffectual, it becomes necessary to resort to the second. A Prince should, therefore, understand how to use well both the man and the beast. And this lesson has been covertly taught by the ancient writers, who relate how Achilles and many others of these old Princes were given over to be brought up and trained by Chiron the Centaur; since the only meaning of their having for instructor one who was half man and half beast is, that it is necessary for a Prince to know how to use both natures, and that the one without the other has no stability.

But since a Prince should know how to use the beast's nature wisely, he ought of beasts to choose both the lion and the fox; for the lion cannot guard himself from the toils, nor the fox from wolves. He must therefore be a fox to discern toils, and a lion to drive off wolves.

To rely wholly on the lion is unwise; and for this reason a prudent Prince neither can nor ought to keep his word when to keep it is hurtful to him and the causes which led him to pledge it are removed. If all men were good, this would not be good advice, but since they are dishonest and do not keep faith with you, you, in return, need not keep faith with them; and no prince was ever at a loss for plausible reasons to cloak a breach of faith. Of this numberless recent instances could be given, and it might be shown how many solemn treaties and engagements have been rendered inoperative and idle through want of faith in Princes, and that he who was best known to play the fox has had the best success.

It is necessary, indeed, to put a good colour on this nature, and to be skilful in simulating and dissembling. But men are so simple, and governed so absolutely by their present needs, that he who wishes to deceive will never fail in finding willing dupes. One recent example I will not omit. Pope Alexander VI had no care or thought but how to deceive, and always found material to work on. No man ever had a more effective manner of asseverating, or made promises with more solemn protestations, or observed them less. And yet, because he understood this side of human nature, his frauds always succeeded.

It is not essential, then, that a Prince should have all the good qualities which I have enumerated above, but it is most essential that he should seem to have them; I will even venture to affirm that if he has and invariably practises them all, they are hurtful, whereas the appearance of having them is useful. Thus, it is well to seem merciful, faithful, humane, religious, and upright, and also to be so; but the mind should remain so balanced that were it needful not to be so, you should be able and know how to change to the contrary.

And you are to understand that a Prince, and most of all a new Prince, cannot observe all those rules of conduct in respect whereof men are accounted good, being often forced, in order to preserve his Princedom, to act in opposition to good faith, charity, humanity, and religion. He must therefore keep his mind ready to shift as the winds and tides of Fortune turn, and, as I have already said, he ought not to quit good courses if he can help it, but should know how to follow evil courses if he must.

A Prince should therefore be very careful that nothing ever escapes his lips which is not replete with the five qualities above named, so that to see and hear him, one would think him the embodiment of mercy, good faith, integrity, humanity, and religion. And there is no virtue which it is more necessary for him to seem to possess than this last; because men in general judge rather by the eye than by the hand, for every one can see but few can touch. Every one sees what you seem, but few know what you are, and these few dare not oppose themselves to the opinion of the many who have the majesty of the State to back them up.

Moreover, in the actions of all men, and most of all of Princes, where there is no tribunal to which we can appeal, we look to results. Wherefore if a Prince succeeds in establishing and maintaining his authority, the means will always be judged honourable and be approved by every one. For the vulgar are always taken by appearances and by results, and the world is made up of the vulgar, the few only finding room when the many have no longer ground to stand on.

A certain Prince of our own days, whose name it is as well not to mention, is always preaching peace and good faith, although the mortal enemy of both; and both, had he practised them as he preaches them, would, oftener than once, have lost him his kingdom and authority.

CHAPTER XIX

THAT A PRINCE SHOULD SEEK TO ESCAPE CONTEMPT AND HATRED

HAVING now spoken of the chief of the qualities above referred to, the rest I shall dispose of briefly with these general remarks, that a Prince, as has already in part been said, should consider how he may avoid such courses as would make him hated or despised; and that whenever he succeeds in keeping clear of these, he has performed his part, and runs no risk though he incur other infamies.

A Prince, as I have said before, sooner becomes hated by being rapacious and by interfering with the property and with the women of his subjects, than in any other way. From these, therefore, he should abstain. For so long as neither their property nor their honour is touched, the mass of mankind live contentedly, and the Prince has only to cope with the ambition of a few, which can in many ways and easily be kept within bounds.

A Prince is despised when he is seen to be fickle, frivolous, effeminate, pusillanimous, or irresolute, against which defects he ought therefore most carefully to guard, striving so to bear himself that greatness, courage, wisdom, and strength may appear in all his actions. In his private dealings with his subjects his decisions should be irrevocable, and his reputation such that no one would dream of overreaching or cajoling him.

The Prince who inspires such an opinion of himself is greatly esteemed, and against one who is greatly esteemed conspiracy is difficult; nor, when he is known to be an excellent Prince and held in reverence by his subjects, will it be easy to attack him. For a Prince is exposed to two dangers, from within in respect of his subjects, from without in respect of foreign powers. Against the latter he will defend himself with good arms and good allies, and if he have good arms he will always have good allies; and when things are settled abroad, they will always be settled at home, unless disturbed by conspiracies; and even should there be hostility from without, if he has taken those measures, and has lived in the way I have recommended, and if he never abandons hope, he will withstand every attack; as I have said was done by Nabis the Spartan.

As regards his own subjects, when affairs are quiet abroad, he has to fear they may engage in secret plots; against which a Prince best secures himself when he escapes being hated or despised, and keeps on good terms with his people; and this, as I have already shown at length, it is essential he should do. Not to be hated or despised by the body of his subjects, is one of the surest safeguards that a Prince can have against conspiracy. For he who conspires always reckons on pleasing the people by putting the Prince to death; but when he sees that instead of pleasing he will offend them, he cannot summon courage to carry out his design. For the difficulties that attend conspirators are infinite, and we know from experience that while there have been many conspiracies, few of them have succeeded.

He who conspires cannot do so alone, nor can he assume as his companions any save those whom he believes to be discontented; but so soon as you impart your design to a discontented man, you supply him with the means of removing his discontent, since by betraying you he can procure for himself every advantage; so that seeing on the one hand certain gain, and on the other a doubtful and dangerous risk, he must either be a rare friend to you, or the mortal enemy of his Prince, if he keep your secret.

To put the matter shortly, I say that on the side of the conspirator there are distrust, jealousy, and dread of punishment to deter him, while on the side of the Prince there are the laws, the majesty of the throne, the protection of friends and of the government to defend him; to which if the general good-will of the people be added, it is hardly possible that any should be rash enough to conspire. For while in ordinary cases, the conspirator has ground for fear only before the execution of his villainy, in this case he has also cause to fear after the crime has been perpetrated, since he has the people for his enemy, and is thus cut off from every hope of shelter.

Of this, endless instances might be given, but I shall content myself with one that happened within the recollection of our fathers. Messer Annibale Bentivoglio, Lord of Bologna and grandfather of the present Messer Annibale, was conspired against and murdered by the Canneschi, leaving behind none belonging to him save Messer Giovanni, then an infant in arms. Immediately upon the murder, the people rose and put all the Canneschi to death. This resulted from the general goodwill with which the House of the Bentivogli was then regarded in Bologna; which feeling was so strong, that when upon the death of Messer Annibale no one was left who could govern the State, there being reason to believe that a descendant of the family (who up to that time had been thought to be the son of a smith), was living in Florence, the citizens of Bologna came there for him, and entrusted him with the government of their city; which he retained until Messer Giovanni was old enough to govern.

To be brief, a Prince has little to fear from conspiracies when his subjects are well disposed towards him; but when they are hostile and hold him in detestation, he has then reason to fear everything and every one. And well ordered States and wise Princes have provided with extreme care that the nobility shall not be driven to desperation, and that the commons shall be kept satisfied and contented; for this is one of the most important matters that a Prince has to look to.

Among the well ordered and governed Kingdoms of our day is that of France, wherein we find an infinite number of wise institutions, upon which depend the freedom and the security of the King, and of which the most important are the Parliament and its authority. For he who gave its constitution to this Realm, knowing the ambition and arrogance of the nobles, and judging it necessary to bridle and restrain them, and on the other hand knowing the hatred, originating in fear, entertained against them by the commons, and desiring that they should be safe, was unwilling that the responsibility for this should rest on the King; and to relieve him of the ill-will which he might incur with the nobles by favouring the commons, or with the commons by favouring the nobles, appointed a third party to be arbitrator, who without committing the King, might depress the nobles and uphold the commons. Nor could there be any better, wiser, or surer safeguard for the King and the Kingdom. And hence we may draw another notable lesson, namely, that Princes should devolve on others those matters that entail responsibility, and reserve to themselves those that relate to grace and favour. And again I say that a Prince should esteem the great, but must not make himself odious to the people.

To some it may perhaps appear, that if the lives and deaths of many of the Roman Emperors be considered, they offer examples opposed to the views expressed by me; since we find that some among them who had always lived good lives, and shown themselves possessed of great qualities, were nevertheless deposed and even put to death by their subjects who had conspired against them.

In answer to such objections, I shall examine the characters of several Emperors, and show that the causes of their downfall were in no way different from those which I have indicated. In doing this I shall submit for consideration such matters only as must strike every one who reads the history of these times; and it will be enough for my purpose to take those Emperors who reigned from the time of Marcus the Philosopher to the time of Maximinus, who were, inclusively, Marcus, Commodus his son, Pertinax, Julianus, Severus, Caracalla his son, Macrinus, Heliogabalus, Alexander, and Maximinus.

In the first place, then, we have to note that while in other Princedoms the Prince has only to contend with the ambition of the nobles and the insubordination of the people, the Roman Emperors had a further difficulty to encounter in the cruelty and rapacity of their soldiers, which were so distracting as to cause the ruin of many of these Princes. For it was hardly possible for them to satisfy both the soldiers and the people; the latter loving peace and therefore preferring sober Princes, while the former preferred a Prince of a warlike spirit, however harsh, haughty, or rapacious; being willing that he should exercise these qualities against the people, as the means of procuring for themselves double pay, and indulging their greed and cruelty.

Whence it followed that those Emperors who had not inherited or won for themselves such authority as enabled them to keep both people and soldiers in check, were always ruined. The most of them, and those especially who came to the Empire new and without experience, seeing the difficulty of dealing with these conflicting humours, set themselves to satisfy the soldiers, and made little account of offending the people. And for them this was a necessary course to take; for as Princes cannot escape being hated by some, they should, in the first place, endeavour not to be hated by a class; failing in which, they must do all they can to escape the hatred of that class which is the stronger. Wherefore those Emperors who, by reason of their newness, stood in need of extraordinary support, sided with the soldiery rather than with the people; a course which turned out advantageous or otherwise, according as the Prince knew, or did not know, how to maintain his authority over them.

From the causes indicated it resulted that Marcus, Pertinax, and Alexander, being Princes of a temperate disposition, lovers of justice, enemies of cruelty, gentle, and kindly, had all, save Marcus, an unhappy end. Marcus alone lived and died honoured in the highest degree; and this because he had succeeded to the Empire by right of inheritance, and not through the favour either of the soldiery or of the people; and also because, being endowed with many virtues which made him revered, he kept, while he lived, both factions within bounds, and was never either hated or despised.

But Pertinax was chosen Emperor against the will of the soldiery, who being accustomed to a licentious life under Commodus, could not tolerate the stricter discipline to which his successor sought to bring them back. And having thus made himself hated, and being at the same time despised by reason of his advanced age, he was ruined at the very outset of his reign.

And here it is to be noted that hatred is incurred as well on account of good actions as of bad; for which reason, as I have already said, a Prince who would maintain his authority is often compelled to be other than good. For when the class, be it the people, the soldiers, or the nobles, on whom you judge it necessary to rely for your support, is corrupt, you must needs adapt yourself to its humours, and satisfy these, in which case virtuous conduct will only prejudice you.

Let us now come to Alexander, who was so just a ruler that among the praises ascribed to him it is recorded, that, during the fourteen years he held the Empire, no man was ever put to death by him without trial. Nevertheless, being accounted effeminate, and thought to be governed by his mother, he fell into contempt, and the army conspiring against him, slew him.

When we turn to consider the characters of Commodus, Severus, and Caracalla, we find them all to have been most cruel and rapacious Princes, who to satisfy the soldiery, scrupled not to inflict every kind of wrong upon the people. And all of them, except Severus, came to a bad end. But in Severus there was such strength of character, that, keeping the soldiers his friends, he was able, although he oppressed the people, to reign on prosperously to the last; because his great qualities made him so admirable in the eyes both of the people and the soldiers, that the former remained in a manner amazed and awestruck, while the latter were respectful and contented.

And because his actions, for one who was a new Prince, were thus remarkable, I will point out shortly how well he understood to play the part both of the lion and of the fox, each of which natures, as I have observed before, a Prince should know how to assume.

Knowing the indolent disposition of the Emperor Julianus, Severus persuaded the army which he commanded in Illyria that it was their duty to go to Rome to avenge the death of Pertinax, who had been slain by the Pretorian guards. Under this pretext, and without disclosing his design on the Empire, he put his army in march, and reached Italy before it was known that he had set out. On his arrival in Rome, the Senate, through fear, elected him Emperor and put Julianus to death. After taking this first step, two obstacles still remained to his becoming sole master of the Empire; one in Asia, where Niger who commanded the armies of the East had caused himself to be proclaimed Emperor; the other in the West, where Albinus, who also aspired to the Empire, was in command. And as Severus judged it dangerous to declare open war against both, he resolved to proceed against Niger by arms, and against Albinus by artifice. To the latter, accordingly, he wrote, that having been chosen Emperor by the Senate, he desired to share the dignity with him; that he therefore sent him the title of Caesar, and in accordance with a resolution of the Senate assumed him as his colleague. All which statements Albinus accepted as true. But so soon as Severus had defeated and slain Niger, and restored tranquillity in the East, returning to Rome he complained in the Senate that Albinus, all unmindful of the favours he had received from him, had treacherously sought to destroy him; for which cause he was compelled to go and punish his ingratitude. Whereupon he set forth to seek Albinus in Gaul, where he at once deprived him of his dignities and his life.

Whoever, therefore, examines carefully the actions of this Emperor, will find in him all the fierceness of the lion and all the craft of the fox, and will note how he was feared and respected by the people, yet not hated by the army, and will not be surprised that though a new man, he was able to maintain his hold of so great an Empire. For the splendour of his reputation always shielded him from the odium which the people might otherwise have conceived against him by reason of his cruelty and rapacity.

Caracalla, his son, was likewise a man of great parts, endowed with qualities that made him admirable in the sight of the people, and endeared him to the army, being of a warlike spirit, most patient of fatigue, and contemning all luxury in food and every other effeminacy. Nevertheless, his ferocity and cruelty were so extravagant and unheard of (he having put to death a vast number of the inhabitants of Rome at different times, and the whole of those of Alexandria at a stroke), that he came to be detested by all the world, and so feared even by those whom he had about him, that at the last he was slain by a centurion in the midst of his army.

And here let it be noted that deaths like this which are the result of a deliberate and fixed resolve, cannot be escaped by Princes, since any one who disregards his own life can effect them. A Prince, however, needs the less to fear them as they are seldom attempted. The only precaution he can take is to avoid doing grave wrong to any of those who serve him, or whom he has near him as officers of his Court, a precaution which Caracalla neglected in putting to a shameful death the brother of this centurion, and in using daily threats against the man himself, whom he nevertheless retained as one of his bodyguard. This, as the event showed, was a rash and fatal course.

We come next to Commodus, who, as he took the Empire by hereditary right, ought to have held it with much ease. For being the son of Marcus, he had only to follow in his father's footsteps to content both the people and the soldiery. But being of a cruel and brutal nature, to sate his rapacity at the expense of the people, he sought support from the army, and indulged it in every kind of excess. On the other hand, by an utter disregard of his dignity, in frequently descending into the arena to fight with gladiators, and by other base acts wholly unworthy of the Imperial station, he became contemptible in the eyes of the soldiery; and being on the one hand hated, on the other despised, was at last conspired against and murdered.

The character of Maximinus remains to be touched upon. He was of a very warlike disposition, and on the death of Alexander, of whom we have already spoken, was chosen Emperor by the army who had been displeased with the effeminacy of that Prince. But this dignity he did not long enjoy, since two causes concurred to render him at once odious and contemptible; the one the baseness of his origin, he having at one time herded sheep in Thrace, a fact well known to all, and which led all to look on him with disdain; the other that on being proclaimed Emperor, delaying to repair to Rome and enter on possession of the Imperial throne, he incurred the reputation of excessive cruelty by reason of the many atrocities perpetrated by his prefects in Rome and other parts of the Empire. The result was that the whole world, stirred at once with scorn of his mean birth and with the hatred which the dread of his ferocity inspired, combined against him, Africa leading the way, the Senate and people of Rome and the whole of Italy following. In which conspiracy his own army joined. For they, being engaged in the siege of Aquileja and finding difficulty in reducing it, disgusted with his cruelty, and less afraid of him when they saw so many against him, put him to death.

I need say nothing of Heliogabalus, Macrinus, or Julianus, all of whom being utterly despicable, came to a speedy downfall, but shall conclude these remarks by observing, that the Princes of our own days are less troubled with the difficulty of having to make constant efforts to keep their soldiers in good humour. For though they must treat them with some indulgence, the need for doing so is soon over, since none of these Princes possesses a standing army which, like the armies of the Roman Empire, has strengthened with the growth of his government and the administration of his State. And if it was then necessary to satisfy the soldiers rather than the people, because the soldiers were more powerful than the people, now it is more necessary for all Princes, except the Turk and the Soldan, to satisfy the people rather than the soldiery, since the former are more powerful than the latter.

I except the Turk because he has always about him some twelve thousand foot soldiers and fifteen thousand horse, on whom depend the security and strength of his kingdom, and with whom he must needs keep on good terms, all regard for the people being subordinate. The government of the Soldan is similar, so that he too being wholly in the hands of his soldiers, must keep well with them without regard to the people.

And here you are to note that the State of the Soldan, while it is unlike all other Princedoms, resembles the Christian Pontificate in this, that it can neither be classed as new, nor as hereditary. For the sons of a Soldan who dies do not succeed to the kingdom as his heirs, but he who is elected to the post by those who have authority to make such elections. And this being the ancient and established order of things, the Princedom cannot be accounted new, since none of the difficulties that attend new Princedoms are found in it. For although the Prince be new, the institutions of the State are old, and are so contrived that the elected Prince is accepted as though he were an hereditary Sovereign.

But returning to the matter in hand, I say that whoever reflects on the above reasoning will see that either hatred or contempt was the ruin of the Emperors whom I have named; and will also understand how it happened that some taking one way and some the opposite, one only by each of these roads came to a happy, and all the rest to an unhappy end. Because for Pertinax and Alexander, they being new Princes, it was useless and hurtful to try to imitate Marcus, who was an hereditary Prince; and similarly for Caracalla, Commodus, and Maximinus it was a fatal error to imitate Severus, since they lacked the qualities that would have enabled them to tread in his footsteps.

In short, a Prince new to the Princedom cannot imitate the actions of Marcus, nor is it necessary that he should imitate all those of Severus; but he should borrow from Severus those parts of his conduct which are needed to serve as a foundation for his government, and from Marcus those suited to maintain it, and render it glorious when once established.

CHAPTER XX

Whether Fortresses, and Certain Other Expedients to Which Princes Often Have Recourse, are Profitable or Hurtful

To govern more securely some Princes have disarmed their subjects, others have kept the towns subject to them divided by factions; some have fostered hostility against themselves, others have sought to gain over those who at the beginning of their reign were looked on with suspicion; some have built fortresses, others have dismantled and destroyed them; and though no definite judgment can be pronounced respecting any of these methods, without regard to the special circumstances of the State to which it is proposed to apply them, I shall nevertheless speak of them in as comprehensive a way as the nature of the subject will admit.

It has never chanced that any new Prince has disarmed his subjects. On the contrary, when he has found them unarmed he has always armed them. For the arms thus provided become yours, those whom you suspected grow faithful, while those who were faithful at the first, continue so, and from your subjects become your partisans. And though all your subjects cannot be armed, yet if those of them whom you arm be treated with marked favour, you can deal more securely with the rest. For the difference which those whom you supply with arms perceive in their treatment, will bind them to you, while the others will excuse you, recognizing that those who incur greater risk and responsibility merit greater rewards. But by disarming, you at once give offence, since you show your subjects that you distrust them, either as doubting their courage, or as doubting their fidelity, each of which imputations begets hatred against you. Moreover, as you cannot maintain yourself without arms you must have recourse to mercenary troops. What these are I have already shown, but even if they were good, they could never avail to defend you, at once against powerful enemies abroad and against subjects whom you distrust. Wherefore, as I have said already, new Princes in new Princedoms have always provided for their being armed; and of instances of this History is full.

But when a Prince acquires a new State, which thus becomes joined on like a limb to his old possessions, he must disarm its inhabitants, except such of them as have taken part with him while he was acquiring it; and even these, as time and occasion serve, he should seek to render soft and effeminate; and he must so manage matters that all the arms of the new State shall be in the hands of his own soldiers who have served under him in his ancient dominions.

Our forefathers, even such among them as were esteemed wise, were wont to say that 'Pistoja was to be held by feuds, and Pisa by fortresses,' and on this principle used to promote dissensions in various subject towns with a view to retain them with less effort. At a time when Italy was in some measure in equilibrium, this may have been a prudent course to follow; but at the present day it seems impossible to recommend it as a general rule of policy. For I do not believe that divisions purposely caused can ever lead to good; on the contrary, when an enemy approaches, divided cities are lost at once, for the weaker faction will always side with the invader, and the other will not be able to stand alone.

The Venetians, influenced as I believe by the reasons above mentioned, fostered the factions of Guelf and Ghibelline in the cities subject to them; and though they did not suffer blood to be shed, fomented their feuds, in order that the citizens having their minds occupied with these disputes might not conspire against them. But this, as we know, did not turn out to their advantage, for after their defeat at Vaila, one of the two factions, suddenly taking courage, deprived them of the whole of their territory.

Moreover methods like these argue weakness in a Prince, for under a strong government such divisions would never be permitted, since they are profitable only in time of peace as an expedient whereby subjects may be more easily managed; but when war breaks out their insufficiency is demonstrated.

Doubtless, Princes become great by vanquishing difficulties and opposition, and Fortune, on that account, when she desires to aggrandize a new Prince, who has more need than an hereditary Prince to win reputation, causes enemies to spring up, and urges them on to attack him, to the end that he may have opportunities to overcome them, and make his ascent by the very ladder which they have planted. For which reason, many are of the opinion that a wise Prince, when he has the occasion, ought dexterously to promote hostility to himself in certain quarters, in order that his greatness may be enhanced by crushing it.

Princes, and new Princes especially, have found greater fidelity and helpfulness in those whom, at the beginning of their reign, they have held in suspicion, than in those who at the outset have enjoyed their confidence; and Pandolfo Petrucci, Lord of Siena, governed his State by the instrumentality of those whom he had at one time distrusted, in preference to all others. But on this point it is impossible to lay down any general rule, since the course to be followed varies with the circumstances. This only I will say, that those men who at the beginning of a reign have been hostile, if of a sort requiring support to maintain them, may always be won over by the Prince with much ease, and are the more bound to serve him faithfully because they know that they have to efface by their conduct the unfavourable impression he had formed of them; and in this way a Prince always obtains better help from them, than from those who serving him in too complete security neglect his affairs.

And since the subject suggests it, I must not fail to remind the Prince who acquires a new State through the favour of its inhabitants, to weigh well what were the causes which led those who favoured him to do so; and if it be seen that they have acted not from any natural affection for him, but merely out of discontent with the former government, that he will find the greatest difficulty in keeping them his friends, since it will be impossible for him to content them. Carefully considering the cause of this, with the aid of examples taken from times ancient and modern, he will perceive that it is far easier to secure the friendship of those who being satisfied with things as they stood, were for that very reason his enemies, than of those who sided with him and aided him in his usurpation only because they were discontented.

It has been customary for Princes, with a view to hold their dominions more securely, to build fortresses which might serve as a curb and restraint on such as have designs against them, and as a safe refuge against a first onset. I approve this custom, because it has been followed from the earliest times. Nevertheless, in our own days, Messer Niccolo Vitelli thought it prudent to dismantle two fortresses in Città di Castello in order to secure that town: and Guido Ubaldo, Duke of Urbino, on returning to his dominions, whence he had been driven by Cesare Borgia, razed to their foundations the fortresses throughout the Dukedom, judging that if these were removed, it would not again be so easily lost. A like course was followed by the Bentivogli on their return to Bologna.

Fortresses, therefore, are useful or no, according to circumstances, and if in one way they benefit, in another they injure you. We may state the case thus: the Prince who is more afraid of his subjects than of strangers ought to build fortresses, while he who is more afraid of strangers than of his subjects, should leave them alone. The citadel built by Francesco Sforza in Milan, has been, and will hereafter prove to be, more dangerous to the House of Sforza than any other disorder of that State. So that, on the whole, the best fortress you can have, is in not being hated by your subjects. If they hate you no fortress will save you; for when once the people take up arms, foreigners are never wanting to assist them.

Within our own time it does not appear that fortresses have been

of service to any Prince, unless to the Countess of Forli after her
husband Count Girolamo was murdered; for by this means she was
able to escape the first onset of the insurgents, and awaiting succour
from Milan, to recover her State; the circumstances of the times not
allowing any foreigner to lend assistance to the people. But afterwards, when she was attacked by Cesare Borgia, and the people, out
of hostility to her, took part with the invader, her fortresses were
of little avail. So that, both on this and on the former occasion, it
would have been safer for her to have had no fortresses, than to have
had her subjects for enemies.

All which considerations taken into account, I shall applaud him
who builds fortresses, and him who does not; but I shall blame him
who, trusting in them, reckons it a light thing to be held in hatred
by his people.

CHAPTER XXI

How a Prince Should Bear Himself So As to Acquire Reputation

Nothing makes a Prince so well thought of as to undertake great
enterprises and give striking proofs of his capacity.

Among the Princes of our time Ferdinand of Aragon, the present
King of Spain, may almost be accounted a new Prince, since from
one of the weakest he has become, for fame and glory, the foremost
King in Christendom. And if you consider his achievements you
will find them all great and some extraordinary.

In the beginning of his reign he made war on Granada, which
enterprise was the foundation of his power. At first he carried on
the war leisurely, without fear of interruption, and kept the attention and thoughts of the Barons of Castile so completely occupied
with it, that they had no time to think of changes at home. Meanwhile he insensibly acquired reputation among them and authority
over them. With the money of the Church and of his subjects he
was able to maintain his armies, and during the prolonged contest
to lay the foundations of that military discipline which afterwards
made him so famous. Moreover, to enable him to engage in still
greater undertakings, always covering himself with the cloak of

religion, he had recourse to what may be called *pious cruelty,* in driving out and clearing his Kingdom of the Moors; than which exploit none could be more wonderful or uncommon. Using the same pretext he made war on Africa, invaded Italy, and finally attacked France; and being thus constantly busied in planning and executing vast designs, he kept the minds of his subjects in suspense and admiration, and occupied with the results of his actions, which arose one out of another in such close succession as left neither time nor opportunity to oppose them.

Again, it greatly profits a Prince in conducting the internal government of his State, to follow striking methods, such as are recorded of Messer Bernabo of Milan, whenever the remarkable actions of any one in civil life, whether for good or for evil, afford him occasion; and to choose such ways of rewarding and punishing as cannot fail to be much spoken of. But above all, he should strive by all his actions to inspire a sense of his greatness and goodness.

A Prince is likewise esteemed who is a stanch friend and a thorough foe, that is to say, who without reserve openly declares for one against another, this being always a more advantageous course than to stand neutral. For supposing two of your powerful neighbours come to blows, it must either be that you have, or have not, reason to fear the one who comes off victorious. In either case it will always be well for you to declare yourself, and join in frankly with one side or other. For should you fail to do so you are certain, in the former of the cases put, to become the prey of the victor to the satisfaction and delight of the vanquished, and no reason or circumstance that you may plead will avail to shield or shelter you; for the victor dislikes doubtful friends, and such as will not help him at a pinch; and the vanquished will have nothing to say to you, since you would not share his fortunes sword in hand.

When Antiochus, at the instance of the Aetolians, passed into Greece in order to drive out the Romans, he sent envoys to the Achaians, who were friendly to the Romans, exhorting them to stand neutral. The Romans, on the other hand, urged them to take up arms on their behalf. The matter coming to be discussed in the Council of the Achaians, the legate of Antiochus again urged neutrality, whereupon the Roman envoy answered—'Nothing can be less to your advantage than the course which has been recommended as the best and most useful for your State, namely, to refrain from taking any part in our war, for by standing aloof you will gain neither favour nor fame, but remain the prize of the victor.' And it will always happen that he who is not your friend will invite you to neutrality, while he who is your friend will call on you to declare yourself openly in arms. Irresolute Princes, to escape immediate danger, commonly follow the neutral path, in most instances to their destruction. But when you pronounce valiantly in favour of one side or other, if he to whom you give your adherence conquers, although he be powerful and you are at his mercy, still he is under obligations to you, and has become your friend; and none are so lost to shame as to destroy with manifest ingratitude, one who has helped them. Besides which, victories are never so complete that the victor can afford to disregard all considerations whatsoever, more especially considerations of justice. On the other hand, if he with whom you take part should lose, you will always be favourably regarded by him; while he can he will aid you, and you become his companion in a cause which may recover.

In the second case, namely, when both combatants are of such limited strength that whichever wins you have no cause to fear, it is all the more prudent for you to take a side, for you will then be ruining the one with the help of the other, who were he wise would endeavour to save him. If he whom you help conquers, he remains in your power, and with your aid he cannot but conquer.

And here let it be noted that a Prince should be careful never to join with one stronger than himself in attacking others, unless, as already said, he be driven to it by necessity. For if he whom you join prevails, you are at his mercy; and Princes, so far as in them lies, should avoid placing themselves at the mercy of others. The Venetians, although they might have declined the alliance, joined with France against the Duke of Milan, which brought about their ruin. But when an alliance cannot be avoided, as was the case with the Florentines when the Pope and Spain together led their armies to attack Lombardy, a Prince, for the reasons given, must take a side. Nor let it be supposed that any State can choose for itself a perfectly safe line of policy. On the contrary, it must reckon on every course which it may take being doubtful; for it happens in all human affairs that we never seek to escape one mischief without falling into another. Prudence therefore consists in knowing how to distinguish degrees of disadvantage, and in accepting a less evil as a good.

Again, a Prince should show himself a patron of merit, and should honour those who excel in every art. He ought accordingly to encourage his subjects by enabling them to pursue their callings, whether mercantile, agricultural, or any other, in security, so that this man shall not be deterred from beautifying his possessions from the apprehension that they may be taken from him, or that other refrain from opening a trade through fear of taxes; and he should provide rewards for those who desire so to employ themselves, and for all who are disposed in any way to add to the greatness of his City or State.

He ought, moreover, at suitable seasons of the year to entertain the people with festivals and shows. And because all cities are divided into guilds and companies, he should show attention to these societies, and sometimes take part in their meetings; offering an example of courtesy and munificence, but always maintaining the dignity of his station, which must under no circumstances be compromised.

CHAPTER XXII

OF THE SECRETARIES OF PRINCES

THE choice of Ministers is a matter of no small moment to a Prince. Whether they shall be good or no depends on his prudence, so that the readiest conjecture we can form of the character and sagacity of a Prince, is from seeing what sort of men he has about him. When they are at once capable and faithful, we may always account him wise, since he has known to recognize their merit and to retain their fidelity. But if they be otherwise, we must pronounce unfavourably of him, since he has committed a first fault in making this selection.

There was none who knew Messer Antonio of Venafro, as Minister of Pandolfo Petrucci, Lord of Siena, but thought Pandolfo a most prudent ruler in having him for his servant. And since there are three scales of intelligence, one which understands by itself, a second which understands what is shown it by others, and a third which understands neither by itself nor on the showing of others, the first of which is most excellent, the second good, but the third worthless, we must needs admit that if Pandolfo was not in the first of these degrees, he was in the second; for when one has the judgment to discern the good from the bad in what another says or does, though he be devoid of invention, he can recognize the merits and demerits of his servant, and will commend the former while he corrects the latter. The servant cannot hope to deceive such a master, and will continue good.

As to how a Prince is to know his Minister, this unerring rule may be laid down. When you see a Minister thinking more of himself than of you, and in all his actions seeking his own ends, that man can never be a good Minister or one that you can trust. For he who has the charge of the State committed to him, ought not to think of himself, but only of his Prince, and should never bring to the notice of the latter what does not directly concern him. On the other hand, to keep his Minister good, the Prince should be considerate of him, dignifying him, enriching him, binding him to himself by benefits, and sharing with him the honours as well as the burthens of the State, so that the abundant honours and wealth bestowed upon him may divert him from seeking them at other hands; while the great responsibilities wherewith he is charged may lead him to dread change, knowing that he cannot stand alone without his master's support. When Prince and Minister are upon this footing they can mutually trust one another; but when the contrary is the case, it will always fare ill with one or other of them.

CHAPTER XXIII

That Flatterers Should Be Shunned

One error into which Princes, unless very prudent or very fortunate in their choice of friends, are apt to fall, is of so great importance that I must not pass it over. I mean in respect of flatterers.

These abound in Courts, because men take such pleasure in their own concerns, and so deceive themselves with regard to them, that they can hardly escape this plague; while even in the effort to escape it there is risk of their incurring contempt.

For there is no way to guard against flattery but by letting it be seen that you take no offence in hearing the truth: but when every one is free to tell you the truth respect falls short. Wherefore a prudent Prince should follow a middle course, by choosing certain discreet men from among his subjects, and allowing them alone free leave to speak their minds on any matter on which he asks their opinion, and on none other. But he ought to ask their opinion on everything, and after hearing what they have to say, should reflect and judge for himself. And with these counsellors collectively, and with each of them separately, his bearing should be such, that each and all of them may know that the more freely they declare their thoughts the better they will be liked. Besides these, the Prince should hearken to no others, but should follow the course determined on, and afterwards adhere firmly to his resolves. Whoever acts otherwise is either undone by flatterers, or from continually vacillating as opinions vary, comes to be held in light esteem.

With reference to this matter, I shall cite a recent instance. Father Luke, who is attached to the Court of the present Emperor Maximilian, in speaking of his Majesty told me, that he seeks advice from none, yet never has his own way; and this from his following a course contrary to that above recommended. For being of a secret disposition, he never discloses his intentions to any, nor asks their opinion; and it is only when his plans are to be carried out that they begin to be discovered and known, and at the same time they begin to be thwarted by those he has about him, when he being facile gives way. Hence it happens that what he does one day, he undoes the next; that his wishes and designs are never fully ascertained; and that it is impossible to build on his resolves.

A Prince, therefore, ought always to take counsel, but at such times and seasons only as he himself pleases, and not when it pleases others; nay, he should discourage every one from obtruding advice on matters on which it is not sought. But he should be free in asking advice, and afterwards, as regards the matters on which he has asked it, a patient hearer of the truth, and even displeased should he perceive that any one, from whatever motive, keeps it back.

But those who think that every Prince who has a name for prudence owes it to the wise counsellors he has around him, and not to any merit of his own, are certainly mistaken; since it is an unerring rule and of universal application that a Prince who is not wise himself cannot be well advised by others, unless by chance he surrender himself to be wholly governed by some one adviser who happens to be supremely prudent; in which case he may, indeed, be well advised; but not for long, since such an adviser will soon deprive him of his Government. If he listen to a multitude of advisers, the Prince who is not wise will never have consistent counsels, nor will he know of himself how to reconcile them. Each of his counsellors will study his own advantage, and the Prince will be unable to detect or correct them. Nor could it well be otherwise, for men will always grow rogues on your hands unless they find themselves under a necessity to be honest.

Hence it follows that good counsels, whencesoever they come, have their origin in the prudence of the Prince, and not the prudence of the Prince in wise counsels.

CHAPTER XXIV

Why the Princes of Italy Have Lost Their States

THE lessons above taught if prudently followed will make a new Prince seem like an old one, and will soon seat him in his place more firmly and securely than if his authority had the sanction of time. For the actions of a new Prince are watched much more closely than those of an hereditary Prince; and when seen to be good are far more effectual than antiquity of blood in gaining men over and attaching them to his cause. For men are more nearly touched by things present than by things past, and when they find themselves well off as they are, enjoy their felicity and seek no further; nay, are ready to do their utmost in defence of the new Prince, provided he be not wanting to himself in other respects. In this way there accrues to him a twofold glory, in having laid the foundations of the new

Princedom, and in having strengthened and adorned it with good laws and good arms, with faithful friends and great deeds; as, on the other hand, there is a double disgrace in one who has been born to a Princedom losing it by his own want of wisdom.

And if we contemplate those Lords who in our own times have lost their dominions in Italy, such as the King of Naples, the Duke of Milan, and others, in the first place we shall see, that in respect of arms they have, for reasons already dwelt on, been all alike defective; and next, that some of them have either had the people against them, or if they have had the people with them, have not known how to secure themselves against their nobles. For without such defects as these, States powerful enough to keep an army in the field are never overthrown.

Philip of Macedon, not the father of Alexander the Great, but he who was vanquished by Titus Quintius, had no great State as compared with the strength of the Romans and Greeks who attacked him. Nevertheless, being a Prince of a warlike spirit, and skilful in gaining the good will of the people and in securing the fidelity of the nobles, he maintained himself for many years against his assailants, and in the end, though he lost some towns, succeeded in saving his Kingdom.

Let those Princes of ours, therefore, who, after holding them for a length of years, have lost their dominions, blame not Fortune but their own inertness. For never having reflected in tranquil times that there might come a change (and it is human nature when the sea is calm not to think of storms), when adversity overtook them, they thought not of defence but only of escape, hoping that their people, disgusted with the arrogance of the conqueror, would some day recall them.

This course may be a good one to follow when all others fail, but it were the height of folly, trusting to it, to abandon every other; since none would wish to fall on the chance of some one else being found to lift him up. It may not happen that you are recalled by your people, or if it happen, it gives you no security. It is an ignoble resource, since it does not depend on you for its success; and those modes of defence are alone good, certain and lasting, which depend upon yourself and your own worth.

CHAPTER XXV

What Fortune Can Effect in Human Affairs, and How She May Be Withstood

I AM not ignorant that many have been and are of the opinion that human affairs are so governed by Fortune and by God, that men cannot alter them by any prudence of theirs, and indeed have no remedy against them; and for this reason have come to think that it is not worth while to labour much about anything, but that they must leave everything to be determined by chance.

Often when I turn the matter over, I am in part inclined to agree with this opinion, which has had the readier acceptance in our own times from the great changes in things which we have seen, and every day see happen contrary to all human expectation. Nevertheless, that our free will be not wholly set aside, I think it may be the case that Fortune is the mistress of one half our actions, and yet leaves the control of the other half, or a little less, to ourselves. And I would liken her to one of those wild torrents which, when angry, overflow the plains, sweep away trees and houses, and carry off soil from one bank to throw it down upon the other. Every one flees before them, and yields to their fury without the least power to resist. And yet, though this be their nature, it does not follow that in seasons of fair weather, men cannot, by constructing weirs and moles, take such precautions as will cause them when again in flood to pass off by some artificial channel, or at least prevent their course from being so uncontrolled and destructive. And so it is with Fortune, who displays her might where there is no organized strength to resist her, and directs her onset where she knows that there is neither barrier nor embankment to confine her.

And if you look at Italy, which has been at once the seat of these changes and their cause, you will perceive that it is a field without embankment or barrier. For if, like Germany, France, and Spain, it had been guarded with sufficient skill, this inundation, if it ever came upon us, would never have wrought the violent changes which we have witnessed.

This I think enough to say generally touching resistance to Fortune. But confining myself more closely to the matter in hand, I note that one day we see a Prince prospering and the next day overthrown, without detecting any change in his nature or character. This, I believe, comes chiefly from a cause already dwelt upon, namely, that a Prince who rests wholly on Fortune is ruined when she changes. Moreover, I believe that he will prosper most whose mode of acting best adapts itself to the character of the times; and conversely that he will be unprosperous, with whose mode of acting the times do not accord. For we see that men in these matters which lead to the end that each has before him, namely, glory and wealth, proceed by different ways, one with caution, another with impetuosity, one with violence, another with subtlety, one with patience, another with its contrary; and that by one or other of these different courses each may succeed.

Again, of two who act cautiously, you shall find that one attains his end, the other not, and that two of different temperament, the one cautious, the other impetuous, are equally successful. All which happens from no other cause than that the character of the times accords or does not accord with their methods of acting. And hence it comes, as I have already said, that two operating differently arrive at the same result, and two operating similarly, the one succeeds and the other not. On this likewise depend the vicissitudes of Fortune. For if to one who conducts himself with caution and patience, time and circumstances are propitious, so that his method of acting is good, he goes on prospering; but if these change he is ruined, because he does not change his method of acting.

For no man is found so prudent as to know how to adapt himself to these changes, both because he cannot deviate from the course to which nature inclines him, and because, having always prospered while adhering to one path, he cannot be persuaded that it would be well for him to forsake it. And so when occasion requires the cautious man to act impetuously, he cannot do so and is undone: whereas, had he changed his nature with time and circumstances, his fortune would have been unchanged.

Pope Julius II proceeded with impetuosity in all his undertakings, and found time and circumstances in such harmony with his mode of acting that he always obtained a happy result. Witness his first expedition against Bologna, when Messer Giovanni Bentivoglio was yet living. The Venetians were not favourable to the enterprise; nor was the King of Spain. Negotiations respecting it with the King of France were still open. Nevertheless, the Pope with his wonted hardihood and impetuosity marched in person on the expedition, and by this movement brought the King of Spain and the Venetians to a check, the latter through fear, the former from his eagerness to recover the entire Kingdom of Naples; at the same time, he dragged after him the King of France, who, desiring to have the Pope for an ally in humbling the Venetians, on finding him already in motion saw that he could not refuse him his soldiers without openly offending him. By the impetuosity of his movements, therefore, Julius effected what no other Pontiff endowed with the highest human prudence could. For had he, as any other Pope would have done, put off his departure from Rome until terms had been settled and everything duly arranged, he never would have succeeded. For the King of France would have found a thousand pretexts to delay him, and the others would have menaced him with a thousand alarms. I shall not touch upon his other actions, which were all of a like character, and all of which had a happy issue, since the shortness of his life did not allow him to experience reverses. But if times had overtaken him, rendering a cautious line of conduct necessary, his ruin must have ensued, since he never could have departed from those methods to which nature inclined him.

To be brief, I say that since Fortune changes and men stand fixed in their old ways, they are prosperous so long as there is congruity between them, and the reverse when there is not. Of this, however, I am well persuaded, that it is better to be impetuous than cautious. For Fortune is a woman who to be kept under must be beaten and roughly handled; and we see that she suffers herself to be more readily mastered by those who so treat her than by those who are more timid in their approaches. And always, like a woman, she favours the young, because they are less scrupulous and fiercer, and command her with greater audacity.

CHAPTER XXVI

An Exhortation to Liberate Italy from the Barbarians

TURNING over in my mind all the matters which have above been considered, and debating with myself whether in Italy at the present hour the times are such as might serve to confer honour on a new Prince, and whether a fit opportunity now offers for a prudent and valiant leader to bring about changes glorious for himself and beneficial to the whole Italian people, it seems to me that so many conditions combine to further such an enterprise, that I know of no time so favourable to it as the present. And if, as I have said, it was necessary in order to display the valour of Moses that the children of Israel should be slaves in Egypt, and to know the greatness and courage of Cyrus that the Persians should be oppressed by the Medes, and to illustrate the excellence of Theseus that the Athenians should be scattered and divided, so at this hour, to prove the worth of some Italian hero, it was required that Italy should be brought to her present abject condition, to be more a slave than the Hebrew, more oppressed than the Persian, more disunited than the Athenian, without a head, without order, beaten, spoiled, torn in pieces, over-run and abandoned to destruction in every shape.

But though, heretofore, glimmerings may have been discerned in this man or that, whence it might be conjectured that he was ordained by God for her redemption, nevertheless it has afterwards been seen in the further course of his actions that Fortune has disowned him; so that our country, left almost without life, still waits to know who it is that is to heal her bruises, to put an end to the devastation and plunder of Lombardy, to the exactions and imposts of Naples and Tuscany, and to stanch those wounds of hers which long neglect has changed into running sores.

We see how she prays God to send some one to rescue her from these barbarous cruelties and oppressions. We see too how ready and eager she is to follow any standard were there only some one to raise it. But at present we see no one except in your illustrious House (pre-eminent by its virtues and good fortune, and favoured by God and by the Church whose headship it now holds), who could undertake the part of a deliverer.

But for you this will not be too hard a task, if you keep before your eyes the lives and actions of those whom I have named above. For although these men were singular and extraordinary, after all they were but men, not one of whom had so great an opportunity as now presents itself to you. For their undertakings were not more just than this, nor more easy, nor was God more their friend than yours. The justice of the cause is conspicuous; for that war is just which is necessary, and those arms are sacred from which we derive our only hope. Everywhere there is the strongest disposition to engage in this cause; and where the disposition is strong the difficulty cannot be great, provided you follow the methods observed by those whom I have set before you as models.

But further, we see here extraordinary and unexampled proofs of Divine favour. The sea has been divided; the cloud has attended you on your way; the rock has flowed with water; the manna has rained from heaven; everything has concurred to promote your greatness. What remains to be done must be done by you; since in order not to deprive us of our free will and such share of glory as belongs to us, God will not do everything himself.

Nor is to be marvelled at if none of those Italians I have named has been able to effect what we hope to see effected by your illustrious House; or that amid so many revolutions and so many warlike movements it should always appear as though the military virtues of Italy were spent; for this comes from her old system being defective, and from no one being found among us capable to strike out a new. Nothing confers such honour on the reformer of a State, as do the new laws and institutions which he devises; for these when they stand on a solid basis and have a greatness in their scope, make him admired and venerated. And in Italy material is not wanting for improvement in every form. If the head be weak the limbs are strong, and we see daily in single combats, or where few are engaged, how superior are the strength, dexterity, and intelligence of Italians. But when it comes to armies, they are nowhere, and this from no other reason than the defects of their leaders. For those who are skilful in arms will not obey, and every one thinks himself skilful, since hitherto we have had none among us so raised by merit or by fortune above his fellows that they should yield him the palm. And hence it happens that for the long period of twenty years, during which so many wars have taken place, whenever there has been an army purely Italian it has always been beaten. To this testify, first Taro, then Alessandria, Capua, Genoa, Vaila, Bologna, Mestri.

If then your illustrious House should seek to follow the example of those great men who have delivered their country in past ages, it is before all things necessary, as the true foundation of every such attempt, to be provided with national troops, since you can have no braver, truer, or more faithful soldiers; and although every single man of them be good, collectively they will be better, seeing themselves commanded by their own Prince, and honoured and esteemed by him. That you may be able, therefore, to defend yourself against the foreigner with Italian valour, the first step is to provide yourself with an army such as this.

And although the Swiss and the Spanish infantry are each esteemed formidable, there are yet defects in both, by reason of which troops trained on a different system might not merely withstand them, but be certain of defeating them. For the Spaniards cannot resist cavalry and the Swiss will give way before infantry if they find them as resolute as themselves at close quarters. Whence it has been seen, and may be seen again, that the Spaniards cannot sustain the onset of the French men-at-arms and that the Swiss are broken by the Spanish foot. And although of this last we have no complete instance, we have yet an indication of it in the battle of Ravenna, where the Spanish infantry confronted the German companies who have the same discipline as the Swiss; on which occasion the Spaniards by their agility and with the aid of their bucklers forced their way under the pikes, and stood ready to close with the Germans, who were no longer in a position to defend themselves; and had they not been charged by cavalry, they must have put the Germans to utter rout. Knowing, then, the defects of each of these kinds of troops, you can train your men on some different system, to withstand cavalry and not to fear infantry. To effect this, will not require the creation of any new forces, but simply a change in the discipline of the old. And these are matters in reforming which the new Prince acquires reputation and importance.

This opportunity then, for Italy at last to look on her deliverer, ought not to be allowed to pass away. With what love he would be received in all those Provinces which have suffered from the foreign inundation, with what thirst for vengeance, with what fixed fidelity, with what devotion, and what tears, no words of mine can declare. What gates would be closed against him? What people would refuse him obedience? What jealousy would stand in his way? What Italian but would yield him homage? This barbarian tyranny stinks in all nostrils.

Let your illustrious House therefore take upon itself this enterprise with all the courage and all the hopes with which a just cause is undertaken; so that under your standard this our country may be ennobled, and under your auspices be fulfilled the words of Petrarch:—

> 'Brief will be the strife
> When valour arms against barbaric rage;
> For the bold spirit of the bygone age
> Still warms Italian hearts with life.'

UTOPIA

BY
SIR THOMAS MORE

WITH THE LIFE OF MORE

BY
WILLIAM ROPER

INTRODUCTORY NOTE

THE accompanying intimate account of the life of Sir Thomas More by his son-in-law, William Roper, renders a biographical sketch unnecessary.

While More was a young law student in Lincoln's Inn, he is known to have delivered in the church of St. Lawrence a course of lectures on Saint Augustine's "City of God"; and some have supposed that it was this that suggested to him the composition of the "Utopia." The book itself was begun in Antwerp in 1515, when More was in Flanders engaged in negotiations on behalf of the English wool merchants, and results of his observations among the towns of the Low Countries are evident in some of the details of his imaginary state. The framework seems to have been suggested by an incident related in the narrative of the fourth voyage of Amerigo Vespucci, in whose company Raphael Hythloday is represented as having sailed.

In the elaborating of his model society, More drew on Plato's "Republic" and on Saint Augustine for a number of important features. But the work as a whole is the outcome of the author's own political thinking and observation; though it is not to be supposed that he believed in all the institutions and customs which he describes. In ordinary intercourse, More was fond of a jest, and many, we are told, found it hard to know when he spoke seriously. Much of this whimsical humor is implicit in the "Utopia"; and while it contains elements in which he had a firm belief, it is more than probable that much of it was in the highest degree tentative, and some of it consciously paradoxical.

In spite of this uncertainty as to More's attitude, the influence of the book, both in imaginative literature and in social theory, has been considerable; and it is the ancestor of a long line of ideal commonwealths. Modern reformers are still finding in its pages suggestions for the society of the future.

THE LIFE OF
SIR THOMAS MORE

In hoc ✠ signo vinces.

FORASMUCH as Sir Thomas More, Knight sometime Lord Chancellor of England, a man of singular virtue and of a clear unspotted conscience, (as witnesseth Erasmus), more pure and white than the whitest snow, and of such an angelical wit, as England, he saith, never had the like before, nor never shall again, universally, as well in the laws of our Realm (a study in effect able to occupy the whole life of a man) as in all other sciences, right well studied, was in his days accounted a man worthy famous memory; I William Roper (though most unworthy) his son-in-law by marriage of his eldest daughter, knowing no one man that of him and of his doings understood so much as myself for that I was continually resident in his house by the space of sixteen years and more, thought it therefore my part to set forth such matters touching his life as I could at this present call to remembrance. Among which very many notable things not meet to have been forgotten, through negligence and long continuance of time, are slipped out of my mind. Yet to the intent the same shall not all utterly perish, I have at the desire of divers worshipful friends of mine, though very far from the grace and worthiness of them, nevertheless as far forth as my mean wit, memory and learning would serve me, declared so much thereof as in my poor judgment seemed worthy to be remembered.

This Sir Thomas More after he had been brought up in the Latin tongue at St. Anthony's in London, he was, by his father's procurement received into the house of the right reverend, wise and learned prelate Cardinal Morton, where (though he was young of years, yet) would he at Christmastide suddenly sometimes step in among the players, and never studying for the matter, make a part of his own there presently among them, which made the lookers-on more sport than all the players beside. In whose wit and towardness the Cardinal much delighting, would often say of him unto the nobles that divers times dined with him, "This child here waiting at the table, whosoever shall live to see it, will prove a marvellous man." Whereupon for his learning he placed him at Oxford, where when he was both in the Greek and Latin tongue sufficiently instructed, he was then for the study of the law of the Realm put to an Inn of the Chancery, called New Inn, where for his time, he very well prospered. And from thence was committed to Lincoln's Inn, with very small allowance, continuing there his study until he was made and accounted a worthy utter barrister. After this, to his great commendation, he read for a good space a public lecture of St. Augustine *de Civitate Dei* in the church of St. Laurence in the Old Jewry, whereunto there resorted Doctor Grocyn, an excellent cunning man, and all the chief learned of the city of London. Then was he made Reader of Furnival's Inn, so remaining by the space of three years and more. After which time he gave himself to devotion and prayer in the Charterhouse of London, religiously living there without vow about four years, until he resorted to the house of one Mr. Colt, a gentleman of Essex that had oft invited him thither, having three daughters whose honest conversation and virtuous education provoked him there especially to set his affection. And albeit his mind most served him to the second daughter, for that he thought her the fairest and best favoured, yet when he considered that it would be both great grief and some shame also to the eldest to see her younger sister in marriage preferred before her, he then of a certain pity framed his fancy towards her, and soon after married her, nevertheless not discontinuing his study of the law at Lincoln's Inn, but applying still the same until he was called to the Bench, and had read twice, which is as often as any judge of the law doth read.

Before which time he had placed himself and his wife at Bucklesbury in London, where he had by her three daughters in virtue and learning brought up from their youth, whom he would often exhort to take virtue and learning for their meat, and play but for their sauce.

Who ere ever he had been reader in Court was in the latter time of King Henry the Seventh made a Burgess in the Parliament, wherein there were by the King demanded (as I have heard it reported) about three-fifteenths for the marriage of his eldest daughter, that then should be the Scottish Queen. At the last debating whereof he made such arguments and reasons there against, that the King's demands were thereby overthrown. So that one of the King's privy chamber, named Mr. Tyler, being present thereat, brought word to the King out of the Parliament house, that a beardless boy had disappointed all his purposes. Whereupon the King conceiving great indignation towards him could not be satisfied until he had some way revenged it. And forasmuch as he nothing having, nothing could lose, his grace devised a causeless quarrel against his Father, keeping him in the Tower until he had paid him an hundred pounds fine. Shortly hereupon it fortuned that this Sir Thomas More coming in a suit to Dr. Fox, Bishop of Winchester, one of the King's privy council, they called him aside, and pretending great favour towards him, promised him that if he would be ruled by him, he would not fail but into the King's favour again to restore him, meaning, as it was after conjectured, to cause him thereby to confess his offence against the King, whereby his Highness might with better colour have occasion to revenge his displeasure against him. But when he came from the Bishop, he fell in communication with one Mr. Witford, his familiar friend, then chaplain to that Bishop and after a Father of Sion, and showed him what the Bishop had said unto him, desiring to have his advice therein, who for the passion of God prayed him in no wise to follow his counsel "for my Lord my Master (quoth he) to serve the King's turn will not stick to agree to his own father's death." So Sir Thomas More returned to the Bishop no more. And had not the King soon after died, he was determined to have gone over the sea, thinking that being in the King's indignation he could not live in England without great danger. After he was made one of the under-sheriffs of London, by which office and his learning together as I have heard him say, he gained without grief not so little as four hundred pounds by the year; since there was at that time in none of the Prince's courts of the laws of this realm any matter of importance in controversy wherein he was not with the one party of counsel. Of whom, for his learning, wisdom, and knowledge and experience, men had him in such estimation, that before he was come to the service of King Henry the Eighth, at the suit and instance of the English Merchants, he was, by the King's consent, made twice Ambassador in certain great causes between them and the Merchants of the Stilliard, whose wise and discreet dealing therein to his high commendation, coming to the King's understanding, provoking his Highness to cause Cardinal Wolsey (then Lord Chancellor) to procure him to his service. And albeit the Cardinal according to the King's request earnestly travailed with him therefore, among many other his persuasions alleging unto him, how dear his service must needs be unto his Majesty, which could not of his honour with less than he should yearly lose thereby seem to recompense him, yet he, loath to change his estate, made such means to the King by the Cardinal to the contrary, that his Grace for that time was well satisfied. Now happened there after this a great ship of his that then was Pope to arrive at Southampton, which the King claiming for a forfeiture, the Pope's Ambassador by suit unto his Grace obtained, that he might for his Master the Pope have counsel learned in the Laws of this realm, and the matter in his own presence (being himself a singular civilian) in some public place to be openly heard and discussed. At which time there could none of our law be found so meet to be of counsel with this Ambassador as Sir Thomas More, who could report to the Ambassador in Latin all the reasons and arguments by the learned counsel on both sides alleged. Upon this the Councillors on either party in presence of the Lord Chancellor, and other the judges in the Star Chamber, had audience accordingly. Where Sir Thomas More not only declared to the Ambassador the whole effect of all their opinions, but also in defence on the Pope's side argued so learnedly himself, that both was the foresaid forfeiture to the Pope restored, and himself among all the hearers, for his upright and commendable demeanour therein, so greatly renowned, that for no entreaty would the King from henceforth be induced any longer to forbear his service. At whose first entry thereunto he made him Master of the Requests, having then no better room void, and within a month after, knight and one of his Privy Council, and so from time to time was by the Prince advanced, continuing in his singular favour and trusty service twenty years and above, a good part whereof used the King upon holidays, when he had done his own devotions to send for him into his private room, and there some time in matters of Astronomy, Geometry, Divinity, and such other Faculties, and some time in his worldly affairs, to sit and confer with him, and other whiles would he in the night have him up into the leads, there to consider with him the diversities, courses, motions, and operations of the stars and planets. And because he was of a pleasant disposition, it pleased the King and Queen, after the Council had supped, at the time of their supper for their pleasure commonly to call for him, and to be merry with them. When he perceived so much in his talk to delight, that he could not once in a month get leave to go home to his wife and children (whose company he most desired) and to be absent from the Court two days together, but that he should be thither sent for again, he much misliking this restraint of liberty, began thereupon somewhat to dissemble his nature, and so by little and little from his former mirth to disuse himself, that he was of them from thenceforth no more so ordinarily sent for. Then died one Mr. Weston, Treasurer of the Exchequer, whose office after his death the King of his own offer, without any asking, freely gave unto Sir Thomas More. In the fourteenth year of his Grace's Reign was there a Parliament holden, whereof Sir Thomas More was chosen Speaker, who being very loath to take that Room upon him, made an oration, not now extant, to the King's Highness for his discharge thereof. Whereunto when the King would not consent, he spake unto his Grace in form following: "Since I perceive (most redoubted sovereign) that it standeth not with your Highness' pleasure to reform this election, and cause it to be changed, but have, by the mouth of the Right Reverend Father in God the Legate your Highness' Chancellor, thereunto given your most royal consent, and have of your benignity determined, far above that I may bear, to enable me, and for this office to repute me meet, rather than ye should seem to impute unto your Commons that they had unmeetly chosen, I am therefore, and always shall be, ready obediently to conform myself to the accomplishment of your high commandment. In my most humble wise beseeching your most noble Majesty, that I may, with your Grace's favour, before I farther enter thereunto, make mine humble intercession unto your Highness for two lowly petitions, the one privately concerning myself, the other the whole assembly of your Common House. And for myself (Gracious Sovereign) that if it mishap me in anything hereafter, that is in the behalf of your Commons in your high presence to be declared, to mistake my message, and for lack of good utterance by me misrehearsed, to pervert or impair the prudent instructions, that it may then like your most noble Majesty of your abundant grace, with the eye of your accustomed pity, to pardon my simplicity, giving me leave again to repair to the Common House, and there to confer with them, and to take their substantial advice, what thing, and in what wise I shall on their behalf utter and speak before your noble Grace: to the intent their prudent advices and affairs be not by my simpleness and folly hindered or impaired. Which thing if it should so hap, as it were well likely to mishap in me (if your Grace's benignity relieved not my oversight) it could not fail to be, during my life, a perpetual grudge and heaviness to my heart. The help and remedy whereof in manner aforesaid remembered, is (most Gracious Sovereign) my first lowly suit and humble petition unto your most noble Grace. Mine other humble request, most excellent Prince, is this. Forasmuch as there be of your Commons here, by your high commandment assembled for your Parliament, a great number which are after the accustomed manner appointed in the Common House to treat and advise of the common affairs among themselves apart: and albeit (my liege Lord) that, according to your prudent advice, by your honourable writs everywhere declared, there hath been as due diligence used in sending up to your Highness' Court of Parliament the most discreet persons out of every quarter, that men could esteem meet thereto, whereby it is not to be doubted but that there is a very substantial assembly of right wise and politic persons: yet (most victorious Prince) since among so many wise men, neither is every man wise alike, nor among so many men like well witted, every man like well spoken; and it often happeneth, that likewise as much folly is uttered with painted polished speeches, so many boisterous and rude in language see deep indeed, and give right substantial counsel: and since also in matters of great importance the mind is often so occupied in the matter, that a man rather studieth what to say, than how; by what reason whereof the wisest man and best spoken in a country fortuneth among, while his mind is fervent on the matter, somewhat to speak in such wise, as he would afterward wish to have been uttered otherwise, and yet no worse will had when he spake it, than he hath when he would so gladly change it: Therefore (most Gracious Sovereign) considering that in all your high Courts of Parliament is nothing entreated but of matters of weight and importance concerning your Realm, and your own Royal estate, it could not fail to let and put to silence from the giving of their advice and counsel many of your discreet Commons [except they] were utterly discharged of all doubt and fear how anything that should happen them to speak, should happen of your Highness to be taken: and in this point your well-known benignity putteth every man in right good hope. Yet such is the weight of the matter, such is the reverend dread that the timorous hearts of your natural subjects conceive towards your high Majesty (our most redoubted King and undoubted Sovereign) that they cannot in this point find themselves satisfied, except your gracious bounty herein declared put away the scruple of their timorous minds, and animate and encourage them out of doubt. It may therefore like your most abundant Grace (our most gracious King) to give to all your Commons here assembled, your most gracious licence and pardon freely, without doubt of your dreadful displeasure, every man to discharge his conscience, and boldly in everything incident among, declare his advice, and whatsoever happeneth any man to say, it may like your noble Majesty of your inestimable goodness to take all in good part, interpreting every man's words, how uncunningly soever they be couched, to proceed yet of a good zeal towards the profit of your Realm and honour of your Royal person, the prosperous estate and preservation whereof (most excellent Sovereign) is the thing which we all your most humble loving subjects, according to the most bounden duty of our natural allegiance, most highly desired and pray for." At this Parliament, Cardinal Wolsey found himself much grieved with the Burgesses thereof, for that nothing was so soon done or spoken therein, but that it was immediately blown abroad in every alehouse.

It fortuned at that Parliament a very great subsidy to be demanded, which the Cardinal fearing it would not pass the Common House, determined for the furtherance thereof, to be there present himself; before whose coming after long debating there, whether it were better but with a few of his Lords (as the most opinion of the house was) or with a whole train royally to receive him there amongst them, "Masters," quoth Sir Thomas More, "forasmuch as my Lord Cardinal lately, you note well, laid to our charge the lightness of our tongues for things uttered out of this house, it shall not be amiss in my mind to receive him with all his pomp, with his maces, his pillars, his pollaxes, his crosses, his hat, and great seal too; to the intent that if he find the like fault with us hereafter, we may be the bolder from ourselves to lay the blame upon those that his Grace bringeth with him." Whereunto the House wholly agreeing, he was received accordingly. Where after he had in a solemn oration by many reasons proved how necessary it was the demands there moved to be granted, and further said that less would not serve the King's purpose; he seeing the company still silent, and thereunto nothing answering, and contrary to his expectation showing in themselves towards his requests no towardness of inclination, said unto them: "Masters, ye have many wise and learned men among you, and seeing I am from the King's own person sent hither unto you for the preservation of yourselves and all the Realm, I think it meet you give me a reasonable answer." Whereat every man holding his peace, then began he to speak to one Mr. Marney, who making him no answer neither, he severally asked the same question of divers others accounted the wisest of the company. To whom when none of them all would give so much as one word, being before agreed, as the custom was, by their speaker to make answer: "Masters," quoth the Cardinal, "unless it be the manner of your house (as of likelihood it is) in such causes to utter your minds by the mouth of your speaker, whom ye have chosen for trusty and wise (as indeed he is) here is without doubt a marvellous obstinate silence;" and thereupon required the answer of Mr. Speaker, who reverently upon his knees excusing the silence of the house, abashed at the presence of so noble a personage, able to amaze the wisest and best learned in a realm, and after by many reasons proving, that for them to make answer was it neither expedient, nor agreeable with the ancient liberty of the House; in conclusion for himself showed, that though they had all with their voices trusted him, yet except every of them could put into his own head all their several wits, he alone in so weighty a matter was unmeet to make his Grace answer, whereupon the Cardinal displeased with Sir Thomas More, that had not in this Parliament in all things satisfied his desire, suddenly arose and departed: and after the Parliament ended, uttered unto him all his griefs, saying, "Would to God you had been at Rome, Mr. More, when I made you Speaker." "Your Grace not offended, so would I too, my Lord," quoth he, and to wind such quarrels out of the Cardinal's head, he began to talk of that gallery at Hampton Court, wherewith so wisely brake he off the Cardinal's displeasant talk, the Cardinal at that present, as it seemed, wist not what more to say to him, but for revengement of his displeasure counselled the King to send him Ambassador into Spain, commending unto his Highness his wisdom, learning and meetness for that voyage, and the difficulty of the cause considered, none was there so well able, he said, to serve his Grace therein. Which when the King had broken to Sir Thomas More, and that he had declared unto his Grace, how unfit a journey it was for him, the nature of the country and disposition of his complexion so disagreeing together, that he should never be likely to do his Grace acceptable service therein, knowing right well that if his Grace sent him thither, he should send him to his grave; but showing himself nevertheless ready according to his duty, albeit with the loss of his life, to fulfil his Grace's pleasure therein, the King allowing well his answer, said unto him, "It is not our meaning, Mr. More, to do you hurt, but to do you good we would be glad. We therefore for this purpose will devise upon some other, and employ your service otherwise." And such entire favour did the King bear him, that he made him Chancellor of the Duchy of Lancaster, upon the death of Sir Richard Winfield, who had that office before. And for the pleasure he took in his company, would his Grace suddenly sometimes come home to his house at Chelsea to be merry with him, whither on a time unlooked for he came to dinner, and after dinner in a fair garden of his walked with him by the space of an hour holding his arm about his neck. As soon as his Grace was gone, I rejoicing, told Sir Thomas More, how happy he was, whom the King had so familiarly entertained, as I had never seen him do to any before, except Cardinal Wolsey, whom I saw his Grace once walk with arm in arm. "I thank our Lord, son," quoth he, "I find his Grace my very good lord indeed, and I do believe he doth as singularly favour me as any subject within this Realm. Howbeit (son Roper) I may tell thee, I have no cause to be proud thereof. For if my head would win him a castle in France (for then there was wars between us) it should not fail to go." This Sir Thomas More, among all other his virtues, was of such meekness, that if it had fortuned him with any learned man resorting to him from Oxford, Cambridge, or elsewhere, as there did divers, some for the desire of his acquaintance, some for the famous report of his learning and wisdom, and some for suits of the Universities, to have entered into argument, wherein few were comparable to him, and so far to have discoursed with them therein, that he might perceive they could not, without some inconvenience, hold out much further disputation against him: then, least he should discomfort them, as he that sought not his own glory, but rather would seem conquered than to discourage students in their studies, ever showing himself more desirous to learn than to teach, would he by some witty device courteously break off into some other matters and give over. Of whom for his wisdom and learning had the King such an opinion, that at such time as he attended upon his Highness, taking his progress either to Oxford or Cambridge, where he was received with very eloquent orations, his Grace would always assign him (as one that was most prompt, and ready therein) *ex tempore* to make answer thereunto; whose manner was, whensoever he had any occasion, either here or beyond the sea to be in any University, not only to be present at the reading and disputations there commonly used, but also learnedly to dispute among them himself. Who being Chancellor of the Duchy, was made ambassador twice; joined in commission with Cardinal Wolsey once to the Emperor Charles into Flanders, the other time to the French King into France. Not long after this the Water Bailiff of London (sometime his servant) hearing, where he had been at dinner, certain merchants liberally to rail against his old master, waxed so discontented therewith, that he hastily came to him, and told him what he had heard: "and were I, Sir" (quoth he) "in such favour and authority with my Prince as you are, such men surely should not be suffered so villainously and falsely to mis-report and slander me. Wherefore I would wish you to call them before you, and, to their shame for their lewd malice to punish them." Who smiling upon him said, "Mr. Water Bailiff, would you have me punish them by whom I receive more benefit than by you all that be my friends? Let them a God's name speak as lewdly as they list of me, and shoot never so many arrows at me, so long as they do not hit me, what am I the worse? But if they should once hit me, then would it a little trouble me: howbeit, I trust, by God's help, there shall none of them all be able once to touch me. I have more cause, Mr. Water Bailiff (I assure thee) to pity them, than to be angry with them." Such fruitful communication had he oftentimes with his familiar friends. So on a time walking along the Thames side with me at Chelsea, in talking of other things, he said to me, "Now would to God, son Roper, upon condition three things were well established in Christendom I were put in a sack, and here presently cast into the Thames." "What great things be these, Sir," quoth I, "that should move you so to wish?" "Wouldest thou know, son Roper, what they be?" quoth he. "Yea marry, Sir, with a good will if it please you," quoth I. "I faith, they be these, son," quoth he. "The first is, that whereas the most part of Christian princes be at mortal wars, they were at universal peace. The second, that where the Church of Christ is at this present sore afflicted with many heresies and errors, it were well settled in an uniformity of religion. The third, that where the King's matter of his marriage is now come into question, it were to the glory of God and quietness of all parties brought to a good conclusion:" whereby, as I could gather, he judged, that otherwise it would be a disturbance to a great part of Christendom. Thus did it by his doings throughout the whole course of his life appear, that all his travails and pains, without respect of earthly commodities, either to himself or any of his, were only upon the service of God, the Prince and the Realm, wholly bestowed and employed; whom in his latter time I heard to say, that he never asked of the King himself the value of one penny. As Sir Thomas More's custom was daily, if he were at home, besides his private prayers with his children, to say the seven psalms, litany, and suffrages following, was his guise nightly, before he went to bed, with his wife, children, and household to go to his chapel, and there upon his knees ordinarily to say certain psalms and collects with them: and because he was desirous for godly purposes some time to be solitary, and sequester himself from worldly company; a good distance from his mansion house builded he a place, called the new building, wherein was a chapel, a library, and a gallery, in which as his use was upon other days to occupy himself in prayer and study together, so on the Fridays there usually continued he from morning unto evening, spending his time duly in devout prayers, and spiritual exercises; and to provoke his wife and children to the desire of heavenly things, he would sometimes use these words unto them. "It is now no mastery for you children to go to heaven. For everybody giveth you good counsel, everybody giveth you good example. You see virtue rewarded, and vice punished, so that you are carried up to heaven even by the chins. But if you live in the time, that no man will give you good counsel, nor no man will give you good example, when you shall see virtue punished, and vice rewarded, if you will then stand fast, and firmly stick to God upon pain of life, if you be but half good, God will allow you for whole good." If his wife or any of his children had been diseased, or troubled, he would say to them, "We may not look at our pleasure to go to heaven in feather beds, it is not the way. For our Lord himself went thither with great pain, and by many tribulations, which is the path wherein he walked thither, and the servant may not look to be in better case than his Master." And as he would in this sort persuade them to take their troubles patiently, so would he in like case teach them to withstand the devil and his temptations, valiantly saying, "Whosoever will mark the devil and his temptations shall find him therein much like to an ape. For as an ape not well looked to will be busy and bold to do shrewd turns, and contrariwise being spied will suddenly leap back and adventure no farther: so the devil, seeing a man idle, slothful, and without resistance ready to receive his temptations, waxeth so hardy that he will not fail still to continue with him, until to his purpose he hath brought him: but on the other side, if he see a man with diligence present to prevent and withstand his temptations, he waxeth so weary, that in conclusion he forsaketh him. For as much as the devil by disposition is a spirit of nature so envious, that he feareth any more to assault him, lest that he should thereby not only catch a foul fall himself, but also minister to the man more matter of merit." Thus delighted he evermore not only in virtuous exercises to be occupied himself, but also to exhort his wife, and children, and household to embrace and follow the same. To whom for his notable virtue and godliness God showed, as he seemed, a manifest miraculous token of his special favour towards him, at such time as my wife (as many others that year were) was sick of the sweating sickness, who lying in so great extremity of that disease, as by no invention or devices, that physicians in such case commonly use (of whom she had divers, both expert, wise, and well learned, then continually attendant upon her) she could be kept from sleep: so that both physicians and all others despaired her health and recovery, and gave her over: her father (as he that most entirely tendered her) being in no small heaviness for her, by prayer at God his hands sought to get remedy, whereupon after his usual manner going up into his new lodging, there in his chapel upon his knees with tears most devoutly besought Almighty God, that it would be like his goodness, unto whom nothing was impossible, if it were his blessed will, at his mediation to vouchsafe graciously to hear his petition; where incontinent came into his mind, that a glister should be the only way to help her, which when he had told the physicians, they by-and-by confessed, that if there were any hope of health, that it was the very best help indeed, much marvelling of themselves, that they had not afore remembered it. Then it was immediately ministered unto her sleeping, which she could by no means have been brought unto waking, and albeit after she was thereby thoroughly awaked, God's marks, evident undoubted token of death, plainly appeared upon her, yet she (contrary to all their expectation) was (as it was thought) by her father's fervent prayer miraculously recovered, and at length again to perfect health restored, whom if it had pleased God at that time to have taken to his mercy, her father said he would never have meddled with worldly matters after. Now while Sir Thomas More was Chancellor of the Duchy, the See of Rome chanced to be void, which was cause of much .

trouble. For Cardinal Wolsey, a man very ambitious, and desirous (as good hope, and likelihood he had) to aspire unto that dignity, perceiving himself of his expectation disappointed by means of the Emperor Charles, so highly commending one Cardinal Adrian, sometime his schoolmaster, to the Cardinals of Rome, in the time of their election for his virtue and worthiness, that thereupon was he chosen Pope, who from Spain (where he was then resident) coming on foot to Rome, before his entry into that city did put off his hose and shoes, barefooted and barelegged passing through the streets towards his palace with such humbleness, that all the people had him in great reverence. Cardinal Wolsey waxed so woe therewith, that he studied to invent all ways of revengement of his grief against the Emperor, which as it was the beginning of a lamentable tragedy, so some part thereof not impertinent to my present purpose I reckoned requisite here to put in remembrance. This Cardinal therefore, not ignorant of the King's unconstant and mutable disposition, soon inclined to withdraw his devotion from his own most noble and virtuous wife Queen Katherine, aunt to the Emperor, upon every light occasion; and upon other, to her in nobility, wisdom, virtue, favour and beauty far incomparable to fix his affection, meaning to make his so light disposition an instrument to bring about this his ungodly intent, devised to allure the King (then already contrary to his mind nothing less looking for than falling in love with the Lady Anne Bullen) to cast fancy to one of the French Sisters, which thing, because of enmity and war was at that time between the French King and the Emperor (whom, for the cause afore remembered, he mortally maligned) he was desirous to procure, and for the better achieving thereof requested Langland, Bishop of Lincoln, and ghostly father to the King, to put a scruple into the King's head, that it was not lawful for him to marry his brother's wife; which the King not sorry to hear of, opened it first to Sir Thomas More, whose counsel he required therein, showing him certain places of Scripture, that somewhat seemed to serve his appetite, which when he had perused, and thereupon, as one that never had professed the study of Divinity himself, excused to be unmeet many ways to meddle with such matters; the King, not satisfied with this answer, so sore still pressed upon him, therefore, in conclusion he condescended to his Grace his motion, and further, that the matter was of such importance as needed good advice and deliberation, he besought his Grace of sufficient respect advisedly to consider of it; wherewith the King well contented said unto him; Tunstall and Clarke, Bishops of Durham and Bath, with other learned of his Privy Council should also be dealers therein. So Sir Thomas More departing, conferred those places of Scripture with the exposition of divers of the old holy doctors, and at his coming to the Court, in talking with his Grace of the foresaid matter, he said, "To be plain with your Grace, neither my Lord of Durham, nor my Lord of Bath, though I know them both to be wise, virtuous, and learned, and honourable prelates, nor myself with the rest of your Council, being all your Grace's own servants, for your manifold benefits daily bestowed on us, so most bounden unto you, be in my judgment meet counsellors for your Grace herein; but if your Grace minds to understand the truth, such counsellors may you have devised, as neither for respect of their own worldly commodity, nor for fear of your princely authority, will be inclined to deceive you."

To whom he named St. Jerome, St. Augustine, and divers other holy doctors, both Greeks and Latins: and moreover showed him what authority he had gathered out of them, which although the King did not very well like of (as disagreeable to his Grace's desire), yet were they by Sir Thomas More (who in all his communication with the King in that matter had always most wisely behaved himself) so wisely tempered, that he both presently took them in good part, and oftentimes had thereof conference with him again. After this were there certain questions proposed among his Council, whether the King needed, in this case, to have any scruple at all, and if he had, what way were best to deliver him of it? the most part of whom were of the opinion, that there was good cause, and that, for discharging of it, suit were meet to be made to the See of Rome, where the King, hoping by liberality to obtain his purpose, wherein (as after it appeared) he was far deceived, then was there, for the trial and examination of this matrimony, procured from Rome a Commission, in which Cardinal Campegines and Cardinal Wolsey were joined Commissioners, who, for the determination thereof, sat at the Blackfriars in London. Where a libel was put in for the admitting of the said matrimony, alleging the said marriage between the King and the Queen to be unlawful, and, for proof of the marriage to be lawful, was there brought in a dispensation; in which, after divers disputations thereupon holden, there appeared an imperfection, which by an instrument or brief, upon search found in the treasury of Spain, and sent to the Commissioners into England, was supplied, and so should judgment have been given by the Pope accordingly, had not the King, upon intelligence thereof, before the same judgment, appealed to the next general Council. After whose appellation the Cardinal upon that matter sat no longer. It fortuned before the matter of the said matrimony brought in question, when I, in talk with Sir Thomas More, of a certain joy commended unto him the happy estate of this realm, that had so catholic a Prince, that no heretic durst show his face, so virtuous and learned a clergy, so grave and sound a nobility, so loving and obedient subjects, all in one faith agreeing together: "True it is indeed (son Roper)," quoth he, and in commending all degrees and estates of the same went far beyond me, "and yet (son Roper) I pray God," said he, "that some of us, as high as we seem to sit upon the mountains, treading heretics under our feet like ants, live not the day, that we gladly would wish to be at league and composition with them, to let them have their churches quietly to themselves; so that they would be content to let us have ours quietly to ourselves." After that I had told him many considerations, why he had no cause to say so, "Well, well," said he, "I pray God (son Roper) some of us live not till that day," showing me no reason why I should put any doubt therein. To whom I said, "By my troth, Sir, it is very desperately spoken," that vile term (I cry God mercy) did I give him, who by these words perceiving me in a fume, said merrily unto me, "Well, son Roper, it shall not be so, it shall not be so." Whom in sixteen years and more, being in his house conversant with him, I could never perceive him so much as once to fume. But now to return again where I left: After supplying of imperfections of the dispensation sent (as before is rehearsed) to the Commissioners into England, the King taking the matter for ended, and then meaning no further to proceed in that matter, assigned the Bishop of Durham, and Sir Thomas More to go ambassadors to Cambray, a place neither Imperial nor French, to treat a

peace between the French King, the Emperor, and him, in the con-
cluding whereof Sir Thomas More so worthily handled himself
(procuring in our league far more benefits unto his realm, than at
that time by the King and Council was possible to be compassed),
that for his good service in that voyage, the King, when he after
made him Lord Chancellor, caused the Duke of Norfolk openly to
declare unto the people (as you shall hear hereafter more at large)
how much all England was bound unto him. Now, upon the coming
home of the Bishop of Durham and Sir Thomas More from Cambray, the King was as earnest in persuading Sir Thomas More to
agree unto the matter of his marriage as before, by many and divers
ways provoking him thereunto. For which cause (as it was thought)
he, the rather soon after made him Lord Chancellor, and further
declared unto him, that though at his going over the sea to Cambray, he was in utter despair thereof, yet he had conceived since
some good hope to compass it. For albeit his marriage, being against
the positive law of the Church, and the written law of God, was
holden by the dispensation, yet was there another thing found out
of late, he said, whereby his marriage appeared to be so directly
against the laws of nature, that it could in no wise by the Church
be dispensable, as Dr. Stoksely (whom he had then newly preferred to be Bishop of London, and in that case chiefly credited) was
able to instruct him, with whom he prayed him in that point to
confer. But for all his conference with him, he saw nothing of such
force, as could induce him to change his opinion therein; which notwithstanding the bishop showed himself in his report of him to the
King's highness so good and favourable, that he said, he found him
in his Grace's cause very toward, and desirous to find some good
matter wherewith he might truly serve his Grace to his contentation.
This Bishop Stoksely being by the Cardinal not long before in the
Star Chamber openly put to rebuke, and awarded to the Fleet, not
brooking his contumelious usage, and thinking, that forasmuch as
the Cardinal, for lack of such forwardness in setting first the King's
divorce as his Grace looked for, was out of his Highness' favour, he
had now a good occasion offered him to revenge his quarrel against
him—further to incense the King's displeasure towards him, busily
travailed to invent some colourable device for the King's furtherance

in that behalf. Which (as before is mentioned) he to his Grace revealed, hoping thereby to bring the King to the better liking of himself, and the more misliking of the Cardinal. His Highness therefore was soon after of his office displaced, and to Sir Thomas More (the rather to move him to incline to his side) the same in his stead committed. Who between Dukes of Norfolk and Suffolk being brought through Westminster Hall to his place in the Chancery, the Duke of Norfolk, in audience of all the people there assembled, showed, that he was from the King himself straightly charged by special commission there openly, in the presence of all, to make declaration, how much all England was beholden to Sir Thomas More for his good service, and how worthy he was to have the highest room in the Realm, and how dearly his Grace loved and trusted him; for which, said the Duke, he had great cause to rejoice. Whereunto Sir Thomas More, among many other his humble and wise sayings (not now in my memory) answered, "That although he had good cause to rejoice of his Highness' singular favour towards him, that he had far above his deserts so highly commended him, yet nevertheless he must for his own part needs confess, that in all things by his Grace alleged he had done no more than was his duty. And further disabled himself as unmeet for that room, wherein, considering how wise and honourable a prelate had lately before taken so great a fall, he had," he said, "thereof no cause to rejoice." And as they on the King's behalf charged him uprightly to minister indifferent justice to the people without corruption or affection, so did he likewise charge them again, that if they saw him at any time in anything digress from any part of his duty, in that honourable office, then, as they would discharge their own duty and fidelity to God and the King, so should they not fail to disclose it to his Grace, who otherwise might have just occasion to lay his fault wholly to their charge. While he was Lord Chancellor (being at leisure, as seldom he was) one of his sons-in-law on a time said merrily unto him, "When Cardinal Wolsey was Lord Chancellor, not only divers of his privy chamber, but such also as were his door keepers got great gain, and since he had married one of his daughters, and gave still attendance upon him, he thought he might of reason look for somewhat, where he indeed, because he was ready himself to hear every man, poor and rich, and keep no doors shut from them, could find none, which was to him a great discouragement. And whereas else some for friendship, some for kindred, and some for profit, would gladly have his furtherance in bringing them to his presence, if he should now take anything of them he knew" (he said), "he should do them great wrong, for that they might do as much for themselves, as he could do for them: which condition although he thought in Sir Thomas More very commendable, yet to him" (said he) "being his son he found it nothing profitable." When he had told him this tale, "You say well, son" (quoth he), "I do not mislike that you are of conscience so scrupulous, but many other ways be there (son), that I may do both yourself good, and pleasure your friend also. For sometimes may I in words, stand your friend in stead, and sometime may I by my letter help you and him, or if he have a cause depending before me, at your request I may hear him before another, or if his cause be not all the best, yet may I move the parties to fall to some reasonable end by arbitrament; howbeit, this one thing I assure thee on my faith, that if the parties will at my hand call for justice, then were it my father stood on the one side and the devil on the other side (his cause being good) the devil should have right. So offered he his son (as he thought" he said) "as much favour as with reason he could require." And that he would for no respect digress from justice well appeared by a plain example of another of his sons-in-law, Mr. Heron. For when he, having a matter before him in the Chancery, presuming too much of his favour, would by him in no wise be persuaded to agree to any indifferent order, then made he in conclusion a flat decree against him. This Lord Chancellor used commonly every afternoon to sit in his open hall, to the intent, if any person had any suit unto him, they might the more boldly come to his presence, and there open complaints before him. Whose manner was also to read every bill himself, ere he would award any subpœna, which bearing matter sufficient worthy a subpœna, would he set his hand unto, or else cancel it. Whensoever he passed through Westminster Hall to his place in the Chancery by the Court of the King's Bench, if his father, one of the judges there, had been sat ere he came, he would go into the same court, and there reverently kneeling down in the sight of them all duly ask his father's blessing.

And if it fortuned that his father and he at readings in Lincoln's Inn met together (as they sometime did) notwithstanding his high office, he would offer in argument the pre-eminence to his father, though he for his office sake would refuse to take it. And for the better declaration of his natural affection towards his father, he not only (when he lay on his death-bed) according to his duty ofttimes with comfortable words most kindly came to visit him; but also at his departure out of this world, with tears taking him about the neck, most lovingly kissed and embraced him, commending into the merciful hands of Almighty God, and so departed from him. And as few injunctions as he granted while he was Lord Chancellor, yet were they by some of the judges of the law misliked, which I understanding, declared the same unto Sir Thomas More, who answered me, that they have little cause to find fault with him therefore. And thereupon caused he one Mr. Crooke, chief of the six clerks, to make a docket, containing the whole number and causes of all such injunctions, as either in his time had already passed, or at that present time depended in any of the King's Courts at Westminster before him. Which done he invited all the judges to dinner with him in the Council Chamber at Westminster, where after dinner when he had broken with them what complaints he had heard of his injunctions, and moreover showed them both the number and causes of every of them in order so plainly, that, upon full debating of those matters, they were all enforced to confess, that they, in like case, could have done no otherwise themselves, then offered he this unto them, that if the justices of every court, unto whom the reformation of rigour of the law, by reason of their office, most specially appertained, would, upon reasonable considerations, by their own discretions (as they were, as he thought, in conscience bound) mitigate and reform the rigour of the law themselves, there should from thenceforth by him no more injunctions be granted. Whereupon when they refused to condescend, then said he unto them: "Forasmuch as yourselves, my lords, drive me to that necessity for awarding our injunctions to relieve the people's injury, you cannot hereafter any more justly blame me;" after that he had said secretly unto me: "I perceive, son, why they like not so to do. For they see, that they may, by the verdict of the jury, cast off all quarrels from themselves upon them, which they account their chief defence, and therefore am I compelled to abide the adventure of all such reports." And as little leisure as he had to be occupied in the study of Holy Scripture, and controversies upon religion, and such other like virtuous exercises, being in manner continually busied about the affairs of the King and the Realm, yet such watch and pain in setting forth of divers profitable works in defence of the true Catholic religion against heresies, secretly sown abroad in the Realm, assuredly sustained he, that the bishops, to whose pastoral cure the reformation thereof principally appertained, thinking themselves by his travail (wherein, by their own confession, with him they were not able to make comparison) of their duty discharged, and considering that, for all his pains, and prince's favour, he was no rich man, nor in yearly revenues advanced as his worthiness deserved, therefore at a convocation among themselves and other of the clergy, they agreed together, and concluded upon a sum of four or five thousand pounds at the least (to my remembrance) for his pains to recompense him. To the payment whereof every bishop, abbot, and the rest of the clergy were after the rate of their abilities liberal contributaries, hoping this portion should be to his contentation. Whereupon Tunstall bishop of Durham, Clarke bishop of Bath, and (as far as I can call to mind) Vaysie bishop of Exeter, repaired unto him, declaring how thankfully for his travails to their discharge in God's cause bestowed, they reckoned themselves bound to consider him. And that albeit, they could not according to his deserts so worthily as they gladly would requite him therefore, but reserve that only to the goodness of God, yet for a small part of recompense, in respect of his estate, so unequal to his worthiness, in the name of their whole Convocation, they presented unto him that sum, which they desired him to take in good part, who forsaking it, said, "That like as it were no small comfort unto him, that so wise and learned men so well accepted his simple doing, for which he intended never to receive reward but at the hands of God only, to whom alone was thanks thereof chiefly to be ascribed: so gave he most humble thanks unto their honours all for their bountiful consideration." When they for all their importune pressing upon him, that few would have went he could have refused it, could by no means make him to take

it, then they besought him be content, yet that they might bestow
it upon his wife and children; "Not so, my Lords" (quoth he), "I
had liever see it all cast into the Thames, than I, or any of mine
should have thereof the worth of one penny. For though your offer,
my Lords, be indeed very friendly and honourable, yet set I so much
by my pleasure, and so little by my profit, that I would not (in good
faith) for so much, and much more to have lost the rest of so many
a night's sleep, as was spent upon the same. And yet wish I would,
for all that, upon conditions that all heresies were suppressed, that
all my books were burned, and my labour utterly lost." Thus
departing, were they fain to restore to every man his own again.
This Lord Chancellor albeit he was to God and the world well
known of notable virtue, though not so of every man considered, yet
for the avoidance of singularity would he appear no otherwise than
other men in his apparel and other outward behaviour. And albeit
he appeared honourable outwardly, and like one of his calling, yet
inwardly he no such vanities esteeming, secretly next his body wore
a shirt of hair, which my sister More, a young gentlewoman in the
summer, as he sat at supper singly in his doublet and hose, wearing
thereupon a plain shirt without ruff or collar, chancing to espy, began
to laugh at it. My wife not ignorant of his manner, perceiving the
same privily told him of it, and he being sorry that she saw it,
presently amended it. He used also sometimes to punish his body
with whips, the cords knotted, which was known only to my wife
his eldest daughter, whom for her secrecy above all other he specially
trusted, caused her, as need required, to wash the same shirt of hair.
Now shortly upon his entry into the high office of the Chancellorship,
the King oftsoons again moved him to weigh and consider his
greatest matter, who falling down upon his knees, humbly besought
his Highness to stand his gracious Sovereign, as ever since his entry
into his gracious service he had found him, saying, "There was
nothing in the world had been so grievous to his heart as to remember he was not able, as he willingly would, with the loss of one of
his limbs, for that matter to find anything whereby he could serve
his Grace's contentment, as he that always bare in mind the most
godly words, that his Highness spake unto him at his first coming
into his noble service, the most virtuous lesson that ever prince

taught his servant, willing him first to look unto God, and after God
to him, as in good faith," he said, "he did, or else might his Grace
well account him his most unworthy servant." To this the King
answered, "that if he could not with his conscience serve him, he
was content to accept his service otherwise, and use the advice of
other his learned Council, whose consciences could well enough
agree thereto, he would nevertheless continue his gracious favour
towards him, and never with that matter molest his conscience after."
But Sir Thomas More, in process of time, seeing the King fully
determined to proceed forth in the marriage of Queen Anne, and
when he with the bishops and nobles of the Higher House of Parliament, were, or the furtherance of that marriage, commanded by the
King to go down to the Common House to show to them both what
the Universities as well of other parts beyond the seas, as at Oxford
and Cambridge had done in that behalf, and their seals also testify-
ing the same: all which matters, at the King's request (not showing
of what mind himself was therein), he opened to the Lower House
of the Parliament: nevertheless doubting lest further attempts should
after follow, which, contrary to his conscience, by reason of his office
he was likely to be put unto, he made suit to the Duke of Norfolk,
his singular dear friend, to be a mean to the King, that he might,
with his Grace's favour, be discharged of that chargeable room of
Chancellorship, wherein for certain infirmities of his body, he pretended himself unable any longer to serve. This Duke coming on a
time to Chelsea to dine with him, fortuned to find him at church
singing in the choir with a surplice on his back; to whom after
service, as they went home together arm in arm, the Duke said,
"God body, God body (my Lord Chancellor) a parish clerk, a parish
clerk, you dishonour the King and his office." "Nay," quoth Sir
Thomas More, smiling upon the Duke, "your Grace may not think,
that the King, your master and mine, will with me for serving God
his Master be offended, or thereby count his office dishonoured."
When the Duke, being thereunto solicited by importunate suit, had at
length obtained for Sir Thomas More a clear discharge of his office,
then at a time convenient, by his Highness' appointment, repaired
he to his Grace, to yield up unto him the great seal, which, as his
Grace with thanks and praise for his worthy service in that office

courteously at his hands received, so pleased it his Highness to say
more unto him, that for the good service he before had done him in
any suit which he should after have unto him, that either should
concern his honour (for that word it liked his Highness to use unto
him) or that should appertain unto his profit, he would find his
Highness a good and gracious lord unto him. After he had thus
given over his Chancellorship, and placed all his gentlemen and
yeomen with bishops and noblemen, and his eight watermen with
the Lord Audley, that after in the same office succeeded him, to
whom also he gave his great barge, then calling us that were his
children unto him, and asking our advice, how we might now, in
this decay of his ability, by the surrender of his office so impaired,
that he could not, as he was wont, and gladly would bear out the
whole charges of them all himself, from henceforth be able to live and
continue together, as he wished we should; when he saw us all silent,
and in that case not ready to show our opinions unto him, "Then
will I" (said he) "show my poor mind unto you. I have been
brought up at Oxford, at an Inn of Chancery, at Lincoln's Inn, and
in the King's Court, so forth from the lowest degree to the highest,
and yet have I in yearly revenues little more than one hundred
pounds by the year at this present left me. So that we must hereafter, if we like to live together. But by my counsel it shall not be
best for us to fall to the lowest fare first. We will not therefore
descend to Oxford fare, nor to the fare of New Inn, but we will
begin with Lincoln's Inn diet, where many right worshipful and of
good years do live full well, which if we find not ourselves the first
year able to maintain, then will we the next year after go one step
down to New Inn fare, wherewith many an honest man is well contented. If that exceed our ability too, then will we the next year after
descend to Oxford fare, where many grave, ancient, and learned
Fathers be conversant continually, which if our ability stretch not
to maintain neither, then may we yet with bags and wallets go
a-begging together, and hoping that for pity some good folks will
give their charity at every man's door to sing *salve Regina,* and so
still keep company merrily together." And whereas you have heard
before he was by the King from a very worshipful living taken unto
his Grace's service, with whom all the great and weighty causes that

concerned his Highness, of the Realm, he consumed and spent with painful cares, travail, and trouble as well beyond the seas, as within the Realm, in effect the whole substance of his life, yet with all the gain he got thereby (being never no wasteful spender thereof) was he not able, after the resignation of his office of the Lord Chancellor, for the maintenance of himself, and such as necessarily belonged unto him, sufficiently to find meat, drink, fuel, apparel, and such other necessary charges. All the land that ever he purchased before he was Lord Chancellor, was not, I am well assured, above the value of twenty marks by the year, and after his debts paid he had not I know (his chain excepted) in gold and silver left him the worth of one hundred pounds. And whereas, upon the holidays, during High Chancellorship, one of his gentlemen, when service at the church was down, ordinarily used to come to my Lady, his wife's pew and say, "Madam, my Lord is gone," the next holiday after the surrender of his office, and departure of his gentlemen he came unto my Lady, his wife's pew, himself, and making a low curtsey, said unto her, "Madam, my Lord is gone." In the time somewhat before his trouble, he would talk with his wife and children of the joys of heaven and the pains of hell, of the lives of holy martyrs, and of their grievous martyrdom, of their marvellous patience, and of their passions and deaths, that they suffered rather than they would offend God, and what an happy and a blessed thing it was for the love of God to suffer loss of goods, imprisonment, loss of lands, and life also. He would further say unto them, that upon his faith, if he might perceive his wife and children would encourage him to die in a good cause, it should so comfort him, that for very joy thereof, it would make him merrily to run to death. He showed them afore what trouble might fall unto him wherewith, and the like virtuous talk he had so long before his trouble encouraged them, that when he after fell in the trouble indeed, his trouble to him was a great deal the less, *quia spicula prævisa minus lædunt.* Now upon this resignment of his office came Sir Thomas Cromwell (then in the King's high favour) to Chelsea to him on a message from the King, wherein when they had throughly communed together, "Mr. Cromwell" (quoth he), "you are now entered into the service of a most noble, wise, and liberal prince; if you will follow my poor advice you shall, in council giving unto his Grace, ever tell him what he ought to do, but never tell him what he is able to do, so shall you show yourself a true faithful servant, and a right worthy Councillor. For if the lion knew his own strength, hard were it for any man to rule him." Shortly thereupon was there a commission directed to Cranmer, then Archbishop of Canterbury, to determine the matter of the matrimony between the King and Queen Katherine at St. Alban's, where according to the King's mind that was throughly finished, who pretending that he had no justice at the Pope's hands, from thenceforth sequestered himself from the See of Rome, and so married the Lady Anne Bullen, which Sir Thomas More understanding, said unto me, "God give grace, son, that these matters within a while be not confirmed with oaths." I, at that time, seeing no likelihood thereof, yet fearing lest for his forespeaking that would the sooner come to pass, waxed therefore for his saying much offended with him. It fortuned not long before the coming of the Queen Anne through the streets of London from the Tower to Westminster to her Coronation, that he received a letter from the Bishops of Durham, Bath, and Winchester, requesting him to bear them company from the Tower to the Coronation and also to take £20 that by the bearer thereof they had sent him to buy a gown with, which he thankfully received, and at home still tarrying, at their next meeting said merrily unto them, "My Lords, in the letters which you lately sent me, you required two things of me, the one whereof since I was so well contented to grant you, the other therefore I thought I might be the bolder to deny you."

In continuance when the King saw that he could by no manner of benefits win him to his side, then went he about by terrors and threats to drive him thereunto, the beginning of which trouble grew by occasion of a certain nun dwelling in Canterbury, for her virtue and holiness among the people not a little esteemed, unto whom for that cause many religious persons, Doctors of Divinity, and divers other of good worship of the laity used to resort, who affirming that she had revelations from God to give the King warning of his wicked life, and of the abuses of the sword and authority committed to him by God, and understanding my Lord of Rochester, Bishop

Fisher, to be a man of notable virtuous living and learning, repaired to Rochester, and there disclosed unto him all her revelations, desiring his advice and counsel therein, which the Bishop perceiving might well stand with the laws of God and his Church advised her (as she before had warning and intended) to go to the King herself, and to let him understand the whole circumstance thereof, whereupon she went unto the King, and told him all her revelations, and returned home again. And in short space after, she making a voyage to the Nun of Sion by the means of one Mr. Reynolds, a father of that house there fortuned concerning such secrets as she had revealed unto her, some part whereof seemed to touch the matter of the King's supremacy and marriage (which shortly thereupon followed) to enter into talk with Sir Thomas More; who notwithstanding he might well at that time without danger of any law (though after, as himself had prognosticated before, those matters were established by statutes and confirmed by oaths) freely and safely have talked with her therein; nevertheless, in all the communication between them (as in process of time it appeared) had always so discreetly demeaned himself, that he deserved not to be blamed, but contrariwise to be commended and praised. And had he not been one that in all his great office, and doings for the King and Realm together, had from all corruption of wrong doing, or bribes taking, kept himself so clear; that no man was able therewith to blemish him, it would without doubt (in this troublesome time of the King's wrath and indignation towards him) have been deeply laid to his charge, and of the King's Highness favourably accepted, as in the case of one Parnell that most manifestly appeared: against whom Sir Thomas More while he was Lord Chancellor, at the suit of one Vaughan his adversary had made a decree. This Parnell to the King's Highness had grievously complained that Sir Thomas More, for making the decree, had of the same Vaughan (unable for the gout to travel abroad himself) by the hands of his wife taken a fair great gilt cup for a bribe, who thereupon by the King's appointment being called before the Council, where that matter was heinously laid to his charge, forthwith confessed, that forasmuch as that cup was long after the aforesaid decree brought unto him for a new year's gift, he upon her importunate pressing upon him, therefore of courtesy refused not to take it. Then the Lord of Wiltshire (for hatred of his religion preferrer of this suit) with which rejoicing said unto the Lords, "Lo my Lords, lo, did I not tell you that you should find this matter true?" Whereupon Sir Thomas More desired their worships, that as they had courteously heard him tell the one part of his tale, so they would vouchsafe of their honours indifferently to hear the other, after which obtained, he further declared unto them, that albeit indeed, he had with much work received that cup, yet immediately thereupon he caused his butler to fill that with wine, and of that cup drank to her, and that when she had pledged him, then as freely as her husband had given it unto him, even so freely gave he the same unto her again, to give unto her husband for his new year's gift, which at his instant request, though much against her will, yet at length she was fain to receive, as herself and certain other there presently deposed before them. Thus was the great mountain turned scarce unto a mole-hill. So I remember that another time on a new year's day there came unto him one Mrs. Crocker, a rich widow (for whom with no small pains he had made a decree in the Chancery against the Lord of Arundel) to present him with a pair of gloves and £40 in angels in them for a New Year's gift, of whom he thankfully received the gloves, but refusing the money said unto her, "Mistress, since that were against good manners to forsake a gentlewoman's New Year's gift, I am content to receive your gloves, but as for your money I utterly refuse:" so much against her mind enforced he her to take her gold again. And one Mr. Gresham likewise having a cause depending in the Chancery against him, sent him for a New Year's gift a fair gilt cup the fashion whereof he very well liking caused one of his own (though not in his fantasy of so good a fashion) yet better in value, to be brought out of his chamber, which he willed the messenger to deliver to his mistress in recompense, and under other conditions would he in no wise receive it. Many things more of like effect for the declaration of his innocence and clearness from corruption, or evil affection, could I here rehearse besides, which for tediousness omitting, I refer to the readers by these few fore-remembered examples with their own judgments wisely to consider. At this Parliament was there put into the Lords' House a bill to attaint the nun, and divers other religious persons of high treason; and the Bishop of Rochester, Sir Thomas More, and certain others of misprision of treason: the King presupposing of likelihood this bill would be to Sir Thomas More so troublous and terrible, that that would force him to relent and condescend to his request, wherein his Grace was much deceived. To which bill Sir Thomas More was a suitor personally to be received in his own defence to make answer, but the King not liking that, assigned the Archbishop of Canterbury, the Lord Chancellor, the Duke of Norfolk, and Mr. Cromwell, at a day and place appointed to call Sir Thomas More before them, at which time I thinking I had good opportunity, earnestly advised him to labour unto these Lords for the help of his discharge out of the Parliament Bill; who answered me, he would: and at his coming before them according to their appointment, they entertained him very friendly, willing him to sit down with them, which in no wise he would. Then began the Lord Chancellor to declare unto him how many ways the King had showed his love and favour toward him, how fain he would have had him continue in his office, how glad he would have been to have heaped more benefits upon him, and finally, how he could ask no worldly honour, or profit at his Highness' hands, that were likely to be denied him; hoping by the declaration of the King's kindness and favour towards him to provoke him to recompense his Grace with the like again, and unto those things that the Parliament, the Bishops, and Universities had already passed to yield his consent. To this Sir Thomas More mildly answered saying, "No man living is there (my Lords) that would with better will do the thing that should be acceptable to the King's Highness than I, which must needs confess his manifold benefits, and bountiful goodness most benignly bestowed on me. Howbeit I verily hoped that I should never have heard of this matter more, considering that I have from time to time always from the beginning so plainly and truly declared my mind unto his Grace, which his Highness to me ever seemed, like a most gracious prince, very well to accept, never minding, as he said, to molest me more therewith. Since which time any further thing that was able to move me to any change could I never find, and if I could, there is none in all the world that could have been gladder of it than I." Many things more were there of like sort on both sides uttered. But in the end when they saw they could by no means of persuasions remove him from his former determinations, then began they more terribly to touch him, telling him that the King's Highness had given them in commandment (if they could by no gentleness win him) in his name with his great ingratitude to charge him, that never was there servant to his master so villainous, nor subject to his prince so traitorous as he. For he by his subtle sinister sleights, most unnaturally procuring and provoking him to set forth a book of the assertion of Seven Sacraments, and in maintenance of the Pope's authority, had caused him to his dishonour throughout all Christendom to put a sword in the Pope's hands to fight against himself. When they had thus laid forth all the terrors they could imagine against him: "My Lords" (quoth he) "These terrors be the arguments for children, and not for me. But to answer that wherewith you do chiefly burden me, I believe the King's Highness of his honour will never lay that to my charge. For none is there that in that point can say more in mine excuse than his Highness himself, who right well knoweth that I was never procurer or councillor of his Majesty thereunto but after that it was finished, by his Grace's appointment, and consent of the makers of the same, only a sorter out, and placer of the principal matters therein contained; wherein when I found the Pope's authority highly advanced, and with strong arguments mightly defended, I said unto his Grace, *I must put your Grace in remembrance of one thing, and that is this, The Pope (as your Grace knoweth) is a Prince as you are, and in league with all other Christian Princes, that may hereafter so fall out, that your Grace and he may vary upon some points of the league, whereupon may grow some breach of amity and war between you both; I think it best therefore that that place be amended, and his authority more slenderly touched.* Nay (quoth his Grace) that it shall not, we are so much bounden unto the See of Rome, that we cannot do too much honour unto it. Then did I put him further in remembrance of the statute of Praemunire, whereby a good part of the Pope's pastoral cure here was paid away. To that answered his Highness, *whatsoever impediment be to the contrary, we will set forth that authority to the uttermost. For we received from that See our Crown Imperial;* which till his Grace with his own mouth told me I never heard of before. So that I trust when his Grace shall be truly informed of this, and call to his gracious remembrance my doings in that behalf, his Highness will never speak of it more, but clear me throughly therein himself." And thus displeasantly departed they. Then took Sir Thomas More his boat towards his house at Chelsea, wherein by the way he was very merry, and for that was I nothing sorry, hoping that he had gotten himself discharged out of the Parliament Bill. When he was come home, then walked we two alone into his garden together, where I desirous to know how he had sped, said, "Sir, I trust all is well, because you are so merry." "That is so, indeed (son Roper) I thank God" (quoth he). "Are you put out of the Parliament Bill then?" said I. "By my troth (son Roper)," quoth he, "I never remembered it." "Never remembered it, Sir?" quoth I. "A case that toucheth yourself so near, and us all for your sake. I am sorry to hear it. For I verily trusted when I saw you so merry, that all had been well." Then said he, "Wilt thou know, son Roper, why I was so merry?" "That would I gladly, Sir," quoth I. "In good faith I rejoice, son," (quoth he), "that I had given the devil so foul a fall, and that with those Lords I had gone so far, as without great shame, I could never go back again." At which words waxed I very sad. For though himself liked it well, yet liked it me but a little. Now upon the report made by the Lord Chancellor, and the other Lords unto the King of all their whole discourse had with Sir Thomas More, the King was so highly offended with him, that he plainly told them he was fully determined the said Parliament Bill should undoubtedly proceed forth against him. To whom my Lord Chancellor and the rest of the Lords said, that they perceived the Lords of the Upper House so precisely bent to hear him, in his own case, make answer for himself, that if he were not put out of the Parliament Bill, it would without fail be utterly an overthrow of all. But for all this needs would the King have his own will therein, or else he said that at the passing thereof he would be personally present himself. Then the Lord Audley and the rest, seeing him so vehemently set thereupon, on their knees most humbly besought his Majesty to forbear the same, considering, that if he should in his own presence receive an overthrow, it would not only encourage his subjects ever after to

contemn him, but also throughout all Christendom, redound to his
dishonour for ever adding thereunto, that they mistrusted not in
time to find some meet matter to serve his Grace's turn better. For
in this case of the nun he was accounted so innocent and clear, that
for his dealing therein men reckoned him worthier of praise than
reproof. Whereupon at length through their earnest persuasion, he
was content to condescend to their petition. And on the morrow
after, Mr. Cromwell meeting me in the Parliament House willed me
to tell my father, that he was put out of the Parliament Bill. But
because I had appointed to dine that day in London, I sent the
message by my servant to my wife at Chelsea, whereof she informed
her father, "in faith Meg" (quoth he) *"Quod defertur, non aufertur."*
After this as the Duke of Norfolk and Sir Thomas More chanced to
fall in familiar talk together, the Duke said unto him, "By the Mass
(Mr. More) it is perilous striving with Princes and therefore I
would wish you somewhat to incline to the King's pleasure. For by
God's body (Mr. More) *Indignatio principis mors est."* "Is that all,
my Lord?" (quoth he). "Is there (in good faith) no more difference between your Grace and me, but that I shall die to-day and
you to-morrow?" So fell it out within a month or thereabout after
the making of the Statute for the oath of Supremacy and Matrimony,
that all the priests of London and Westminster, and no temporal
men but he were sent to appear at Lambeth before the Bishop of
Canterbury, the Lord Chancellor, and Secretary Cromwell, Commissioners, there, to tender the oath unto them. Then Sir Thomas
More, as his accustomed manner was always ere he entered into any
matter of importance (as when he was first chosen of the King's
Privy Council, when he was sent Ambassador, appointed Speaker
of the Parliament, made Lord Chancellor, or when he took any like
weighty matter upon him) to go to the church, and to be confessed,
to hear mass, and be housled; so did he likewise in the morning
early the selfsame day, that he was summoned to appear before the
Lords at Lambeth. And whereas he used evermore before, at his
departure from his house and children (whom he loved tenderly)
to have them bring him to his boat, and there to kiss them all, and
bid them farewell, then would he suffer none of them forth of the
gate to follow him, but pulled the wicket after him, and shut them

all from him, and with an heavy heart (as by his countenance it appeared) with me, and our four servants, there took his boat towards Lambeth. Wherein sitting still sadly awhile, at the last he rounded me in the ear and said, "Son Roper, I thank our Lord, the field is won." What he meant thereby, then, I wist not. Yet loath to seem ignorant I answered, "Sir, I am thereof very glad." But as I conjectured afterwards it was for that the love he had to God wrought in him so effectually, that it conquered in him all his carnal affections utterly. At his coming to Lambeth, how wisely he behaved himself before the Commissioners, at the ministration of the oath unto him, may be found in certain letters of his (sent to my wife) remaining in a great book of his works: where by the space of four days, he was betaken to the custody of the Abbot of Westminster, during which time the King consulted with his Council what order were meet to be taken with him. And albeit in the beginning they were resolved, that with an oath not to be known whether he had to the supremacy been sworn, or what he thought thereof, he should be discharged, yet did Queen Anne, by her importunate clamour, so sore exasperate the King against him, that, contrary to his former resolution, he caused the oath of the supremacy to be ministered unto him, who, albeit he made a discreet qualified answer, nevertheless was forthwith committed to the Tower, who as he was going thitherward, wearing, as he commonly did, a chain of gold about his neck, Sir Richard Cromwell (that had the charge of his conveyance thither) advised him to send home his chain to his wife, or some of his children, "Nay, Sir (quoth he), that will I not. For if I were taken in the field by my enemies, I would they should somewhat fare the better by me." At whose landing Mr. Lieutenant at the Tower gate was ready to receive him, where the porter demanded of him his upper garment. "Mr. Porter" (quoth he) "here it is," and took off his cap and delivered him, saying, "I am very sorry it is no better for you." "Nay, Sir" (quoth the Porter), "I must have your gown," and so was he by Mr. Lieutenant conveyed into his lodging, where he called unto him one John Awood his own servant there appointed to attend upon him, who could neither write nor read, and swore him before the Lieutenant that if he should hear, or see him at any time, speak or write any manner of

thing against the King, the Council, or the state of the Realm, he
should open it to the Lieutenant, that the Lieutenant might incontinent reveal it to the Council. Now when Sir Thomas More had
remained in the Tower a little more than a month, my wife, longing
to see her father, by her earnest suit at length gat leave to go to
him. At whose coming (after the seven psalms and litany said,
which whensoever she came to him, ere he fell in talk of any worldly
matters, he used accustomably to say with her) among other communication he said unto her, "I believe (Meg) that they that have
put me here, ween they have done me a high displeasure. But I
assure you on my faith, mine own dear daughter, if it had not been
for my wife and you that be my children, whom I account the chief
part of my charge, I would not have failed, long ere this, to have
closed myself in as strait a room and straiter too. But since I come
hither without mine own desert, I trust that God of his goodness
will discharge me of my care, and with his gracious help supply my
want among you. I find no cause (I thank God, Meg) to reckon
myself in worse case here, than in mine own house. For methinketh
God maketh me a wanton, and setteth me on his lap and dandleth
me." Thus by his gracious demeanour in tribulations appeared it,
that all the troubles that ever chanced unto him by his patient suf-
ferance thereof were to him no painful punishment, but of his
patience profitable exercises. And at another time, when he had first
questioned with my wife a while of the order of his wife and children, and state of his house in his absence, he asked her how Queen
Anne did: "In faith, father" (quoth she), "never better." "Never
better, Meg?" quoth he. "Alas (Meg) alas, it pitieth me to remember, in what misery she (poor soul) shortly shall come." After this
Mr. Lieutenant coming into his chamber to visit him, rehearsed the
benefits and friendships that he had many times received at his
hands, and how much bounden he was therefore friendly to entertain him and make him good cheer, which since (the case standing
as it did) he could not do without the King's indignation, he trusted
(he said) he would accept his good will, and such poor cheer as he
had. "Mr. Lieutenant" (quoth he again), "I verily believe, as you
may, so are you my good friends indeed, and would (as you say)
with your best cheer entertain me, for the which I most heartily

thank you. And assure yourself (Mr. Lieutenant)," quote he, "I do not mislike my cheer, but whensoever I do so, then thrust me out of your doors." Whereas the oath confirming the supremacy and matrimony was by the first statute comprised in few words, the Lord Chancellor and Mr. Secretary did of their own heads add more words unto it, to make it appear to the King's ears more pleasant and plausible. And that oath so amplified caused they to be ministered to Sir Thomas More and to all other throughout the Realm, which Sir Thomas perceiving said unto my wife: "I may tell thee (Meg) they that have committed me hither for refusing of the oath, not agreeable with the statute, are not able by their own law to justify my imprisonment. And surely (daughter) it is a great pity that a Christian prince should (by a flexible council ready to follow his affections, and by a weak clergy lacking grace constantly to stand to their learning) with flattery so shameful to be abused." But at length the Lord Chancellor and Mr. Secretary, espying their oversight in that behalf, were fain afterwards to find the means that another statute should be made for the confirmation of the oath so amplified with their additions. After Sir Thomas More had given over his office and all other worldly doings therewith, to the intent he might from thenceforth the more quietly set himself to the service of God, then made he a conveyance for the disposition of his lands, reserving for himself an estate thereof only for the term of his life, and after his decease assuring some part of the same to his wife, some to his son's wife for a jointure, in consideration that she was an inheritrix in possession of more than an hundred pounds land by the year, and some to me and my wife in recompense of our marriage money with divers remainders over, all which conveyance and assurance was perfectly finished long before that matter, whereupon she was attainted, was made an offence, and yet after by statute clearly voided; and so were all his lands, that he had to his wife and children by the said conveyance in such sort assured, contrary to the order of law, taken away from them, and brought into the King's hands, saving that portion that he had appointed to my wife and me, which although he had in the foresaid conveyance reserved, as he did the rest, for term of his life unto himself, nevertheless, upon further consideration after by another conveyance he gave that same immediately to me, and my wife in possession. And so because the statute had undone only the first conveyance, giving no more to the King but so much as passed by that, the second conveyance, whereby it was given unto my wife and me, being dated two days after was without the compass of the statute, and so was our portion to us by that means clearly reserved. As Sir Thomas More in the Tower chanced on a time looking out of his window to behold one Mr. Reynolds, a religious, learned and virtuous father of Sion, and three monks of the Charterhouse for the matter of the supremacy going out of the Tower to execution, he, as one longing in that journey to have accompanied them, said unto my wife, then standing there beside him, "Lo, dost thou not see (Meg) that these blessed fathers be now as cheerful going to their deaths, as bridegrooms to their marriages? Wherefore thereby mayest thou see (mine own good daughter) what a difference there is between such as have in effect spent all their days in a strait, hard, penitential, and painful life religiously, and such as have in the world, like worldly wretches, as thy poor father hath done, consumed all the time in pleasure and ease licentiously. For God, considering their long-continued life in most sore and grievous penance, will not longer suffer them to remain here in this vale of misery, and iniquity, but speedily hence take them to the fruition of his everlasting deity: whereas thy silly father (Meg) that, like a most wicked caitiff, hath passed forth the whole course of his miserable life most pitifully, God, thinking him not worthy so soon to come to that eternal felicity, leaveth him here yet, still in the world further to be plunged and turmoiled with misery." Within a while after Mr. Secretary (coming to him into the Tower from the King) pretended much friendship towards him, and for his comfort told him, that the King's Highness was his good and gracious lord and minded not with any matter, wherein he should have any cause of scruple, from henceforth to trouble his conscience. As soon as Mr. Secretary was gone, to express what comfort he conceived of his words, he wrote with a coal (for ink then he had none) these verses following:—

> *"Ay flattering fortune look you never so fair,*
> *Nor never so pleasantly begin to smile,*
> *As though thou wouldst my ruins all repair*

During my life thou shalt not me beguile,
Trust I shall, God, to enter in a while
Thy haven of heaven sure and uniform,
Ever after thy calm look I for no storm."

When Sir Thomas More had continued a good while in the Tower, my lady his wife obtained licence to see him, who at her first coming like a simple woman, and somewhat worldly too, with this manner of salutations bluntly saluted him, "What the good year, Mr. More," quoth she, "I marvel that you, that have been always hitherunto taken for so wise a man, will now so play the fool to lie here in this close filthy prison, and be content to be shut up among mice and rats, when you might be abroad at your liberty, and with the favour and good will both of the King and his Council, if you would but do as all the bishops and best learned of this Realm have done. And seeing you have at Chelsea a right fair house, your library, your books, your gallery, your garden, your orchards, and all other necessaries so handsomely about you, where you might, in the company of me your wife, your children, and household be merry, I muse what a God's name you mean here still thus fondly to tarry." After he had a while quietly heard her, with a cheerful countenance he said unto her, "I pray thee good Mrs. Alice, tell me, tell me one thing." "What is that?" (quoth she). "Is not this house as nigh heaven as mine own?" To whom she, after her accustomed fashion, not liking such talk, answered, *"Tille valle, tille valle."* "How say you, Mrs. Alice, is it not so?" He quoth. *"Bone Deus, bone Deus,* man, will this gear never be left?" quoth she. "Well then, Mrs. Alice, if it be so, it is very well. For I see no great cause why I should much joy of my gay house, or of anything belonging thereunto, when, if I should but seven years lie buried under the ground, and then arise and come thither again, I should not fail to find some therein that would bid me get out of the doors, and tell me that were none of mine. What cause have I then to like such an house as would so soon forget his master?" So her persuasions moved him but a little. Not long after came there to him the Lord Chancellor, the Dukes of Norfolk and Suffolk, with Mr. Secretary, and certain others of the Privy Council at two separate times, by all policies possible procuring him either precisely to confess the supremacy, or precisely to deny it. Whereunto (as appeareth by his examination in the said great book) they could never bring him. Shortly hereupon Mr. Rich (afterwards Lord Rich) then newly the King's Solicitor, Sir Richard Southwell, and Mr. Palmer, servant to the Secretary, were sent to Sir Thomas More into the Tower, to fetch away his books from him. And while Sir Richard Southwell and Mr. Palmer were busy in trussing up of his books, Mr. Rich pretending friendly talk with him, among other things of a set course, as it seemed, said thus unto him: "Forasmuch as it is well known (Mr. More) that you are a man both wise and well learned, as well in the laws of the Realm, as otherwise, I pray you therefore, Sir, let me be so bold as of good will to put unto you this case. Admit there were, Sir," quoth he, "an Act of Parliament, that all the Realm should take me for the King, would not you (Mr. More) take me for the King?" "Yes, Sir," quoth Sir Thomas More, "that would I." "I put the case further" (quoth Mr. Rich) "that there were an Act of Parliament that all the Realm should take me for the Pope; would then not you, Mr. More, take me for the Pope?" "For answer," quoth Sir Thomas More, "to your first case, the Parliament may well (Mr. Rich) meddle with the state of temporal princes; but to make answer to your second case, I will put you this case. Suppose the Parliament would make a law, that God should not be God, would you then, Mr. Rich, say God were not God?" "No, Sir," quoth he, "that would I not, since no Parliament may make any such law." "No more" (said Sir Thomas More, as Mr. Rich reported of him) "could the Parliament make the King supreme head of the Church." Upon whose only report was Sir Thomas More indicted of treason upon the Statute in which it was made treason to deny the King to be supreme head of the Church, into which indictment were put these words, *maliciously, traitorously, and diabolically.* When Sir Thomas More was brought from the Tower to Westminster Hall to answer the indictment, and at the King's Bench bar before the judges thereupon arraigned, he openly told them that he would upon that indictment have abiden in law, but he thereby should have been driven to confess of himself the matter indeed, which was the denial of the King's supremacy, which he protested was untrue, wherefore thereto he pleaded not guilty, and so reserved unto himself advantage to be taken of the body of the matter after verdict, to avoid that indictment. And moreover added, "if those only odious terms, *maliciously, traitorously, and diabolically* were put out of the indictment, he saw nothing therein justly to charge him." And for proof to the jury that Sir Thomas More was guilty to this treason, Mr. Rich was called by them to give evidence unto them, as he did; against whom Sir Thomas More began in this wise to say: "If I were a man (my Lords) that did not regard an oath, I need not (as it is well known) in this place, at this time, nor in this case to stand as an accused person. And if this oath of yours (Mr. Rich) be true, then pray I that I may never see God in the face, which I would not say, were it otherwise, to win the whole world." Then recited he unto the discourse of all their communication in the Tower according to the truth, and said, "In faith, Mr. Rich, I am sorrier for your perjury than for mine own peril, and you shall understand that neither I, nor no man else to my knowledge ever took you to be a man of such credit as in any matter of importance I, or any other would at any time vouchsafe to communicate with you. And (as you know) of no small while I have been acquainted with you and your conversation, who have known you from your youth hitherto. For we long dwelled both in one parish together, where, as yourself can tell (I am sorry you compel me so to say) you were esteemed very light of your tongue, a great dicer, and of not commendable fame. And so in your house at the Temple (where hath been your chief bringing up) were you likewise accounted. Can it therefore seem likely unto your honourable Lordships, that I would, in so weighty a cause, so far overshoot myself, as to trust Mr. Rich (a man of me always reputed for one of so little truth, as your Lordships have heard) so far above my sovereign Lord the King, or any of his noble councillors, that I would unto him utter the secrets of my conscience touching the King's supremacy, the special point and only mark at my hands so long sought for? A thing which I never did, nor never would, after the Statute thereof made, reveal it, either to the King's Highness himself, or to any of his honourable councillors, as it is not unknown unto your house, at sundry times, and several, sent from his Grace's own person unto the Tower to me for none other purpose. Can this in your judgments (my Lords) seem likely to be true? And if I had so done indeed, my Lords, as Mr. Rich hath sworn, seeing it was spoke but in familiar secret talk, nothing affirming, and only in putting of cases, without other displeasant circumstances, it cannot justly be taken to be spoken maliciously. And where there is no malice there can be no offence. And over this I can never think (my Lords) that so many worthy bishops, so many honourable personages, and many other worshipful, virtuous, wise, and well-learned men, as at the making of that law were in the Parliament assembled, ever meant to have any man punished by death, in whom there could be found no malice, taking *malitia pro malevolentia*. For if *malitia* be generally taken for sin, no man is there then that can thereof excuse himself. *Quia si dixerimus quod peccatum non habemus, nosmetipsos seducimus, et veritas in nobis non est.* And only this word *maliciously* is in the Statute material, as this term *forcible* is in the statute of forcible entries; by which statute if a man enter peaceably, and put not his adversary out forcibly, it is no offence, but if he put him out forcibly, then by that statute it is an offence. And so shall he be punished by this term *forcible.* Besides this, the manifold goodness of my sovereign Lord the King's Highness himself that hath been so many ways my singular good Lord and Gracious Sovereign, that hath so dearly loved me, and trusted me even at my first coming into his noble service with the dignity of his honourable Privy Council, vouchsafing to admit me to offices of great credit, and worship most liberally advanced me, and finally with that weighty room of his Grace's high Chancellorship (the like whereof he never did to temporal men before) next to his own royal person the highest officer in this noble realm, so far above my merits or qualities able and meet therefore, of his incomparable benignity honoured and exalted me by the space of twenty years and more, showing his continual favour towards me; and (until, at mine own poor suit, it pleased his Highness, giving me licence, with his Majesty's favour, to bestow the residue of my life wholly for the provision of my soul in the service of God, of his special goodness thereof to discharge and unburden me) most benignly heaped honours more and more upon me; all this his Highness' goodness, I say, so long continued towards me, were, in my mind (my Lords), matter sufficient to convince this

slanderous surmise (by this man) so wrongfully imagined against
me." Mr. Rich seeing himself so disproved, and his credit so foully
defaced, caused Sir Richard Southwell and Mr. Palmer, that at that
time of their communication were in the chamber, to be sworn what
words had passed betwixt them. Whereupon Mr. Palmer on his
deposition said, that he was so busy about the trussing up Sir Thomas
More's books in a sack, that he took no heed to their talk. Sir
Richard Southwell likewise upon his deposition said, that because
he was appointed only to look to the conveyance of his books, he
gave no ear unto them. After this, were there many other reasons
(not now in my rememberance) by Sir Thomas More in his own
defence alleged, to the discredit of Mr. Rich his foresaid evidence,
and proof of the clearness of his own conscience. All which notwithstanding the jury found him guilty, and incontinent upon the
verdict the Lord Chancellor (for that matter chief commissioner)
beginning in judgment against him, Sir Thomas More said to him,
"My Lord, when I was towards the law, the manner in such case
was to ask the prisoner before judgment, why judgment should not
be given against him?" Whereupon the Lord Chancellor staying his
judgment, wherein he had partly proceeded, demanded of him what
he was able to say to the contrary? Who then in this sort mildly
made answer: "Forasmuch as, my Lord" (quoth he), "this indictment is grounded upon an Act of Parliament, directly oppugnant to
the laws of God and his holy Church, the supreme government of
which, or of any part thereof, may no temporal prince presume by
any law to take upon him as rightfully belonging to the See of
Rome, a spiritual pre-eminence by the mouth of our Saviour himself,
personally present upon the earth, to St. Peter and his successors,
bishops of the same see, by special prerogative, granted, it is therefore in law amongst Christian men insufficient to charge any
Christian." And for proof thereof like as amongst divers other
reasons and authorities he declared that this Realm, being but one
member and small part of the Church, might not make a particular
law dischargeable with the general law of Christ's holy Catholic
Church, no more than the City of London, being but one poor member in respect of the whole Realm, might make a law against an
Act of Parliament to bind the whole Realm unto: so further showed

he, that it was contrary both to the laws and statutes of this land, yet unrepealed, as they might evidently perceive in *Magna charta, Quod Ecclesia Anglicana libera sit et habeat omnia jura sua integra, at libertates suas illæsas,* and contrary to that sacred oath which the King's Highness himself, and every other Christian prince always at their coronations received, alleging moreover, that no more might this Realm of England refuse obedience to the See of Rome, than might the child refuse obedience to his natural father. For as St. Paul said of the Corinthians, "I have regenerated you my children in Christ," so might St. Gregory Pope of Rome (of whom by St. Augustine his messenger we first received the Christian faith) of us English men truly say, "You are my children, because I have given to you everlasting salvation, a far better inheritance than any carnal father can leave unto his child, and by spiritual generation have made you my spiritual children in Christ." Then was it thereunto by the Lord Chancellor answered, that seeing all the bishops, universities, and best learned men of the Realm had to this Act agreed, it was much marvelled that he alone against them all would so stiffly stick and vehemently argue there against. To that Sir Thomas More replied saying, "If the number of bishops and universities be so material, as your Lordships seemeth to take it, then see I little cause (my Lords) why that thing in my conscience should make any change. For I nothing doubt, but that though not in this Realm, yet in Christendom about they be not the least part, that be of my mind therein. But if I should speak of those that be already dead (of whom many be now saints in heaven) I am very sure it is the far greater part of them, that all the while they lived, thought in this case that way that I think now. And therefore am I not bound (my Lords) to conform my conscience to the council of one realm against the General Council of Christendom." Now when Sir Thomas More, for the avoiding of the indictment, had taken as many exceptions as he thought meet and more reasons than I can now remember alleged, the Lord Chancellor, loath to have the burden of the judgment wholly to depend upon himself, then openly asked the advice of the Lord Fitz-James, then the Lord Chief Justice of the King's Bench, and joined in commission with him, whether this indictment were sufficient or not? Who like a wise man answered, "My Lords all, by St. Julian" (that was ever his oath) "I must needs confess, that if the Act of Parliament be not unlawful, then is not the indictment in my conscience insufficient." Whereupon the Lord Chancellor said to the rest of the Lords, "Lo, my Lords, lo, you hear what my Lord Chief Justice saith," and so immediately gave the judgment against him. After which ended, the commissioners yet courteously offered him, if he had anything else to allege for his defence to grant him favourable audience, who answered, "More have I not to say (my Lords) but like as the blessed Apostle St. Paul, as we read in the Acts of the Apostles, was present, and consented to the death of St. Stephen, and kept their clothes that stoned him to death, and yet be they now both twain holy saints in heaven, and shall continue there friends for ever, so I verily trust and shall therefore right heartily pray, that though your Lordships have now in earth been judges to my condemnation, we may yet hereafter in heaven merrily all meet together to our everlasting salvation." Thus much touching Sir Thomas More's arraignment, being not thereat present myself, have I by the credible report of Sir Anthony Sumtleger Knight, and partly of Sir Richard Heywood, and John Webb Gentleman, with others of good credit, at the hearing thereof present themselves, as far forth as my poor wit and memory would serve me, here truly rehearsed unto you. Now after this arraignment departed he from the bar to the Tower again, led by Sir William Kingston, a tall, strong, and comely knight, Constable of the Tower, his very dear friend, who, when he had brought him from Westminster to the Old Swan towards the Tower, there with a heavy heart, the tears running down his cheeks, bade him farewell. Sir Thomas More seeing him so sorrowful, comforted him with as good words as he could, saying, "Good Mr. Kingston, trouble not yourself, but be of good cheer. For I will pray for you, and my good Lady your wife, that we may meet in heaven together, where we shall be merry for ever and ever." Soon after Sir William Kingston talking with me of Sir Thomas More, said, "In faith Mr. Roper I was ashamed of myself, that at my departure from your father, I found my heart so feeble, and his so strong, that he was fain to comfort me which should rather have comforted him." When Sir Thomas More came from Westminster to the Towerward again his daughter my wife, desirous to see her father, whom she thought she should never see in this world after, and also to have his final blessing, gave attendance about the Tower wharf, where she knew he should pass by, ere he could enter into the Tower. There tarrying for his coming home, as soon as she saw him, after his blessings on her knees reverently received, she, hasting towards, without consideration of care of herself, pressing in amongst the midst of the throng and the Company of the Guard, that with halbards and bills were round about him, hastily ran to him, and there openly in the sight of all them embraced and took him about the neck and kissed him, who well liking her most daughterly love and affection towards him, gave her his fatherly blessing, and many godly words of comfort besides, from whom after she was departed, she not satisfied with the former sight of her dear father, having respect neither to herself, nor to the press of the people and multitude that were about him, suddenly turned back again, and ran to him as before, took him about the neck, and divers times together most lovingly kissed him, and at last with a full heavy heart was fain to depart from him; the beholding whereof was to many of them that were present thereat so lamentable, that it made them for very sorrow to mourn and weep. So remained Sir Thomas More in the Tower more than a sevennight after his judgment. From whence the day before he suffered he sent his shirt of hair, not willing to have it seen, to my wife, his dearly beloved daughter, and a letter, written with a coal, contained in the foresaid book of his works, plainly expressing the fervent desire he had to suffer on the morrow in these words: "I cumber you, good Margaret, much, but I would be sorry if it should be any longer than to-morrow. For to-morrow is St. Thomas' even, and the Octave of St. Peter, and therefore to-morrow long I to go to God, that were a day very meet and convenient for me. And I never liked your manners better, than when you kissed me last. For I like when daughterly love, and dear charity hath no leisure to look to worldly courtesy." And so upon the next morning, being Tuesday, St. Thomas' even, and the Octave of St. Peter in the year of our Lord God 1537, according as he in his letter the day before had wished, early in the morning came to him Sir Thomas Pope, his singular friend, on message from the King and his Council, that he should before nine of the clock in the same morning suffer death, and that therefore forthwith he should prepare himself thereto. "Mr. Pope," saith he, "for your good tidings I most heartily thank you. I have been always bounden much to the King's Highness for the benefits and honours which he hath still from time to time most bountifully heaped upon me, and yet more bounded I am to his Grace for putting me into this place, where I have had convenient time and space to have remembrance of my end, and so help me God most of all, Mr. Pope, am I bound to his Highness, that it pleased him so shortly to rid me of the miseries of this wretched world. And therefore will I not fail most earnestly to pray for his Grace both here, and also in another world." "The King's pleasure is further," quoth Mr. Pope, "that at your execution you shall not use many words." "Mr. Pope" (quoth he), "you do well that you give me warning of his Grace's pleasure. For otherwise, had I purposed at that time somewhat to have spoken, but of no matter wherewith his Grace, or any other should have had cause to be offended. Nevertheless, whatsoever I intend I am ready obediently to conform myself to his Grace's commandment. And I beseech you, good Mr. Pope, to be a mean unto his Highness, that my daughter Margaret may be present at my burial." "The King is well contented already" (quoth Mr. Pope) "that your wife, children, and other friends shall have free liberty to be present thereat." "O how much beholden," then said Sir Thomas More, "am I to his Grace, that unto my poor burial vouchsafeth to have so gracious consideration." Wherewithal Mr. Pope taking his leave of him could not refrain from weeping, which Sir Thomas More perceiving, comforted him in this wise, "Quiet yourself, good Mr. Pope, and be not discomforted. For I trust that we shall once in heaven see each other full merrily, where we shall be sure to live and love together in joyful bliss eternally." Upon whose departure Sir Thomas More, as one that had been invited to a solemn feast, changed himself into his best apparel; which Mr. Lieutenant espying, advised him to put it off, saying, That he that should have it was but a worthless fellow. "What Mr. Lieutenant" (quoth he), "shall I account him a worthless fellow, that will do me this day so singular a benefit? Nay, I assure you, were it cloth of gold I would account it well bestowed on him, as St. Cyprian did, who gave his executioner thirty pieces of gold." And albeit at length, through Mr. Lieutenant's persuasions, he altered his apparel, yet, after the example of that holy martyr St. Cyprian, did he of that little money that was left him, send one angel of gold to his executioner. And so was he brought by Mr. Lieutenant out of the Tower, and from thence led towards the place of execution, where going up the scaffold, which was so weak that it was ready to fall, he said to Mr. Lieutenant, "I pray you, I pray you, Mr. Lieutenant, see me safe up, and for my coming down let me shift for myself." Then desired he all the people thereabouts to pray for him, and to bear witness with him, that he should then suffer death in and for the faith of the holy Catholic Church, which done he kneeled down, and after his prayers said, he turned to the executioner, and with a cheerful countenance spake unto him. "Pluck up thy spirits, man, and be not afraid to do thine office, my neck is very short. Take heed therefore thou shoot not awry for saving thine honesty." So passed Sir Thomas More out of this world to God upon the very same day in which himself had most desired. Soon after whose death came intelligence thereof to the Emperor Charles, whereupon he sent for Sir Thomas Eliott, our English Ambassador, and said unto him, "My Lord Ambassador, we understand that the King your master hath put his faithful servant and grave wise councillor Sir Thomas More to death." Whereunto Sir Thomas Eliott answered, that he understood nothing thereof. "Well," said the Emperor, "it is very true, and this will we say, that if we had been master of such a servant, of whose doings ourselves have had these many years no small experience, we would rather have lost the best city of our dominions, than have lost such a worthy councillor." Which matter was by Sir Thomas Eliott to myself, to my wife, to Mr. Clement and his wife, to Mr. John Haywood and his wife, and divers others of his friends accordingly reported.

UTOPIA

THE most victorious and triumphant King of England, Henry the Eighth of that name, in all royal virtues, prince most peerless, had of late in controversy with the right high and mighty King of Castile, weighty matters and of great importance. For the debatement and final determination whereof, the King's Majesty sent me ambassador into Flanders, joined in commission with Cuthbert Tunstall, a man doubtless out of comparison, and whom the King's Majesty of late, to the great rejoicing of all men, did prefer to the office of Master of the Rolls.

But of this man's praises I will say nothing, not because I do fear that small credence shall be given to the testimony that cometh out of a friend's mouth: but because his virtue and learning be greater, and of more excellency, than that I am able to praise them: and also in all places so famous and so perfectly well known, that they need not, nor ought not of me to be praised, unless I would seem to show and set forth the brightness of the sun with a candle, as the proverb saith. There met us at Bruges (for thus it was before agreed) they whom their Prince had for that matter appointed commissioners: excellent men all. The chief and the head of them was the Margrave (as they call him) of Bruges, a right honourable man: but the wisest and the best spoken of them was George Temsice, provost of Cassel, a man, not only by learning, but also by nature of singular eloquence, and in the laws profoundly learned: but in reasoning and debating of matters, what by his natural wit, and what by daily exercise, surely he had few fellows. After that we had once or twice met, and upon certain points or articles could not fully and thoroughly agree, they for a certain space took their leave of us, and departed to Brussels, there to know their Prince's pleasure. I in the meantime (for so my business lay) went straight thence to Antwerp. Whiles I was there abiding, oftentimes among other, but which to me was more welcome than any other, did visit me one Peter Giles, a citizen of Antwerp, a man there in his country of honest reputation, and also preferred to high promotions, worthy truly of the highest. For it is hard to say, whether the young man be in learning, or in honesty more excellent. For he is both of wonderful virtuous conditions, and also singularly well learned, and towards all sorts of people exceeding gentle: but towards his friends so kind-hearted, so loving, so faithful, so trusty, and of so earnest affection, that it were very hard in any place to find a man, that with him in all points of friendship may be compared. No man can be more lowly or courteous. No man useth less simulation or dissimulation, in no man is more prudent simplicity. Besides this, he is in his talk and communication so merry and pleasant, yea and that without harm, that through his gentle entertainment, and his sweet and delectable communication, in me was greatly abated and diminished the fervent desire, that I had to see my native country, my wife and my children, whom then I did much long and covet to see, because that at that time I had been more than four months from them. Upon a certain day when I had heard the divine service in our Lady's church, which is the fairest, the most gorgeous and curious church of building in all the city and also most frequented of people, and, the service being done, was ready to go home to my lodging, I chanced to espy this foresaid Peter talking with a certain stranger, a man well stricken in age, with a black sunburned face, a long beard, and a cloak cast homely about his shoulders, whom by his favour and apparel forthwith I judged to be a mariner. But when this Peter saw me, he cometh to me and saluteth me.

And as I was about to answer him: see you this man, saith he (and therewith he pointed to the man, that I saw him talking with before); I was minded, quoth he, to bring him straight home to you.

He should have been very welcome to me, said I, for your sake.

Nay (quoth he) for his own sake, if you knew him: for there is no man this day living, that can tell you of so many strange and unknown peoples, and countries, as this man can. And I know well that you be very desirous to hear of such news.

Then I conjectured not far amiss (quoth I) for even at the first sight I judged him to be a mariner.

Nay (quoth he) there ye were greatly deceived: he hath sailed indeed, not as the mariner Palinure, but as the expert and prudent prince Ulysses: yea, rather as the ancient and sage philosopher Plato. For this same Raphael Hythloday (for this is his name) is very well learned in the Latin tongue: but profound and excellent in the Greek tongue. Wherein he ever bestowed more study than in the Latin, because he had given himself wholly to the study of philosophy. Whereof he knew that there is nothing extant in the Latin tongue that is to any purpose, saving a few of Seneca's, and Cicero's doings. His patrimony that he was born unto, he left to his brethren (for he is a Portugal born) and for the desire that he had to see, and know the far countries of the world, he joined himself in company with Amerigo Vespucci, and in the three last voyages of those four that be now in print and abroad in every man's hands, he continued still in his company, saving that in the last voyage he came not home again with him. For he made such means and shift, what by entreatance, and what by importune suit, that he got licence of master Amerigo (though it were sore against his will) to be one of the twenty-four which in the end of the last voyage were left in the country of Gulike. He was therefore left behind for his mind sake, as one that took more thought and care for travelling than dying: having customably in his mouth these sayings: he that hath no grave, is covered with the sky: and, the way to heaven out of all places is of like length and distance. Which fantasy of his (if God had not been his better friend) he had surely bought full dear. But after the departing of master Vespucci, when he had travelled through and about many countries with five of his companions Gulikians, at the last by marvellous chance he arrived in Taprobane, from whence he went to Caliquit, where he chanced to find certain of his country ships, wherein he returned again into his country, nothing less than looked for.

All this when Peter had told me, I thanked him for his gentle kindness, that he had vouchsafed to bring me to the speech of that

man, whose communication he thought should be to me pleasant
and acceptable. And therewith I turned me to Raphael. And when
we had saluted each other, and had spoken these common words,
that be customably spoken at the first meeting and acquaintance of
strangers, we went thence to my house, and there in my garden upon
a bench covered with green turf we sat down talking together. There
he told us, how that after the departing of Vespucci, he and his fellows, that tarried behind in Gulike, began by little and little, through
fair and gentle speech, to win the love and favour of the people of
that country, insomuch that within short space, they did dwell
amongst them, not only harmless, but also occupied with them very
familiarly. He told us also, that they were in high reputation and
favour with a certain great man (whose name and country is now
quite out of my remembrance) which of his mere liberality did bear
the costs and charges of him and his five companions. And besides
that gave them a trusty guide to conduct them in their journey
(which by water was in boats, and by land in waggons) and to bring
them to other princes, with very friendly commendations. Thus after
many days' journeys, he said, they found towns and cities and weal
publics, full of people, governed by good and wholesome laws. For
under the line equinoctial, and of both sides of the same, as far as
the sun doth extend his course, lieth (quoth he) great and wide
deserts and wildernesses, parched, burned, and dried up with continual and intolerable heat. All things be hideous, terrible, loathsome, and unpleasant to behold: all things out of fashion and
comeliness, inhabited with wild beasts and serpents, or at the leastwise, with people, that be no less savage, wild and noisome, than
the very beasts themselves be. But a little farther beyond that,
all things begin by little and little to wax pleasant; the air soft, temperate, and gentle; the ground covered with green grass; less wild-
ness in the beasts. At the last shall ye come again to people, cities,
and towns wherein is continual intercourse and occupying of merchandise and chaffer, not only among themselves and with their
borderers, but also with merchants of far countries, both by land and
water. There I had occasion (said he) to go to many countries of
every side. For there was no ship ready to any voyage or journey,
but I and my fellows were into it very gladly received. The ships
that they found first were made plain, flat and broad in the bottom,

trough-wise. The sails were made of great rushes, or of wickers, and in some places, of leather. Afterward they found ships with ridged keels, and sails of canvas, yea, and shortly after, having all things like ours. The shipmen also very expert and cunning, both in the sea and in the weather. But he said that he found great favour and friendship among them, for teaching them the feat and use of the load-stone, which to them before that time was unknown. And therefore they were wont to be very timorous and fearful upon the sea; nor to venture upon it, but only in the summer time. But now they have such a confidence in that stone, that they fear not stormy winter: in so doing farther from care than jeopardy; insomuch, that it is greatly to be doubted, lest that thing, through their own foolish hardiness, shall turn them to evil and harm, which at the first was supposed should be to them good and commodious.

But what he told us that he saw in every country where he came, it were very long to declare; neither is it my purpose at this time to make rehearsal thereof. But peradventure in another place I will speak of it, chiefly such things as shall be profitable to be known, as in special be those decrees and ordinances, that he marked to be well and wisely provided and enacted among such peoples, as do live together in a civil policy and good order. For of such things did we busily inquire and demand of him, and he likewise very willingly told us of the same. But as for monsters, because they be no news, of them we were nothing inquisitive. For nothing is more easy to be found, then be barking Scyllas, ravening Celenos, and Læstrygonians devourers of people, and such like great, and incredible monsters. But to find citizens ruled by good and wholesome laws, that is an exceeding rare, and hard thing. But as he marked many fond, and foolish laws in those new found lands, so he rehearsed many acts, and constitutions, whereby these our cities, nations, countries, and kingdoms may take example to amend their faults, enormities, and errors. Whereof in another place (as I said) I will treat.

Now at this time I am determined to rehearse only that he told us of the manners, customs, laws, and ordinances of the Utopians. But first I will repeat our former communication by the occasion, and (as I might say) the drift whereof, he was brought into the mention of that weal public.

For, when Raphael had very prudently touched divers things that be amiss, some here and some there, yea, very many of both parts; and again had spoken of such wise and prudent laws and decrees, as be established and used, both here among us and also there among them, as a man so cunning, and expert in the laws, and customs of every several country, as though into what place soever he came guestwise, there he had led all his life: then Peter much marvelling at the man: Surely Master Raphael (quoth he) I wonder greatly, why you get you not into some king's court. For I am sure there is no prince living, that would not be very glad of you, as a man not only able highly to delight him with your profound learning, and this your knowledge of countries, and peoples, but also are meet to instruct him with examples, and help him with counsel. And thus doing, you shall bring yourself in a very good case, and also be in ability to help all your friends and kinsfolk.

As concerning my friends and kinsfolk (quoth he) I pass not greatly for them. For I think I have sufficiently done my part towards them already. For these things, that other men do not depart from, until they be old and sick, yea, which they be then very loath to leave, when they can no longer keep, those very same things did I being not only lusty and in good health, but also in the flower of my youth, divide among my friends and kinsfolks. Which I think with this my liberality ought to hold them contented, and not to require nor to look that besides this, I should for their sakes give myself in bondage to kings.

Nay, God forbid (quoth Peter), it is not my mind that you should be in bondage to kings, but as a retainer to them at your pleasure. Which surely I think is the nighest way that you can devise how to bestow your time fruitfully, not only for the private commodity of your friends and for the general profit of all sorts of people, but also for the advancement of yourself to a much wealthier state and condition, than you be now in.

To a wealthier condition (quoth Raphael) by that means, that my mind standeth clean against? Now I live at liberty after my own mind and pleasure, which I think very few of these great states and peers of realms can say. Yea and there be enough of them that seek for great men's friendships: and therefore think it no great hurt, if they have not me, nor two or three such other as I am.

Well, I perceive plainly friend Raphael (quoth I) that you be desirous neither of riches nor of power. And truly I have in no less reverence and estimation a man that is of your mind, than any of them all that be so high in power and authority. But you shall do as it becometh you: yea, and according to this wisdom, and this high and free courage of yours, if you can find in your heart so to appoint and dispose yourself, that you may apply your wit and diligence to the profit of the weal public, though it be somewhat to your own pain and hindrance. And this shall you never so well do, nor with so great profit perform, as if you be of some great prince's council, and put into his head (as I doubt not but you will) honest opinions and virtuous persuasions. For from the prince, as from a perpetual well spring, cometh among the people the flood of all that is good or evil. But in you is so perfect learning, that without any experience, and again so great experience, that without any learning you may well be any king's councillor.

You be twice deceived, Master More (quoth he), first in me, and again in the thing itself. For neither is in me that ability that you force upon me, and if it were never so much, yet in disquieting mine own quietness I should nothing further the weal public. For first of all, the most part of all princes have more delight in warlike matters and feats of chivalry (the knowledge whereof I neither have nor desire) than in the good feats of peace: and employ much more study, how by right or by wrong to enlarge their dominions, than how well and peaceably to rule and govern that they have already. Moreover, they that be councillors to kings, every one of them either is of himself so wise indeed, that he need not, or else he thinketh himself so wise, that he will not allow another man's counsel, saving that they do shamefully and flatteringly give assent to the fond and foolish sayings of certain great men. Whose favours, because they be in high authority with their prince, by assentation and flattery they labour to obtain. And verily it is naturally given to all men to esteem their own inventions best. So both the raven and the ape think their own young ones fairest. Then if a man in such a company, where some disdain and have despite at other men's inventions, and some count their own best, if among such men (I say) a man should bring forth anything, that he hath read done in times past, or that he hath seen done in other places: there the hearers fare as though the whole existimation of their wisdom were in jeopardy to be overthrown, and that ever after they should be counted for very fools, unless they could in other men's inventions pick out matter to reprehend, and find fault at. If all other poor helps fail, then this is their extreme refuge. These things (say they) pleased our forefathers and ancestors; would God we could be so wise as they were: and as though they had wittily concluded the matter, and with this answer stopped every man's mouth, they sit down again. As who should say, it were a very dangerous matter, if a man in any point should be found wiser than his forefathers were.

And yet be we content to suffer the best and wittiest of their decrees to lie unexecuted: but if in anything a better order might have been taken, than by them was, there we take fast hold, and find many faults. Many times have I chanced upon such proud, lewd, overthwart and wayward judgments, yea, and once in England.

I pray you sir (quoth I) have you been in our country?

Yea forsooth (quoth he) and there I tarried for the space of four or five months together, not long after the insurrection, that the western Englishmen made against their king, which by their own miserable and pitiful slaughter was suppressed and ended. In the mean season I was much bound and beholden to the right reverend father, John Morton, Archbishop and Cardinal of Canterbury, and at that time also Lord Chancellor of England: a man, Master Peter (for Master More knoweth already that I will say), not more honourable for his authority, than for his prudence and virtue. He was of a mean stature, and though stricken in age, yet bare he his body upright. In his face did shine such an amiable reverence, as was pleasant to behold, gentle in communication, yet earnest, and sage. He had great delight many times with rough speech to his suitors, to prove, but without harm, what prompt wit and what bold spirit were in every man. In the which, as in a virtue much agreeing with his nature, so that therewith were not joined impudence, he took great delectation. And the same person, as apt and meet to have an administration in the weal public, he did lovingly embrace. In his

speech he was fine, eloquent, and pithy. In the law he had profound
knowledge, in wit he was incomparable, and in memory wonderful
excellent. These qualities, which in him were by nature singular,
he by learning and use had made perfect. The king put much trust
in his counsel, the weal public also in a manner leaned unto him,
when I was there. For even in the chief of his youth he was taken
from school into the court, and there passed all his time in much
trouble and business, and was continually tumbled and tossed in the
waves of divers misfortunes and adversities. And so by many and
great dangers he learned the experience of the world, which so being
learned can not easily be forgotten. It chanced on a certain day,
when I sat at his table, there was also a certain layman cunning in
the laws of your realm. Which, I cannot tell whereof taking occasion, began diligently and busily to praise that strait and rigorous
justice, which at that time was there executed upon felons, who, as
he said, were for the most part twenty hanged together upon one
gallows. And, seeing so few escaped punishment, he said he could
not choose, but greatly wonder and marvel, how and by what evil
luck it should so come to pass, that thieves nevertheless were in every
place so rife and rank. Nay, sir, quoth I (for I durst boldly speak my
mind before the Cardinal), marvel nothing hereat: for this punishment of thieves passeth the limits [of] justice, and is also very hurtful
to the weal public. For it is too extreme and cruel a punishment
for theft, and yet not sufficient to refrain men from theft. For simple
theft is not so great an offence, that it ought to be punished with
death. Neither there is any punishment so horrible, that it can keep
them from stealing, which have no other craft, whereby to get their
living. Therefore in this point, not you only, but also the most part of
the world, be like evil schoolmasters, which be readier to beat, than
to teach their scholars. For great and horrible punishments be appointed for thieves, whereas much rather provision should have been
made, that there were some means, whereby they might get their
living, so that no man should be driven to this extreme necessity, first
to steal, and then to die. Yes (quoth he) this matter is well enough
provided for already. There be handicrafts, there is husbandry to
get their living by, if they would not willingly be nought. Nay,
quoth I, you shall not 'scape so: for first of all, I will speak nothing

of them, that come home out of war, maimed and lame, as not long
ago, out of Blackheath field, and a little before that, out of the wars
in France: such, I say, as put their lives in jeopardy for the weal public's or the king's sake, and by the reason of weakness and lameness
be not able to occupy their old crafts, and be too aged to learn new:
of them I will speak nothing, because war like the tide ebbeth and
floweth. But let us consider those things that chance daily before
our eyes. First there is a great number of gentlemen, which cannot
be content to live idle themselves, like drones, of that which other
have laboured for: their tenants I mean, whom they poll and shave
to the quick by raising their rents (for this only point of frugality
do they use, men else through their lavish and prodigal spending,
able to bring themselves to very beggary) these gentlemen, (I say), do
not only live in idleness themselves, but also carry about with them
at their tails a great flock or train of idle and loitering serving-men,
which never learned any craft whereby to get their livings. These
men as soon as their master is dead, or be sick themselves, be incontinent thrust out of doors. For gentlemen had rather keep idle persons, than sick men, and many times the dead man's heir is not able
to maintain so great a house, and keep so many serving-men as his
father did. Then in the mean season they that be thus destitute of
service, either starve for hunger, or manfully play the thieves. For
what would you have them to do? When they have wandered
abroad so long, until they have worn threadbare their apparel, and
also impaired their health, then gentlemen because of their pale and
sick faces, and patched coats, will not take them into service. And
husbandmen dare not set them a work, knowing well enough that he
is nothing meet to do true and faithful service to a poor man with a
spade and a mattock for small wages and hard fare, which being
daintily and tenderly pampered up in idleness and pleasure, was
wont with a sword and a buckler by his side to strut through the
street with a bragging look, and to think himself too good to be any
man's mate. Nay, by Saint Mary, sir (quoth the lawyer) not so.
For this kind of men must we make most of. For in them as men
of stouter stomachs, bolder spirits, and manlier courages than handicraftsmen and ploughmen be, doth consist the whole power, strength,
and puissance of our host, when we must fight in battle. Forsooth,

sir, as well you might say (quoth I) that for war's sake you must cherish thieves. For surely you shall never lack thieves, whiles you have them. No, nor thieves be not the most false and faint-hearted soldiers, nor soldiers be not the cowardliest thieves: so well these two crafts agree together. But this fault, though it be much used among you, yet is it not peculiar to you only, but common also almost to all nations. Yet France besides this is troubled and infected with a much sorer plague. The whole realm is filled and besieged with hired soldiers in peace time (if that be peace) which be brought in under the same colour and pretence that hath persuaded you to keep these idle serving-men. For these wise fools and very archdolts thought the wealth of the whole country herein to consist, if there were ever in a readiness a strong and a sure garrison, specially of old practiced soldiers, for they put no trust at all in men unexercised. And therefore they must be fain to seek for war, to the end they may ever have practiced soldiers and cunning manslayers, lest that (as it is prettily said of Sallust) their hands and their minds through idleness or lack of exercise should wax dull. But how pernicious and pestilent a thing it is to maintain such beasts, the Frenchmen, by their own harms have learned, and the examples of the Romans, Carthaginians, Syrians, and of many other countries do manifestly declare. For not only the empire but also the fields and cities of all these, by divers occasions have been overrun and destroyed of their own armies beforehand had in a readiness. Now how unnecessary a thing this is, hereby it may appear: that the French soldiers, which from their youth have been practiced and inured in feats of arms, do not crack nor advance themselves to have very often got the upper hand and mastery of your new-made and unpracticed soldiers. But in this point I will not use many words, lest perchance I may seem to flatter you. No, nor those same handicraftsmen of yours in cities, nor yet the rude and uplandish ploughmen of the country, are not supposed to be greatly afraid of your gentlemen's idle serving-men, unless it be such as be not of body or stature correspondent to their strength and courage, or else whose bold stomachs be discouraged through poverty. Thus you may see, that it is not to be feared lest they should be effeminated, if they were brought up in good crafts and laboursome works, whereby to get their living, those stout and sturdy bodies (for gentlemen vouchsafe to corrupt and spoil none but picked and chosen men) now either by reason of rest and idleness be brought to weakness: or else by too easy and womanly exercises be made feeble and unable to endure hardness. Truly, howsoever the case standeth, this methinketh is nothing available to the weal public, for war's sake, which you never have, but when you will yourselves, to keep and maintain an innumerable flock of that sort of men, that be so troublesome and annoyous in peace, whereof you ought to have a thousand times more regard than of war. But yet this is not only the necessary cause of stealing. There is another, which, as I suppose, is proper and peculiar to you Englishmen alone. What is that, quoth the Cardinal? forsooth (quoth I) your sheep that were wont to be so meek and tame, and so small eaters, now, as I hear say, be become so great devourers and so wild, that they eat up, and swallow down the very men themselves. They consume, destroy, and devour whole fields, houses, and cities. For look in what parts of the realm doth grow the finest and therefore dearest wool, there noblemen and gentlemen, yea and certain abbots, holy men God wot not contenting themselves with the yearly revenues and profits, that were wont to grow to their forefathers and predecessors of their lands, nor being content that they live in rest and pleasure nothing profiting, yea much annoying the weal public, leave no ground for tillage, they inclose all in pastures; they throw down houses; they pluck down towns, and leave nothing standing, but only the church to make of it a sheep-house. And as though you lost no small quantity of ground by forests, chases, lawns, and parks, those good holy men turn all dwelling-places and all glebeland into desolation and wilderness. Therefore that one covetous and insatiable cormorant and very plague of his native country may compass about and inclose many thousand acres of ground together within one pale or hedge, the husbandmen be thrust out of their own, or else either by cunning and fraud, or by violent oppression they be put besides it, or by wrongs and injuries they be so wearied, that they be compelled to sell all: by one means therefore or by other, either by hook or crook they must needs depart away, poor, silly, wretched souls, men, women, husbands, wives, fatherless children, widows, woeful mothers, with their young babes, and their whole households small in substance and much in number, as husbandry requireth many hands. Away they trudge, I say, out of their known and accustomed houses, finding no places to rest in. All their household stuff, which is very little worth, though it might well abide the sale: yet being suddenly thrust out, they be constrained to sell it for a thing of nought. And when they, have wandering about, soon spent that, what can they else do but steal, and then justly, God wot, be hanged, or else go about a begging. And yet then also they be cast in prison as vagabonds, because they go about and work not: whom no man will set a work, though they never so willingly offer themselves thereto. For one shepherd or herdsman is enough to eat up that ground with cattle, to the occupying whereof about husbandry many hands were requisite. And this is also the cause that victuals be now in many places dearer. Yea, besides this the price of wool is so risen, that poor folks, which were wont to work it and make cloth of it, be now able to buy none at all. And by this means very many be fain to forsake work, and to give themselves to idleness. For after that so much ground was inclosed for pasture, an infinite multitude of sheep died of the rot, such vengeance God took of their inordinate and insatiable covetousness, sending among the sheep that pestiferous murrain, which much more justly should have fallen on the sheepmasters' own heads. And though the number of sheep increase never so fast, yet the price falleth not one mite, because there be so few sellers. For they be almost all come into a few rich men's hands, whom no need driveth to sell before they lust, and they lust not before they may sell as dear as they lust. Now the same cause bringeth in like dearth of the other kinds of cattle, yea and that so much the more, because that after farms plucked down and husbandry decayed, there is no man that passeth for the breeding of young store. For these rich men bring not up the young ones of great cattle as they do lambs. But first they buy them abroad very cheap and afterward, when they be fatted in their pastures, they sell them again exceeding dear. And therefore (as I suppose) the whole incommodity hereof is not yet felt. For yet they make dearth only in those places where they sell. But when they shall fetch them away from thence where they be bred faster than they can be brought up: then shall there also be felt great dearth, when store beginneth to fail, there where the ware is brought. Thus the unreasonable covetousness of a few hath turned that thing to the utter undoing of your island, in the which thing the chief felicity of your realm did consist. For this great dearth of victuals causeth every man to keep as little houses and as small hospitality as he possible may, and to put away their servants: whether, I pray you, but a begging: or else (which these gentle bloods and stout stomachs will sooner set their minds unto) a stealing? Now to amend the matters, to this wretched beggary and miserable poverty is joined great wantonness, importunate superfluity, and excessive riot. For not only gentlemen's servants, but also handicraftsmen: yea and almost the ploughmen of the country, with all other sorts of people, use much strange and proud newfangleness in their apparel, and too much prodigal riot and sumptuous fare at their table. Now bawds, queans, whores, harlots, strumpets, brothel-houses, stews, and yet another stews, winetaverns, ale houses and tippling houses, with so many naughty, lewd, and unlawful games, as dice, cards, tables, tennis, bowls, quoits, do not all these send the haunters of them straight a stealing when their money is gone? Cast out these pernicious abominations, make a law, that they, which plucked down farms and towns of husbandry, shall build them up again, or else yield and uprender the possession of them to such as will go to the cost of building them anew. Suffer not these rich men to buy up all, to engross and forestall, and with their monopoly to keep the market alone as please them. Let not so many be brought up in idleness, let husbandry and tillage be restored again, let clothworking be renewed, that there may be honest labours for this idle sort to pass their time in profitably, which hitherto either poverty hath caused to be thieves, or else now be either vagabonds, or idle serving men, and shortly will be thieves. Doubtless unless you find a remedy for these enormities, you shall in vain advance yourselves of executing justice upon felons. For this justice is more beautiful than just or profitable. For by suffering your youth wantonly and viciously to be brought up, and to be infected, even from their tender age, by little and little with vice: then a God's name to be punished, when they commit the same faults after they be come to man's state, which from their youth they were ever like to do: In this point, I pray you, what other thing do you, than make thieves and then punish them? Now as I was thus speaking, the lawyer began to make himself ready to answer, and was determined with himself to use the common fashion and trade of disputers, which be more diligent in rehearsing than answering, as thinking the memory worthy of the chief praise. Indeed, sir, quoth he, you have said well, being but a stranger and one that might rather hear something of these matters, than have any exact or perfect knowledge of the same, as I will incontinent by open proof make manifest and plain. For first I will rehearse in order all that you have said: then I will declare in what thing you be deceived, through lack of knowledge, in all our fashions, manners and customs: and last of all I will answer to your arguments and confute them every one. First therefore, I will begin where I promised. Four things you seemed to me. Hold your peace, quoth the Cardinal: for be like you will make no short answer, which make such a beginning. Wherefore at this time you shall not take the pains to make your answer, but keep it to your next meeting, which I would be right glad, that it might be even to-morrow next, unless either you or Master Raphael have any earnest let. But now, Master Raphael, I would very gladly hear of you, why you think theft not worthy to be punished with death, or what other punishment you can devise more expedient to the weal public. For I am sure you are not of that mind, that you would have theft escape unpunished. For if now the extreme punishment of death cannot cause them to leave stealing, then if ruffians and robbers should be sure of their lives; what violence, what fear were able to hold their hands from robbing, which would take the mitigation of the punishment, as a very provocation to the mischief? Surely my lord, quoth I, I think it not right nor justice, that the loss of money should cause the loss of man's life. For mine opinion is, that all the goods in the world are not able to countervail man's life. But if they would thus say: that the breaking of justice, and the transgression of the laws is recompensed with this punishment, and not the loss of the money, then why may not this extreme justice well be called extreme injury? For neither so cruel governance, so strait rules, and unmerciful laws be allowable, that if a small offence be committed, by-and-by the sword should be drawn: nor so stoical ordinances are to be borne withal, as to count all offences of such equality that the killing of a man, or the taking of his money from him were both a matter, and the one no more heinous offence than the other: between the which two, if we have any respect to equity, no similitude or equality consisteth. God commandeth us that we shall not kill. And be we then so hasty to kill a man for taking a little money? And if any man would understand killing by this commandment of God to be forbidden after no larger wise, than man's constitutions define killing to be lawful, then why may it not likewise by man's constitutions be determined after what sort whoredom, fornication and perjury may be lawful? For whereas, by the permission of God, no man hath power to kill neither himself, nor yet any other man: then if a law made by the consent of men, concerning slaughter of men, ought to be of such strength, force and virtue, that they which, contrary to the commandment of God, have killed those, whom this constitution of man commanded to be killed, be clean quit and exempt out of the bonds and danger of God's commandment: shall it not then by this reason follow, that the power of God's commandment shall extend no further than man's law doth define, and permit? And so shall it come to pass, that in like manner man's constitutions in all things shall determine how far the observation of all God's commandments shall extend. To be short, Moses' law, though it were ungentle and sharp, as a law that was given to bondmen; yea, and them very obstinate, stubborn, and stiff-necked; yet it punished theft by the purse, and not with death. And let us not think that God in the new law of clemency and mercy, under the which he ruleth us with fatherly gentleness, as his dear children, hath given us greater scope and license to execute cruelty, one upon another. Now, ye have heard the reasons whereby I am persuaded that this punishment is unlawful. Furthermore I think there is nobody that knoweth not how unreasonable, yea, how pernicious a thing it is to the weal public, that a thief and an homicide or murderer, should suffer equal and like punishment. For the thief seeing that man, that is condemned for theft in no less jeopardy, nor judged to no less punishment, than him that is convict of manslaughter; through this cogitation only he is strongly and forcibly provoked, and in a manner constrained to kill him whom else he would have but robbed. For

the murder once done, he is in less care, and in more hope that the
deed shall not be bewrayed or known, seeing the party is now dead
and rid out of the way, which only might have uttered and disclosed
it. But if he chance to be taken and discrived, yet he is in no more
danger and jeopardy, than if he had committed but single felony.
Therefore whiles we go about with such cruelty to make thieves
afraid, we provoke them to kill good men. Now as touching this
question, what punishment were more commodious and better; that
truly in my judgment is easier to be found than what punishment
were worse. For why should we doubt that to be a good and a
profitable way for the punishment of offenders, which we know did
in times past so long please the Romans, men in the administration
of a weal public most expert, politic, and cunning? Such as among
them were convict of great and heinous trespasses, them they condemned into stone quarries, and into mines to dig metal, there to
be kept in chains all the days of their life. But as concerning this
matter, I allow the ordinance of no nation so well as that I saw, whiles
I travelled abroad about the world, used in Persia among the people
that commonly be called the Polylerites. Whose land is both large
and ample, and also well and wittily governed: and the people in
all conditions free and ruled by their own laws, saving that they pay
a yearly tribute to the great king of Persia. But because they be
far from the sea, compassed and closed in almost round about with
high mountains, and do content themselves with the fruits of their
own land, which is of itself very fertile and fruitful: for this cause
neither they go to other countries, nor other come to them. And
according to the old custom of the land, they desire not to enlarge
the bounds of their dominions: and those that they have, by reason
of the high hills be easily defended: and the tribute which they pay
to their chief lord and king setteth them quiet and free from warfare. Thus their life is commodious rather than gallant, and may
better be called happy or lucky, than notable or famous. For they
be not known as much as by name, I suppose, saving only to their
next neighbours and borderers. They that in this land be attainted
and convict of felony, make restitution of that they stole, to the right
owner, and not (as they do in other lands) to the king: whom they
think to have no more right to the thief-stolen thing, than the thief

himself hath. But if the thing be lost or made away, then the value of it is paid of the goods of such offenders, which else remaineth all whole to their wives and children. And they themselves be condemned to be common labourers, and, unless the theft be very heinous, they be neither locked in prison nor fettered in gyves, but be untied and go at large, labouring in the common works. They that refuse labour, or go slowly and slackly to their work, be not only tied in chains, but also pricked forward with stripes. They that be diligent about their work live without check or rebuke. Every night they be called in by name, and be locked in their chambers. Beside their daily labour, their life is nothing hard or incommodious. Their fare is indifferent good, borne at the charges of the weal public, because they be common servants to the commonwealth. But their charges in all places of the land is not borne alike. For in some parts that is bestowed upon them is gathered of alms. And though that way be uncertain, yet the people be so full of mercy and pity, that none is found more profitable or plentiful. In some places certain lands be appointed hereunto, of the revenues whereof they be maintained. And in some places every man giveth a certain tribute for the same use and purpose. Again in some parts of the land these serving-men (for so be these condemned persons called) do no common work, but as every private man needeth labourers, so he cometh into the market place, and there hireth some of them for meat and drink, and a certain limited wages by the day, somewhat cheaper than he should hire a free man. It is also lawful for them to chastise the sloth of these serving-men with stripes. By this means they never lack work, and besides their meat and drink, every one of them bringeth daily something into the common treasury. All and every one of them be apparelled in one colour. Their heads be not polled or shaven, but rounded a little above the ears. And the tip of the one ear is cut off. Every one of them may take meat and drink of their friends, and also a coat of their own colour: but to receive money is death, as well to the giver, as to the receiver. And no less jeopardy it is for a free man to receive money of a serving-man for any manner of cause: and likewise for serving-men to touch weapons. The serving-men of every several shire be distinct and known from other by their several and distinct badges: which to cast away is death: as it is also to be seen out of the precincts of their own shire, or to talk with a serving-man of another shire. And it is no less danger to them, for to intend to run away than to do it indeed. Yea and to conceal such an enterprise in a serving-man it is death, in a free man servitude. Of the contrary part, to him that openeth and uttereth such counsels, be decreed large gifts; to a free man a great sum of money, to a serving-man freedom: and to them both forgiveness and pardon of that they were of counsel in that pretence. So that it can never be so good for them to go forward in their evil purpose, as by repentance to turn back. This is the law and order in this behalf, as I have showed you. Wherein what humanity is used, how far it is from cruelty, and how commodious it is, you do plainly perceive: forasmuch as the end of their wrath and punishment intendeth nothing else, but the destruction of vices, and saving of men: with so using and ordering them, that they cannot choose but be good, and what harm soever they did before, in the residue of their life to make amends for the same. Moreover it is so little feared, that they should turn again to their vicious conditions, that wayfaring men will for their safeguard choose them to their guides before any other, in every shire changing and taking new. For if they would commit robbery, they have nothing about them meet for that purpose. They may touch no weapons: money found about them should betray the robbery. They should be no sooner taken with the manner, but forthwith they should be punished. Neither they can have any hope at all to 'scape away by flying. For how should a man, that in no part of his apparel is like other men, fly privily and unknown, unless he would run away naked? Howbeit so also flying he should be discrived by his rounding and his ear-mark. But it is a thing to be doubted, that they will lay their heads together, and conspire against the weal public. No, no, I warrant you. For the serving-men of one shire alone could never hope to bring to pass such an enterprise, without soliciting, enticing, and alluring the serving-men of many other shires to take their parts. Which thing is to them so impossible, that they may not as much as speak or talk together, or salute one another. No, it is not to be thought that they would make their own countrymen and companions of their counsel in such a matter which they know well should be jeopardy to the concealer thereof, and great commodity and goodness to the opener of the same. Whereas on the other part, there is none of them all hopeless or in despair to recover again his freedom, by humble obedience, by patient suffering and by giving good tokens and likelihood of himself, that he will, ever after that, live like a true and an honest man. For every year divers be restored again to their freedom: through the commendation of their patience. When I had thus spoken, saying moreover that I could see no cause why this order might not be had in England with much more profit, than the justice which the lawyer so highly praised: Nay, quoth the lawyer, this could never be so established in England, but that it must needs bring the weal public into great jeopardy and hazard. And as he was thus saying, he shaked his head, and made a wry mouth, and so held his peace. And all that were there present, with one assent agreed to his saying. Well, quoth the Cardinal, yet it were hard to judge without a proof, whether this order would do well here or no. But when the sentence of death is given, if then the king should command execution to be deferred and spared, and would prove this order and fashion: taking away the privileges of all sanctuaries: if then the proof would declare the thing to be good and profitable, then it were well done that it were established; else the condemned and reprieved persons may as well and as justly be put to death after this proof, as when they were first cast. Neither any jeopardy can in the mean space grow hereof. Yea, and methinketh that these vagabonds may very well be ordered after the same fashion, against whom we have hitherto made so many laws, and so little prevailed. When the Cardinal had thus said, then every man gave great praise to my sayings, which a little before they had disallowed. But most of all was esteemed that which was spoken of vagabonds, because it was the Cardinal's own addition. I cannot tell whether it were best to rehearse the communication that followed, for it was not very sad. But yet you shall hear it, for there was no evil in it, and partly it pertained to the matter beforesaid. There chanced to stand by a certain jesting parasite, or scoffer, which would seem to resemble and counterfeit the fool. But he did in such wise counterfeit, that he was almost the very same indeed that he laboured to represent: he so studied with words and sayings brought forth so out of time and place to make sport and move laughter, that he himself was oftener laughed at than his jests were. Yet the foolish fellow brought out now and then such indifferent and reasonable stuff, that he made the proverb true, which saith: he that shooteth oft at the last shall hit the mark. So that when one of the company said, that through my communication a good order was found for thieves, and that the Cardinal also had well provided for vagabonds, so that only remained some good provision to be made for them that through sickness and age were fallen into poverty, and were become so impotent and unwieldy, that they were not able to work for their living: Tush (quoth he) let me alone with them: you shall see me do well enough with them. For I had rather than any good, that this kind of people were driven some whether out of my sight, they have so sore troubled me many times and oft, when they have with their lamentable tears begged money of me: and yet they could never to my mind so tune their song, that thereby they ever got of me one farthing. For evermore the one of these two chanced: either that I would not, or else that I could not, because I had it not. Therefore now they be waxed wise. When they see me go by, because they will not lose their labour, they let me go and say not one word to me. So they look for nothing of me, no in good sooth no more, than if I were a priest. But I will make a law, that all these beggars shall be distributed and bestowed into houses of religion. The men shall be made lay brethren, as they call them, and the women nuns. Hereat the Cardinal smiled, and allowed it in jest, yea and all the residue in good earnest. But a certain friar, graduate in divinity, took such pleasure and delight in this jest of priests and monks, that he also being else a man of grisly and stern gravity, began merrily and wantonly to jest and taunt. Nay, quoth he, you shall not so be rid and despatched of beggars, unless you make some provision also for us friars. Why, quoth the jester, that is done already, for my lord himself set a very good order for you, when he decreed that vagabonds should be kept strait and set to work: for you be the greatest and veriest vagabonds that be. This jest also, when they saw the Cardinal not disprove it, every man took it gladly, saving only the friar. For he (and that no marvel) when he was thus touched on the quick, and hit on the gall, so fret, so fumed, and chafed at it, and was in such a rage, that he could not refrain himself from chiding, scolding, railing and reviling. He called the fellow ribald, villain, javel, back-biter, slanderer, and the son of perdition: citing therewith terrible threatening out of Holy Scripture. Then the jesting scoffer began to play the scoffer indeed, and verily he was good at it, for he could play a part in that play no man better. Patient yourself, good master friar, quoth he, and be not angry, for Scripture saith: in your patience you shall save your souls. Then the friar (for I will rehearse his own very words), No, gallows wretch, I am not angry (quoth he) or at the leastwise, I do not sin: for the Psalmist saith, be you angry, and sin not. Then the Cardinal spake gently to the friar, and desired him to quiet himself. No my lord, quoth he, I speak not but of a good zeal as I ought: for holy men had a good zeal. Wherefore it is said: the zeal of the house hath eaten me. And it is sung in the church, the scorners of Helizeus, whiles he went up into the house of God, felt the zeal of the bald, as peradventure this scorning villain ribald shall feel. You do it (quoth the Cardinal) perchance of a good mind and affection: but methinketh you should do, I cannot tell whether more holily, certes more wisely, if you would not set your wit to a fool's wit, and with a fool take in hand a foolish contention. No forsooth, my lord (quoth he) I should not do more wisely. For Solomon the wise saith: Answer a fool according to his foolishness, like as I do now, and do show him the pit that he shall fall into, if he take not heed. For if many scorners of Helizeus, which was but one bald man, felt the zeal of the bald, how much more shall one scorner of many friars feel, among whom be many bald men? And we have also the pope's bulls, whereby all that mock and scorn us be excommunicate, suspended and accursed. The Cardinal, seeing that none end would be made, sent away the jester by a privy beck, and turned the communication to another matter. Shortly after, when he was risen from the table, he went to hear his suitors, and so dismissed us. Look, Master More, with how long and tedious a tale I have kept you, which surely I would have been ashamed to have done, but that you so earnestly desired me, and did after such a sort give ear unto it, as though you would not that any parcel of that communication should be left out. Which though I have done somewhat briefly, yet could I not choose but rehearse it, for the judg-

ment of them, which when they had improved and disallowed
my sayings, yet incontinent, hearing the Cardinal allow them, did
themselves also approve the same: so impudently flattering him, that
they were nothing ashamed to admit, yea almost in good earnest,
his jester's foolish inventions: because that he himself by smiling at
them did seem not to disprove them. So that hereby you may right
well perceive how little the courtiers would regard and esteem me
and my sayings.

I ensure you, Master Raphael, quoth I, I took great delectation in
hearing you: all things that you said were spoken so wittily and so
pleasantly. And me thought myself to be in the meantime, not
only at home in my country, but also through the pleasant remembrance of the Cardinal, in whose house I was brought up of a child,
to wax a child again. And, friend Raphael, though I did bear very
great love towards you before, yet seeing you do so earnestly favour
this man, you will not believe how much my love towards you is
now increased. But yet, all this notwithstanding, I can by no means
change my mind, but that I must needs believe, that you, if you be
disposed, and can find in your heart to follow some prince's court,
shall with your good counsels greatly help and further the commonwealth. Wherefore there is nothing more appertaining to your duty,
that is to say, to the duty of a good man. For whereas your Plato
judgeth that weal publics shall by this means attain perfect felicity,
either if philosophers be kings, or else if kings give themselves to the
study of philosophy, how far I pray you, shall commonwealths then
be from this felicity, if philosophers will [not] vouchsafe to instruct
kings with their good counsel?

They be not so unkind (quoth he) but they would gladly do it,
yea, many have done it already in books that they have put forth, if
kings and princes would be willing and ready to follow good counsel.
But Plato doubtless did well foresee, unless kings themselves would
apply their minds to the study of Philosophy, that else they would
never thoroughly allow the counsel of philosophers, being themselves
before even from their tender age infected, and corrupt with perverse and evil opinions. Which thing Plato himself proved true in
King Dionysius. If I should propose to any king wholesome decrees,
doing my endeavour to pluck out of his mind the pernicious original

causes of vice and naughtiness, think you not that I should forthwith either be driven away, or else made a laughing stock? Go to, suppose that I were with the French king, and there sitting in his council, whiles that in that most secret consultation, the king himself there being present in his own person, they beat their brains and search the very bottoms of their wits to discuss by what craft and means the king may still keep Milan, and draw to him again fugitive Naples, and then how to conquer the Venetians, and how to bring under his jurisdiction all Italy, then how to win the dominion of Flanders, Brabant, and of all Burgundy: with divers other lands, whose kingdoms he hath long ago in mind and purpose invaded. Here whiles one counselleth to conclude a league of peace with the Venetians, which shall so long endure, as shall be thought meet and expedient for their purpose, and to make them also of their counsel, yea, and besides that to give them part of the prey, which afterward, when they have brought their purpose about after their own minds, they may require and claim again. Another thinketh best to hire the Germans. Another would have the favour of the Swiss won with money. Another's advice is to appease the puissant power of the Emperor's majesty with gold, as with a most pleasant and acceptable sacrifice. Whiles another giveth counsel to make peace with the King of Arragon, and to restore unto him his own kingdom of Navarre, as a full assurance of peace. Another cometh in with his five eggs, and adviseth to hook in the King of Castile with some hope of affinity or alliance, and to bring to their part certain peers of his court for great pensions. Whiles they all stay at the chiefest doubt of all, what to do in the meantime with England, and yet agree all in this to make peace with the Englishmen, and with most sure and strong bonds to bind that weak and feeble friendship, so that they must be called friends, and had in suspicion as enemies. And that therefore the Scots must be had in a readiness, as it were in a standing, ready at all occasions, if peradventure the Englishmen should stir never so little, incontinent to set upon them. And moreover privily and secretly (for openly it may not be done by the truce that is taken) privily therefore I say to make much of some peer of England that is banished his country, which must claim title to the crown of the realm, and affirm himself just inheritor thereof, that by this subtle means they may hold to them the king, in whom else they have but small trust and affiance. Here I say, where so great and high matters be in consultation, where so many noble and wise men counsel their king only to war, here if I silly man should rise up and will them to turn over the leaf, and learn a new lesson, saying that my counsel is not to meddle with Italy, but to tarry still at home, and that the kingdom of France alone is almost greater, than that it may well be governed of one man: so that the king should not need to study how to get more; and then should propose unto them the decrees of the people that be called the Achoriens, which be situate over against the island of Utopia on the southeast side. These Achoriens once made war in their king's quarrel for to get him another kingdom, which he laid claim unto, and advanced himself right inheritor to the crown thereof, by the title of an old alliance. At the last when they had gotten it, and saw that they had even as much vexation and trouble in keeping it, as they had in getting it, and that either their new conquered subjects by sundry occasions were making daily insurrections to rebel against them, or else that other countries were continually with divers inroads and foragings invading them: so that they were ever fighting either for them, or against them, and never could break up their camps: seeing themselves in the mean season pilled and impoverished: their money carried out of the realm: their own men killed to maintain the glory of another nation; when they had no war, peace nothing better than war, by reason that their people in war had inured themselves to corrupt and wicked manners, that they had taken a delight and pleasure in robbing and stealing: that through manslaughter they had gathered boldness to mischief: that their laws were had in contempt, and nothing set by or regarded: that their king being troubled with the charge and governance of two kingdoms, could not nor was not able perfectly to discharge his office towards them both: seeing again that all these evils and troubles were endless: at the last laid their heads together, and like faithful and loving subjects gave to their king free choice and liberty to keep still the one of these two kingdoms whether he would: alleging that he was not able to keep both, and that they were more than might well be governed of half a king: forasmuch as no man would be content to take him for his muleteer, that keepeth another man's mules besides his. So this good prince was constrained to be content with his old kingdom and to give over the new to one of his friends. Which shortly after was violently driven out. Furthermore if I should declare unto them, that all this busy preparance to war, whereby so many nations for his sake should be brought into a troublesome hurly-burly, when all his coffers were emptied, his treasures wasted and his people destroyed, should at the length through some mischance be in vain and to none effect: and that therefore it were best for him to content himself with his own kingdom of France, as his forefathers and predecessors did before him; to make much of it, to enrich it, and to make it as flourishing as he could, to endeavour himself to love his subjects, and again to be beloved of them, willingly to live with them, peaceably to govern them, and with other kingdoms not to meddle, seeing that which he hath already is even enough for him, yea, and more than he can well turn him to: this mine advice, Master More, how think you it would be heard and taken?

So God help me not very thankfully, quoth I.

Well let us proceed then, quoth he. Suppose that some king and his council were together whetting their wits, and devising what subtle craft they might invent to enrich the king with great treasures of money. First one counselleth to raise and enhance the valuation of money when the king must pay any: and again to call down the value of coin to less than it is worth, when he must receive or gather any. For thus great sums shall be paid with a little money, and where little is due much shall be received. Another counselleth to feign war, that when under this colour and pretence the king hath gathered great abundance of money, he may, when it shall please him, make peace with great solemnity and holy ceremonies, to blind the eyes of the poor commonalty, as taking pity and compassion God wot upon man's blood, like a loving and a merciful prince. Another putteth the king in remembrance of certain old and moth-eaten laws, that of long time have not been put in execution, which because no man can remember that they were made, every man hath transgressed. The fines of these laws he counselleth the king to require: for there is no way so profitable nor more honourable, as the which hath a show and colour of justice. Another adviseth him to forbid many things under great penalties and fines, specially such things as is for the people's profit not to be used, and afterward to dispense for money with them, which by this prohibition sustain loss and damage. For by this means the favour of the people is won, and profit riseth two ways. First by taking forfeits of them whom covetousness of gains hath brought in danger of this statute, and also by selling privileges and licenses, which the better that the prince is, forsooth the dearer he selleth them: as one that is loath to grant to any private person anything that is against the profit of his people. And therefore may sell none but at an exceeding dear price. Another giveth the king counsel to endanger unto his grace the judges of the realm, that he may have them ever on his side, which must in every matter dispute and reason for the king's right. And they must be called into the king's palace and be desired to argue and discuss his matters in his own presence. So there shall be no matter of his so openly wrong and unjust, wherein one or other of them, either because he will have something to allege and object, or that he is ashamed to say that which is said already, or else to pick a thank with his prince, will not find some hole open to set a snare in, wherewith to take the contrary part in a trip. Thus whiles the judges cannot agree among themselves, reasoning and arguing of that which is plain enough, and bringing the manifest truth in doubt: in the mean season the king may take a fit occasion to understand the law as shall most make for his advantage, whereunto all other for shame, or for fear will agree. Then the judges may be bold to pronounce of the king's side. For he that giveth sentence for the king, cannot be without a good excuse. For it shall be sufficient for him to have equity of his part, or the bare words of the law, or a writhen and wrested understanding of the same, or else (which with good and just judges is of greater force than all laws be) the king's indisputable prerogative. To conclude, all the councillors agree and consent together with the rich Crassus, that no abundance of gold can be sufficient for a prince, which must keep and maintain an army: furthermore that a king, though he would, can do nothing unjustly. For all that all men have, yea also the men themselves be all his. And that every man hath so much of his own, as the king's gentleness hath not taken from him. And that it shall be most for the king's advantage, that his subjects have very little or nothing in their possession, as whose safeguard doth herein consist, that his people do not wax wanton and wealthy through riches and liberty, because where these things be, there men be not wont patiently to obey hard, unjust, and unlawful commandments; whereas on the other part need and poverty doth hold down and keep under stout courages, and maketh them patient perforce, taking from them bold and rebelling stomachs. Here again if I should rise up, and boldly affirm that all these counsels be to the king dishonour and reproach, whose honour and safety is more and rather supported and upholden by the wealth and riches of his people, than by his own treasures: and if I should declare that the commonalty chooseth their king for their own sake and not for his sake: for this intent, that through his labour and study they might all live wealthily, safe from wrongs and injuries: and that therefore the king ought to take more care for the wealth of his people, than for his own wealth, even as the office and duty of a shepherd is in that he is a shepherd, to feed his sheep rather than himself. For as touching this, that they think the defence and maintenance of peace to consist in the poverty of the people, the thing itself showeth that they be far out of the way. For where shall a man find more wrangling, quarrelling, brawling, and chiding, than among beggars? Who be more desirous of new mutations and alterations, than they that be not content with the present state of their life? Or finally who be bolder stomached to bring all in hurly-burly (thereby trusting to get some windfall) than they that have now nothing to lose? And if so be that there were any king that were so smally regarded, so behated of his subjects, that other ways he could not keep them in awe, but only by open wrongs, by polling and shaving, and by bringing them to beggary, surely it were better for him to forsake his kingdom, than to hold it by this means: whereby though the name of a king be kept, yet the majesty is lost. For it is against the dignity of a king to have rule over beggars, but rather over rich and wealthy men. Of this mind was the hardy and courageous Fabricius, when he said, that he had rather be a ruler of rich men, than be rich himself. And verily one man to live in pleasure and wealth, whiles all other weep and smart for it, that is the part, not of a king, but of a jailer. To be short, as he is a foolish physician, that cannot cure his patient's disease, unless he cast him in another sickness, so he that cannot amend the lives of his subjects, but by taking from them the wealth and commodity of life, he must needs grant that he knoweth not the feat how to govern free men. But let him rather amend his own life, renounce unhonest pleasures, and forsake pride. For these be the chief vices that cause him to run in the contempt or hatred of his people. Let him live of his own, hurting no man. Let him do cost not above his power. Let him restrain wickedness. Let him prevent vices, and take away the occasions of offences by well ordering his subjects, and not by suffering wickedness to increase afterward to be punished. Let him not be too hasty in calling again laws, which a custom hath abrogated: specially such as have been long forgotten, and never lacked nor needed. And let him never under the cloak and pretence of transgression take such fines and forfeits, as no judge will suffer a private person to take, as unjust and full of guile. Here if I should bring forth before them the law of the Macariens, which be not far distant from Utopia: whose king the day of his coronation is bound by a solemn oath, that he shall never at any time have in his treasure above a thousand pounds of gold or silver. They say a very good king, which took more care for the wealth and commodity of his country, than for the enriching of himself, made this law to be a stop and a bar to kings for heaping and hoarding up so much money as might impoverish their people. For he foresaw that this sum of treasure would suffice to support the king in battle against his own people, if they should chance to rebel: and also to maintain his wars against the invasions of his foreign enemies. Again he perceived the same stock of money to be too little and insufficient to encourage and enable him wrongfully to take away other men's goods: which was the chief cause why the law was made. Another cause was this. He thought that by this provision his people should not lack money, wherewith to maintain their daily occupying and chaffer. And seeing the king could not choose but lay out and bestow all that came in above the prescript sum of his stock, he thought he would seek no occasions to do his subjects injury. Such a king shall be feared of evil men, and loved of good men. These, and such other informations, if I should use among men wholly inclined and given to the contrary part, how deaf hearers think you should I have?

Deaf hearers doubtless (quoth I) and in good faith no marvel. And to speak as I think, truly I cannot allow that such communication shall be used, or such counsel given, as you be sure shall never be regarded nor received. For how can so strange informations be profitable, or how can they be beaten into their heads, whose minds be already prevented with clean contrary persuasions? This school philosophy is not unpleasant among friends in familiar communication, but in the councils of kings, where great matters be debated and reasoned with great authority, these things have no place.

That is it which I meant (quoth he) when I said philosophy had no place among kings.

Indeed (quoth I) this school philosophy hath not, which thinketh all things meet for every place. But there is another philosophy more civil, which knoweth, as ye would say, her own stage, and thereafter ordering and behaving herself in the play that she hath in hand, playeth her part accordingly with comeliness, uttering nothing out of due order and fashion. And this is the philosophy that you must use. Or else whiles a comedy of Plautus is playing, and the vile bondmen scoffing and trifling among themselves, if you should suddenly come upon the stage in a philosopher's apparel, and rehearse out of Octavia the place wherein Seneca disputeth with Nero: had it not been better for you to have played the dumb person, than by rehearsing that, which served neither for the time nor place, to have made such a tragical comedy or gallimaufry? For by bringing in other stuff that nothing appertaineth to the present matter, you must needs mar and pervert the play that is in hand, though the stuff that you bring be much better. What part soever you have taken upon you, play that as well as you can and make the best of it: and do not therefore disturb and bring out of order the whole matter, because that another, which is merrier, and better, cometh to your remembrance. So the case standeth in a commonwealth, and so it is in the consultations of kings and princes. If evil opinions and naughty persuasions cannot be utterly and quite plucked out of their hearts, if you cannot, even as you would, remedy vices, which use and custom hath confirmed: yet for this cause you must not leave

and forsake the commonwealth: you must not forsake the ship in a
tempest, because you cannot rule and keep down the winds. No, nor
you must not labour to drive into their heads new and strange informations, which you know well shall be nothing regarded with them
that be of clean contrary minds. But you must with a crafty wile
and a subtle train study and endeavour yourself, as much as in you
lieth, to handle the matter wittily and handsomely for the purpose,
and that which you cannot turn to good, so to order it that it be not
very bad. For it is not possible for all things to be well, unless all
men were good. Which I think will not be yet this good many years.

By this means (quoth he) nothing else will be brought to pass,
but whiles that I go about to remedy the madness of others, I should
be even as mad as they. For if I would speak things that be true, I
must needs speak such things; but as for to speak false things,
whether that be a philosopher's part or no; I cannot tell, truly it is
not my part. Howbeit this communication of mine, though peradventure it may seem unpleasant to them, yet can I not see why it
should seem strange, or foolishly newfangled. If so be that I should
speak those things that Plato feigneth in his weal public: or that the
Utopians do in theirs, these things though they were (as they be
indeed) better, yet they might seem spoken out of place. Forasmuch as here amongst us, every man hath his possessions several to
himself, and there all things be common. But what was in my communication contained, that might not, and ought not in any place
to be spoken? Saving that to them which have thoroughly decreed
and determined with themselves to roam headlong the contrary
way, it cannot be acceptable and pleasant, because it calleth them
back, and showeth them the jeopardies. Verily if all things that evil
and vicious manners have caused to seem inconvenient and nought
should be refused, as things unmeet and reproachful, then we must
among Christian people wink at the most part of all those things,
which Christ taught us, and so strictly forbade them to be winked at,
that those things also which he whispered in the ears of his disciples,
he commanded to be proclaimed in open houses. And yet the most
part of them is more dissident from the manners of the world nowadays, than my communication was. But preachers, sly and wily
men, following your counsel (as I suppose) because they saw men

evil willing to frame their manners to Christ's rule, they have wrested and perverted his doctrine, and like a rule of lead have applied it to men's manners: that by some means at the leastways, they might agree together. Whereby I cannot see what good they have done: but that men may more sickerly be evil. And I truly should prevail even as much in king's councils. For either I must say otherways than they say, and then I were as good to say nothing, or else I must say the same that they say, and (as Mitio saith in Terence) help to further their madness. For that crafty wile, and subtle train of yours, I cannot perceive to what purpose it serveth, wherewith you would have me to study and endeavour myself, if all things cannot be made good, yet to handle them wittily and handsomely for the purpose, that as far forth as is possible they may not be very evil. For there is no place to dissemble in, nor to wink in. Naughty counsels must be openly allowed and very pestilent decrees must be approved. He shall be counted worse than a spy, yea almost as evil as a traitor, that with a faint heart doth praise evil and noisome decrees. Moreover, a man can have no occasion to do good chancing into the company of them which will sooner make nought a good man, than be made good themselves: through whose evil company he shall be marred, or else if he remain good and innocent, yet the wickedness and foolishness of others shall be imputed to him, and laid in his neck. So that it is impossible with that crafty wile and subtle train to turn anything to better. Wherefore Plato by a goodly similitude declareth, why wise men refrain to meddle in the commonwealth. For when they see the people swarm into the streets, and daily wet to the skin with rain, and yet cannot persuade them to go out of the rain and to take their houses, knowing well, that if they should go out to them, they should nothing prevail, nor win ought by it, but be wet also in the rain, they do keep themselves within their houses, being content that they be safe themselves, seeing they cannot remedy the folly of the people. Howbeit doubtless, Master More (to speak truly as my mind giveth me) where soever possessions be private, where money beareth all the stroke, it is hard and almost impossible that there the weal public may justly be governed, and prosperously flourish. Unless you think thus: that justice is there executed, where all things come into the hands of evil men;

or that prosperity there flourisheth, where all is divided among a few; which few nevertheless do not lead their lives very wealthily, and the residue live miserably, wretched and beggarly. Wherefore when I consider with myself and weigh in my mind the wise and godly ordinances of the Utopians, among whom with very few laws all things be so well and wealthily ordered, that virtue is had in price and estimation, and yet, all things being there common, every man hath abundance of everything. Again on the other part, when I compare with them so many nations ever making new laws, yet none of them all well and sufficiently furnished with laws; where every man calleth that he hath gotten, his own proper and private goods; where so many new laws daily made be not sufficient for every man to enjoy, defend, and know from another man's that which he calleth his own; which thing the infinite controversies in the law, that daily rise never to be ended, plainly declare to be true. These things (I say) when I consider with myself, I hold well with Plato, and do nothing marvel, that he would make no laws for them, that refused those laws, whereby all men should have and enjoy equal portions of wealths and commodities. For the wise man did easily foresee, that this is the one and only way to the wealth of a commonalty, if equality of all things should be brought in and established. Which I think is not possible to be observed, where every man's goods be proper and peculiar to himself. For where every man under certain titles and pretences draweth and plucketh to himself as much as he can, and so a few divide among themselves all the riches that there is, be there never so much abundance and store, there to the residue is left lack and poverty. And for the most part it chanceth, that this latter sort is more worthy to enjoy that state of wealth, than the other be: because the rich men be covetous, crafty and unprofitable. On the other part the poor be lowly, simple, and by their daily labour more profitable to the commonwealth than to themselves. Thus I do fully persuade myself, that no equal and just distribution of things can be made, nor that perfect wealth shall ever be among men, unless this propriety be exiled and banished. But so long as it shall continue, so long shall remain among the most and best part of men the heavy and inevitable burden of poverty and wretchedness. Which, as I grant that it may be somewhat eased, so I utterly deny that it can wholly be taken away. For if there were a statute made, that no man should possess above a certain measure of ground, and that no man should have in his stock above a prescript and appointed sum of money: if it were by certain laws decreed, that neither the king should be of too great power, neither the people too proud and wealthy, and that offices should not be obtained by inordinate suit, or by bribes and gifts: that they should neither be bought nor sold, nor that it should be needful for the officers, to be at any cost or charge in their offices: for so occasion is given to the officers by fraud and ravin to gather up their money again, and by reason of gifts and bribes the offices be given to rich men, which should rather have been executed of wise men: by such laws I say, like as sick bodies that be desperate and past cure, be wont with continual good cherishing to be kept up: so these evils also might be lightened and mitigated. But that they may be perfectly cured, and brought to a good and upright state, it is not to be hoped for, whiles every man is master of his own to himself. Yea, and whiles you go about to do your cure of one part, you shall make bigger the sore of another part, so the help of one causeth another's harm: forasmuch as nothing can be given to any man unless that be taken from another.

But I am of a contrary opinion (quoth I) for methinketh that men shall never there live wealthily, where all things be common. For how can there be abundance of goods, or of anything, where every man withdraweth his hand from labour? Whom the regard of his own gains driveth not to work, and the hope that he hath in other men's travails maketh him slothful. Then when they be pricked with poverty, and yet no man can by any law or right defend that for his own, which he hath gotten with the labour of his own hands, shall not there of necessity be continual sedition and blood-shed? Specially the authority and reverence of magistrates being taken away, which, what place it may have with such men among whom is no difference, I cannot devise.

I marvel not (quoth he) that you be of this opinion. For you conceive in your mind either none at all, or else a very false image and similitude of this thing. But if you had been with me in Utopia and had presently seen their fashions and laws, as I did, which lived there five years and more, and would never have come thence, but only to make that new land known here: then doubtless you would grant, that you never saw people well ordered, but only there.

Surely (quoth Master Peter) it shall be hard for you to make me believe, that there is better order in that new land, than is here in these countries that we know. For good wits be as well here as there: and I think our commonwealths be ancienter than theirs; wherein long use and experience hath found out many things commodious for man's life, besides that many things here among us have been found by chance, which no wit could ever have devised.

As touching the ancientness (quoth he) of commonwealths, then you might better judge, if you had read the histories and chronicles of that land, which if we may believe, cities were there, before there were men here. Now what thing soever hitherto by wit hath been devised, or found by chance, that might be as well there as here. But I think verily, though it were so that we did pass them in wit: yet in study and laboursome endeavour they far pass us. For (as their chronicles testify) before our arrival there, they never heard anything of us, whom they call the ultra-equinoctials: saving that once about 1200 years ago, a certain ship was lost by the isle of Utopia, which was driven thither by tempest. Certain Romans and Egyptians were cast on land. Which after that never went thence. Mark now what profit they took of this one occasion through diligence and earnest travail. There was no craft nor science within the empire of Rome, whereof any profit could rise, but they either learned it of these strangers, or else of them taking occasion to search for it, found it out. So great profit was it to them that ever any went thither from hence. But if any like chance before this hath brought any man from thence hither, that is as quite out of remembrance, as this also perchance in time to come shall be forgotten, that ever I was there. And like as they quickly, almost at the first meeting, made their own whatsoever is among us wealthily devised: so I suppose it would be long before we would receive anything that among them is better instituted than among us. And this I suppose is the chief cause why their commonwealths be wiselier governed, and do flourish in more wealth than ours, though we neither in wit nor riches be their inferiors.

Therefore gentle Master Raphael (quoth I) I pray you and beseech you describe unto us the island. And study not to be short: but declare largely in order their grounds, their rivers, their cities, their people, their manners, their ordinances, their laws, and to be short, all things, that you shall think us desirous to know. And you shall think us desirous to know whatsoever we know not yet.

There is nothing (quoth he) that I will do gladlier. For all these things I have fresh in mind. But the matter requireth leisure.

Let us go in therefore (quoth I) to dinner, afterward we will bestow the time at our pleasure.

Content (quoth he) be it.

So we went in and dined. When dinner was done, we came into the same place again, and sat us down upon the same bench, commanding our servants that no man should trouble us. Then I and Master Peter Giles desired Master Raphael to perform his promise. He therefore seeing us desirous and willing to hearken to him, when he had sat still and paused a little while, musing and bethinking himself, thus he began to speak.

THE END OF THE FIRST BOOK.

THE SECOND BOOK

The Second Book of the Communication of Raphael Hythloday, concerning the best state of a commonwealth, containing the description of Utopia, with a large declaration of the Godly government, and of all the good laws and orders of the same Island.

THE island of Utopia containeth in breadth in the middle part of it (for there it is broadest) two hundred miles. Which breadth continueth through the most part of the land, saving that by little and little it cometh in, and waxeth narrower towards both the ends. Which fetching about a circuit or compass of five hundred miles, do fashion the whole island like to the new moon. Between these two corners the sea runneth in, dividing them asunder by the distance of eleven miles or thereabouts, and there surmounteth into a large and wide sea, which by reason that the land on every side compasseth it about, and sheltereth it from the winds, is not rough, nor mounteth not with great waves, but almost floweth quietly, not much unlike a great standing pool: and maketh almost all the space within the belly of the land in manner of a haven: and to the great commodity of the inhabitants receiveth in ships towards every part of the land. The forefronts or frontiers of the two corners, what with fords and shelves, and what with rocks be very jeopardous and dangerous. In the middle distance between them both standeth up above the water a great rock, which therefore is nothing perilous because it is in sight. Upon the top of this rock is a fair and a strong tower builded, which they hold with a garrison of men. Other rocks there be that lie hid under the water, and therefore be dangerous. The channels be known only to themselves. And therefore it seldom chanceth that any stranger unless he be guided by a Utopian can come into this haven. Insomuch that they themselves could scarcely enter without jeopardy, but that their way is directed and ruled by certain landmarks standing on the shore. By turning, translating, and removing these marks into other places they may destroy their enemies' navies, be they never so many. The outside of the land is also full of havens, but the landing is so surely defenced, what by nature, and what by workmanship of man's hand, that a few defenders may drive back many armies. Howbeit as they say, and as the fashion of the place itself doth partly show, it was not ever compassed about with the sea. But King Utopus, whose name, as conqueror the island beareth (for before that time it was called Abraxa) which also brought the rude and wild people to that excellent perfection in all good fashions, humanity, and civil gentleness, wherein they now go beyond all the people of the world: even at his first arriving and entering upon the land, forthwith obtaining the victory, caused fifteen miles space of uplandish ground, where the sea had no passage, to be cut and digged up.

And so brought the sea round about the land. He set to this work not only the inhabitants of the island (because they should not think it done in contumely and despite) but also all his own soldiers. Thus the work being divided into so great a number of workmen, was with exceeding marvellous speed despatched. Insomuch that the borderers, which at the first began to mock, and to jest at this vain enterprise, then turned their laughter to marvel at the success, and to fear. There be in the island fifty-four large and fair cities, or shire towns, agreeing all together in one tongue, in like manners, institutions and laws. They be all set and situate alike, and in all points fashioned alike, as far forth as the place or plot suffereth.

Of these cities they that be nighest together be twenty-four miles asunder. Again there is none of them distant from the next above one day's journey afoot. There come yearly to Amaurote out of every city three old men wise and well experienced, there to entreat and debate, of the common matters of the land. For this city (because it standeth just in the midst of the island, and is therefore most meet for the ambassadors of all parts of the realm) is taken for the chief and head city. The precincts and bounds of the shires be so commodiously appointed out, and set forth for the cities, that never a one of them all hath of any side less than twenty miles of ground, and of some side also much more, as of that part where the cities be of farther distance asunder. None of the cities desire to enlarge the bounds and limits of their shires. For they count themselves rather the good husbands than the owners of their lands. They have in the country in all parts of the shire houses or farms builded, well appointed and furnished with all sorts of instruments and tools belonging to husbandry. These houses be inhabited of the citizens, which come thither to dwell by course. No household or farm in the country hath fewer than forty persons, men and women, besides two bondmen, which be all under the rule and order of the good man, and the good wife of the house, being both very sage and discreet persons. And every thirty farms or families have one head ruler, which is called a philarch, being as it were a head bailiff. Out of every one of these families or farms cometh every year into the city twenty persons which have continued two years before in the country. In their place so many fresh be sent thither out of the city, which of them that have been there a year already, and be therefore expert and cunning in husbandry, shall be instructed and taught. And they the next year shall teach other. This order is used for fear that either scarceness of victuals, or some other like incommodity should chance, through lack of knowledge, if they should be altogether new, and fresh, and unexpert in husbandry. This manner and fashion of yearly changing and renewing the occupiers of husbandry, though it be solemn and customably used, to the intent that no man shall be constrained against his will to continue long in that hard and sharp kind of life, yet many of them have such a pleasure and delight in husbandry, that they obtain a longer space of years. These husbandmen plough and till the ground, and breed up cattle, and make ready wood, which they carry to the city either by land, or by water, as they may most conveniently. They bring up a great multitude of poultry, and that by a marvellous policy. For the hens do not sit upon the eggs: but by keeping them in a certain equal heat they bring life into them, and hatch them. The chickens, as soon as they be come out of the shell, follow men and women instead of the hens. They bring up very few horses: nor none, but very fierce ones: and for none other use or purpose, but only to exercise their youth in riding and feats of arms. For oxen be put to all the labour of ploughing and drawing. Which they grant to be not so good as horses at a sudden brunt, and (as we say) at a dead lift, but yet they hold opinion that they will abide and suffer much more labour and pain than horses will. And they think that they be not in danger and subject unto so many diseases. and that they be kept and maintained with much less cost and charge: and finally that they be good for meat, when they be past labour. They sow corn only for bread. For their drink is either wine made of grapes, or else of apples, or pears, or else it is clean water. And many times mead made of honey or liquorice sodden in water, for thereof they have great store. And though they know certainly (for they know it perfectly indeed) how much victuals the city with the whole country or shire round about it doth spend: yet they sow much more corn, and breed up much more cattle, than serveth for their own use, and the overplus they part among their borderers. Whatsoever necessary things be lacking in the country, all such stuff they fetch out of the city: where without any exchange they easily obtain it of the magistrates of the city. For every month many of them go into the city on the holy day. When their harvest day draweth near and is at hand, then the philarchs, which be the head officers and bailiffs of husbandry, send word to the magistrates of the city what number of harvest men is needful to be sent to them out of the city. The which company of harvest men being there ready at the day appointed, almost in one fair day despatcheth all the harvest work.

Of the Cities, and namely of Amaurote

As for their cities, he that knoweth one of them, knoweth them all: they be all so like one to another, as farforth as the nature of the place permitteth. I will describe therefore to you one or other of them, for it skilleth not greatly which: but which rather than Amaurote? Of them all this is the worthiest and of most dignity. For the residue acknowledge it for the head city, because there is the council house. Nor to me any of them all is better beloved, as wherein I lived five whole years together. The city of Amaurote standeth upon the side of a low hill in fashion almost four square. For the breadth of it beginneth a little beneath the top of the hill, and still continueth by the space of two miles, until it come to the river of Anyder. The length of it, which lieth by the river's side, is somewhat more. The river of Anyder riseth twenty-four miles above Amaurote out of a little spring. But being increased by other small floods and brooks that run into it, and among other two somewhat big ones, before the city it is half a mile broad, and farther broader. And sixty miles beyond the city it falleth into the Ocean sea. By all that space that lieth between the sea and the city, and a good sort of miles also above the city, the water ebbeth and floweth six hours together with a swift tide. When the sea floweth in, for the length of thirty miles it filleth all the Anyder with salt water, and driveth back the fresh water of the river. And somewhat further it changeth the sweetness of the fresh water with saltness. But a little beyond that the river waxeth sweet, and runneth forby the city fresh and pleasant. And when the sea ebbeth, and goeth back again, the fresh water followeth it almost even to the very fall into the sea. There goeth a bridge over the river made not of piles of timber, but of stonework with gorgeous and substantial arches at that part of the city that is farthest from the sea: to the intent that ships may go along forby all the side of the city without let. They have also another river which indeed is not very great. But it runneth gently and pleasantly. For it riseth even out of the same hill that the city standeth upon, and runneth down a slope through the midst of the city into Anyder. And because it riseth a little without the city, the Amaurotians have inclosed the head spring of it with strong fences and bulwarks, and so have joined it to the city. This is done to the intent that the water should not be stopped nor turned away, or poisoned, if their enemies should chance to come upon them. From thence the water is derived and brought down in canals of brick divers ways into the lower parts of the city. Where that cannot be done, by reason that the place will not suffer it, there they gather the rain water in great cisterns, which doth them as good service. The city is compassed about with a high and thick wall full of turrets and bulwarks. A dry ditch, but deep, and broad, and overgrown with bushes, briers and thorns, goeth about three sides or quarters of the city. To the fourth side the river itself serveth for a ditch. The streets be appointed and set forth very commodious and handsome, both for carriage, and also against the winds. The houses be of fair and gorgeous building, and in the street side they stand joined together in a long row through the whole street without any partition or separation. The streets be twenty feet broad. On the back side of the houses through the whole length of the street, lie large gardens which be closed in round about with the back part of the streets. Every house hath two doors, one into the street, and a postern door on the back side into the garden. These doors be made with two leaves, never locked nor bolted, so easy to be opened, that they will follow the least drawing of a finger, and shut again by themselves. Every man that will, may go in, for there is nothing within the houses that is private, or any man's own. And every tenth year they change their houses by lot. They set great store by their gardens. In them they have vineyards, all manner of fruit, herbs, and flowers, so pleasant, so well furnished and so finely kept, that I never saw thing more fruitful, nor better trimmed in any place. Their study and diligence herein cometh not only of pleasure, but also of a certain strife and contention that is between street and street, concerning the trimming, husbanding, and furnishing of their gardens: every man for his own part. And verily you shall not lightly find in all the city anything, that is more commodious, either for the profit of the citizens, or for pleasure. And therefore it may seem that the first founder of the city minded nothing so much as he did these gardens. For they say that King Utopus himself, even at the first beginning appointed and drew forth the platform of the city into this fashion and figure that it hath now, but the gallant garnishing, and the beautiful setting forth of it, whereunto he saw that one man's age would not suffice: that he left to his posterity. For their chronicles, which they keep written with all diligent circumspection, containing the history of 1760 years, even from the first conquest of the island, record and witness that the houses in the beginning were very low, and like homely cottages or poor shepherd houses, made at all adventures of every rude piece of wood, that came first to hands, with mud walls and ridged roofs, thatched over with straw. But now the houses be curiously builded after a gorgeous and gallant sort, with three stories one over another. The outsides of the walls be made either of hard flint, or of plaster, or else of brick, and the inner sides be well strengthened with timber work.

The roofs be plain and flat, covered with a certain kind of plaster that is of no cost, and yet so tempered that no fire can hurt or perish it, and withstandeth the violence of the weather better than any lead. They keep the wind out of their windows with glass, for it is there much used, and somewhere also with fine linen cloth dipped in oil or amber, and that for two commodities. For by this means more light cometh in, and the wind is better kept out.

Of the Magistrates

Every thirty families or farms, choose them yearly an officer, which in their old language is called the syphogrant, and by a newer name, the philarch. Every ten syphogrants, with all their 300 families be under an officer which was once called the tranibore, now the chief philarch. Moreover as concerning the election of the prince, all the syphogrants, which be in number 200, first be sworn to choose him whom they think most meet and expedient. Then by a secret election, they name prince, one of those four whom the people before named unto them. For out of the four quarters of the city there be four chosen, out of every quarter one, to stand for the election: which be put up to the council. The prince's office continueth all his lifetime, unless he be deposed or put down for suspicion of tyranny. They choose the tranibores yearly, but lightly they change them not. All the other offices be but for one year. The tranibores every third day, and sometimes, if need be, oftener come into the council house with the prince. Their council is concerning the commonwealth. If there be any controversies among the commoners, which be very few, they despatch and end them by-and-by. They take ever two syphogrants to them in counsel, and every day a new couple. And it is provided that nothing touching the commonwealth shall be confirmed and ratified unless it have been reasoned of and debated three days in the council, before it be decreed. It is death to have any consultation for the commonwealth out of the council, or the place of the common election. This statute, they say, was made to the intent that the prince and tranibores might not easily conspire together to oppress the people by tyranny, and to change the state of the weal public. Therefore matters of great weight and importance be brought to the election house of the syphogrants, which open the matter to their families. And afterward, when they have consulted among themselves, they show their device to the council. Sometimes the matter is brought before the council of the whole island. Furthermore this custom also the council useth, to dispute or reason of no matter the same day that it is first proposed or put forth, but to defer it to the next sitting of the council. Because that no man when he hath rashly there spoken that cometh first to his tongue's end, shall then afterward rather study for reasons wherewith to defend and confirm his first foolish sentence, than for the commodity of the commonwealth: as one rather willing the harm or hindrance of the weal public than any loss or diminution of his own existimation. And as one that would not for shame (which is a very foolish shame) be counted anything overseen in the matter at the first. Who at the first ought to have spoken rather wisely, than hastily, or rashly.

Of Sciences, Crafts, and Occupations

Husbandry is a science common to them all in general, both men and women, wherein they be all expert and cunning. In this they be all instruct even from their youth: partly in schools with traditions and precepts, and partly in the country nigh the city, brought up as it were in playing, not only beholding the use of it, but by occasion of exercising their bodies practising it also. Besides husbandry, which (as I said) is common to them all, every one of them learneth one or other several and particular science, as his own proper craft. That is most commonly either clothworking in wool or flax, or masonry, or the smith's craft, or the carpenter's science. For there is none other occupation that any number to speak of doth use there. For their garments, which throughout all the island be of one fashion (saving that there is a difference between the man's garment and the woman's, between the married and the unmarried) and this one continueth for evermore unchanged, seemly and comely to the eye, no let to the moving and wielding of the body, also fit both for winter and summer: as for these garments (I say) every family maketh their own. But of the other foresaid crafts every man learneth one. And not only the men, but also the women. But the women, as the weaker sort, be put to the easier crafts: they work wool and flax. The other more laboursome sciences be committed to the men. For the most part every man is brought up in his father's craft. For most commonly they be naturally thereto bent and inclined. But if a man's mind stand to any other, he is by adoption put into a family of that occupation, which he doth most fantasy. Whom not only his father, but also the magistrates do diligently look to, that he be put to a discreet and an honest householder. Yea, and if any person, when he hath learned one craft, be desirous to learn also another, he is likewise suffered and permitted.

When he hath learned both, he occupieth whether he will: unless the city have more need of the one, than of the other. The chief and almost the only office of the syphogrants is, to see and take heed that no man sit idle: but that every one apply his own craft with earnest diligence. And yet for all that, not to be wearied from early in the morning, to late in the evening, with continual work, like labouring and toiling beasts.

For this is worse than the miserable and wretched condition of bondmen. Which nevertheless is almost everywhere the life of workmen and artificers, saving in Utopia. For they dividing the day and the night into twenty-four just hours, appoint and assign only six of those hours to work; three before noon, upon the which they go straight to dinner: and after dinner, when they have rested two hours, then they work three and upon that they go to supper. About eight of the clock in the evening (counting one of the clock at the first hour after noon) they go to bed: eight hours they give to sleep. All the void time, that is between the hours of work, sleep, and meat, that they be suffered to bestow, every man as he liketh best himself. Not to the intent that they should misspend this time in riot or slothfulness: but being then licensed from the labour of their own occupations, to bestow the time well and thriftly upon some other good science, as shall please them. For it is a solemn custom there, to have lectures daily early in the morning, where to be present they only be constrained that be namely chosen and appointed to learning. Howbeit a great multitude of every sort of people, both men and women, go to hear lectures, some one and some another, as every man's nature is inclined. Yet, this notwithstanding, if any man had rather bestow this time upon his own occupation (as it chanceth in many, whose minds rise not in the contemplation of any science liberal) he is not letted, nor prohibited, but is also praised and commended, as profitable to the commonwealth. After supper they bestow one hour in play: in summer in their gardens: in winter in their common halls: where they dine and sup. There they exercise themselves in music, or else in honest and wholesome communication. Diceplay, and such other foolish and pernicious games they know not. But they use two games not much unlike the chess. The one is the battle of numbers, wherein one number stealeth away another. The other is wherein vices fight with virtues, as it were in battle array, or a set field. In the which game is very properly showed, both the strife and discord that vices have among themselves, and again their unity and concord against virtues. And also what vices be repugnant to what virtues: with what power and strength they assail them openly: by what wiles and subtlety they assault them secretly: with what help and aid the virtues resist and overcome the puissance of the vices: by what craft they frustrate their purposes: and finally by what sleight or means the one getteth the victory. But here lest you be deceived, one thing you must look more narrowly upon. For seeing they bestow but six hours in work, perchance you may think that the lack of some necessary things hereof may ensue. But this is nothing so. For that small time is not only enough but also too much for the store and abundance of all things that be requisite, either for the necessity, or commodity of life. The which thing you also shall perceive, if you weigh and consider with yourselves how great a part of the people in other countries liveth idle. First almost all women, which be the half of the whole number: or else if the women be anywhere occupied, there most commonly in their stead the men be idle. Besides this how great, and how idle a company is there of priests, and religious men, as they call them? put thereto all rich men, especially all landed men, which commonly be called gentlemen, and noblemen. Take into this number also their servants: I mean all that flock of stout bragging rush bucklers. Join to them also sturdy and valiant beggars, cloaking their idle life under the colour of some disease or sickness. And truly you shall find them much fewer than you thought, by whose labour all these things be gotten that men use and live by. Now consider with yourself, of these few that do work, how few be occupied, in necessary works. For where money beareth all the swing, there many vain and superfluous occupations must needs be used, to serve only for riotous superfluity and unhonest pleasure. For the same multitude that now is occupied in work, if they were divided into so few occupations as the necessary use of nature requireth; in so great plenty of things as then of necessity would ensue, doubtless the prices would be too little for the artificers to maintain their livings. But if all these, that be now busied about unprofitable occupations, with all the whole flock of them that live idly and slothfully, which consume and waste every one of them more of these things that come by other men's labour, than two of the workmen themselves do: if all these (I say) were set to profitable occupations, you easily perceive how little time would be enough, yea and too much to store us with all things that may be requisite either for necessity, or for commodity, yea or for pleasure, so that the same pleasure be true and natural. And this in Utopia the thing itself maketh manifest and plain. For there in all the city, with the whole country, or shire adjoining to it scarcely 500 persons of all the whole number of men and women, that be neither too old, nor too weak to work, be licensed from labour. Among them be the syphogrants which (though they be by the laws exempt and privileged from labour) yet they exempt not themselves: to the intent they may the rather by their example provoke other to work. The same vacation from labour do they also enjoy, to whom the people persuaded by the commendation of the priests, and secret election of the syphogrants, have given a perpetual license from labour to learning. But if any one of them prove not according to the expectation and hope of him conceived, he is forthwith plucked back to the company of artificers. And contrariwise, often it chanceth that a handicraftsman doth so earnestly bestow his vacant and spare hours in learning, and through diligence so profit therein, that he is taken from his handy occupation, and promoted to the company of the learned. Out of this order of the learned be chosen ambassadors, priests, tranibores, and finally the prince himself. Whom they in their old tongue call Barzanes, and by a newer name, Adamus. The residue of the people being neither idle nor occupied about unprofitable exercises, it may be easily judged in how few hours how much good work by them may be done towards those things that I have spoken of. This commodity they have also above other, that in the most part of necessary occupations they need not so much work, as other nations do. For first of all the building or repairing of houses asketh everywhere so many men's continual labour, because that the unth[r]ifty heir suffereth the houses that his father builded in continuance of time to fall in decay. So that which he might have upholden with little cost, his successor is constrained to build it again anew, to his great charge. Yea many times also the house that stood one man in much money, another is of so nice and so delicate a mind, that he setteth nothing by it. And it being neglected, and therefore shortly falling into ruin, he buildeth up another in another place with no less cost and charge. But among the Utopians, where all things be set in a good order, and the commonwealth in a good stay, it very seldom chanceth, that they choose a new plot to build an house upon. And they do not only find speedy and quick remedies for present faults: but also prevent them that be like to fall. And by this means their houses continue and last very long with little labour and small reparations: insomuch that this kind of workmen sometimes have almost nothing to do. But that they be commanded to hew timber at home, and to square and trim up stones, to the intent that if any work chance, it may the speedier rise. Now, sir, in their apparel, mark (I pray you) how few workmen they need. First of all, whilst they be at work, they be covered homely with leather or skins, that will last seven years. When they go forth abroad they cast upon them a cloak, which hideth the other homely apparel. These cloaks throughout the whole island be all of one colour, and that is the natural colour of the wool. They therefore do not only spend much less woollen cloth than is spent in other countries, but also the same standeth them in much less cost. But linen cloth is made with less labour, and is therefore had more in use. But in linen cloth only whiteness, in woollen only cleanliness is regarded. As for the smallness or fineness of the thread, that is nothing passed for. And this is the cause wherefore in other places four or five cloth gowns of divers colours, and as many silk coats be not enough for one man. Yea and if he be of the delicate and nice sort ten be too few: whereas there one garment will serve a man most commonly two years. For why should he desire more? Seeing if he had them, he should not be the better wrapped or covered from cold, neither in his apparel any whit the comelier. Wherefore, seeing they be all exercised in profitable occupations, and that few artificers in the same crafts be sufficient, this is the cause that plenty of all things being among them, they do sometimes bring forth an innumerable company of people to amend the highways, if any be broken. Many times also, when they have no such work to be occupied about, an open proclamation is made, that they shall bestow fewer hours in work. For the magistrates do not exercise their citizens against their wills in unneedful labours. For why? in the institution of that weal public, this end is only and chiefly pretended and minded, that what time may possibly be spared from the necessary occupations and affairs of the commonwealth, all that the citizens should withdraw from the bodily service to the free liberty of the mind, and garnishing of the same. For herein they suppose the felicity of this life to consist.

Of their living and mutual conversation together

But now will I declare how the citizens use themselves one towards another: what familiar occupying and entertainment there is among the people, and what fashion they use in distributing every thing. First the city consisteth of families, the families most commonly be made of kindreds. For the women, when they be married at a lawful age, they go into their husbands' houses. But the male children with all the whole male offspring continue still in their own family and be governed of the eldest and ancientest father, unless he dote for age: for then the next to him in age is put in his room. But to the intent the prescript number of the citizens should neither decrease, nor above measure increase, it is ordained that no family which in every city be six thousand in the whole, besides them of the country, shall at once have fewer children of the age of fourteen years or thereabout than ten or more than sixteen, for of children under this age no number can be appointed. This measure or number is easily observed and kept, by putting them that in fuller families be above the number into families of smaller increase. But if chance be that in the whole city the store increase above the just number, therewith they fill up the lack of other cities. But if so be that the multitude throughout the whole island pass and exceed the due number, then they choose out of every city certain citizens, and build up a town under their own laws in the next land where the inhabitants have much waste and unoccupied ground, receiving also of the inhabitants to them, if they will join and dwell with them. They thus joining and dwelling together do easily agree in one fashion of living, and that to the great wealth of both the peoples. For they so bring the matter about by their laws, that the ground which before was neither good nor profitable for the one nor for the other, is now sufficient and fruitful enough for them both. But if the inhabitants of that land will not dwell with them to be ordered by their laws, then they drive them out of those bounds which they have limited, and appointed out for themselves. And if they resist and rebel, then they make war against them. For they count this the most just cause of war, when any people holdeth a piece of ground void and vacant, to no good nor profitable use, keeping other from the use and possession of it, which notwithstanding by the law of nature ought thereof to be nourished and relieved. If any chance do so much diminish the number of any of their cities, that it cannot be filled up again, without the diminishing of the just number of the other cities (which they say chanced but twice since the beginning of the land through a great pestilent plague) then they make up the number with citizens fetched out of their own foreign towns, for they had rather suffer their foreign towns to decay and perish, than any city of their own island to be diminished. But now again to the conversation of the citizens among themselves. The eldest (as I said) ruleth the family. The wives be ministers to their husbands, the children to their parents, and to be short the younger to their elders. Every city is divided into four equal parts. In the midst of every quarter there is a market place of all manner of things. Thither the works of every family be brought into certain houses. And every kind of thing is laid up in several barns or store-houses. From hence the father of every family, or every householder

fetcheth whatsoever he and his have need of, and carrieth it away
with him without money, without exchange, without any gage, or
pledge. For why should any thing be denied unto him? Seeing
there is abundance of all things, and that it is not to be feared, lest
any man will ask more than he needeth. For why should it be
thought that that man would ask more than enough, which is sure
never to lack? Certainly in all kinds of living creatures either fear
of lack doth cause covetousness and ravin, or in man only pride,
which counteth it a glorious thing to pass and excel other in the
superfluous and vain ostentation of things. The which kind of vice
among the Utopians can have no place. Next to the market places
that I spake of, stand meat markets: whither be brought not only
all sorts of herbs, and the fruits of trees, with bread, but also fish, and
all manner of four-footed beasts, and wild fowl that be man's meat.
But first the filthiness and ordure thereof is clean washed away in
the running river without the city in places appointed meet for the
same purpose. From thence the beasts [be] brought in killed, and
clean washed by the hands of their bondmen. For they permit not
their free citizens to accustom themselves to the killing of beasts,
through the use whereof they think that clemency, the gentlest affection of our nature, doth by little and little decay and perish. Neither
they suffer any thing that is filthy, loathsome, or uncleanly, to be
brought into the city, lest the air by the stench thereof infected and
corrupt, should cause pestilent diseases. Moreover every street hath
certain great large halls set in equal distance one from another, every
one known by a several name. In these halls dwell the syphogrants.
And to every one of the same halls be appointed thirty families, on
either side fifteen. The stewards of every hall at a certain hour come
into the meat markets, where they receive meat according to the
number of their halls. But first and chiefly of all, respect is had to the
sick, that be cured in the hospitals. For in the circuit of the city, a little
without the walls, they have four hospitals, so big, so wide, so ample,
and so large, that they may seem four little towns, which were devised of that bigness partly to the intent the sick, be they never so
many in number, should not lie too throng or strait, and therefore
uneasily and incommodiously: and partly that they which were
taken and holden with contagious diseases, such as be wont by infec-

tion to creep from one to another, might be laid apart far from the company of the residue. These hospitals be so well appointed, and with all things necessary to health so furnished, and moreover so diligent attendance through the continual presence of cunning physicians is given, that though no man be sent thither against his will, yet notwithstanding there is no sick person in all the city, that had not rather lie there than at home in his own house. When the steward of the sick hath received such meats as the physicians have prescribed, then the best is equally divided among the halls, according to the company of every one, saving that there is had a respect to the prince, the bishop, the tranibores, and to ambassadors and all strangers, if there be any, which be very few and seldom. But they also when they be there, have certain houses appointed and prepared for them. To these halls at the set hours of dinner and supper cometh all the whole syphogranty or ward, warned by the noise of a brazen trumpet: except such as be sick in the hospitals, or else in their own houses. Howbeit no man is prohibited or forbid, after the halls be served, to fetch home meat out of the market to his own house, for they know that no man will do it without a cause reasonable. For though no man be prohibited to dine at home, yet no man doth it willingly: because it is counted a point of small honesty. And also it were a folly to take the pain to dress a bad dinner at home, when they may be welcome to good and fine fare so nigh hand at the hall. In this hall all vile service, all slavery, and drudgery, with all laboursome toil and business, is done by bondmen. But the women of every family by course have the office and charge of cookery for seething and dressing the meat, and ordering all things thereto belonging. They sit at three tables or more, according to the number of their company. The men sit upon the bench next the wall, and the women against them on the other side of the table, that if any sudden evil should chance to them, as many times happeneth to women with child, they may rise without trouble or disturbance of anybody, and go thence into the nursery. The nurses sit several alone with their young sucklings in a certain parlour appointed and deputed to the same purpose, never without fire and clean water, nor yet without cradles, that when they will they may lay down the young infants, and at their pleasure take them out of

their swathing clothes, and hold them to the fire, and refresh them
with play. Every mother is nurse to her own child, unless either
death, or sickness be the let. When that chanceth, the wives of the
syphogrants quickly provide a nurse. And that is not hard to be
done. For they that can do it, do proffer themselves to no service so
gladly as to that. Because that there this kind of pity is much
praised: and the child that is nourished, ever after taketh his nurse
for his own natural mother. Also among the nurses sit all the children that be under the age of five years. All the other children of
both kinds, as well boys as girls, that be under the age of marriage,
do either serve at the tables, or else if they be too young thereto, yet
they stand by with marvellous silence. That which is given to them
from the table they eat, and other several dinner-time they have none.
The syphogrant and his wife sit in the midst of the high table, forasmuch as that is counted the honourablest place, and because from
thence all the whole company is in their sight. For that table
standeth overthwart the over end of the hall. To them be joined
two of the ancientest and eldest. For at every table they sit four at
a mess. But if there be a church standing in that syphogranty or
ward, then the priest and his wife sitteth with the syphogrant, as
chief in the company. On both sides of them sit young men, and
next unto them again old men. And thus throughout all the house
equal of age be set together, and yet be mixed with unequal ages.
This, they say, was ordained, to the intent that the sage gravity and
reverence of the elders should keep the younger from wanton license
of words and behaviour. Forasmuch as nothing can be so secretly
spoken or done at the table, but either they that sit on the one side or
on the other must needs perceive it. The dishes be not set down in
order from the first place, but all the old men (whose places be
marked with some special token to be known) be first served of their
meat, and then the residue equally. The old men divide their dainties as they think best to the younger that sit on each side of them.

Thus the elders be not defrauded of their due honour, and nevertheless equal commodity cometh to every one. They begin every
dinner and supper of reading something that pertaineth to good
manners and virtue. But it is short, because no man shall be grieved
therewith. Hereof the elders take occasion of honest communica-

tion, but neither sad nor unpleasant. Howbeit they do not spend all the whole dinner-time themselves with long and tedious talks: but they gladly hear also the young men: yea, and do purposely provoke them to talk, to the intent that they may have a proof of every man's wit, and towardness, or disposition to virtue, which commonly in the liberty of feasting doth show and utter itself. Their dinners be very short: but their suppers be somewhat longer, because that after dinner followeth labour, after supper sleep and natural rest, which they think to be of more strength and efficacy to wholesome and healthful digestion. No supper is passed without music. Nor their banquets lack no conceits nor junkets. They burn sweet gums and spices for perfumes, and pleasant smells, and sprinkle about sweet ointments and waters, yea, they leave nothing undone that maketh for the cheering of the company. For they be much inclined to this opinion: to think no kind of pleasure forbidden, whereof cometh no harm. Thus therefore and after this sort they live together in the city, but in the country they that dwell alone far from any neighbours, do dine and sup at home in their own houses. For no family there lacketh any kind of victuals, as from whom cometh all that the citizens eat and live by.

Of their journeying or travelling abroad, with divers other matters cunningly reasoned, and wittily discussed

But if any be desirous to visit either their friends that dwell in another city, or to see the place itself: they easily obtain licence of their syphogrants and tranibores, unless there be some profitable let. No man goeth out alone but a company is sent forth together with their prince's letters, which do testify that they have licence to go that journey, and prescribeth also the day of their return. They have a waggon given them, with a common bondman, which driveth the oxen, and taketh charge of them. But unless they have women in their company, they send home the waggon again, as an impediment and a let. And though they carry nothing forth with them, yet in all their journey they lack nothing. For wheresoever they come they be at home. If they tarry in a place longer than one day, then there every one of them falleth to his own occupation, and be very gently entertained of the workmen and companies of the same crafts. If any man of his own head and without leave, walk out of his precinct and bounds, taken without the prince's letters, he is brought again for a fugitive or a runaway with great shame and rebuke, and is sharply punished. If he be taken in that fault again, he is punished with bondage. If any be desirous to walk abroad into the fields, or into the country that belongeth to the same city that he dwelleth in, obtaining the goodwill of his father, and the consent of his wife, he is not prohibited. But into what part of the country soever he cometh he hath no meat given him until he have wrought out his forenoon's task, or else despatched so much work, as there is wont to be wrought before supper. Observing this law and condition, he may go whither he will within the bounds of his own city. For he shall be no less profitable to the city, than if he were within it. Now you see how little liberty they have to loiter: how they can have no cloak or pretence to idleness. There be neither wine taverns, nor ale-houses, nor stews, nor any occasion of vice or wickedness, no lurking corners, no places of wicked counsels or unlawful assemblies. But they be in the present sight, and under the eyes of every man. So that of necessity they must either apply their accustomed labours, or else recreate themselves with honest and laudable pastimes.

This fashion being used among the people, they must of necessity have store and plenty of all things. And seeing they be all thereof partners equally, therefore can no man there be poor or needy. In the council of Amaurote, whither, as I said, every city sendeth three men apiece yearly, as soon as it is perfectly known of what things there is in every place plenty, and again what things be scant in any place: incontinent the lack of the one is performed and filled up with the abundance of the other. And this they do freely without any benefit, taking nothing again of them, to whom the things is given, but those cities that have given of their store to any other city that lacketh, requiring nothing again of the same city, do take such things as they lack of another city, to whom they gave nothing. So the whole island is as it were one family, or household. But when they have made sufficient provision of store for themselves (which they think not done, until they have provided for two years following because of the uncertainty of the next year's proof) then of those things, whereof they have abundance, they carry forth into other countries great plenty: as grain, honey, wool, flax, wood, madder, purple dyed fells, wax, tallow, leather, and living beasts. And the seventh part of all these things they give frankly and freely to the poor of that country. The residue they sell at a reasonable and mean price. By this trade of traffic or merchandise, they bring into their own country, not only great plenty of gold and silver, but also all such things as they lack at home, which is almost nothing but iron. And by reason they have long used this trade, now they have more abundance of these things, than any man will believe. Now therefore they care not whether they sell for ready money, or else upon trust to be paid at a day, and to have the most part in debts. But in so doing they never follow the credence of private men: but the assurance or warrantys of the whole city, by instruments and writings made in that behalf accordingly. When the day of payment is come and expired, the city gathereth up the debt of the private debtors, and putteth it into the common box and so long hath the use and profit of it, until the Utopians their creditors demand it. The most part of it they never ask. For that thing which is to them no profit to take it from other, to whom it is profitable: they think it no right nor conscience. But if the case so stand, that they must lend part of that money to another people, then they require their debt: or when they have war. For the which purpose only they keep at home all the treasure which they have, to be holpen and succoured by it either in extreme jeopardies, or in sudden dangers. But especially and chiefly to hire therewith, and that for unreasonable great wages, strange soldiers. For they had rather put strangers in jeopardy, than their own countrymen: knowing that for money enough, their enemies themselves many times may be bought and sold, or else through treason be set together by the ears among themselves. For this cause they keep an inestimable treasure. But yet not as a treasure: but so they have it, and use it, as in good faith I am ashamed to show: fearing that my words shall not be believed. And this I have more cause to fear, for that I know how difficulty and hardly I myself would have believed another man telling the same, if I had not presently seen it with mine own eyes.

For it must needs be, that how far a thing is dissonant and disagreeing from the guise and trade of the hearers, so far shall it be out of their belief. Howbeit, a wise and indifferent esteemer of things will not greatly marvel perchance, seeing all their other laws and customs do so much differ from ours, if the use also of gold and silver among them be applied, rather to their own fashions than to ours. I mean in that they occupy not money themselves, but keep it for that chance, which as it may happen, so it may be that it shall never come to pass. In the meantime gold and silver, whereof money is made, they do so use, as none of them doth more esteem it, than the very nature of the thing deserveth. And then who doth not plainly see how far it is under iron: as without the which men can no better live than without fire and water. Whereas to gold and silver nature hath given no use, that we may not well lack: if that the folly of men had not set it in higher estimation for the rareness sake. But of the contrary part, nature as a most tender and loving mother, hath placed the best and most necessary things open abroad: as the air, the water and the earth itself. And hath removed and hid farthest from us vain and unprofitable things. Therefore if these metals among them should be fast locked up in some tower, it might be suspected, that the prince and the council (as the people is ever foolishly imagining) intended by some subtilty to deceive the commons, and to take same profit of it to themselves. Furthermore if they should make thereof plate and such other finely and cunningly wrought stuff: if at any time they should have occasion to break it, and melt it again, and therewith to pay their soldiers' wages, they see and perceive very well, that men would be loath to part from those things, that they once began to have pleasure and delight in. To remedy all this they have found out a means, which, as it is agreeable to all their other laws and customs, so it is from ours, where gold is so much set by and so diligently kept, very far discrepant and repugnant: and therefore incredible, but only to them that be wise. For whereas they eat and drink in earthen and glass vessels, which indeed be curiously and properly made, and yet be of very small value: of gold and silver they make commonly chamber pots, and other like vessels, that serve for most vile uses, not only in their common halls, but in every man's private house. Furthermore of the same metals they make great chains, with fetters, and gyves wherein they tie their bondmen. Finally whosoever for any offence be infamed, by their ears hang rings of gold, upon their fingers they wear rings of gold, and about their necks chains of gold, and in conclusion their heads be tied about with gold. Thus by all means that may be they procure to have gold and silver among them in reproach and infamy. And therefore these metals, which other nations do as grievously and sorrowfully forgo, as in a manner from their own lives: if they should altogether at once be taken from the Utopians, no man there would think that he had lost the worth of one farthing. They gather also pearls by the sea-side, and diamonds and carbuncles upon certain rocks, and yet they seek not for them: but by chance finding them, they cut and polish them. And therewith they deck their young infants. Which like as in the first years of their childhood, they make much and be fond and proud of such ornaments, so when they be a little more grown in years and discretion, perceiving that none but children do wear such toys and trifles: they lay them away even of their own shamefacedness, without any bidding of their parents: even as our children, when they wax big, do cast away nuts, brooches, and puppets. Therefore these laws and customs, which be so far different from all other nations, how divers fantasies also and minds they do cause, did I never so plainly perceive, as in the ambassadors of the Anemolians.

These ambassadors came to Amaurote whilest I was there. And because they came to entreat of great and weighty matters, those three citizens apiece out of every city were come thither before them. But all the ambassadors of the next countries, which had been there before, and knew the fashions and manners of the Utopians, among whom they perceived no honour given to sumptuous and costly apparel, silks to be contemned, gold also to be infamed and reproachful, were wont to come thither in very homely and simple apparel. But the Anemolians, because they dwell far thence and had very little acquaintance with them, hearing that they were all apparelled alike, and that very rudely and homely: thinking them not to have the things which they did not wear: being therefore more proud, than wise: determined in the gorgeousness of their apparel to represent very gods, and with the bright shining and

glistering of their gay clothing to dazzle the eyes of the silly poor
Utopians. So there came in three ambassadors with one hundred
servants all apparelled in changeable colours: the most of them in
silks: the ambassadors themselves (for at home in their own country
they were noblemen) in cloth of gold, with great chains of gold,
with gold hanging at their ears, with gold rings upon their fingers,
with brooches and aglets of gold upon their caps, which glistered full
of pearls and precious stones: to be short, trimmed and adorned
with all those things, which among the Utopians were either the
punishment of bondmen, or the reproach of infamed persons, or else
trifles for young children to play withal. Therefore it would have
done a man good at his heart to have seen how proudly they displayed their peacock's feathers, how much they made of their
painted sheaths, and how loftily they set forth and advanced themselves, when they compared their gallant apparel with the poor raiment of the Utopians. For all the people were swarmed forth into
the streets. And on the other side it was no less pleasure to consider
how much they were deceived, and how far they missed of their
purpose, being contrariwise taken than they thought they should
have been. For to the eyes of all the Utopians, except very few,
which had been in other countries for some reasonable cause, all
that gorgeousness of apparel seemed shameful and reproachful. Insomuch that they most reverently saluted the vilest and most abject of
them for lords: passing over the ambassadors themselves without
any honour: judging them by their wearing of golden chains to be
bondmen. Yea you should have seen children also, that had cast
away their pearls and precious stones, when they saw the like stick-
ing upon the ambassadors' caps, dig and push their mothers under
the sides, saying thus to them. Look, mother, how great a lubber
doth yet wear pearls and precious stones, as though he were a little
child still. But the mother, yea, and that also in good earnest: peace,
son, saith she: I think he be some of the ambassadors' fools. Some
found fault at their golden chains, as to no use nor purpose, being
so small and weak, that a bondman might easily break them, and
again so wide and large, that when it pleased him, he might cast
them off, and run away at liberty whither he would. But when the
ambassadors had been there a day or two and saw so great abun-

dance of gold so lightly esteemed, yea in no less reproach, than it was with them in honour: and besides that more gold in the chains and gyves of one fugitive bondman, than all the costly ornaments of them three was worth: they began to abate their courage, and for very shame laid away all that gorgeous array, whereof they were so proud. And specially when they had talked familiarly with the Utopians, and had learned all their fashions and opinions.

For they marvel that any men be so foolish, as to have delight and pleasure in the glistering of a little trifling stone, which may behold any of the stars, or else the sun itself. Or that any man is so mad, as to count himself the nobler for the smaller or finer thread of wool, which selfsame wool (be it now in never so fine a spun thread) did once a sheep wear: and yet was she all that time no other thing than a sheep. They marvel also that gold, which of the own nature is a thing so unprofitable, is now among all people in so high estimation, that man himself, by whom, yea and for the use of whom it is so much set by, is in much less estimation than the gold itself. Insomuch that a lumpish blockheaded churl, and which hath no more wit than an ass, yea and as full of worthless-ness and foolishness, shall have nevertheless many wise and good men in subjection and bondage, only for this, because he hath a great heap of gold. Which if it should be taken from him by any fortune, or by some subtle wile of the law (which no less than fortune doth raise up the low and pluck down the high), and be given to the most vile slave and abject drudge of all his household, then shortly after he shall go into the service of his servant, as an augmentation or an overplus beside his money. But they much more marvel at and detest the madness of them which to those rich men, in whose debt and danger they be not, do give almost divine honours, for none other consideration, but because they be rich: and yet knowing them to be such niggardly penny-fathers, that they be sure as long as they live, not the worth of one farthing of that heap of gold shall come to them.

These and such like opinions have they conceived, partly by educa-tion, being brought up in that commonwealth, whose laws and cus-toms be far different from these kinds of folly, and partly by good literature and learning. For though there be not many in every city, which be exempt and discharged of all other labours, and appointed only to learning; that is to say, such in whom even from their very childhood they have perceived a singular towardness, a fine wit, and a mind apt to good learning: yet all in their childhood be instruct in learning. And the better part of the people, both men and women throughout all their whole life do bestow in learning those spare hours, which we said they have vacant from bodily labours. They be taught learning in their own native tongue. For it is both copious in words, and also pleasant to the ear, and for the utterance of a man's mind very perfect and sure. The most part of all that side of the world useth the same language, saving that among the Utopians it is finest and purest, and according to the diversity of the countries it is diversely altered. Of all these philosophers, whose names be here famous in this part of the world to us known, before our coming thither not as much as the fame of any of them was come among them. And yet in music, logic, arithmetic, and geometry they have found out in a manner all that our ancient philosophers have taught. But as they in all things be almost equal to our old ancient clerks, so our new logicians in subtle inventions have far passed and gone beyond them. For they have not devised one of all those rules of restrictions, amplifications and suppositions, very wittily invented in the small logicals, which here our children in every place do learn. Furthermore, they were never yet able to find out the second intentions: insomuch that none of them all could ever see man himself in common, as they call him, though he be (as you know) bigger than ever was any giant, yea and pointed to of us even with our finger. But they be in the course of the stars, and the movings of the heavenly spheres very expert and cunning. They have also wittily excogitated and devised instruments of divers fashions: wherein is exactly comprehended and contained the movings and situations of the sun, the moon, and of all the other stars, which appear in their horizon. But as for the amities and dissensions of the planets, and all that deceitful divination by the stars, they never as much as dreamed thereof. Rains, winds, and other courses of tempests they know before by certain tokens, which they have learned by long use and observation. But of the causes of all these things and of the ebbing, flowing and saltness of the sea, and finally of the original beginning and nature of heaven and of the world, they hold partly the same opinions that our old philosophers hold, and partly, as our philosophers vary among themselves, so they also, whiles they bring new reasons of things, do disagree from all them, and yet among themselves in all points they do not accord. In that part of philosophy, which treateth of manners and virtue, their reasons and opinions agree with ours. They dispute of the good qualities of the soul, of the body and of fortune. And whether the name of goodness may be applied to all these, or only to the endowments and gifts of the soul.

They reason of virtue and pleasure. But the chief and principal question is in what thing, be it one or more, the felicity of man consisteth. But in this point they seem almost too much given and inclined to the opinion of them which defend pleasure, wherein they determine either all or the chiefest part of man's felicity to rest. And (which is more to be marvelled at) the defence of this so dainty and delicate an opinion they fetch even from their grave, sharp, bitter, and rigorous religion. For they never dispute of felicity or blessedness, but they join to the reasons of philosophy certain principles taken out of religion: without the which to the investigation of true felicity they think reason of itself weak and imperfect. Those principles be these and such like: That the soul is immortal, and by the bountiful goodness of God ordained to felicity. That to our virtues and good deeds rewards be appointed after this life, and to our evil deeds, punishments. Though these be pertaining to religion, yet they think it meet that they should be believed and granted by proofs of reason. But if these principles were condemned and disannulled, then without any delay they pronounce no man to be so foolish, which would not do all his diligence and endeavour to obtain pleasure by right or wrong, only avoiding this inconvenience, that the less pleasure should not be a let or hindrance to the bigger: or that he laboured not for that pleasure, which would bring after it displeasure, grief, and sorrow. For they judge it extreme madness to follow sharp and painful virtue, and not only to banish the pleasure of life, but also willingly to suffer grief without any hope of profit thereof. For what profit can there be, if a man, when he hath passed over all his life unpleasantly, that is to say, wretchedly, shall have no reward after his death? But now, sir, they think not felicity to rest in all pleasure, but only in that pleasure that is good and honest, and that hereto, as to perfect blessedness our nature is allured and drawn even of virtue, whereto only they that be of the contrary opinion do attribute felicity. For they define virtue to be a life ordered according to nature, and that we be hereunto ordained of God. And that he doth follow the course of nature, which in desiring and refusing things is ruled by reason. Furthermore, that reason doth chiefly and principally kindle in men the love and veneration of the divine majesty. Of whose goodness it is that we be, and that we be in possibility to attain felicity. And that secondly, it moveth and provoketh us to lead our life out of care in joy and mirth, and to help all other in respect of the society of nature to obtain the same. For there was never man so earnest and painful a follower of virtue and hater of pleasure, that would so enjoin you labours, watchings and fastings, but he would also exhort you to ease and lighten, to your power, the lack and misery of others, praising the same as a deed of humanity and pity. Then if it be a point of humanity for man to bring health and comfort to man, and specially (which is a virtue most peculiarly belonging to man) to mitigate and assuage the grief of others, and by taking from them the sorrow and heaviness of life, to restore them to joy, that is to say, to pleasure: why may it not then be said, that nature doth provoke every man to do the same to himself? For a joyful life, that is to say, a pleasant life, is either evil, and if it be so, then thou shouldest not only help no man thereto, but rather, as much as in thee lieth, help all men from it, as noisome and hurtful, or else if thou not only mayst, but also of duty art bound to procure it to others, why not chiefly to thyself, to whom thou art bound to show as much favour as to other? For when nature biddeth thee to be good and gentle to other she commandeth thee not to be cruel and ungentle to thyself. Therefore even very nature (say they) prescribeth to us a joyful life, that is to say, pleasure as the end of all our operations. And they define virtue to be life ordered according to the prescript of nature. But in that, that nature doth allure and provoke men one to help another to live merrily (which surely she doth not without a good cause, for no man is so far above the lot of man's state or condition, that nature doth cark and care for him only, which equally favoureth all that be comprehended under the communion of one shape, form and fashion) verily she commandeth thee to use diligent circumspection, that thou do not so seek for thine own commodities, that thou procure others incommodities. Wherefore their opinion is, that not only covenants and bargains made among private men ought to be well and faithfully fulfilled, observed, and kept, but also common laws, which either a good prince hath justly published, or else the people neither oppressed with tyranny, neither deceived by fraud and guile, hath by their common consent constituted and ratified, concerning the partition of the commodities of life, that is to say, the matter of pleasure. These laws not offended, it is wisdom, that thou look to thine own wealth. And to do the same for the commonwealth is no less than thy duty, if thou bearest any reverent love or any natural zeal and affection to thy native country. But to go about to let another man of his pleasure, whilst thou procurest thine own, that is open wrong. Contrariwise to withdraw something from thyself to give to other, that is a point of humanity and gentleness; which never taketh away so much commodity, as it bringeth again. For it is recompensed with the return of benefits; and the conscience of the good deed, with the remembrance of the thankful love and benevolence of them to whom thou hast done it, doth bring more pleasure to thy mind, than that which thou hast withholden from thyself could have brought to thy body. Finally (which to a godly disposed and a religious mind is easy to be persuaded) God recompenseth the gift of a short and small pleasure with great and everlasting joy. Therefore the matter diligently weighed and considered, thus they think, that all our actions, and in them the virtues themselves, be referred at the last to pleasure, as their end and felicity. Pleasure they call every motion and state of the body or mind wherein man hath naturally delectation. Appetite they join to nature, and that not without a good cause. For like as, not only the senses, but also right reason coveteth whatsoever is naturally pleasant, so that it may be gotten without wrong or injury, not letting or debarring a greater pleasure, nor causing painful labour, even so those things that men by vain imagination do feign against nature to be pleasant (as though it lay in their power to change the things, as they do the names of things) all such pleasures they believe to be of so small help and furtherance to felicity, that they count them great let and hindrance. Because that in whom they have once taken place, all his mind they possess with a false opinion of pleasure. So that there is no place left for true and natural delectations. For there be many things, which of their own nature contain no pleasantness: yea the most part of them much grief and sorrow. And yet through the perverse and malicious flickering enticements of lewd and unhonest desires, be taken not only for special and sovereign pleasures, but also be counted among the chief causes of life. In this counterfeit kind of pleasure they put them that I spake of before; which the better gown they have on, the better men they think themselves. In the which thing they do twice err. For they be no less deceived in that they think their gown the better, than they be, in that they think themselves the better. For if you consider the profitable use of the garment, why should wool of a finer spun thread be thought better, than the wool of a coarse spun thread? Yet they, as though the one did pass the other by nature, and not by their mistaking, advance themselves, and think the price of their own persons thereby greatly increased. And therefore the honour, which in a coarse gown they durst not have looked for, they require, as it were of duty, for their finer gown's sake. And if they be passed by without reverence, they take it angrily and disdainfully. And again is it not a like madness to take a pride in vain and unprofitable honours? For what natural or true pleasure dost thou take of another man's bare head, or bowed knees? Will this ease the pain of thy knees, or remedy the frenzy of thy head? In this image of counterfeit pleasure, they be of a marvellous madness, which for the opinion of nobility, rejoice much in their own conceit. Because it was their fortune to come of such ancestors, whose stock of long time hath been counted rich (for now nobility is nothing else) specially rich in lands. And though their ancestors left them not one foot of land, yet they think themselves not the less noble therefore of one hair. In this number also they count them that take pleasure and delight (as I said) in gems and precious stones, and think themselves almost gods, if they chance to get an excellent one, specially of that kind, which in that time of their own countrymen is had in highest estimation. For one kind of stone keepeth not his price still in all countries and at all times. Nor they buy them not, but taken out of the gold and bare: no, nor so neither, before they have made the seller to swear, that he will warrant and assure it to be a true stone, and no counterfeit gem. Such care they take lest a counterfeit stone should deceive their eyes instead of a right stone. But why shouldst thou not take even as much pleasure in beholding a counterfeit stone, which thine eye cannot discern from a right stone? They should both be of like value to thee, even as to a blind man. What shall I say of them, that keep superfluous riches, to take delectation only in the beholding, and not in the use or occupying thereof? Do they take true pleasure, or else be they deceived with false pleasure? Or of them that be in a contrary vice, hiding the gold which they shall never occupy, nor peradventure never see more; and whiles they take care lest they shall lose it, do lose it indeed? For what is it else, when they hide it in the ground, taking it both from their own use, and perchance from all other men's also? And yet thou, when thou hast hid thy treasure, as one out of all care, hoppest for joy. The which treasure, if it should chance to be stolen, and thou ignorant of the theft shouldst die ten years after: all that ten years' space that thou livedst after thy money was stolen, what matter was it to thee, whether it had been taken away or else safe as thou leftest it? Truly both ways like profit came to thee. To these so foolish pleasures they join dicers, whose madness they know by hearsay and not by use. Hunters also, and hawkers, For what pleasure is there (say they) in casting the dice upon a table; which thou hast done so often, that if there were any pleasure in it, yet the oft use might make thee weary thereof? Or what delight can there be, and not rather displeasure in hearing the barking and howling of dogs? Or what greater pleasure is there to be felt when a dog followeth an hare, than when a dog followeth a dog? for one thing is done in both, that is to say, running, if thou hast pleasure therein. But if the hope of slaughter and the expectation of tearing in pieces the beast doth please thee: thou shouldest rather be moved with pity to see a silly innocent hare murdered of a dog, the weak of the stronger, the fearful of the fierce, the innocent of the cruel and unmerciful. Therefore all this exercise of hunting, as a thing unworthy to be used of free men, the Utopians have rejected to their butchers, to the which craft (as we said before) they appoint their bondmen. For they count hunting the lowest, the vilest, and most abject part of butchery, and the other parts of it more profitable and more honest, as which do bring much more commodity, and do kill beasts only for necessity. Whereas the hunter seeketh nothing but pleasure of the silly and woful beasts' slaughter and murder. The which pleasure, in beholding death, they think doth rise in the very beasts, either of a cruel affection of mind, or else to be changed in continuance of time into cruelty, by long use of so cruel a pleasure. These therefore and all such like, which be innumerable, though the common sort of people doth take them for pleasures, yet they, seeing there is no natural pleasantness in them, do plainly determine them to have no affinity with true and right pleasure. For as touching that they do commonly move the sense with delectation (which seemeth to be a work of pleasure) this doth nothing diminish their opinion. For not the nature of the thing, but their perverse and lewd custom is the cause hereof, which causeth them to accept bitter or sour things for sweet things. Even as women with child in their viciated and corrupt taste, think pitch and tallow sweeter than any honey. Howbeit no man's judgment depraved and corrupt, either by sickness, or by custom, can change the nature of pleasure, more than it can do the nature of other things.

They make divers kinds of true pleasures. For some they attribute to the soul, and some to the body. To the soul they give intelligence and that delectation that cometh of the contemplation of truth. Hereunto is joined the pleasant remembrance of the good life past. The pleasure of the body they divide into two parts. The first is when delectation is sensibly felt and perceived. The second part of bodily pleasure, they say, is that which consisteth and resteth in the quiet and upright state of the body. And that truly is every man's own proper health, intermingled and disturbed with no grief. For this, if it be not let nor assaulted with no grief, is delectable of itself, though it be moved with no external or outward pleasure. For though it be not so plain and manifest to the sense, as the greedy lust of eating and drinking, yet nevertheless many take it for the chiefest pleasure. All the Utopians grant it to be a right great pleasure, and as you would say, the foundation and ground of all pleasures, as which even alone is able to make the state and condition of life delectable and pleasant. And it being once taken away, there is no place left for any pleasure. For to be without grief not having health, that they call insensibility, and not pleasure. The Utopians have long ago rejected and condemned the opinion of them which said that steadfast and quiet health (for this question also hath been diligently debated among them) ought not therefore to be counted a pleasure, because they say it cannot be presently and sensibly perceived and felt by some outward motion. But of the contrary part now they agree almost all in this, that health is a most sovereign pleasure. For seeing that in sickness (say they) is grief, which is a mortal enemy to pleasure, even as sickness is to health, why should not then pleasure be in the quietness of health? For they say it maketh nothing to this matter, whether you say that sickness is a grief, or that in sickness is grief, for all cometh to one purpose. For whether health be a pleasure itself, or a necessary cause of pleasure, as fire is of heat, truly both ways it followeth that they cannot be without pleasure that be in perfect health. Furthermore whilest we eat (say they) then health, which began to be impaired, fighteth by the help of food against hunger. In the which fight, whilest health by little and little getteth the upper hand, that same proceeding, and (as ye would say) that onwardness to the wonted strength, ministreth that pleasure, whereby we be so refreshed. Health therefore, which in the conflict is joyful, shall it not be merry, when it hath gotten the victory? But as soon as it hath recovered the pristinate strength, which thing only in all the fight it coveted, shall it incontinent be astonished? Nor shall it not know nor embrace the own wealth and goodness? For that it is said, health cannot be felt: this, they think, is nothing true. For what man waking, say they, feeleth not himself in health, but he that is not? Is there any man so possessed with stonish insensibility, or with the sleeping sickness, that he will not grant health to be acceptable to him, and delectable? But what other thing is delectation, than that which by another name is called pleasure? They embrace chiefly the pleasures of the mind. For them they count the chiefest and most principal of all. The chief part of them they think doth come of the exercise of virtue,

and conscience of good life. Of these pleasures that the body ministreth, they give the pre-eminence to health. For the delight of eating and drinking, and whatsoever hath any like pleasantness, they determine to be pleasures much to be desired, but no other ways than for
health's sake. For such things of their own proper nature be not
pleasant, but in that they resist sickness privily stealing on. Therefore like as it is a wise man's part, rather to avoid sickness, than to
wish for medicines, and rather to drive away and put to flight careful griefs, than to call for comfort: so it is much better not to need
this kind of pleasure, than in curing the contrary grief to be eased of
the same. The which kind of pleasure, if any man take for his
felicity, that man must needs grant, that then he shall be in most
felicity, if he live that life, which is led in continual hunger, thirst,
itching, eating, drinking, scratching and rubbing. The which life
how not only foul it is, but also miserable and wretched who perceiveth not? These doubtless be the basest pleasures of all, as impure
and imperfect. For they never come, but accompanied with their
contrary griefs. As with the pleasure of eating is joined hunger, and
that after no very equal sort. For of these two the grief is both the
more vehement, and also of longer continuance. For it riseth before
the pleasure, and endeth not until the pleasure die with it. Wherefore such pleasures they think not greatly to be set by, but in that
they be necessary. Howbeit they have delight also in these, and
thankfully acknowledge the tender love of mother nature, which
with most pleasant delectation allureth her children to that, which
of necessity they be driven often to use. For how wretched and
miserable should our life be, if these daily griefs of hunger and
thirst could not be driven away, but with bitter potions and sour
medicines, as the other diseases be, wherewith we be seldomer
troubled? But beauty, strength, nimbleness, these as peculiar and
pleasant gifts of nature they make much of. But those pleasures
which be received by the ears, the eyes and the nose, which nature
willeth to be proper and peculiar to man (for no other kind of living
beasts doth behold the fairness and the beauty of the world, or is
moved with any respect of savours, but only for the diversity of
meats, neither perceiveth the concordant and discordant distances
of sounds and tunes) these pleasures, I say, they accept and allow

as certain pleasant rejoicings of life. But in all things this precaution they use, that a less pleasure hinder not a bigger, and that the pleasure be no cause of displeasure, which they think to follow of necessity, if the pleasure be unhonest. But yet to despise the comeliness of beauty, to waste the bodily strength, to turn nimbleness into sluggishness, to consume and make feeble the body with fasting, to do injury to health, and to reject the other pleasant motions of nature unless a man neglect these his commodities, whilest he doth with a fervent zeal procure the wealth of others, or the common profit, for the which pleasure forborn, he is in hope of a greater pleasure at God's hand; else for a vain shadow of virtue, for the wealth and profit of no man, to punish himself, or to the intent he may be able courageously to suffer adversities, which perchance shall never come to him; this to do they think it a point of extreme madness, and a token of a man cruelly minded towards himself, and unkind toward nature, as one so disdaining to be in her danger, that he renounceth and refuseth all her benefits.

This is their sentence and opinion of virtue and pleasure. And they believe that by man's reason none can be found truer than this, unless any godlier be inspired into man from heaven. Wherein whether they believe well or no, neither the time doth suffer us to discuss, neither it is now necessary. For we have taken upon us to show and declare their lores and ordinances, and not to defend them. But this thing I believe verily, howsoever these decrees be, that there is in no place of the world, neither a more excellent people, neither a more flourishing commonwealth. They be light and quick of body, full of activity and nimbleness, and of more strength than a man would judge them by their stature, which for all that is not too low. And though their soil be not very fruitful, nor their air very wholesome, yet against the air they so defend them with temperate diet, and so order and husband their ground with diligent travail, that in no country is greater increase, and plenty of corn and cattle, nor men's bodies of longer life, and subject or apt to fewer diseases. There therefore, a man may see well and diligently exploited and furnished, not only those things which husbandmen do commonly in other countries, as by craft and cunning to remedy the barrenness of the ground; but also a whole wood by the hands of the people plucked up by the roots in one place, and set again in another place. Wherein was had regard and consideration, not of plenty but of commodious carriage, that wood and timber might be nigher to the sea, or the rivers or the cities. For it is less labour and business to carry grain far by land, than wood. The people be gentle, merry, quick, and fine witted, delighting in quietness, and when need requireth, able to abide and suffer much bodily labour. Else they be not greatly desirous and fond of it; but in the exercise and study of the mind they be never weary. When they had heard me speak of the Greek literature or learning (for in Latin there was nothing that I thought they would greatly allow, besides historians and poets) they made wonderful earnest and importunate suit unto me that I would teach and instruct them in that tongue and learning. I began therefore to read unto them, at the first truly more because I would not seem to refuse the labour, than that I hoped that they would anything profit therein. But when I had gone forward a little, and perceived incontinent by their diligence, that my labour should not be bestowed in vain; for they began so easily to fashion their letters, so plainly to pronounce the words, so quickly to learn by heart, and so surely to rehearse the same, that I marvelled at it, saving that the most part of them were fine and chosen wits and of ripe age, picked out of the company of the learned men, which not only of their own free and voluntary will, but also by the commandment of the council, undertook to learn this language. Therefore in less than three years' space there was nothing in the Greek tongue that they lacked. They were able to read good authors without any stay, if the book were not false. This kind of learning, as I suppose, they took so much the sooner, because it is somewhat allied to them. For I think that this nation took their beginning of the Greeks, because their speech, which in all other points is not much unlike the Persian tongue, keepeth divers signs and tokens of the Greek language in the names of their cities and of their magistrates. They have of me (for when I was determined to enter into my fourth voyage, I cast into the ship in the stead of merchandise a pretty fardel of books, because I intended to come again rather never, than shortly) the most part of Plato's works, more of Aristotle's, also Theophrastus of plants, but in divers places (which I am sorry for) imperfect. For whilst we were sailing, a marmoset chanced upon the book, as it was negligently laid by, which wantonly playing therewith plucked out certain leaves, and tore them in pieces. Of them that have written the grammar, they have only Lascaris. For Theodorus I carried not with me, nor never a dictionary but Hesychius, and Dioscorides. They set great store by Plutarch's books. And they be delighted with Lucian's merry conceits and jests. Of the poets they have Aristophanes, Homer, Euripides, and Sophocles in Aldus' small print. Of the historians they have Thucydides, Herodotus, and Herodian. Also my companion, Tricius Apinatus, carried with him physic books, certain small works of Hippocrates and Galen's Microtechne. The which book they have in great estimation. For though there be almost no nation under heaven that hath less need of physic than they, yet this notwithstanding, physic is nowhere in greater honour; because they count the knowledge of it among the goodliest and most profitable parts of philosophy. For whilest they by the help of this philosophy search out the secret mysteries of nature, they think that they not only receive thereby wonderful great pleasure, but also obtain great thanks and favour of the author and maker thereof. Whom they think, according to the fashion of other artificers, to have set forth the marvellous and gorgeous frame of the world for man to behold. Whom only he hath made of wit and capacity to consider and understand the excellence of so great a work. And therefore (say they) doth he bear more goodwill and love to the curious and diligent beholder and viewer of his work and marveller at the same, than he doth to him, which like a very beast without wit and reason, or as one without sense or moving, hath no regard to so great and so wonderful a spectacle. The wits therefore of the Utopians, inured and exercised in learning, be marvellous quick in the invention of feats helping anything to the advantage and wealth of life. Howbeit two feats they may thank us for. That is, the science of imprinting, and the craft of making paper. And yet not only us but chiefly and principally themselves.

For when we showed to them Aldus his print in books of paper, and told them of the stuff whereof paper is made, and of the feat of graving letters, speaking somewhat more, than we could plainly declare (for there was none of us, that knew perfectly either the one or the other) they forthwith very wittily conjectured the thing. And whereas before they wrote only in skins, in barks of trees, and in reeds, now they have attempted to make paper, and to imprint letters. And though at the first it proved not all of the best, yet by often assaying the same they shortly got the feat of both. And have so brought the matter about that if they had copies of Greek authors, they could lack no books. But now they have no more than I rehearsed before, saving that by printing of books they have multiplied and increased the same into many thousands of copies. Whosoever cometh thither to see the land, being excellent in any gift of wit, or through much and long journeying well experienced and seen in the knowledge of many countries (for the which cause we were very welcome to them) him they receive and entertain wonders gently and lovingly. For they have delight to hear what is done in every land, howbeit very few merchantmen come thither, for what should they bring thither, unless it were iron, or else gold and silver, which they had rather carry home again? Also such things as are to be carried out of their land, they think it more wisdom to carry that gear forth themselves, than that others should come thither to fetch it, to the intent they may the better know the outlands on every side of them, and keep in use the feat and knowledge of sailing.

Of Bondmen, Sick Persons, Wedlock, and divers other matters

They neither make bondmen of prisoners taken in battle, unless it be in battle that they fought themselves, nor of bondmen's children, nor to be short, any man whom they can get out of another country, though he were there a bondman. But either such as among themselves for heinous offences be punished with bondage, or else such as in the cities of other lands for great trespasses be condemned to death. And of this sort of bondmen they have most store.

For many of them they bring home sometimes paying very little for them, yea most commonly getting them gratis. These sorts of bondmen they keep not only in continual work and labour, but also in bands. But their own men they handle hardest, whom they judge more desperate, and to have deserved greater punishment, because they being so godly brought up to virtue in so excellent a commonwealth, could not for all that be refrained from misdoing. Another kind of bondmen they have, when a vile drudge being a poor labourer in another country doth choose of his own free will to be a bondman among them. These they handle and order honestly, and entertain almost as gently as their own free citizens, saving that they put them to a little more labour, as thereto accustomed. If any such be disposed to depart thence (which seldom is seen) they neither hold him against his will, neither send him away with empty hands. The sick (as I said) they see to with great affection, and let nothing at all pass concerning either physic or good diet whereby they may be restored again to their health. Them that be sick of incurable diseases they comfort with sitting by them, with talking with them, and to be short, with all manner of helps that may be. But if the disease be not only incurable, but also full of continual pain and anguish; then the priests and the magistrates exhort the man, seeing he is not able to do any duty of life, and by overliving his own death is noisome and irksome to other, and grievous to himself, that he will determine with himself no longer to cherish that pestilent and painful disease. And seeing his life is to him but a torment, that he will not be unwilling to die, but rather take a good hope to him, and either despatch himself out of that painful life, as out of a prison, or a rack of torment, or else suffer himself willingly to be rid out of it by other. And in so doing they tell him he shall do wisely, seeing by his death he shall lose no commodity, but end his pain. And because in that act he shall follow the counsel of the priests, that is to say, of the interpreters of God's will and pleasure, they show him that he shall do like a godly and a virtuous man. They that be thus persuaded, finish their lives willingly, either with hunger, or else die in their sleep without any feeling of death. But they cause none such to die against his will, nor they use no less diligence and attendance about him, believing this to be an honourable death. Else he that killeth himself before that the priests and the council have allowed the cause of his death, him as unworthy both of the earth and of fire, they cast unburied into some stinking marsh. The woman is not married before she be eighteen years old. The man is four years older before he marry.

If either the man or the woman be proved to have bodily offended before their marriage with another, he or she whether it be is sharply punished. And both the offenders be forbidden ever after in all their life to marry: unless the fault be forgiven by the prince's pardon. But both the goodman and the goodwife of the house where that offence was done, as being slack and negligent in looking to their charge, be in danger of great reproach and infamy. That offence is so sharply punished, because they perceive, that unless they be diligently kept from the liberty of this vice, few will join together in the love of marriage, wherein all the life must be led with one, and also all the griefs and displeasures that come therewith must patiently be taken and borne. Furthermore in choosing wives and husbands they observe earnestly and straitly a custom, which seemed to us very fond and foolish. For a sad and an honest matron showeth the woman, be she maid or widow, naked to the wooer. And likewise a sage and discreet man exhibiteth the wooer naked to the woman. At this custom we laughed and disallowed it as foolish. But they on the other part do greatly wonder at the folly of all other nations, which in buying a colt, whereas a little money is in hazard, be so chary and circumspect, that though he be almost all bare, yet they will not buy him, unless the saddle and all the harness be taken off, lest under those coverings be hid some gall or sore. And yet in choosing a wife, which shall be either pleasure, or displeasure to them all their life after, they be so reckless, that all the residue of the woman's body being covered with clothes, they esteem her scarcely by one hand-breadth (for they can see no more but her face), and so do join her to them not without great jeopardy of evil agreeing together, if anything in her body afterward do offend and mislike them.

For all men be not so wise, as to have respect to the virtuous conditions of the party. And the endowments of the body cause the virtues of the mind more to be esteemed and regarded: yea even in the marriages of wise men. Verily so foul deformity may be hid under those coverings, that it may quite alienate and take away the man's mind from his wife, when it shall not be lawful for their bodies to be separate again. If such deformity happen by any chance after the marriage is consummate and finished, well, there is no remedy but patience. Every man must take his fortune, well-a-worth. But it were well done that a law were made whereby all such deceits might be eschewed and avoided beforehand.

And this were they constrained more earnestly to look upon, because they only of the nations in that part of the world be content every man with one wife apiece.

And matrimony is there never broken, but by death; except adultery break the bond, or else the intolerable wayward manners of either party. For if either of them find themselves for any such cause grieved, they may by the licence of the council change and take another. But the other party liveth ever after in infamy and out of wedlock. But for the husband to put way his wife for no fault, but for that some mishap is fallen to her body, this by no means they will suffer. For they judge it a great point of cruelty, that anybody in their most need of help and comfort should be cast off and forsaken, and that old age, which both bringeth sickness with it, and is a sickness itself, should unkindly and unfaithfully be dealt withal. But now and then it chanceth, whereas the man and the woman cannot well agree between themselves, both of them finding other, with whom they hope to live more quietly and merrily, that they by the full consent of them both be divorced asunder and new married to other. But that not without the authority of the council; which agreeth to no divorces, before they and their wives have diligently tried and examined the matter. Yea and then also they be loath to consent to it, because they know this to be the next way to break love between man and wife, to be in easy hope of a new marriage. Breakers of wedlock be punished with most grievous bondage. And if both the offenders were married, then the parties which in that behalf have suffered wrong, be divorced from the adulterers, if they will, and be married together, or else to whom they list. But if either of them both do still continue in love toward so unkind a bedfellow, the use of wedlock is not to them forbidden, if the party be disposed to follow in toiling and drudgery the person which for that offence is condemned to bondage. And very oft it chanceth that the repentance of the one, and the earnest diligence of the other, doth so move the prince with pity and compassion, that he restoreth the bond person from servitude to liberty and freedom again. But if the same party be taken again in that fault there

is no other way but death. To other trespassers there is no prescript
punishment appointed by any law. But according to the heinous-
ness of the offence, or contrary, so the punishment is moderated by
the discretion of the council. The husbands chastise their wives,
and the parents their children, unless they have done any so horrible
an offence, that the open punishment thereof maketh much for the
advancement of honest manners. But most commonly the most
heinous faults be punished with the incommodity of bondage. For
that they suppose to be to the offenders no less grief, and to the
commonwealth more profitable, than if they should hastily put them
to death, and make them out of the way. For there cometh more
profit of their labour, than of their death, and by their example they
fear other the longer from like offences. But if they being thus used,
do rebel and kick again, then forsooth they be slain as desperate and
wild beasts, whom neither prison nor chain could restrain and keep
under. But they which take their bondage patiently be not left all
hopeless. For after they have been broken and tamed with long
miseries, if then they show such repentance, whereby it may be perceived that they be sorrier for their offence than for their punishment,
sometimes by the prince's prerogative, and sometimes by the voice
and consent of the people, their bondage either is mitigated, or else
clean remitted and forgiven. He that moveth to adultery is in no
less danger and jeopardy than if he had committed adultery indeed.
For in all offences they count the intent and pretensed purpose as
evil as the act or deed itself, for they think that no let ought to excuse
him that did his best to have no let. They set great store by fools.
And as it is great reproach to do to any of them hurt or injury, so
they prohibit not to take pleasure of foolishness. For that, they
think, doth much good to the fools. And if any man be so sad and
stern, that he cannot laugh neither at their words, nor at their deeds,
none of them be committed to his tuition; for fear lest he would not
order them gently and favourably enough, to whom they should
bring no delectation (for other goodness in them is none) much
less any profit should they yield him. To mock a man for his deformity, or for that he lacketh any part or limb of his body, is
counted great dishonesty and reproach, not to him that is mocked,
but to him that mocketh. Which unwisely doth upbraid any man of

that as a vice which was not in his power to eschew. Also as they count and reckon very little wit to be in him, that regardeth not natural beauty and comeliness, so to help the same with paintings, is taken for a vain and a wanton pride, not without great infamy. For they know, even by very experience, that no comeliness of beauty doth so highly commend and advance the wives in the conceit of their husbands, as honest conditions and lowliness. For as love is oftentimes won with beauty, so it is not kept, preserved and continued, but by virtue and obedience. They do not only fear their people from doing evil by punishments, but also allure them to virtue with rewards of honour. Therefore they set up in the market-place the images of notable men, and of such as have been great and bountiful benefactors to the commonwealth, for the perpetual memory of their good acts, and also that the glory and renown of the ancestors may stir and provoke their posterity to virtue. He that inordinately and ambitiously desireth promotions is left all hopeless for ever attaining any promotion as long as he liveth. They live together lovingly. For no magistrate is either haughty or fearful. Fathers they be called, and like fathers they use themselves. The citizens (as it is their duty) do willingly exhibit unto them due honour without any compulsion. Nor the prince himself is not known from the other by his apparel, nor by a crown or diadem, or cap of maintenance, but by a little sheaf of corn carried before him. And so a taper of wax is borne before the bishop, whereby only he is known. They have but few laws. For to people so instruct and institute very few do suffice. Yea this thing they chiefly reprove among other nations, that innumerable books of laws and expositions upon the same be not sufficient. But they think it against all right and justice that men should be bound to those laws, which either be in number more than be able to be read, or else blinder and darker, than that any man can well understand them. Furthermore they utterly exclude and banish all proctors, and sergeants at the law; which craftily handle matters, and subtly dispute of the laws. For they think it most meet, that every man should plead his own matter, and tell the same tale before the judge that he would tell to his man of law. So shall there be less circumstance of words, and the truth shall sooner come to light, whiles the judge with a discreet

judgment doth weigh the words of him whom no lawyer hath instruct with deceit, and whiles he helpeth and beareth out simple
wits against the false and malicious circumventions of crafty children. This is hard to be observed in other countries, in so infinite a
number of blind and intricate laws. But in Utopia every man is a
cunning lawyer. For (as I said) they have very few laws; and the
plainer and grosser that any interpretation is, that they allow as
most just. For all laws (say they) be made and published only to
the intent that by them every man should be put in remembrance
of his duty. But the crafty and subtle interpretation of them can
put very few in that remembrance (for they be but few that do perceive them), whereas the simple, the plain and gross meaning of the
laws is open to every man.

Else as touching the vulgar sort of the people, which be both most
in number, and have most need to know their duties, were it not
as good for them, that no law were made at all, as when it is made,
to bring so blind an interpretation upon it, that without great wit
and long arguing no man can discuss it? To the finding out whereof
neither the gross judgment of the people can attain, neither the
whole life of them that be occupied in working for their livings can
suffice thereto. These virtues of the Utopians have caused their next
neighbours and borderers, which live free and under no subjection
(for the Utopians long ago, have delivered many of them from
tyranny) to take magistrates of them, some for a year, and some for
five years' space. Which when the time of their office is expired,
they bring home again with honour and praise, and take new ones
again with them into their country. These nations have undoubtedly
very well and wholesomely provided for their commonwealths.
For seeing that both the making and the marring of the weal public
doth depend and hang upon the manners of the rulers and magistrates, what officers could they more wisely have chosen, than those
which cannot be led from honesty by bribes (for to them that shortly
after shall depart thence into their own country money should be
unprofitable) nor yet be moved either with favour, or malice towards
any man, as being strangers, and unacquainted with the people?
The which two vices of affection and avarice, where they take place
in judgments, incontinent they break justice, the strongest and

surest bond of a commonwealth. These peoples which fetch their officers and rulers from them, the Utopians call their fellows. And other to whom they have been beneficial, they call their friends. As touching leagues, which in other places beween country and country be so oft concluded, broken and made again, they never make none with any nation. For to what purpose serve leagues? say they. As though nature had not set sufficient love between man and man. And who so regardeth not nature, think you that he will pass for words? They be brought into this opinion chiefly, because that in those parts of the world, leagues between princes be wont to be kept and observed very slenderly. For here in Europe, and especially in these parts where the faith and religion of Christ reigneth, the majesty of leagues is everywhere esteemed holy and inviolable, partly through the justice and goodness of princes, and partly through the reverence of great bishops. Which like as they make no promise themselves but they do very religiously perform the same, so they exhort all princes in any wise to abide by their promises, and them that refuse or deny so to do, by their pontifical power and authority they compel thereto. And surely they think well that it might seem a very reproachful thing, if in the leagues of them which by a peculiar name be called faithful, faith should have no place. But in that new found part of the world, which is scarcely so far from us beyond the line equinoctial as our life and manners be dissident from theirs, no trust nor confidence is in leagues. But the more and holier ceremonies the league is knit up with, the sooner it is broken by some cavillation found in the words, which many times of purpose be so craftily put in and placed, that the bands can never be so sure nor so strong, but they will find some hole open to creep out at, and to break both league and truth. The which crafty dealing, yea the which fraud and deceit, if they should know it to be practised among private men in their bargains and contracts, they would incontinent cry out at it with a sour countenance, as an offence most detestable, and worthy to be punished with a shameful death: yea even very they that advance themselves authors of like council given to princes. Wherefore it may well be thought, either that all justice is but a base and a low virtue, and which abaseth itself far under the high dignity of kings; or at the least-

wise, that there be two justices, the one meet for the inferior sort of
the people, going afoot and creeping below on the ground, and
bound down on every side with many bands because it shall not run
at rovers; the other a princely virtue, which like as it is of much
higher majesty than the other poor justice, so also it is of much more
liberty, as to the which nothing is unlawful that it lusteth after.
These manners of princes (as I said) which be there so evil keepers
of leagues, cause the Utopians, as I suppose, to make no leagues at
all, which perchance would change their mind if they lived here.
Howbeit they think that though leagues be never so faithfully
observed and kept, yet the custom of **making** leagues was very evil
begun. For this causeth men (as though nations which be separate
asunder, by the space of a little hill or a river, were coupled together
by no society or bond of nature) to think themselves born adversaries
and enemies one to another, and that it is lawful for the one to seek
the death and destruction of the other, if leagues were not: yea, and
that after the leagues be accorded, friendship doth not grow and
increase; but the licence of robbing and stealing doth still remain, as
farforth as for lack of foresight and advisement in writing the
words of the league, any sentence or clause to the contrary is not
therein sufficiently comprehended. But they be of a contrary opinion.
That is, that no man ought to be counted an enemy, which hath
done no injury. And that the fellowship of nature is a strong league;
and that men be better and more surely knit together by love and
benevolence, than by covenants of leagues; by hearty affection of
mind, than by words.

Of Warfare

War or battle as a thing very beastly, and yet to no kind of beasts
in so much use as it is to man, they do detest and abhor. And contrary to the custom almost of all other nations, they count nothing
so much against glory, as glory gotten in war. And therefore
though they do daily practise and exercise themselves in the discipline of war, and that not only the men, but also the women upon
certain appointed days, lest they should be to seek in the feat of
arms, if need should require, yet they never [to] go to battle, but

either in the defence of their own country, or to drive out of their
friends' land the enemies that have invaded it, or by their power
to deliver from the yoke and bondage of tyranny some people, that
be oppressed with tyranny. Which thing they do of mere pity and
compassion. Howbeit they send help to their friends; not ever in
their defence, but sometimes also to requite and revenge injuries
before to them done. But this they do not unless their counsel and
advice in the matter be asked, whilest it is yet new and fresh. For
if they find the cause probable, and if the contrary part will not
restore again such things as be of them justly demanded, then they
be the chief authors and makers of the war. Which they do not only
as oft as by inroads and invasions of soldiers, preys and booties be
driven away, but then also much more mortally, when their friends'
merchants in any land, either under the pretence of unjust laws, or
else by the wresting and wrong understanding of good laws, do
sustain an unjust accusation under the colour of justice. Neither
the battle which the Utopians fought for the Nephelogetes against
the Alaopolitanes a little before our time was made for any other
cause, but that the Nephelogete merchantmen, as the Utopians
thought, suffered wrong of the Alaopolitanes, under the pretence of
right. But whether it were right or wrong, it was with so cruel and
mortal war revenged, the countries round about joining their help
and power to the puissance and malice of both parties, that most
flourishing and wealthy peoples, being some of them shrewdly
shaken, and some of them sharply beaten, the mischiefs were not
finished nor ended, until the Alaopolitanes at the last were yielded
up as bondmen into the jurisdiction of the Nephelogetes. For the
Utopians fought not this war for themselves. And yet the Nephelogetes before the war, when the Alaopolitanes flourished in wealth,
were nothing to be compared with them. So eagerly the Utopians
prosecute the injuries done to their friends, yea, in money matters;
and not their own likewise. For if they by cunning or guile be defrauded of their goods, so that no violence be done to their bodies,
they wreak their anger by abstaining from occupying with that
nation, until they have made satisfaction. Not for because they set
less store by their own citizens, than by their friends; but that they
take the loss of their friends' money more heavily than the loss of

their own. Because that their friends' merchantmen, forasmuch as that they lose is their own private goods, sustain great damage by the loss. But their own citizens lose nothing but of the common goods, and of that which was at home plentiful and almost superfluous, else had it not been sent forth. Therefore no man feeleth the loss. And for this cause they think it too cruel an act, to revenge that loss with the death of many, the incommodity of the which loss no man feeleth neither in his life, neither in his living. But if it chance that any of their men in any other country be maimed or killed, whether it be done by a common or a private counsel, knowing and trying out the truth of the matter by their ambassadors, unless the offenders be rendered unto them in recompense of the injury, they will not be appeased; but incontinent they proclaim war against them. The offenders yielded, they punish either with death or with bondage. They be not only sorry, but also ashamed to achieve the victory with much bloodshed, counting it great folly to buy precious wares too dear. They rejoice and avaunt themselves, if they vanquish and oppress their enemies by craft and deceit. And for that act they make a general triumph, and as if the matter were manfully handled, they set up a pillar of stone in the place where they so vanquished their enemies, in token of the victory. For then they glory, then they boast and crack that they have played the men indeed, when they have so overcome, as no other living creature but only man could; that is to say, by the might and puissance of wit. For with bodily strength (say they) bears, lions, boars, wolves, dogs and other wild beasts do fight. And as the most part of them do pass us in strength and fierce courage, so in wit and reason we be much stronger than they all. Their chief and principal purpose in war, is to obtain that thing, which if they had before obtained, they would not have moved battle. But if that be not possible, they take so cruel vengeance of them, which be in the fault, that ever after they be afraid to do the like. This is their chief and principal intent, which they immediately and first of all prosecute, and set forward. But yet so, that they be more circumspect in avoiding and eschewing jeopardies, than they be desirous of praise and renown. Therefore immediately after that war is once solemnly denounced, they procure many proclamations signed with their own common seal to be

set up privily at one time in their enemies' land, in places most
frequented. In these proclamations they promise great rewards to
him that will kill their enemies' prince, and somewhat less gifts, but
them very great also, for every head of them, whose names be in
the said proclamations contained. They be those whom they count
their chief adversaries, next unto the prince. Whatsoever is prescribed unto him that killeth any of the proclaimed persons, that is
doubled to him that bringeth any of the same to them alive; yea,
and to the proclaimed persons themselves, if they will change their
minds and come into them, taking their parts, they proffer the same
great rewards with pardon and surety of their lives. Therefore it
quickly cometh to pass that they have all other men in suspicion,
and be unfaithful and mistrusting among themselves one to another,
living in great fear, and in no less jeopardy. For it is well known,
that divers times the most part of them (and specially the prince
himself) hath been betrayed of them, in whom they put their most
hope and trust. So that there is no manner of act nor deed that gifts
and rewards do not enforce men unto. And in rewards they keep
no measure. But remembering and considering into how great
hazard and jeopardy they call them, endeavour themselves to recompense the greatness of the danger with like great benefits. And
therefore they promise not only wonderful great abundance of gold,
but also lands of great revenues lying in most safe places among their
friends. And their promises they perform faithfully without any
fraud or deceit. This custom of buying and selling adversaries among
other people is disallowed, as a cruel act of a base and a cowardish
mind. But they in this behalf think themselves much praiseworthy,
as who like wise men by this means despatch great wars without
any battle or skirmish. Yea they count it also a deed of pity and
mercy, because that by the death of a few offenders the lives of a
great number of innocents, as well of their own men as also of their
enemies, be ransomed and saved, which in fighting should have
been slain. For they do no less pity the base and common sort of
their enemies' people, than they do their own; knowing that they
be driven to war against their wills by the furious madness of their
princes and heads. If by none of these means the matter go forward
as they would have it, then they procure occasions of debate and

dissension to be spread among their enemies. As by bringing the
prince's brother, or some of the noblemen, in hope to obtain the
kingdom. If this way prevail not, then they raise up the people that
be next neighbours and borderers to their enemies, and them they
set in their necks under the colour of some old title of right, such as
kings do never lack. To them they promise their help and aid in
their war. And as for money they give them abundance. But of
their own citizens they send to them few or none. Whom they
make so much of and love so entirely, that they would not be willing
to change any of them for their adversary's prince. But their gold
and silver, because they keep it all for this only purpose, they lay it
out frankly and freely; as who should live even as wealthily, if they
had bestowed it every penny. Yea, and besides their riches, which
they keep at home, they have also an infinite treasure abroad, by
reason that (as I said before) many nations be in their debt. Therefore they hire soldiers out of all countries and send them to battle,
but chiefly of the Zapoletes. This people is five hundred miles from
Utopia eastward. They be hideous, savage and fierce, dwelling in
wild woods and high mountains, where they were bred and brought
up. They be of an hard nature, able to abide and sustain heat, cold
and labour, abhorring from all delicate dainties, occupying no husbandry nor tillage of the ground, homely and rude both in the
building of their houses and in their apparel, given unto no goodness, but only to the breeding and bringing up of cattle. The most
part of their living is by hunting and stealing. They be born only
to war, which they diligently and earnestly seek for. And when
they have gotten it, they be wonders glad thereof. They go forth of
their country in great companies together, and whosoever lacketh
soldiers, there they proffer their service for small wages. This is
only the craft that they have to get their living by. They maintain
their life by seeking their death. For them with whom they be in
wages they fight hardily, fiercely, and faithfully. But they bind themselves for no certain time. But upon this condition they enter into
bonds, that the next day they will take part with the other side for
greater wages, and the next day after that, they will be ready to
come back again for a little more money. There be few wars there-
away, wherein is not a great number of them in both parties. There-

fore it daily chanceth that nigh kinsfolk, which were hired together on one part, and there very friendly and familiarly used themselves one with another, shortly after being separate into contrary parts, run one against another enviously and fiercely, and forgetting both kindred and friendship, thrust their swords one in another. And that for none other cause, but that they be hired of contrary princes for a little money. Which they do so highly regard and esteem, that they will easily be provoked to change parts for a halfpenny more wages by the day. So quickly they have taken a smack in covetousness. Which for all that is to them no profit. For that they get by fighting, immediately they spend unthriftily and wretchedly in riot. This people fight for the Utopians against all nations, because they give them greater wages than any other nation will. For the Utopians like as they seek good men to use well, so they seek these evil and vicious men to abuse. Whom, when need requireth, with promises of great rewards they put forth into great jeopardies. From whence the most part of them never cometh again to ask their rewards. But to them that remain alive they pay that which they promised faithfully, that they may be the more willing to put themselves in like dangers another time. Nor the Utopians pass not how many of them they bring to destruction. For they believe that they should do a very good deed for all mankind, if they could rid out of the world all that foul stinking den of that most wicked and cursed people. Next unto these they use the soldiers of them whom they fight for. And then the help of their other friends. And last of all, they join to their own citizens. Among whom they give to one of tried virtue and prowess the rule, governance, and conduction of the whole army. Under him they appoint two other, which, whilest he is safe, be both private and out of office. But if he be taken or slain, the one of the other two succeedeth him, as it were by inheritance. And if the second miscarry, then the third taketh his room, lest that (as the chance of battle is uncertain and doubtful) the jeopardy or death of the captain should bring the whole army in hazard. They choose soldiers, out of every city, those which put forth themselves willingly. For they thrust no man forth into war against his will. Because they believe, if any man be fearful and faint-hearted of nature, he will not only do no manful and hardy act himself, but also be occasion of cowardice to his fellows. But if any battle be made against their own country, then they put these cowards (so that they be strong-bodied) in ships among other bold-hearted men. Or else they dispose them upon the walls, from whence they may not fly. Thus what for shame that their enemies be at hand, and what for because they be without hope of running away, they forget all fear. And many times extreme necessity turneth cowardice into prowess and manliness. But as none of them is thrust forth of his country into war against his will, so women that be willing to accompany their husbands in times of war be not prohibited or stopped. Yet they provoke and exhort them to it with praises. And in set field the wives do stand every one by her own husband's side. Also every man is compassed next about with his own children, kinsfolks, and alliance; that they, whom nature chiefly moveth to mutual succour, thus standing together, may help one another. It is a great reproach and dishonesty for the husband to come home without his wife, or the wife without her husband, or the son without his father. And therefore if the other part stick so hard by it that the battle come to their hands, it is fought with great slaughter and bloodshed, even to the utter destruction of both parts. For as they make all the means and shifts that may be to keep themselves from the necessity of fighting, so that they may despatch the battle by their hired soldiers; so when there is no remedy, but that they must needs fight themselves, then they do as courageously fall to it, as before, whiles they might, they did wisely avoid it. Nor they be not most fierce at the first brunt. But in continuance by little and little their fierce courage increaseth, with so stubborn and obstinate minds, that they will rather die than give back an inch. For that surety of living, which every man hath at home being joined with no careful anxiety or remembrance how their posterity shall live after them (for this pensiveness oftentimes breaketh and abateth courageous stomachs) maketh them stout and hardy, and disdainful to be conquered. Moreover their knowledge in chivalry and feats of arms putteth them in a good hope. Finally the wholesome and virtuous opinions, wherein they were brought up even from their childhood, partly through learning, and partly through the good ordinances and laws of their weal public, augment and increase their manful courage. By reason whereof they neither set so little store by their lives, that they will rashly and unadvisedly cast them away: nor they be not so far in lewd and fond love therewith, that they will shamefully covet to keep them, when honesty biddeth leave them. When the battle is hottest and in all places most fierce and fervent, a band of chosen and picked young men, which be sworn to live and die together, take upon them to destroy their adversary's captain. Him they invade, now with privy wiles, now by open strength. At him they strike both near and far off. He is assailed with a long and a continual assault, fresh men still coming in the wearied men's places. And seldom it chanceth (unless he save himself by flying) that he is not either slain, or else taken prisoner and yielded to his enemies alive. If they win the field, they persecute not their enemies with the violent rage of slaughter. For they had rather take them alive than kill them. Neither they do so follow the chase and pursuit of their enemies, but they leave behind them one part of their host in battle array under their standards. Insomuch that if all their whole army be discomfited and overcome saving the rearward, and that they therewith achieve the victory, then they had rather let all their enemies 'scape, than to follow them out of array. For they remember, it hath chanced unto themselves more than once; the whole power and strength of their host being vanquished and put to flight, whilest their enemies rejoicing in the victory have persecuted them flying some one way and some another; a few of their men lying in an ambush, there ready at all occasions, have suddenly risen upon them thus dispersed and scattered out of array, and through presumption of safety unadvisedly pursuing the chase, and have incontinent changed the fortune of the whole battle, and spite of their teeth wresting out of their hands the sure and undoubted victory, being a little before conquered, have for their part conquered the conquerors. It is hard to say whether they be craftier in laying an ambush, or wittier in avoiding the same. You would think they intend to fly, when they mean nothing less. And contrariwise when they go about that purpose, you would believe it were the least part of their thought. For if they perceive themselves either overmatched in number, or closed in too narrow a place, then they remove their camp either in the night season with silence, or

by some policy they deceive their enemies, or in the daytime they
retire back so softly, that it is no less jeopardy to meddle with them
when they give back, than when they press on. They fence and
fortify their camp surely with a deep and a broad trench. The earth
thereof is cast inward. Nor they do not set drudges and slaves awork
about it. It is done by the hands of the soldiers themselves. All the
whole army worketh upon it, except them that watch in harness
before the trench for sudden adventures. Therefore by the labour
of so many a large trench closing in a great compass of ground is
made in less time than any man would believe. Their armour or
harness, which they wear, is sure and strong to receive strokes, and
handsome for all movings and gestures of the body, insomuch that
it is not unwieldy to swim in. For in the discipline of their warfare
among other feats they learn to swim in harness. Their weapons be
arrows afar off, which they shoot both strongly and surely, not only
footmen, but also horsemen. At hand strokes they use not swords
but pollaxes, which be mortal, as well in sharpness, as in weight,
both for foins and down strokes. Engines for war they devise and
invent wonders wittily. Which when they be made they keep very
secret, lest if they should be known before need require, they should
be but laughed at and serve to no purpose. But in making them,
hereunto they have chief respect, that they be both easy to be carried,
and handsome to be moved and turned about. Truce taken with
their enemies for a short time they do so firmly and faithfully keep,
that they will not break it; no, not though they be thereunto provoked. They do not waste nor destroy their enemies' land with
foragings, nor they burn not up their corn. Yea, they save it as much
as may be from being overrun and trodden down either with men
or horses, thinking that it groweth for their own use and profit.
They hurt no man that is unarmed, unless he be an espial. All cities
that be yielded unto them they defend. And such as they win by
force of assault, they neither despoil nor sack, but them that withstood and dissuaded the yielding up of the same, they put to death;
the other soldiers they punish with bondage. All the weak multitude
they leave untouched. If they know that any citizens counselled to
yield and render up the city, to them they give part of the condemned
men's goods. The residue they distribute and give freely among

them, whose help they had in the same war. For none of themselves taketh any portion of the prey. But when the battle is finished and ended, they put their friends to never a penny cost of all the charges that they were at, but lay it upon their necks that be conquered. Them they burden with the whole charge of their expenses, which they demand of them partly in money to be kept for like use of battle, and partly in lands of great revenues to be paid unto them yearly for ever. Such revenues they have now in many countries. Which by little and little rising of divers and sundry causes be increased above seven hundred thousand ducats by the year. Thither they send forth some of their citizens as lieutenants, to live there sumptuously like men of honour and renown. And yet, this notwithstanding, much money is saved, which cometh to the common treasury; unless it so chance that they had rather trust the country with the money. Which many times they do so long, until they have need to occupy it. And it seldom happeneth that they demand all. Of these lands they assign part unto them which, at their request and exhortation, put themselves in such jeopardies as I spake of before. If any prince stir up war against them, intending to invade their land, they meet him incontinent out of their own borders with great power and strength. For they never lightly make war in their own countries. Nor they be never brought into so extreme necessity as to take help out of foreign lands into their own island.

Of the Religions in Utopia

There be divers kinds of religion not only in sundry parts of the island, but also in divers places of every city. Some worship for God, the sun; some, the moon; some, some other of the planets. There be that give worship to a man that was once of excellent virtue or of famous glory, not only as God, but also as the chiefest and highest God. But the most and the wisest part (rejecting all these) believe that there is a certain godly power unknown, everlasting, incomprehensible, inexplicable, far above the capacity and reach of man's wit, dispersed throughout all the world, not in bigness, but in virtue and power. Him they call the father of all. To him alone they attribute the beginnings, the increasings, the proceedings, the changes and the ends of all things. Neither they give divine honours to any other than to him. Yea all the other also, though they be in divers opinions, yet in this point they agree all together with the wisest sort, in believing that there is one chief and principal God, the maker and ruler of the whole world: whom they all commonly in their country language call Mithra. But in this they disagree, that among some he is counted one, and among some another. For every one of them, whatsoever that is which he taketh for the chief God, thinketh it to be the very same nature, to whose only divine might and majesty the sum and sovereignty of all things by the consent of all people is attributed and given. Howbeit they all begin by little and little to forsake and fall from this variety of superstitions, and to agree together in that religion which seemeth by reason to pass and excel the residue. And it is not to be doubted, but all the other would long ago have been abolished, but that whatsoever unprosperous thing happened to any of them, as he was minded to change his religion, the fearfulness of people did take it, not as a thing coming by chance, but as sent from God out of heaven. As though the God whose honour he was forsaking would revenge that wicked purpose against him. But after they heard us speak of the name of Christ, of his doctrine, laws, miracles, and of the no less wonderful constancy of so many martyrs, whose blood willingly shed brought a great number of nations throughout all parts of the world into their sect; you will not believe with how glad minds, they agreed unto the same: whether it were by the secret inspiration of God, or else for that they thought it next unto that opinion, which among them is counted the chiefest. Howbeit I think this was no small help and furtherance in the matter, that they heard us say, that Christ instituted among his, all things common; and that the same community doth yet remain amongst the rightest Christian companies. Verily howsoever, it came to pass, many of them consented together in our religion, and were washed in the holy water of baptism. But because among us four (for no more of us was left alive, two of our company being dead) there was no priest; which I am right sorry for; they being entered and instructed in all other points of our religion, lack only those sacraments, which here none but priests do minister. Howbeit they understand and perceive them and be very desirous of the same. Yea, they reason and dispute the matter earnestly among themselves, whether without the sending of a Christian bishop, one chosen out of their own people may receive the order of priesthood. And truly they were minded to choose one. But at my departure from them they had chosen none. They also which do not agree to Christ's religion, fear no man from it, nor speak against any man that hath received it. Saving that one of our company in my presence was sharply punished. He as soon as he was baptised began against our wills, with more earnest affection than wisdom, to reason of Christ's religion; and began to wax so hot in his matter, that he did not only prefer our religion before all other, but also did utterly despise and condemn all other, calling them profane, and the followers of them wicked and devilish and the children of everlasting damnation. When he had thus long reasoned the matter, they laid hold on him, accused him and condemned him into exile, not as a despiser of religion, but as a seditious person and a raiser up of dissension among the people. For this is one of the ancientest laws among them; that no man shall be blamed for reasoning in the maintenance of his own religion. For King Utopus, even at the first beginning, hearing that the inhabitants of the land were, before his coming thither, at continual dissension and strife among themselves for their religions; perceiving also that this common dissension (whilest every several sect took several parts in fighting for their country) was the only occasion of his conquest over them all: as soon as he had gotten the victory, first of all he made a decree, that it should be lawful for every man to favour and follow what religion he would, and that he might do the best he could to bring other to his opinion, so that he did it peaceably, gently, quietly, and soberly, without haste and contentious rebuking and inveighing against other. If he could not by fair and gentle speech induce them unto his opinion yet he should use no kind of violence, and refrain from displeasant and seditious words. To him that would vehemently and fervently in this cause strive and contend was decreed banishment or bondage. This law did King Utopus make not only for the maintenance of peace, which he saw through continual contention and mortal hatred utterly extinguished; but also because he thought this decree should make

for the furtherance of religion. Whereof he durst define and determine nothing unadvisedly, as doubting whether God desiring manifold and divers sorts of honour, would inspire sundry men with
sundry kinds of religion. And this surely he thought a very unmeet
and foolish thing, and a point of arrogant presumption, to compel
all other by violence and threatenings to agree to the same that thou
believest to be true. Furthermore though there be one religion which
alone is true, and all other vain and superstitious, yet did he well
foresee (so that the matter were handled with reason, and sober
modesty) that the truth of its own power would at the last issue
out and come to light. But if contention and debate in that behalf
should continually be used, as the worst men be most obstinate and
stubborn, and in their evil opinion most constant; he perceived that
then the best and holiest religion would be trodden underfoot and
destroyed by most vain superstitions, even as good corn is by thorns
and weeds overgrown and choked. Therefore all this matter he left
undiscussed, and gave to every man free liberty and choice to believe
what he would. Saving that he earnestly and straightly charged
them, that no man should conceive so vile and base an opinion of
the dignity of man's nature, as to think that the souls do die and
perish with the body; or that the world runneth at all adventures
governed by no divine providence. And therefore they believe that
after this life vices be extremely punished and virtues bountifully
rewarded. Him that is of a contrary opinion they count not in the
number of men, as one that hath abased the high nature of his soul
to the vileness of brute beasts' bodies, much less in the number of
their citizens, whose laws and ordinances, if it were not for fear, he
would nothing at all esteem. For you may be sure that he will study
either with craft privily to mock, or else violently to break the common laws of his country, in whom remaineth no further fear than of
the laws, nor no further hope than of the body. Wherefore he that
is thus minded is deprived of all honours, excluded from all offices
and rejected from all common administrations in the weal public.
And thus he is of all sort despised, as of an unprofitable and of a base
and vile nature. Howbeit they put him to no punishment, because
they be persuaded that it is in no man's power to believe what he list.
No, nor they constrain him not with threatenings to dissemble his

mind and show countenance contrary to his thought. For deceit and falsehood and all manner of lies, as next unto fraud, they do marvellously detest and abhor. But they suffer him not to dispute in his opinion, and that only among the common people. For else apart among the priests and men of gravity they do not only suffer, but also exhort him to dispute and argue, hoping that at the last, that madness will give place to reason. There be also other, and of them no small number, which be not forbidden to speak their minds, as grounding their opinion upon some reason, being in their living neither evil nor vicious. Their heresy is much contrary to the other. For they believe that the souls of brute beasts be immortal and everlasting. But nothing to be compared with ours in dignity, neither ordained and predestinate to like felicity. For all they believe certainly and surely that man's bliss shall be so great, that they do mourn and lament every man's sickness, but no man's death, unless it be one whom they see depart from his life carefully and against his will. For this they take for a very evil token, as though the soul being in despair and vexed in conscience, through some privy and secret forefeeling of the punishment now at hand, were afraid to depart. And they think he shall not be welcome to God, which, when he is called, runneth not to him gladly, but is drawn by force and sore against his will. They therefore that see this kind of death do abhor it, and them that so die they bury with sorrow and silence. And when they have prayed God to be merciful to the soul and mercifully to pardon the infirmities thereof, they cover the dead corse with earth. Contrariwise all that depart merrily and full of good hope, for them no man mourneth, but followeth the hearse with joyful singing, commending the souls to God with great affection. And at the last, not with mourning sorrow, but with a great reverence they burn the bodies. And in the same place they set up a pillar of stone, with the dead man's titles therein graved. When they be come home they rehearse his virtuous manners and his good deeds. But no part of his life is so oft or gladly talked of as his merry death. They think that this remembrance of their virtue and goodness doth vehemently provoke and enforce the quick to virtue. And that nothing can be more pleasant and acceptable to the dead. Whom they suppose to be present among them, when they talk of

them, though to the dull and feeble eyesight of mortal men they
be invisible. For it were an inconvenient thing that the blessed
should not be at liberty to go whither they would. And it were a
point of great unkindness in them to have utterly cast away the
desire of visiting and seeing their friends, to whom they were in their
lifetime joined by mutual love and charity. Which in good men
after their death they count to be rather increased than diminished.
They believe therefore that the dead be presently conversant among
the quick, as beholders and witnesses of all their words and deeds.
Therefore, they go more courageously to their business as having a
trust and affiance in such overseers. And this same belief of the
present conversation of their forefathers and ancestors among them
feareth them from all secret dishonesty. They utterly despise and
mock soothsayings and divinations of things to come by the flight
or voices of birds, and all other divinations of vain superstition,
which in other countries be in great observation. But they highly
esteem and worship miracles that come by no help of nature, as
works and witnesses of the present power of God. And such they
say do chance there very often. And sometimes in great and doubtful matters, by common intercession and prayers, they procure and
obtain them with a sure hope and confidence, and a steadfast belief.

They think that the contemplation of nature and the praise thereof
coming, is to God a very acceptable honour. Yet there be many so
earnestly bent and affectioned to religion, that they pass nothing
for learning, nor give their minds to no knowledge of things. But
idleness they utterly forsake and eschew, thinking felicity after this
life to be gotten and obtained by busy labours and good exercises.
Some therefore of them attend upon the sick, some amend highways, cleanse ditches, repair bridges, dig turfs, gravel and stones,
fell and cleave wood, bring wood, corn, and other things into the
cities in carts, and serve not only in common works, but also in
private labours as servants, yea, more than bondmen. For whatsoever unpleasant, hard and vile work is anywhere, from the which
labour, loathsomeness and desperation doth frighten other, all that
they take upon them willingly and gladly, procuring quiet and rest
to other, remaining in continual work and labour themselves, not
upbraiding others therewith. They neither reprove other men's

lives, nor glory in their own. These men the more serviceable they behave themselves, the more they be honoured of all men. Yet they be divided into two sects. The one is of them that live single and chaste, abstaining not only from the company of women, but also from the eating of flesh, and some of them from all manner of beasts. Which utterly rejecting the pleasures of this present life as hurtful, be all wholly set upon the desire of the life to come by watching and sweating, hoping shortly to obtain it, being in the mean season merry and lusty. The other sect is no less desirous of labour, but they embrace matrimony, not despising the solace thereof, thinking that they cannot be discharged of their bounden duties towards nature without labour and toil, nor towards their native country without procreation of children. They abstain from no pleasure that doth nothing hinder them from labour. They love the flesh of four-footed beasts, because they believe that by that meat they be made hardier and stronger to work. The Utopians count this sect the wiser, but the other the holier. Which, in that they prefer single life before matrimony, and that sharp life before an easier life, if herein they grounded upon reason they would mock them. But now forasmuch as they say they be led to it by religion, they honour and worship them. And these be they whom in their language by a peculiar name, they call Buthrescas, the which word by interpretation signifieth to us men of religion or religious men. They have priests of exceeding holiness, and therefore very few. For there be but thirteen in every city according to the number of their churches, saving when they go forth to battle. For then seven of them go forth with the army; in whose stead so many new be made at home. But the other at their return home again re-enter every one into his own place, they that be above the number, until such time as they succeed into the places of the other at their dying, be in the mean season continually in company with the bishop. For he is the chief head of them all. They be chosen of the people, as the other magistrates be, by secret voices for the avoiding of strife. After their election they be consecrate of their own company. They be overseers of all divine matters, orderers of religions, and as it were judges and masters of manners. And it is a great dishonesty and shame to be rebuked or spoken to by any of them for dissolute and incontinent living. But as it is their office to give good exhortations and counsel, so is it the duty of the prince and the other magistrates to correct and punish offenders, saving that the priests, whom they find exceeding vicious livers, them they excommunicate from having any interest in divine matters. And there is almost no punishment among them more feared. For they run in very great infamy, and be inwardly tormented with a secret fear of religion, and shall not long 'scape free with their bodies. For unless they by quick repentance approve the amendment of their lives to the priests, they be taken and punished of the council, as wicked and irreligious. Both childhood and youth is instructed and taught of them. Nor they be not more diligent to instruct them in learning, than in virtue and good manners. For they use with very great endeavour and diligence to put into the heads of their children, whiles they be yet tender and pliant, good opinions and profitable for the conservation of their weal public. Which when they be once rooted in children, do remain with them all their life after, and be wonders profitable for the defence and maintenance of the state of the commonwealth. Which never decayeth but through vices rising of evil opinions. The priests, unless they be women (for that kind is not excluded from priesthood, howbeit few be chosen, and none but widows and old women), the men priests, I say, take to their wives the chiefest women in all their country. For to no office among the Utopians is more honour and pre-eminence given. Insomuch that if they commit any offence, they be under no common judgment, but be left only to God, and themselves. For they think it not lawful to touch him with man's hand, be he never so vicious, which after so singular a sort was dedicate and consecrate to God, as a holy offering. This manner may they easily observe, because they have so few priests, and do choose them with such circumspection. For it scarcely ever chanceth that the most virtuous among virtuous, which in respect only of his virtue is advanced to so high a dignity, can fall to vice and wickedness. And if it should chance indeed (as man's nature is mutable and frail) yet by reason they be so few and promoted to no might nor power, but only honour, it were not to be feared that any great damage by them should happen and ensue to the commonwealth. They have so rare and few priests, lest if the honour were communicate to many, the dignity of the order, which among them now is so highly esteemed, should run in contempt. Specially because they think it hard to find many so good as to be meet for that dignity, to the execution and discharge whereof it is not sufficient to be endued with mean virtues. Furthermore these priests be not more esteemed of their own countrymen, than they be of foreign and strange countries. Which thing may hereby plainly appear. And I think also that this is the cause of it. For whiles the arm[i]es be fighting together in open field, they a little beside, not far off kneel upon their knees in their hallowed vestments, holding up their hands to heaven, praying first of all for peace, next for victory of their own part, but to neither part a bloody victory. If their host get the upper hand, they run into the main battle and restrain their own men from slaying and cruelly pursuing their vanquished enemies. Which enemies, if they do but see them and speak to them, it is enough for the safeguard of their lives. And the touching of their clothes defendeth and saveth all their goods from ravine and spoil. This thing hath advanced them to so great worship and true majesty among all nations, that many times they have as well preserved their own citizens from the cruel force of their enemies, as they have their enemies from the furious rage of their own men. For it is well known, that when their own army hath reculed and in despair turned back and run away, their enemies fiercely pursuing with slaughter and spoil, then the priests coming between have stayed the murder, and parted both the hosts. So that peace hath been made and concluded between both parts upon equal and indifferent conditions. For there was never any nation, so fierce, so cruel and rude, but they had them in such reverence, that they counted their bodies hallowed and sanctified, and therefore not to be violently and unreverently touched.

They keep holy day the first and the last day of every month and year, dividing the year into months, which they measure by the course of the moon, as they do the year by the course of the sun. The first days they call in their language Cynemernes and the last Trapemernes, the which words may be interpreted, primifest and finifest, or else in our speech, first feast and last feast. Their churches be very gorgeous and not only of fine and curious workmanship, but also (which in the fewness of them was necessary) very wide and large, and able to receive a great company of people. But they be all somewhat dark. Howbeit that was not done through ignorance in building, but as they say, by the counsel of the priests. Because they thought that over much light doth disperse men's cogitations, whereas in dim and doubtful light they be gathered together, and more earnestly fixed upon religion and devotion; which because it is not there of one sort among all men, and yet all the kinds and fashions of it, though they be sundry and manifold, agree together in the honour of the divine nature as going divers ways to one end; therefore nothing is seen nor heard in the churches, which seemeth not to agree indifferently with them all. If there be a distinct kind of sacrifice peculiar to any several sect, that they execute at home in their own houses. The common sacrifices be so ordered, that they be no derogation nor prejudice to any of the private sacrifices and religions. Therefore, no image of any god is seen in the church, to the intent it may be free for every man to conceive God by their religion after what likeness and similitude they will. They call upon no peculiar name of God, but only Mithra, in the which word they all agree together in one nature of the divine majesty whatsoever it be. No prayers be used but such as every man may boldly pronounce without the offending of any sect. They come therefore to the church the last day of every month and year, in the evening yet fasting, there to give thanks to God for that they have prosperously passed over the year or month, whereof that holy day is the last day. The next day they come to the church early in the morning, to pray to God that they may have good fortune and success all the new year or month which they do begin of that same holy day. But in the holy days that be the last days of the months and years before they come to the church, the wives fall down prostrate before their husbands' feet at home and the children before the feet of their parents, confessing and acknowledging that they have offended either by some actual deed, or by omission of their duty, and desire pardon for their offence. Thus, if any cloud of privy displeasure was risen at home, by this satisfaction it is overblown, that they may be present at the sacrifices with pure and charitable minds. For they be afraid to come there with troubled consciences. Therefore, if they know themselves to bear any hatred or grudge towards any man, they presume not to come to the sacrifices, before they have reconciled themselves and purged their consciences, for fear of great vengeance and punishment for their offence. When they come thither, the men go into the right side of the church and the women into the left side. There they place themselves in such order, that all they which be of the male kind in every household sit before the goodman of the house, and they of the female kind before the goodwife. Thus it is foreseen that all their gestures and behaviours be marked and observed abroad of them by whose authority and discipline they be governed at home. This also they diligently see unto, that the younger evermore be coupled with his elder, lest if children be joined together, they should pass over that time in childish wantonness, wherein they ought principally to conceive a religious and devout fear towards God, which is the chief and almost the only incitation to virtue. They kill no living beast in sacrifice, nor they think not that the merciful clemency of God hath delight in blood and slaughter, which hath given life to beasts to the intent they should live. They burn frankincense and other sweet savours, and light also a great number of wax candles and tapers, not supposing this gear to be anything available to the divine nature, as neither the prayers of men. But this unhurtful and harmless kind of worship pleaseth them. And by these sweet savours and lights, and other such ceremonies men feel themselves secretly lifted up and encouraged to devotion with more willing and fervent hearts. The people weareth in the church white apparel. The priest is clothed in changeable colours. Which in workmanship be excellent, but in stuff not very precious. For their vestments be neither embroidered with gold, nor set with precious stones. But they be wrought so finely and cunningly with divers feathers of fowls, that the estimation of no costly stuff is able to countervail the price of the work. Furthermore in these birds' feathers, and in the due order of them, which is observed in their setting, they say, is contained certain divine mysteries. The interpretation whereof known, which is diligently taught by the priests, they be put in remembrance of the bountiful benefits of God toward them; and of the love and honour which of their behalf is due to God; and also of their duties one

toward another. When the priest first cometh out of the vestry thus
apparelled, they fall down incontinent every one reverently to the
ground, with so still silence on every part, that the very fashion of
the thing striketh into them a certain fear of God, as though he
were there personally present. When they have lain a little space on
the ground, the priest giveth them a sign for to rise. Then they sing
praises unto God, which they intermix with instruments of music,
for the most part of other fashions than these that we use in this
part of the world. And like as some of ours be much sweeter than
theirs, so some of theirs do far pass ours. But in one thing doubtless
they go exceeding far beyond us. For all their music, both that
they play upon instruments, and that they sing with man's voice,
doth so resemble and express natural affections, the sound and tune
is so applied and made agreeable to the thing, that whether it be a
prayer, or else a ditty of gladness, of patience, of trouble, of mourning, or of anger; the fashion of the melody doth so represent the
meaning of the thing, that it doth wonderfully move, stir, pierce
and inflame the hearers' minds. At the last the people and the priest
together rehearse solemn prayers in words, expressly pronounced,
so made that every man may privately apply to himself that which
is commonly spoken of all. In these prayers every man recogniseth
and acknowledgeth God to be his maker, his governor and the
principal cause of all other goodness, thanking him for so many
benefits received at his hand. But namely that through the favour
of God he hath chanced into that public weal, which is most happy
and wealthy, and hath chosen that religion, which he hopeth to be
most true. In the which thing if he do anything err, or if there be
any other better than either of them is, being more acceptable to
God, he desireth him that he will of his goodness let him have
knowledge thereof, as one that is ready to follow what way soever
he will lead him. But if this form and fashion of a commonwealth
be best, and his own religion most true and perfect, then he desireth
God to give him a constant steadfastness in the same, and to bring
all other people to the same order of living and to the same opinion
of God, unless there be anything that in this diversity of religions
doth delight his unsearchable pleasure. To be short, he prayeth him
that after his death he may come to him. But how soon or late that

he dare not assign or determine. Howbeit, if it might stand with his majesty's pleasure, he would be much gladder to die a painful death and so to go to God, than by long living in worldly prosperity to be away from him. When this prayer is said they fall down to the ground again and a little after they rise up and go to dinner. And the residue of the day they pass over in plays and exercise of chivalry.

Now I have declared and described unto you, as truly as I could the form and order of that commonwealth, which verily in my judgment is not only the best, but also that which alone of good right may claim and take upon it the name of a commonwealth or public weal. For in other places they speak still of the commonwealth, but every man procureth his own private wealth. Here where nothing is private, the common affairs be earnestly looked upon. And truly on both parts they have good cause so to do as they do. For in other countries who knoweth not that he shall starve for hunger, unless he make some several provision for himself, though the commonwealth flourish never so much in riches? And therefore he is compelled even of very necessity to have regard to himself, rather than to the people, that is to say, to other. Contrariwise, there where all things be common to every man, it is not to be doubted that any man shall lack anything necessary for his private uses, so that the common storehouses and barns be sufficiently stored. For there nothing is distributed after a niggish sort, neither there is any poor man or beggar. And though no man have anything, yet every man is rich. For what can be more rich, than to live joyfully and merrily, without all grief and pensiveness; not caring for his own living, nor vexed or troubled with his wife's importunate complaints, not dreading poverty to his son, nor sorrowing for his daughter's dowry? Yea they take no care at all for the living and wealth of themselves and all theirs, of their wives, their children, their nephews, their children's children, and all the succession that ever shall follow in their posterity. And yet besides this there is no less provision for them that were once labourers and be now weak and impotent, than for them that do now labour and take pain. Here now would I see, if any man dare be so bold as to compare with this equity, the justice of other nations; among whom, I forsake God, if I can find any sign or token of equity and justice. For what justice is this, that a rich goldsmith, or an usurer, or to be short, any of them which either do nothing at all, or else that which they do is such that it is not very necessary to the commonwealth, should have a pleasant and a wealthy living, either by idleness, or by unnecessary business; when in the meantime poor labourers, carters, ironsmiths, carpenters and ploughmen, by so great and continual toil, as drawing and bearing beasts be scant able to sustain, and again so necessary toil, that without it no commonwealth were able to continue and endure one year, do yet get so hard and poor a living, and live so wretched and miserable a life, that the state and condition of the labouring beasts may seem much better and wealthier? For they be not put to so continual labour, nor their living is not much worse, yea to them much pleasanter, taking no thought in the mean season for the time to come. But these silly poor wretches be presently tormented with barren and unfruitful labour. And the remembrance of their poor indigent and beggarly old age killeth them up. For their daily wages is so little, that it will not suffice for the same day, much less it yieldeth any overplus, that may daily be laid up for the relief of old age. Is not this an unjust and an unkind public weal, which giveth great fees and rewards to gentlemen, as they call them, and to goldsmiths, and to such other, which be either idle persons, or else only flatterers, and devisers of vain pleasures; and of the contrary part maketh no gentle provision for poor ploughmen, colliers, labourers, carters, ironsmiths, and carpenters: without whom no commonwealth can continue. But when it hath abused the labours of their lusty and flowering age, at the last when they be oppressed with old age and sickness, being needy, poor, and indigent of all things, then forgetting their so many painful watchings, not remembering their so many and so great benefits, recompenseth and acquitteth them most unkindly with miserable death. And yet besides this the rich men not only by private fraud, but also by common laws, do every day pluck and snatch away from the poor some part of their daily living. So whereas it seemed before unjust to recompense with unkindness their pains that have been beneficial to the public weal, now they have to this their wrong and unjust dealing (which is yet a much worse point) given the name of justice, yea and that by force of a law. Therefore, when I consider and weigh in my mind all these commonwealths, which nowadays anywhere do flourish, so God help me, I can perceive nothing but a certain conspiracy of rich men procuring their own commodities under the name and title of the commonwealth. They invent and devise all means and crafts, first how to keep safely, without fear of losing, that they have unjustly gathered together, and next how to hire and abuse the work and labour of the poor for as little money as may be. These devices, when the rich men have decreed to be kept and observed for the commonwealth's sake, that is to say for the wealth also of the poor people, then they be made laws. But these most wicked and vicious men, when they have by their insatiable covetousness divided among themselves all those things, which would have sufficed all men, yet how far be they from the wealth and felicity of the Utopian commonwealth? Out of the which, in that all the desire of money with the use thereof is utterly secluded and banished, how great a heap of cares is cut away! How great an occasion of wickedness and mischief is plucked up by the roots! For who knoweth not, that fraud, theft, ravine, brawling, quarreling, brabling, strife, chiding, contention, murder, treason, poisoning, which by daily punishments are rather revenged than refrained, do die when money dieth? And also that fear, grief, care, labours and watchings do perish even the very same moment that money perisheth? Yea poverty itself, which only seemed to lack money, if money were gone, it also would decrease and vanish away. And that you may perceive this more plainly, consider with yourselves some barren and unfruitful year, wherein many thousands of people have starved for hunger. I dare be bold to say, that in the end of that penury so much corn or grain might have been found in the rich men's barns, if they had been searched, as being divided among them whom famine and pestilence have killed, no man at all should have felt that plague and penury. So easily might men get their living, if that same worthy princess, lady money, did not alone stop up the way between us and our living, which a God's name was very excellently devised and invented, that by her the way thereto should be opened. I am sure the rich men perceive this, nor they be not ignorant how much better it were to lack no necessary thing, than to abound with overmuch superfluity; to be rid out of innumerable cares and troubles, than to be besieged with great riches. And I doubt not that either the respect of every man's private commodity, or else the authority of our saviour Christ (which for his great wisdom could not but know what were best, and for his inestimable goodness could not but counsel to that which he knew to be best) would have brought all the world long ago into the laws of this weal public, if it were not that one only beast, the princess and mother of all mischief, pride, doth withstand and let it. She measureth not wealth and prosperity by her own commodities, but by the miseries and incommodities of other: she would not by her good will be made a goddess, if there were no wretches left, whom she might be lady over to mock and scorn; over whose miseries her felicity might shine, whose poverty she might vex, torment and increase by gorgeously setting forth her riches. This hell-hound creepeth into men's hearts, and plucketh them back from entering the right path of life, and is so deeply rooted in men's breasts, that she cannot be plucked out. This form and fashion of a weal public, which I would gladly wish unto all nations, I am glad yet that it hath chanced to the Utopians, which have followed those institutions of life, whereby they have laid such foundations of their commonwealth, as shall continue and last not only wealthily, but also, as far as man's wit may judge and conjecture, shall endure for ever. For seeing the chief causes of ambition and sedition with other vices be plucked up by the roots and abandoned at home, there can be no jeopardy of domestical dissension, which alone hath cast under foot and brought to nought the well fortified and strongly-defenced wealth and riches of many cities. But forasmuch as perfect concord remaineth, and wholesome laws be executed at home the envy of all foreign princes be not able to shake or move the empire, though they have many times long ago gone about to do it, being evermore driven back.

Thus when Raphael had made an end of his tale, though many things came to my mind, which in the manners and laws of that people seemed to be instituted and founded of no good reason, not only in the fashion of their chivalry, and in their sacrifices and religions, and in other of their laws, but also, yea and chiefly, in that which is the principal foundation of all their ordinances, that is to say, in the community of their life and living, without any occupying of money, by the which thing only all nobility, magnificence, worship, honour and majesty, the true ornaments and honours, as the common opinion is, of a commonwealth, utterly be overthrown and destroyed; yet because I knew that he was weary of talking, and was not sure whether he could abide that anything should be said against his mind; specially because I remembered that he had reprehended this fault in other, which be afraid lest they should seem not to be wise enough, unless they could find some fault in other men's inventions; therefore I praising both their institutions and his communication, took him by the hand, and led him in to supper; saying that we would choose another time to weigh and examine the same matters, and to talk with him more at large therein. Which would to God it might once come to pass. In the meantime, as I cannot agree and consent to all things that he said, being else without doubt a man singularly well learned, and also in all worldly matters exactly and profoundly experienced, so must I needs confess and grant that many things be in the Utopian weal public, which in our cities I may rather wish for, than hope after.

Thus endeth the afternoon's talk of Raphael Hythloday concerning the laws and institutions of the Island of Utopia.

IMPRINTED AT LONDON BY ABRAHAM VELE,
DWELLING IN PAUL'S CHURCH YARD
AT THE SIGN OF THE LAMB.
ANNO 1551.

To the Right Honourable Hieronymus Buslidius, Provost of Arienn, and Councillor to the Catholic King Charles, Peter Giles, Citizen of Antwerp, wisheth health and felicity.

THOMAS MORE, the singular ornament of this our age, as you yourself (right honourable Buslidius) can witness, to whom he is perfectly well known, sent unto me this other day the Island of Utopia, to very few as yet known, but most worthy; which, as far excelling Plato's commonwealth, all people should be willing to know; specially of a man most eloquent so finely set forth, so cunningly painted out and so evidently subject to the eye, that as oft as I read it, methinketh that I see somewhat more, than when I heard Raphael Hythloday himself (for I was present at that talk as well as Master More) uttering and pronouncing his own words. Yea, though the same man, according to his pure eloquence, did so open and declare the matter, that he might plainly enough appear, to report not things which he had learned of others only by hearsay, but which he had with his own eyes presently seen and thoroughly viewed, and wherein he had no small time been conversant and abiding; a man truly, in mine opinion, as touching the knowledge of regions, peoples, and worldly experience, much passing, yea even the very famous and renowned traveller Ulysses; and indeed such a one, as for the space of these eight hundred years past I think nature into the world brought not forth his like; in comparison of whom Vespucci may be thought to have seen nothing. Moreover, whereas we be wont more effectually and pithily to declare and express things that we have seen, than which we have but only heard, there was besides that in this man a certain peculiar grace, and singular dexterity to describe and set forth a matter withal. Yet the selfsame things as oft as I behold and consider them drawn and painted out with Master More's pencil, I am therewith so moved, so delighted, so inflamed, and so rapt, that sometimes methink I am presently conversant, even in the island of Utopia. And I promise you, I can scant believe that Raphael himself by all that five years' space that he was in Utopia abiding, saw there so much, as here in Master More's description is to be seen and perceived. Which description with so many wonders, and miraculous things is replenished, that I stand in great doubt whereat first and chiefly to muse or marvel; whether at the excellence of his perfect and sure memory, which could well-nigh word by word rehearse so many things once only heard; or else at his singular prudence, who so well and wittily marked and bare away all the original causes and fountains (to the vulgar people commonly most unknown) whereof both issueth and springeth the mortal confusion and utter decay of a commonwealth, and also the advancement and wealthy state of the same may rise and grow; or else at the efficacy and pith of his words, which in so fine a Latin style, with such force of eloquence hath couched together and comprised so many and divers matters, especially being a man continually encumbered with so many busy and troublesome cares, both public and private, as he is. Howbeit all these things cause you little to marvel (right honourable Buslidius) for that you are familiarly and thoroughly acquainted with the notable, yea almost divine wit of the man. But now to proceed to other matters, I surely know nothing needful or requisite to be adjoined unto his writings, only a meter of four verses written in the Utopian tongue, which after Master More's departure Hythloday by chance showed me, that have I caused to be added thereto, with the alphabet of the same nation. For, as touching the situation of the island, that is to say, in what part of the world Utopia standeth, the ignorance and lack whereof not a little troubleth and grieveth Master More, indeed Raphael left not that unspoken of. Howbeit with very few words he lightly touched it, incidentally by the way passing it over, as meaning of likelihood to keep and reserve that to another place. And the same, I wot not how, by a certain evil and unlucky chance escaped us both. For when Raphael was speaking thereof, one of Master More's servants came to him and whispered in his ear. Wherefore I being then of purpose more earnestly addict to hear, one of the company, by reason of cold taken, I think, a shipboard, coughed out so loud, that he took from my hearing certain of his words. But I will never stint nor rest, until I have got the full and exact knowledge hereof; insomuch that I will be able perfectly to instruct you, not only in the longitude or true meridian of the island, but also in the just latitude therof, that is to say, in the sublevation or height of the pole in that region, if our friend Hythloday be in safety and alive. For we hear very uncertain news of him. Some report, that he died in his journey homeward. Some again affirm, that he returned into his country, but partly, for that he could not away with the fashions of his country folk, and partly for that his mind and affection was altogether set and fixed upon Utopia, they say that he hath taken his voyage thitherward again. Now as touching this, that the name of this island is nowhere found among the old and ancient cosmographers, this doubt Hythloday himself very well dissolved. For why it is possible enough (quoth he) that the name, which it had in old time, was afterward changed, or else that they never had knowledge of this island; forasmuch as now in our time divers lands be found, which to the old geographers were unknown. Howbeit, what needeth it in this behalf to fortify the matter with arguments, seeing Master More is author hereof sufficient? But whereas he doubteth of the edition or imprinting of the book, indeed herein I both commend, and also acknowledge the man's modesty. Howbeit unto me it seemeth a work most unworthy to be long suppressed, and most worthy to go abroad into the hands of men, yea, and under the title of your name to be published to the world; either because the singular endowments and qualities of Master More be to no man better known than to you, or else because no man is more fit and meet, than you with good counsels to further and advance the commonwealth, wherein you have many years already continued and travailed with great glory and commendation, both of wisdom and knowledge, and also of integrity and uprightness. Thus, O liberal supporter of good learning, and flower of this our time, I bid you most heartily well to fare. At Antwerp 1516, the first day of November.

THE NINETY-FIVE THESES

ADDRESS TO
THE GERMAN NOBILITY

CONCERNING CHRISTIAN LIBERTY

BY
MARTIN LUTHER

INTRODUCTORY NOTE

MARTIN LUTHER, the leader of the Protestant Reformation, was born at Eisleben, Prussian Saxony, November 10, 1483. He studied jurisprudence at the University of Erfurt, where he later lectured on physics and ethics. In 1505 he entered the Augustinian monastery at Erfurt; two years later was ordained priest; and in 1508 became professor of philosophy at the University of Wittenberg.

The starting-point of Luther's career as a reformer was his posting on the church door of Wittenberg the Ninety-five Theses on October 31, 1517. These formed a passionate statement of the true nature of penitence, and a protest against the sale of indulgences. In issuing the Theses, Luther expected the support of his ecclesiastical superiors; and it was only after three years of controversy, during which he refused a summons to Rome, that he proceeded to publish those works that brought about his expulsion from the Church.

The year 1520 saw the publication of the three great documents which laid down the fundamental principles of the Reformation. In the "Address to the Christian Nobility of the German Nation," Luther attacked the corruptions of the Church and the abuses of its authority, and asserted the right of the layman to spiritual independence. In "Concerning Christian Liberty," he expounded the doctrine of justification by faith, and gave a complete presentation of his theological position. In the "Babylonish Captivity of the Church," he criticized the sacramental system, and set up the Scriptures as the supreme authority in religion.

In the midst of this activity came his formal excommunication, and his renunciation of allegiance to the Pope. He was proscribed by the Emperor Charles V and taken into the protection of prison in the Wartburg by the friendly Elector of Saxony, where he translated the New Testament. The complete translation of the Bible, issued in 1534, marks the establishment of the modern literary language of Germany.

The rest of Luther's life was occupied with a vast amount of literary and controversial activity. He died at Eisleben, February 18, 1546.

INTRODUCTORY LETTER

To the most Reverend Father in Christ and most illustrious Lord, Albert, Archbishop and Primate of the Churches of Magdeburg and Mentz, Marquis of Brandenburg, etc., his lord and pastor in Christ, most gracious and worthy of all fear and reverence—

JESUS

The grace of God be with you, and whatsoever it is and can do.

Spare me, most reverend Father in Christ, most illustrious Prince, if I, the very dregs of humanity, have dared to think of addressing a letter to the eminence of your sublimity. The Lord Jesus is my witness that, in the consciousness of my own pettiness and baseness, I have long put off the doing of that which I have now hardened my forehead to perform, moved thereto most especially by the sense of that faithful duty which I feel that I owe to your most reverend Fatherhood in Christ. May your Highness then in the meanwhile deign to cast your eyes upon one grain of dust, and, in your pontifical clemency, to understand my prayer.

Papal indulgences are being carried about, under your most distinguished authority, for the building of St. Peter's. In respect of these, I do not so much accuse the extravagant sayings of the preachers, which I have not heard, but I grieve at the very false ideas which the people conceive from them, and which are spread abroad in common talk on every side— namely, that unhappy souls believe that, if they buy letters of indulgences, they are sure of their salvation; also, that, as soon as they have thrown their contribution into the chest, souls forthwith fly out of purgatory; and furthermore, that so great is the grace thus conferred, that there is no sin so great—even, as they say, if, by an impossibility, any one had violated the Mother of God—but that it may be pardoned; and again, that by these indulgences a man is freed from all punishment and guilt.

O gracious God! it is thus that the souls committed to your care, most excellent Father, are being taught unto their death, and a most severe account, which you will have to render for all of them, is growing and increasing. Hence I have not been able to keep silence any longer on this subject, for by no function of a bishop's office can a man become sure of salvation, since he does not even become sure through the grace of God infused into him, but the Apostle bids us to be ever working out

247

our salvation in fear and trembling. (Phil. ii. 12.) Even the righteous man—says Peter—shall scarcely be saved. (1 Peter iv. 18.) In fine, so narrow is the way which leads unto life, that the Lord, speaking by the prophets Amos and Zachariah, calls those who are to be saved brands snatched from the burning, and our Lord everywhere declares the difficulty of salvation.

Why, then, by these false stories and promises of pardon, do the preachers of them make the people to feel secure and without fear? since indulgences confer absolutely no good on souls as regards salvation or holiness, but only take away the outward penalty which was wont of old to be canonically imposed.

Lastly, works of piety and charity are infinitely better than indulgences, and yet they do not preach these with such display or so much zeal; nay, they keep silence about them for the sake of preaching pardons. And yet it is the first and sole duty of all bishops, that the people should learn the Gospel and Christian charity: for Christ nowhere commands that indulgences should be preached. What a dreadful thing it is then, what peril to a bishop, if, while the Gospel is passed over in silence, he permits nothing but the noisy outcry of indulgences to be spread among his people, and bestows more care on these than on the Gospel! Will not Christ say to them: "Straining at a gnat, and swallowing a camel"?

Besides all this, most reverend Father in the Lord, in that instruction to the commissaries which has been put forth under the name of your most reverend Fatherhood it is stated—doubtless without the knowledge and consent of your most reverend Fatherhood—that one of the principal graces conveyed by indulgences is that inestimable gift of God, by which man is reconciled to God, and all the pains of purgatory are done away with; and further, that contrition is not necessary for those who thus redeem souls or buy confessional licences.

But what can I do, excellent Primate and most illustrious Prince, save to entreat your reverend Fatherhood, through the Lord Jesus Christ, to deign to turn on us the eye of fatherly care, and to suppress that advertisement altogether and impose on the preachers of pardons another form of preaching, lest perchance some one should at length arise who will put forth writings in confutation of them and of their advertisements, to the deepest reproach of your most illustrious Highness. It is intensely abhorrent to me that this should be done, and yet I fear that it will happen, unless the evil be speedily remedied.

This faithful discharge of my humble duty I entreat that your most illustrious Grace will deign to receive in a princely and bishoplike spirit—

that is, with all clemency—even as I offer it with a most faithful heart, and one most devoted to your most reverend Fatherhood, since I too am part of your flock. May the Lord Jesus keep your most reverend Fatherhood for ever and ever. Amen.

From Wittenberg, on the eve of All Saints, in the year 1517.

If it so please your most reverend Fatherhood, you may look at these Disputations, that you may perceive how dubious a matter is that opinion about indulgences, which they disseminate as if it were most certain.

To your most reverend Fatherhood,

MARTIN LUTHER.

THE NINETY-FIVE THESES

DISPUTATION OF DR. MARTIN LUTHER CONCERNING PENITENCE AND INDULGENCES

IN the desire and with the purpose of elucidating the truth, a disputation will be held on the underwritten propositions at Wittenberg, under the presidency of the Reverend Father Martin Luther, Monk of the Order of St. Augustine, Master of Arts and of Sacred Theology, and ordinary Reader of the same in that place. He therefore asks those who cannot be present and discuss the subject with us orally, to do so by letter in their absence. In the name of our Lord Jesus Christ. Amen.

1. Our Lord and Master Jesus Christ, in saying "Repent ye," [1] etc., intended that the whole life of believers should be penitence.

2. This word cannot be understood of sacramental penance, that is, of the confession and satisfaction which are performed under the ministry of priests.

3. It does not, however, refer solely to inward penitence; nay such inward penitence is naught, unless it outwardly produces various mortifications of the flesh.

4. The penalty[2] thus continues as long as the hatred of self—that is, true inward penitence—continues: namely, till our entrance into the kingdom of heaven.

5. The Pope has neither the will nor the power to remit any penalties, except those which he has imposed by his own authority, or by that of the canons.

6. The Pope has no power to remit any guilt, except by declaring and warranting it to have been remitted by God; or at most by

---

[1] In the Latin, from the Vulgate, *"agite pœnitentiam,"* sometimes translated "Do penance." The effect of the following theses depends to some extent on the double meaning of *"pœnitentia"*—penitence and penance.

[2] I. e. *"Pœna,"* the connection between *"pœna"* and *"pœnitentia"* being again suggestive.

remitting cases reserved for himself; in which cases, if his power were despised, guilt would certainly remain.

7. God never remits any man's guilt, without at the same time subjecting him, humbled in all things, to the authority of his representative the priest.

8. The penitential canons are imposed only on the living, and no burden ought to be imposed on the dying, according to them.

9. Hence the Holy Spirit acting in the Pope does well for us, in that, in his decrees, he always makes exception of the article of death and of necessity.

10. Those priests act wrongly and unlearnedly, who, in the case of the dying, reserve the canonical penances for purgatory.

11. Those tares about changing of the canonical penalty into the penalty of purgatory seem surely to have been sown while the bishops were asleep.

12. Formerly the canonical penalties were imposed not after, but before absolution, as tests of true contrition.

13. The dying pay all penalties by death, and are already dead to the canon laws, and are by right relieved from them.

14. The imperfect soundness or charity of a dying person necessarily brings with it great fear; and the less it is, the greater the fear it brings.

15. This fear and horror is sufficient by itself, to say nothing of other things, to constitute the pains of purgatory, since it is very near to the horror of despair.

16. Hell, purgatory, and heaven appear to differ as despair, almost despair, and peace of mind differ.

17. With souls in purgatory it seems that it must needs be that, as horror diminishes, so charity increases.

18. Nor does it seem to be proved by any reasoning or any scriptures, that they are outside of the state of merit or of the increase of charity.

19. Nor does this appear to be proved, that they are sure and confident of their own blessedness, at least all of them, though we may be very sure of it.

20. Therefore the Pope, when he speaks of the plenary remission of all penalties, does not mean simply of all, but only of those imposed by himself.

21. Thus those preachers of indulgences are in error who say that, by the indulgences of the Pope, a man is loosed and saved from all punishment.

22. For in fact he remits to souls in purgatory no penalty which they would have had to pay in this life according to the canons.

23. If any entire remission of all penalties can be granted to any one, it is certain that it is granted to none but the most perfect—that is, to very few.

24. Hence the greater part of the people must needs be deceived by this indiscriminate and high-sounding promise of release from penalties.

25. Such power as the Pope has over purgatory in general, such has every bishop in his own diocese, and every curate in his own parish, in particular.

26. The Pope acts most rightly in granting remission to souls, not by the power of the keys (which is of no avail in this case), but by the way of suffrage.

27. They preach mad, who say that the soul flies out of purgatory as soon as the money thrown into the chest rattles.

28. It is certain that, when the money rattles in the chest, avarice and gain may be increased, but the suffrage of the Church depends on the will of God alone.

29. Who knows whether all the souls in purgatory desire to be redeemed from it, according to the story told of Saints Severinus and Paschal?

30. No man is sure of the reality of his own contrition, much less of the attainment of plenary remission.

31. Rare as is a true penitent, so rare is one who truly buys indulgences—that is to say, most rare.

32. Those who believe that, through letters of pardon, they are made sure of their own salvation, will be eternally damned along with their teachers.

33. We must especially beware of those who say that these pardons from the Pope are that inestimable gift of God by which man is reconciled to God.

34. For the grace conveyed by these pardons has respect only to the penalties of sacramental satisfaction, which are of human appointment.

35. They preach no Christian doctrine, who teach that contrition is not necessary for those who buy souls out of purgatory or buy confessional licences.

36. Every Christian who feels true compunction has of right plenary remission of pain and guilt, even without letters of pardon.

37. Every true Christian, whether living or dead, has a share in all the benefits of Christ and of the Church given him by God, even without letters of pardon.

38. The remission, however, imparted by the Pope is by no means to be despised, since it is, as I have said, a declaration of the Divine remission.

39. It is a most difficult thing, even for the most learned theologians, to exalt at the same time in the eyes of the people the ample effect of pardons and the necessity of true contrition.

40. True contrition seeks and loves punishment; while the ampleness of pardons relaxes it, and causes men to hate it, or at least gives occasion for them to do so.

41. Apostolical pardons ought to be proclaimed with caution, lest the people should falsely suppose that they are placed before other good works of charity.

42. Christians should be taught that it is not the mind of the Pope that the buying of pardons is to be in any way compared to works of mercy.

43. Christians should be taught that he who gives to a poor man, or lends to a needy man, does better than if he bought pardons.

44. Because, by a work of charity, charity increases and the man becomes better; while, by means of pardons, he does not become better, but only freer from punishment.

45. Christians should be taught that he who sees any one in need, and passing him by, gives money for pardons, is not purchasing for himself the indulgences of the Pope, but the anger of God.

46. Christians should be taught that, unless they have superfluous wealth, they are bound to keep what is necessary for the use of their own households, and by no means to lavish it on pardons.

47. Christians should be taught that, while they are free to buy pardons, they are not commanded to do so.

48. Christians should be taught that the Pope, in granting pardons, has both more need and more desire that devout prayer should be made for him, than that money should be readily paid.

49. Christians should be taught that the Pope's pardons are useful, if they do not put their trust in them; but most hurtful, if through them they lose the fear of God.

50. Christians should be taught that, if the Pope were acquainted with the exactions of the preachers of pardons, he would prefer that the Basilica of St. Peter should be burnt to ashes, than that it should be built up with the skin, flesh and bones of his sheep.

51. Christians should be taught that, as it would be the duty, so it would be the wish of the Pope, even to sell, if necessary, the Basilica of St. Peter, and to give of his own money to very many of those from whom the preachers of pardons extract money.

52. Vain is the hope of salvation through letters of pardon, even if a commissary—nay, the Pope himself—were to pledge his own soul for them.

53. They are enemies of Christ and of the Pope who, in order that pardons may be preached, condemn the word of God to utter silence in other churches.

54. Wrong is done to the word of God when, in the same sermon, an equal or longer time is spent on pardons than on it.

55. The mind of the Pope necessarily is, that if pardons, which are a very small matter, are celebrated with single bells, single processions, and single ceremonies, the Gospel, which is a very great matter, should be preached with a hundred bells, a hundred processions, and a hundred ceremonies.

56. The treasures of the Church, whence the Pope grants indulgences, are neither sufficiently named nor known among the people of Christ.

57. It is clear that they are at least not temporal treasures, for these are not so readily lavished, but only accumulated, by many of the preachers.

58. Nor are they the merits of Christ and of the saints, for these, independently of the Pope, are always working grace to the inner man, and the cross, death, and hell to the outer man.

59. St. Lawrence said that the treasures of the Church are the poor

of the Church, but he spoke according to the use of the word in his time.

60. We are not speaking rashly when we say that the keys of the Church, bestowed through the merits of Christ, are that treasure.

61. For it is clear that the power of the Pope is alone sufficient for the remission of penalties and of reserved cases.

62. The true treasure of the Church is the Holy Gospel of the glory and grace of God.

63. This treasure, however, is deservedly most hateful, because it makes the first to be last.

64. While the treasure of indulgences is deservedly most acceptable, because it makes the last to be first.

65. Hence the treasures of the gospel are nets, wherewith of old they fished for the men of riches.

66. The treasures of indulgences are nets, wherewith they now fish for the riches of men.

67. Those indulgences, which the preachers loudly proclaim to be the greatest graces, are seen to be truly such as regards the promotion of gain.

68. Yet they are in reality in no degree to be compared to the grace of God and the piety of the cross.

69. Bishops and curates are bound to receive the commissaries of apostolical pardons with all reverence.

70. But they are still more bound to see to it with all their eyes, and take heed with all their ears, that these men do not preach their own dreams in place of the Pope's commission.

71. He who speaks against the truth of apostolical pardons, let him be anathema and accursed.

72. But he, on the other hand, who exerts himself against the wantonness and licence of speech of the preachers of pardons, let him be blessed.

73. As the Pope justly thunders against those who use any kind of contrivance to the injury of the traffic in pardons.

74. Much more is it his intention to thunder against those who, under the pretext of pardons, use contrivances to the injury of holy charity and of truth.

75. To think that Papal pardons have such power that they could

absolve a man even if—by an impossibility—he had violated the Mother of God, is madness.

76. We affirm, on the contrary, that Papal pardons cannot take away even the least of venal sins, as regards its guilt.

77. The saying that, even if St. Peter were now Pope, he could grant no greater graces, is blasphemy against St. Peter and the Pope.

78. We affirm, on the contrary, that both he and any other Pope have greater graces to grant—namely, the Gospel, powers, gifts of healing, etc. (1 Cor. xii. 9.)

79. To say that the cross set up among the insignia of the Papal arms is of equal power with the cross of Christ, is blasphemy.

80. Those bishops, curates, and theologians who allow such discourses to have currency among the people, will have to render an account.

81. This licence in the preaching of pardons makes it no easy thing, even for learned men, to protect the reverence due to the Pope against the calumnies, or, at all events, the keen questionings of the laity.

82. As for instance:—Why does not the Pope empty purgatory for the sake of most holy charity and of the supreme necessity of souls— this being the most just of all reasons—if he redeems an infinite number of souls for the sake of that most fatal thing, money, to be spent on building a basilica—this being a very slight reason?

83. Again: why do funeral masses and anniversary masses for the deceased continue, and why does not the Pope return, or permit the withdrawal of the funds bequeathed for this purpose, since it is a wrong to pray for those who are already redeemed?

84. Again: what is this new kindness of God and the Pope, in that, for money's sake, they permit an impious man and an enemy of God to redeem a pious soul which loves God, and yet do not redeem that same pious and beloved soul, out of free charity, on account of its own need?

85. Again: why is it that the penitential canons, long since abrogated and dead in themselves in very fact and not only by usage, are yet still redeemed with money, through the granting of indulgences, as if they were full of life?

86. Again: why does not the Pope, whose riches are at this day

more ample than those of the wealthiest of the wealthy, build the one Basilica of St. Peter with his own money, rather than with that of poor believers?

87. Again: what does the Pope remit or impart to those who, through perfect contrition, have a right to plenary remission and participation?

88. Again: what greater good would the Church receive if the Pope, instead of once, as he does now, were to bestow these remissions and participations a hundred times a day on any one of the faithful?

89. Since it is the salvation of souls, rather than money, that the Pope seeks by his pardons, why does he suspend the letters and pardons granted long ago, since they are equally efficacious?

90. To repress these scruples and arguments of the laity by force alone, and not to solve them by giving reasons, is to expose the Church and the Pope to the ridicule of their enemies, and to make Christian men unhappy.

91. If, then, pardons were preached according to the spirit and mind of the Pope, all these questions would be resolved with ease— nay, would not exist.

92. Away, then, with all those prophets who say to the people of Christ, "Peace, peace," and there is no peace!

93. Blessed be all those prophets who say to the people of Christ, "The cross, the cross," and there is no cross!

94. Christians should be exhorted to strive to follow Christ their Head through pains, deaths, and hells,

95. And thus trust to enter heaven through many tribulations, rather than in the security of peace.

PROTESTATION

I, Martin Luther, Doctor, of the Order of Monks at Wittenberg, desire to testify publicly that certain propositions against pontifical indulgences, as they call them, have been put forth by me. Now although, up to the present time, neither this most celebrated and renowned school of ours, nor any civil or ecclesiastical power has condemned me, yet there are, as I hear, some men of headlong and audacious spirit, who dare to pronounce me a heretic, as though the matter had been thoroughly looked into and studied. But on my part, as I have often done before, so now too, I implore all men, by the faith of Christ, either to point out to me a better way, if such a way has been divinely revealed to any, or at least to submit their opinion to the judgment of God and of the Church. For I am neither so rash as to wish that my sole opinion should be preferred to that of all other men, nor so senseless as to be willing that the word of God should be made to give place to fables, devised by human reason.

DEDICATORY LETTER

To the respected and worthy Nicolaus von Amsdorff, Licentiate in the Holy Scriptures and Canon of Wittenberg,[1] *my particular and affectionate friend.*   Dr. Martinus Luther.

THE grace and peace of God be with you, respected, worthy Sir, and dear friend!

The time for silence is gone, and the time to speak has come, as we read in Ecclesiastes (iii. 7). I have, in conformity with our resolve, put together some few points concerning the *reformation of the Christian estate,* with the intent of placing the same before the *Christian nobility of the German nation,* in case it may please God to help His Church by means of the laity, inasmuch as the clergy, whom this task rather befitted, have become quite careless. I send all this to your worship, to judge and to amend where needed. I am well aware that I shall not escape the reproach of taking far too much upon me in presuming, insignificant and forsaken as I am, to address such high estates on such weighty and great subjects, as if there were no one in the world but Dr. Luther to have a care for Christianity and to give advice to such wise people.

Let who will blame me, I shall not offer any excuse. Perhaps I still owe God and the world another folly. This debt I have now resolved honestly to discharge, as well as may be, and to be Court fool for once in my life; if I fail, I shall at any rate gain this advantage: that no one need buy me a fool's cap or shave my poll. But it remains to be seen which shall hang the bells on the other. I must fulfil the proverb, "When anything is to be done in the world, a monk must be in it, were it only as a painted figure." I suppose it has often happened that a fool has spoken wisely, and wise men have often done foolishly, as St. Paul says, "If any man among you seemeth to be wise in this world, let him become a fool, that he may be wise" (1 Cor. iii. 18).

Now, inasmuch as I am not only a fool, but also a sworn doctor of the Holy Scriptures, I am glad that I have an opportunity of fulfilling my oath, just in this fool's way. I beg you to excuse me to the moderately wise, for I know not how to deserve the favour and grace of the

---

[1] Nicolaus von Amsdorff (1483–1565) was a colleague of Luther at the university of Wittenberg, and one of his most zealous fellow-workers in the cause of the Reformation.

supremely wise, which I have so often sought with much labour, but now for the future shall neither have nor regard.

God help us to seek not our glory, but His alone. Amen.

Wittenberg, in the monastry of St. Augustine, on the eve of St. John the Baptist in the year 1520.

JESUS

ADDRESS TO THE NOBILITY

INTRODUCTION

*To his most Serene and Mighty Imperial Majesty and to the Christian
Nobility of the German Nation.*

Dr. Martinus Luther.

THE grace and might of God be with you, Most Serene
Majesty, most gracious, well-beloved gentlemen!

It is not out of mere arrogance and perversity that I, an
individual poor man, have taken upon me to address your lordships.
The distress and misery that oppress all the Christian estates, more
especially in Germany, have led not only myself, but every one else,
to cry aloud and to ask for help, and have now forced me too to
cry out and to ask if God would give His Spirit to any one to reach
a hand to His wretched people. Councils have often put forward
some remedy, but it has adroitly been frustrated, and the evils have
become worse, through the cunning of certain men. Their malice
and wickedness I will now, by the help of God, expose, so that,
being known, they may henceforth cease to be so obstructive and
injurious. God has given us a young and noble sovereign,[2] and by
this has roused great hopes in many hearts; now it is right that we
too should do what we can, and make good use of time and grace.

The first thing that we must do is to consider the matter with
great earnestness, and, whatever we attempt, not to trust in our own
strength and wisdom alone, even if the power of all the world were
ours; for God will not endure that a good work should be begun
trusting to our own strength and wisdom. He destroys it; it is all
useless, as we read in Psalm xxxiii., "There is no king saved by the
multitude of a host; a mighty man is not delivered by much
strength." And I fear it is for that reason that those beloved princes
the Emperors Frederick, the First and the Second, and many other

---

[2] Charles V. was at that time not quite twenty years of age.

German emperors were, in former times, so piteously spurned and oppressed by the popes, though they were feared by all the world. Perchance they trusted rather in their own strength than in God; therefore they could not but fall; and how would the sanguinary tyrant Julius II. have risen so high in our own days but that, I fear, France, Germany, and Venice trusted to themselves? The children of Benjamin slew forty-two thousand Israelites, for this reason: that these trusted to their own strength (Judges xx., etc.).

That such a thing may not happen to us and to our noble Emperor Charles, we must remember that in this matter we wrestle not against flesh and blood, but against the rulers of the darkness of this world (Eph. vi. 12), who may fill the world with war and bloodshed, but cannot themselves be overcome thereby. We must renounce all confidence in our natural strength, and take the matter in hand with humble trust in God; we must seek God's help with earnest prayer, and have nothing before our eyes but the misery and wretchedness of Christendom, irrespective of what punishment the wicked may deserve. If we do not act thus, we may begin the game with great pomp; but when we are well in it, the spirits of evil will make such confusion that the whole world will be immersed in blood, and yet nothing be done. Therefore let us act in the fear of God and prudently. The greater the might of the foe, the greater is the misfortune, if we do not act in the fear of God and with humility. If popes and Romanists have hitherto, with the devil's help, thrown kings into confusion, they may still do so, if we attempt things with our own strength and skill, without God's help.

THE THREE WALLS OF THE ROMANISTS

The Romanists have, with great adroitness, drawn three walls round themselves, with which they have hitherto protected themselves, so that no one could reform them, whereby all Christendom has fallen terribly.

Firstly, if pressed by the temporal power, they have affirmed and maintained that the temporal power has no jurisdiction over them, but, on the contrary, that the spiritual power is above the temporal.

Secondly, if it were proposed to admonish them with the Scriptures, they objected that no one may interpret the Scriptures but the Pope.

Thirdly, if they are threatened with a council, they pretend that no one may call a council but the Pope.

Thus they have secretly stolen our three rods, so that they may be unpunished, and intrenched themselves behind these three walls, to act with all the wickedness and malice, which we now witness. And whenever they have been compelled to call a council, they have made it of no avail by binding the princes beforehand with an oath to leave them as they were, and to give moreover to the Pope full power over the procedure of the council, so that it is all one whether we have many councils or no councils, in addition to which they deceive us with false pretences and tricks. So grievously do they tremble for their skin before a true, free council; and thus they have overawed kings and princes, that these believe they would be offending God, if they were not to obey them in all such knavish, deceitful artifices.

Now may God help us, and give us one of those trumpets that overthrew the walls of Jericho, so that we may blow down these walls of straw and paper, and that we may set free our Christian rods for the chastisement of sin, and expose the craft and deceit of the devil, so that we may amend ourselves by punishment and again obtain God's favour.

(a) THE FIRST WALL

That the Temporal Power has no Jurisdiction over the Spiritualty

Let us, in the first place, attack the first wall.

It has been devised that the Pope, bishops, priests, and monks are called the *spiritual estate,* princes, lords, artificers, and peasants are the *temporal estate.* This is an artful lie and hypocritical device, but let no one be made afraid by it, and that for this reason: that all Christians are truly of the spiritual estate, and there is no difference among them, save of office alone. As St. Paul says (1 Cor. xii.), we are all one body, though each member does its own work, to serve the others. This is because we have one baptism, one Gospel, one faith, and are all Christians alike; for baptism, Gospel, and faith, these alone make spiritual and Christian people.

As for the unction by a pope or a bishop, tonsure, ordination, consecration, and clothes differing from those of laymen—all this may make a hypocrite or an anointed puppet, but never a Christian or a spiritual man. Thus we are all consecrated as priests by baptism, as St. Peter says: "Ye are a royal priesthood, a holy nation" (1 Peter ii. 9); and in the book of Revelations: "and hast made us unto our God (by Thy blood) kings and priests" (Rev. v. 10). For, if we had not a higher consecration in us than pope or bishop can give, no priest could ever be made by the consecration of pope or bishop, nor could he say the mass, or preach, or absolve. Therefore the bishop's consecration is just as if in the name of the whole congregation he took one person out of the community, each member of which has equal power, and commanded him to exercise this power for the rest; in the same way as if ten brothers, co-heirs as king's sons, were to choose one from among them to rule over their inheritance, they would all of them still remain kings and have equal power, although one is ordered to govern.

And to put the matter even more plainly, if a little company of pious Christian laymen were taken prisoners and carried away to a desert, and had not among them a priest consecrated by a bishop, and were there to agree to elect one of them, born in wedlock or not, and were to order him to baptise, to celebrate the mass, to absolve, and to preach, this man would as truly be a priest, as if all the bishops and all the popes had consecrated him. That is why in cases of necessity every man can baptise and absolve, which would not be possible if we were not all priests. This great grace and virtue of baptism and of the Christian estate they have quite destroyed and made us forget by their ecclesiastical law. In this way the Christians used to choose their bishops and priests out of the community; these being afterwards confirmed by other bishops, without the pomp that now prevails. So was it that St. Augustine, Ambrose, Cyprian, were bishops.

Since, then, the temporal power is baptised as we are, and has the same faith and Gospel, we must allow it to be priest and bishop, and account its office an office that is proper and useful to the

Christian community. For whatever issues from baptism may boast that it has been consecrated priest, bishop, and pope, although it does not beseem every one to exercise these offices. For, since we are all priests alike, no man may put himself forward or take upon himself, without our consent and election, to do that which we have all alike power to do. For, if a thing is common to all, no man may take it to himself without the wish and command of the community. And if it should happen that a man were appointed to one of these offices and deposed for abuses, he would be just what he was before. Therefore a priest should be nothing in Christendom but a functionary; as long as he holds his office, he has precedence of others; if he is deprived of it, he is a peasant or a citizen like the rest. Therefore a priest is verily no longer a priest after deposition. But now they have invented *characteres indelebiles*,[3] and pretend that a priest after deprivation still differs from a simple layman. They even imagine that a priest can never be anything but a priest—that is, that he can never become a layman. All this is nothing but mere talk and ordinance of human invention.

It follows, then, that between laymen and priests, princes and bishops, or, as they call it, between spiritual and temporal persons, the only real difference is one of office and function, and not of estate; for they are all of the same spiritual estate, true priests, bishops, and popes, though their functions are not the same—just as among priests and monks every man has not the same functions. And this, as I said above, St. Paul says (Rom. xii.; 1 Cor. xii.), and St. Peter (1 Peter ii.): "We, being many, are one body in Christ, and severally members one of another." Christ's body is not double or twofold, one temporal, the other spiritual. He is one Head, and He has one body.

We see, then, that just as those that we call spiritual, or priests, bishops, or popes, do not differ from other Christians in any other or higher degree but in that they are to be concerned with the word of God and the sacraments—that being their work and office—in the same way the temporal authorities hold the sword and the rod in their hands to punish the wicked and to protect the good. A cobbler,

[3] In accordance with a doctrine of the Roman Catholic Church, the act of ordination impresses upon the priest an indelible character; so that he immutably retains the sacred dignity of priesthood.

a smith, a peasant, every man, has the office and function of his calling, and yet all alike are consecrated priests and bishops, and every man should by his office or function be useful and beneficial to the rest, so that various kinds of work may all be united for the furtherance of body and soul, just as the members of the body all serve one another.

Now see what a Christian doctrine is this: that the temporal authority is not above the clergy, and may not punish it. This is as if one were to say the hand may not help, though the eye is in grievous suffering. Is it not unnatural, not to say unchristian, that one member may not help another, or guard it against harm? Nay, the nobler the member, the more the rest are bound to help it. Therefore I say, Forasmuch as the temporal power has been ordained by God for the punishment of the bad and the protection of the good, therefore we must let it do its duty throughout the whole Christian body, without respect of persons, whether it strikes popes, bishops, priests, monks, nuns, or whoever it may be. If it were sufficient reason for fettering the temporal power that it is inferior among the offices of Christianity to the offices of priest or confessor, or to the spiritual estate—if this were so, then we ought to restrain tailors, cobblers, masons, carpenters, cooks, cellarmen, peasants, and all secular workmen, from providing the Pope or bishops, priests and monks, with shoes, clothes, houses or victuals, or from paying them tithes. But if these laymen are allowed to do their work without restraint, what do the Romanist scribes mean by their laws? They mean that they withdraw themselves from the operation of temporal Christian power, simply in order that they may be free to do evil, and thus fulfil what St. Peter said: "There shall be false teachers among you, . . . and in covetousness shall they with feigned words make merchandise of you" (2 Peter ii. 1, etc.).

Therefore the temporal Christian power must exercise its office without let or hindrance, without considering whom it may strike, whether pope, or bishop, or priest: whoever is guilty, let him suffer for it.

Whatever the ecclesiastical law has said in opposition to this is merely the invention of Romanist arrogance. For this is what St. Paul says to all Christians: "Let every soul" (I presume including the popes) "be subject unto the higher powers; for they bear not the sword in vain: they serve the Lord therewith, for vengeance on evildoers and for praise to them that do well" (Rom. xiii. 1-4). Also St. Peter: "Submit yourselves to every ordinance of man for the Lord's sake, . . . for so is the will of God" (1 Peter ii. 13, 15). He has also foretold that men would come who should despise government (2 Peter ii.), as has come to pass through ecclesiastical law.

Now, I imagine, the first paper wall is overthrown, inasmuch as the temporal power has become a member of the Christian body; although its work relates to the body, yet does it belong to the spiritual estate. Therefore, it must do its duty without let or hindrance upon all members of the whole body, to punish or urge, as guilt may deserve, or need may require, without respect of pope, bishops, or priests, let them threaten or excommunicate as they will. That is why a guilty priest is deprived of his priesthood before being given over to the secular arm; whereas this would not be right, if the secular sword had not authority over him already by Divine ordinance.

It is, indeed, past bearing that the spiritual law should esteem so highly the liberty, life, and property of the clergy, as if laymen were not as good spiritual Christians, or not equally members of the Church. Why should your body, life, goods, and honour be free, and not mine, seeing that we are equal as Christians, and have received alike baptism, faith, spirit, and all things? If a priest is killed, the country is laid under an interdict[4]: why not also if a peasant is killed? Whence comes this great difference among equal Christians? Simply from human laws and inventions.

It can have been no good spirit, either, that devised these evasions and made sin to go unpunished. For if, as Christ and the Apostles bid us, it is our duty to oppose the evil one and all his works and words, and to drive him away as well as may be, how then should we remain quiet and be silent when the Pope and his followers are guilty of devilish works and words? Are we for the sake of men to allow the commandments and the truth of God to be defeated, which at our baptism we vowed to support with body and soul? Truly we

[4] By the *Interdict*, or general excommunication, whole countries, districts, or towns, or their respective rulers, were deprived of all the spiritual benefits of the Church, such as Divine service, the administering of the sacraments, etc.

should have to answer for all souls that would thus be abandoned and led astray.

Therefore it must have been the arch-devil himself who said, as we read in the ecclesiastical law, If the Pope were so perniciously wicked, as to be dragging souls in crowds to the devil, yet he could not be deposed. This is the accursed and devilish foundation on which they build at Rome, and think that the whole world is to be allowed to go to the devil rather than they should be opposed in their knavery. If a man were to escape punishment simply because he is above the rest, then no Christian might punish another, since Christ has commanded each of us to esteem himself the lowest and the humblest (Matt. xviii. 4; Luke ix. 48).

Where there is sin, there remains no avoiding the punishment, as St. Gregory says, We are all equal, but guilt makes one subject to another. Now let us see how they deal with Christendom. They arrogate to themselves immunities without any warrant from the Scriptures, out of their own wickedness, whereas God and the Apostles made them subject to the secular sword; so that we must fear that it is the work of antichrist, or a sign of his near approach.

(*b*) The Second Wall

That no one may interpret the Scriptures but the Pope

The second wall is even more tottering and weak: that they alone pretend to be considered masters of the Scriptures; although they learn nothing of them all their life. They assume authority, and juggle before us with impudent words, saying that the Pope cannot err in matters of faith, whether he be evil or good, albeit they cannot prove it by a single letter. That is why the canon law contains so many heretical and unchristian, nay unnatural, laws; but of these we need not speak now. For whereas they imagine the Holy Ghost never leaves them, however unlearned and wicked they may be, they grow bold enough to decree whatever they like. But were this true, where were the need and use of the Holy Scriptures? Let us burn them, and content ourselves with the unlearned gentlemen at Rome, in whom the Holy Ghost dwells, who, however, can dwell in pious souls only. If I had not read it, I could never have believed that the devil should have put forth such follies at Rome and find a following.

But not to fight them with our own words, we will quote the Scriptures. St. Paul says, "If anything be revealed to another that sitteth by, let the first hold his peace" (1 Cor. xiv. 30). What would be the use of this commandment, if we were to believe him alone that teaches or has the highest seat? Christ Himself says, "And they shall be all taught of God." (St. John vi. 45). Thus it may come to pass that the Pope and his followers are wicked and not true Christians, and not being taught by God, have no true understanding, whereas a common man may have true understanding. Why should we then not follow him? Has not the Pope often erred? Who could help Christianity, in case the Pope errs, if we do not rather believe another who has the Scriptures for him?

Therefore it is a wickedly devised fable—and they cannot quote a single letter to confirm it—that it is for the Pope alone to interpret the Scriptures or to confirm the interpretation of them. They have assumed the authority of their own selves. And though they say that this authority was given to St. Peter when the keys were given to him, it is plain enough that the keys were not given to St. Peter alone, but to the whole community. Besides, the keys were not ordained for doctrine or authority, but for sin, to bind or loose; and what they claim besides this from the keys is mere invention. But what Christ said to St. Peter: "I have prayed for thee that thy faith fail not" (St. Luke xxii. 32), cannot relate to the Pope, inasmuch as the greater part of the Popes have been without faith, as they are themselves forced to acknowledge; nor did Christ pray for Peter alone, but for all the Apostles and all Christians, as He says, "Neither pray I for these alone, but for them also which shall believe on Me through their word" (St. John xvii.). Is not this plain enough?

Only consider the matter. They must needs acknowledge that there are pious Christians among us that have the true faith, spirit, understanding, word, and mind of Christ: why then should we reject their word and understanding, and follow a pope who has neither understanding nor spirit? Surely this were to deny our whole faith and the Christian Church. Moreover, if the article of our faith is right, "I believe in the holy Christian Church," the Pope

cannot alone be right; else we must say, "I believe in the Pope of
Rome," and reduce the Christian Church to one man, which is a
devilish and damnable heresy. Besides that, we are all priests, as
I have said, and have all one faith, one Gospel, one Sacrament; how
then should we not have the power of discerning and judging what
is right or wrong in matters of faith? What becomes of St. Paul's
words, "But he that is spiritual judgeth all things, yet he himself is
judged of no man" (1 Cor. ii. 15), and also, "we having the same
spirit of faith"? (2 Cor. iv. 13). Why then should we not perceive
as well as an unbelieving pope what agrees or disagrees with our
faith?

By these and many other texts we should gain courage and freedom, and should not let the spirit of liberty (as St. Paul has it) be
frightened away by the inventions of the popes; we should boldly
judge what they do and what they leave undone by our own believing understanding of the Scriptures, and force them to follow the
better understanding, and not their own. Did not Abraham in old
days have to obey his Sarah, who was in stricter bondage to him
than we are to any one on earth? Thus, too, Balaam's ass was wiser
than the prophet. If God spoke by an ass against a prophet, why
should He not speak by a pious man against the Pope? Besides, St.
Paul withstood St. Peter as being in error (Gal. ii.). Therefore it
behoves every Christian to aid the faith by understanding and
defending it and by condemning all errors.

(c) The Third Wall

That no one may call a council but the Pope

The third wall falls of itself, as soon as the first two have fallen;
for if the Pope acts contrary to the Scriptures, we are bound to stand
by the Scriptures, to punish and to constrain him, according to
Christ's commandment, "Moreover, if thy brother shall trespass
against thee, go and tell him his fault between thee and him alone;
if he shall hear thee, thou hast gained thy brother. But if he will not
hear thee, then take with thee one or two more, that in the mouth
of two or three witnesses every word may be established. And if he

shall neglect to hear them, tell it unto the Church; but if he neglect to hear the Church, let him be unto thee as a heathen man and a publican" (St. Matt. xviii. 15–17). Here each member is commanded to take care for the other; much more then should we do this, if it is a ruling member of the community that does evil, which by its evil-doing causes great harm and offence to the others. If then I am to accuse him before the Church, I must collect the Church together. Moreover, they can show nothing in the Scriptures giving the Pope sole power to call and confirm councils; they have nothing but their own laws; but these hold good only so long as they are not injurious to Christianity and the laws of God. Therefore, if the Pope deserves punishment, these laws cease to bind us, since Christendom would suffer, if he were not punished by a council. Thus we read (Acts xv.) that the council of the Apostles was not called by St. Peter, but by all the Apostles and the elders. But if the right to call it had lain with St. Peter alone, it would not have been a Christian council, but a heretical *conciliabulum*. Moreover, the most celebrated council of all—that of Nicæa—was neither called nor confirmed by the Bishop of Rome, but by the Emperor Constantine; and after him many other emperors have done the same, and yet the councils called by them were accounted most Christian. But if the Pope alone had the power, they must all have been heretical. Moreover, if I consider the councils that the Pope has called, I do not find that they produced any notable results.

Therefore when need requires, and the Pope is a cause of offence to Christendom, in these cases whoever can best do so, as a faithful member of the whole body, must do what he can to procure a true free council. This no one can do so well as the temporal authorities, especially since they are fellow-Christians, fellow-priests, sharing one spirit and one power in all things, and since they should exercise the office that they have received from God without hindrance, whenever it is necessary and useful that it should be exercised. Would it not be most unnatural, if a fire were to break out in a city, and every one were to keep still and let it burn on and on, whatever might be burnt, simply because they had not the mayor's authority, or because the fire perchance broke out at the mayor's house? Is not every citizen bound in this case to rouse and call in the rest? How much more should this be done in the spiritual city of Christ, if a fire of offence breaks out, either at the Pope's government or wherever it may! The like happens if an enemy attacks a town. The first to rouse up the rest earns glory and thanks. Why then should not he earn glory that descries the coming of our enemies from hell and rouses and summons all Christians?

But as for their boasts of their authority, that no one must oppose it, this is idle talk. No one in Christendom has any authority to do harm, or to forbid others to prevent harm being done. There is no authority in the Church but for reformation. Therefore if the Pope wished to use his power to prevent the calling of a free council, so as to prevent the reformation of the Church, we must not respect him or his power; and if he should begin to excommunicate and fulminate, we must despise this as the doings of a madman, and, trusting in God, excommunicate and repel him as best we may. For this his usurped power is nothing; he does not possess it, and he is at once overthrown by a text from the Scriptures. For St. Paul says to the Corinthians "that God has given us authority for edification, and not for destruction" (2 Cor. x. 8). Who will set this text at nought? It is the power of the devil and of antichrist that prevents what would serve for the reformation of Christendom. Therefore we must not follow it, but oppose it with our body, our goods, and all that we have. And even if a miracle were to happen in favour of the Pope against the temporal power, or if some were to be stricken by a plague, as they sometimes boast has happened, all this is to be held as having been done by the devil in order to injure our faith in God, as was foretold by Christ: "There shall arise false Christs and false prophets, and shall show great signs and wonders, insomuch that, if it were possible, they shall deceive the very elect" (Matt. xxiv. 23); and St. Paul tells the Thessalonians that the coming of antichrist shall be "after the working of Satan with all power and signs and lying wonders" (2 Thess. ii. 9).

Therefore let us hold fast to this: that Christian power can do nothing against Christ, as St. Paul says, "For we can do nothing against Christ, but for Christ" (2 Cor. xiii. 8). But, if it does anything against Christ, it is the power of antichrist and the devil, even if it rained and hailed wonders and plagues. Wonders and plagues prove nothing, especially in these latter evil days, of which false wonders are foretold in all the Scriptures. Therefore we must hold fast to the words of God with an assured faith; then the devil will soon cease his wonders.

And now I hope the false, lying spectre will be laid with which the Romanists have long terrified and stupefied our consciences. And it will be seen that, like all the rest of us, they are subject to the temporal sword; that they have no authority to interpret the Scriptures by force without skill; and that they have no power to prevent a council, or to pledge it in accordance with their pleasure, or to bind it beforehand, and deprive it of its freedom; and that if they do this, they are verily of the fellowship of antichrist and the devil, and have nothing of Christ but the name.

OF THE MATTERS TO BE CONSIDERED IN THE COUNCILS

Let us now consider the matters which should be treated in the councils, and with which popes, cardinals, bishops, and all learned men should occupy themselves day and night, if they love Christ and His Church. But if they do not do so, the people at large and the temporal powers must do so, without considering the thunders of their excommunications. For an unjust excommunication is better than ten just absolutions, and an unjust absolution is worse than ten just excommunications. Therefore let us rouse ourselves, fellow-Germans, and fear God more than man, that we be not answerable for all the poor souls that are so miserably lost through the wicked, devilish government of the Romanists, and that the dominion of the devil should not grow day by day, if indeed this hellish government can grow any worse, which, for my part, I can neither conceive nor believe.

1. It is a distressing and terrible thing to see that the head of Christendom, who boasts of being the vicar of Christ and the successor of St. Peter, lives in a worldly pomp that no king or emperor can equal, so that in him that calls himself most holy and most spiritual there is more worldliness than in the world itself. He wears a triple crown, whereas the mightiest kings only wear one crown.

If this resembles the poverty of Christ and St. Peter, it is a new sort of resemblance. They prate of its being heretical to object to this; nay, they will not even hear how unchristian and ungodly it is. But I think that if he should have to pray to God with tears, he would have to lay down his crowns; for God will not endure any arrogance. His office should be nothing else than to weep and pray constantly for Christendom and to be an example of all humility.

However this may be, this pomp is a stumbling-block, and the Pope, for the very salvation of his soul, ought to put it off, for St. Paul says, "Abstain from all appearance of evil" (1 Thess. v. 21), and again, "Provide things honest in the sight of all men" (2 Cor. viii. 21). A simple mitre would be enough for the pope: wisdom and sanctity should raise him above the rest; the crown of pride he should leave to antichrist, as his predecessors did some hundreds of years ago. They say, He is the ruler of the world. This is false; for Christ, whose vicegerent and vicar he claims to be, said to Pilate, "My kingdom is not of this world" (John xviii. 36). But no vicegerent can have a wider dominion than his Lord, nor is he a vicegerent of Christ in His glory, but of Christ crucified, as St. Paul says, "For I determined not to know anything among you save Jesus Christ, and Him crucified" (2 Cor. ii. 2), and "Let this mind be in you, which was also in Christ Jesus, who made Himself of no reputation, and took upon Himself the form of a servant" (Phil. ii. 5, 7). Again, "We preach Christ crucified" (1 Cor. i.). Now they make the Pope a vicegerent of Christ exalted in heaven, and some have let the devil rule them so thoroughly that they have maintained that the Pope is above the angels in heaven and has power over them, which is precisely the true work of the true antichrist.

2. What is the use in Christendom of the people called "cardinals"? I will tell you. In Italy and Germany there are many rich convents, endowments, fiefs, and benefices, and as the best way of getting these into the hands of Rome, they created cardinals, and gave them the sees, convents, and prelacies, and thus destroyed the service of God. That is why Italy is almost a desert now: the convents are destroyed, the sees consumed, the revenues of the prelacies and of all the churches drawn to Rome; towns are decayed, the country and the people ruined, because there is no more any worship of God or

preaching; why? Because the cardinals must have all the wealth. No Turk could have thus desolated Italy and overthrown the worship of God.

Now that Italy is sucked dry, they come to Germany and begin very quietly; but if we look on quietly Germany will soon be brought into the same state as Italy. We have a few cardinals already. What the Romanists mean thereby the drunken Germans[5] are not to see until they have lost everything—bishoprics, convents, benefices, fiefs, even to their last farthing. Antichrist must take the riches of the earth, as it is written (Dan. xi. 8, 39, 43). They begin by taking off the cream of the bishoprics, convents and fiefs; and as they do not dare to destroy everything as they have done in Italy, they employ such holy cunning to join together ten or twenty prelacies, and take such a portion of each annually that the total amounts to a considerable sum. The priory of Würzburg gives one thousand guilders; those of Bamberg, Mayence, Treves, and others also contribute. In this way they collect one thousand or ten thousand guilders, in order that a cardinal may live at Rome in a state like that of a wealthy monarch.

After we have gained this, we will create thirty or forty cardinals on one day, and give one St. Michael's Mount,[6] near Bamberg, and likewise the see of Würzburg, to which belong some rich benefices, until the churches and the cities are desolated; and then we shall say, We are the vicars of Christ, the shepherds of Christ's flocks; those mad, drunken Germans must submit to it. I advise, however, that there be made fewer cardinals, or that the Pope should have to support them out of his own purse. It would be amply sufficient if there were twelve, and if each of them had an annual income of one thousand guilders.

What has brought us Germans to such a pass that we have to suffer this robbery and this destruction of our property by the Pope? If the kingdom of France has resisted it, why do we Germans suffer ourselves to be fooled and deceived? It would be more endurable if they did nothing but rob us of our property; but they destroy the

[5] The epithet "drunken" was formerly often applied by the Italians to the Germans.

[6] Luther alludes here to the Benedictine convent standing on the *Mönchberg*, or St. Michael's Mount.

Church and deprive Christ's flock of their good shepherds, and overthrow the service and word of God. Even if there were no cardinals at all, the Church would not perish, for they do nothing for the good of Christendom; all they do is to traffic in and quarrel about prelacies and bishoprics, which any robber could do as well.

3. If we took away ninety-nine parts of the Pope's Court and only left one hundredth, it would still be large enough to answer questions on matters of belief. Now there is such a swarm of vermin at Rome, all called papal, that Babylon itself never saw the like. There are more than three thousand papal secretaries alone; but who shall count the other office-bearers, since there are so many offices that we can scarcely count them, and all waiting for German benefices, as wolves wait for a flock of sheep? I think Germany now pays more to the Pope than it formerly paid the emperors; nay, some think more than three hundred thousand guilders are sent from Germany to Rome every year, for nothing whatever; and in return we are scoffed at and put to shame. Do we still wonder why princes, noblemen, cities, foundations, convents, and people grow poor? We should rather wonder that we have anything left to eat.

Now that we have got well into our game, let us pause a while and show that the Germans are not such fools as not to perceive or understand this Romish trickery. I do not here complain that God's commandments and Christian justice are despised at Rome; for the state of things in Christendom, especially at Rome, is too bad for us to complain of such high matters. Nor do I even complain that no account is taken of natural or secular justice and reason. The mischief lies still deeper. I complain that they do not observe their own fabricated canon law, though this is in itself rather mere tyranny, avarice, and worldly pomp, than a law. This we shall now show.

Long ago the emperors and princes of Germany allowed the Pope to claim the *annates*[7] from all German benefices; that is, half of the first year's income from every benefice. The object of this concession was that the Pope should collect a fund with all this money to fight against the Turks and infidels, and to protect Christendom, so that the nobility should not have to bear the burden of the struggle alone, and that the priests should also contribute. The popes have made

[7] The duty of paying *annates* to the Pope was established by John XXII. in 1319.

such use of this good simple piety of the Germans that they have taken this money for more than one hundred years, and have now made of it a regular tax and duty; and not only have they accumulated nothing, but they have founded out of it many posts and offices at Rome, which are paid by it yearly, as out of a ground-rent.

Whenever there is any pretence of fighting the Turks, they send out some commission for collecting money, and often send out indulgences under the same pretext of fighting the Turks. They think we Germans will always remain such great and inveterate fools that we will go on giving money to satisfy their unspeakable greed, though we see plainly that neither *annates,* nor absolution money, nor any other—not one farthing—goes against the Turks, but all goes into the bottomless sack. They lie and deceive, form and make covenants with us, of which they do not mean to keep one jot. And all this is done in the holy name of Christ and St. Peter.

This being so, the German nation, the bishops and princes, should remember that they are Christians, and should defend the people, who are committed to their government and protection in temporal and spiritual affairs, from these ravenous wolves in sheep's clothing that profess to be shepherds and rulers; and since the *annates* are so shamefully abused, and the covenants concerning them not carried out, they should not suffer their lands and people to be so piteously and unrighteously flayed and ruined; but by an imperial or a national law they should either retain the *annates* in the country, or abolish them altogether. For since they do not keep to the covenants, they have no right to the *annates;* therefore bishops and princes are bound to punish this thievery and robbery, or prevent it, as justice demands. And herein should they assist and strengthen the Pope, who is perchance too weak to prevent this scandal by himself, or, if he wishes to protect or support it, restrain and oppose him as a wolf and tyrant; for he has no authority to do evil or to protect evil-doers. Even if it were proposed to collect any such treasure for use against the Turks, we should be wise in future, and remember that the German nation is more fitted to take charge of it than the Pope, seeing that the German nation by itself is able to provide men enough, if the money is forthcoming. This matter of the *annates* is like many other Romish pretexts.

Moreover, the year has been divided among the Pope and the ruling bishops and foundations in such wise that the Pope has taken every other month—six in all—to give away the benefices that fall in his month; in this way almost all the benefices are drawn into the hands of Rome, and especially the best livings and dignities. And those that once fall into the hands of Rome never come out again, even if they never again fall vacant in the Pope's month. In this way the foundations come very short of their rights, and it is a downright robbery, the object of which is not to give up anything again. Therefore it is now high time to abolish the Pope's months and to take back again all that has thereby fallen into the hands of Rome. For all the princes and nobles should insist that the stolen property shall be returned, the thieves punished, and that those who abuse their powers shall be deprived of them. If the Pope can make a law on the day after his election by which he takes our benefices and livings to which he has no right, the Emperor Charles should so much the more have a right to issue a law for all Germany on the day after his coronation[8] that in future no livings and benefices are to fall to Rome by virtue of the Pope's month, but that those that have so fallen are to be freed and taken from the Romish robbers. This right he possesses authoritatively by virtue of his temporal sword.

But the see of avarice and robbery at Rome is unwilling to wait for the benefices to fall in one after another by means of the Pope's month; and in order to get them into its insatiable maw as speedily as possible, they have devised the plan of taking livings and benefices in three other ways:—

First, if the incumbent of a free living dies at Rome or on his way thither, his living remains for ever the property of the see of Rome, or I rather should say, the see of robbers, though they will not let us call them robbers, although no one has ever heard or read of such robbery.

Secondly, if a "servant" of the Pope or of one of the cardinals takes a living, or if, having a living, he becomes a "servant" of the Pope or of a cardinal, the living remains with Rome. But who can count

²'At the time when the above was written—June, 1520—the Emperor Charles had been elected, but not yet crowned.

the "servants" of the Pope and his cardinals, seeing that if he goes out riding, he is attended by three or four thousand mule-riders, more than any king or emperor? For Christ and St. Peter went on foot, in order that their vicegerents might indulge the better in all manner of pomp. Besides, their avarice has devised and invented this: that in foreign countries also there are many called "papal servants," as at Rome; so that in all parts this single crafty little word "papal servant" brings all benefices to the chair at Rome, and they are kept there for ever. Are not these mischievous, devilish devices? Let us only wait a while, Mayence, Magdeburg, and Halberstadt will fall very nicely to Rome, and we shall have to pay dearly for our cardinal.[9] Hereafter all the German bishops will be made cardinals, so that there shall remain nothing to ourselves.

Thirdly, whenever there is any dispute about a benefice; and this is, I think, well-nigh the broadest and commonest road by which benefices are brought to Rome. For where there is no dispute numberless knaves can be found at Rome who are ready to scrape up disputes, and attack livings wherever they like. In this way many a good priest loses his living, or has to buy off the dispute for a time with a sum of money. These benefices, confiscated by right or wrong of dispute, are to be for ever the property of the see of Rome. It would be no wonder, if God were to rain sulphur and fire from heaven and cast Rome down into the pit, as He did formerly to Sodom and Gomorrah. What is the use of a pope in Christendom, if the only use made of his power is to commit these supreme villainies under his protection and assistance? Oh noble princes and sirs, how long will you suffer your lands and your people to be the prey of these ravening wolves?

But these tricks did not suffice, and bishoprics were too slow in falling into the power of Roman avarice. Accordingly our good friend Avarice made the discovery that all bishoprics are abroad in name only, but that their land and soil is at Rome; from this it fol-

---

[9] Luther alludes here to the Archbishop Albert of Mayence, who was, besides, Archbishop of Magdeburg and administrator of the bishopric of Halberstadt. In order to be able to defray the expense of the archiepiscopal tax due to Rome, amounting to thirty thousand guilders, he had farmed the sale of the Pope's indulgences, employing the notorious Tetzel as his agent and sharing the profits with the Pope. In 1518 Albert was appointed cardinal. See Ranke, *Deutsche Geschichte*, etc., vol. i., p. 309, etc.

lows that no bishop may be confirmed until he has bought the "Pall" [10] for a large sum, and has with a terrible oath bound himself a servant of the Pope. That is why no bishop dare oppose the Pope. This was the object of the oath, and this is how the wealthiest bishoprics have come to debt and ruin. Mayence, I am told, pays twenty thousand guilders. These are true Roman tricks, it seems to me. It is true that they once decreed in the canon law that the *Pall* should be given free, the number of the Pope's servants diminished, disputes made less frequent, that foundations and bishops should enjoy their liberty; but all this brought them no money. They have therefore reversed all this: bishops and foundations have lost all their power; they are mere ciphers, without office, authority, or function; all things are regulated by the chief knaves at Rome, even the offices of sextons and bell-ringers in all churches. All disputes are transferred to Rome; each one does what he will, strong through the Pope's power.

What has happened in this very year? The Bishop of Strasburg, wishing to regulate his see in a proper way and reform it in the matter of Divine service, published some Divine and Christian ordinances for that purpose. But our worthy Pope and the holy chair at Rome overturn altogether this holy and spiritual order on the requisition of the priests. This is what they call being the shepherd of Christ's sheep—supporting priests against their own bishops and protecting their disobedience by Divine decrees. Antichrist, I hope, will not insult God in this open way. There you have the Pope, as you have chosen to have him; and why? Why, because if the Church were to be reformed, there would be danger that it would spread further, so that it might also reach Rome. Therefore it is better to prevent priests from being at one with each other; they should rather, as they have done hitherto, sow discord among kings and princes, and flood the world with Christian blood, lest Christian unity should trouble the holy Roman see with reforms.

So far we have seen what they do with the livings that fall vacant. Now there are not enough vacancies for this delicate greed; therefore it has also taken prudent account of the benefices that are

[10] The *Pallium* was since the fourth century the symbol of archiepiscopal power, and had to be redeemed from the Pope by means of a large sum of money and a solemn oath of obedience.

still held by their incumbents, so that they may become vacant, though they are in fact not vacant, and this they effect in many ways.

First, they lie in wait for fat livings or sees which are held by an old or sick man, or even by one afflicted by an imaginary incompetence; him the Roman see gives a *coadjutor,* that is an assistant without his asking or wishing it, for the benefit of the coadjutor, because he is a papal servant, or pays for the office, or has otherwise earned it by some menial service rendered to Rome. Thus there is an end of free election on the part of the chapter, or of the right of him who had presented to the living; and all goes to Rome.

Secondly, there is a little word: *commendam,* that is, when the Pope gives a rich and fat convent or church into the charge of a cardinal or any other of his servants, just as I might command you to take charge of one hundred guilders for me. In this way the convent is neither given, nor lent, nor destroyed, nor is its Divine service abolished, but only entrusted to a man's charge, not, however, for him to protect and improve it, but to drive out the one he finds there, to take the property and revenue, and to install some apostate[11] runaway monk, who is paid five or six guilders a year, and sits in the church all day and sells symbols and pictures to the pilgrims; so that neither chanting nor reading in the church goes on there any more. Now if we were to call this the destruction of convents and abolition of Divine service we should be obliged to accuse the Pope of destroying Christianity and abolishing Divine service—for truly he is doing this effectually—but this would be thought harsh language at Rome; therefore it is called a *commendam,* or an order to take charge of the convent. In this way the Pope can make *commendams* of four or more convents a year, any one of which produces a revenue of more than six thousand guilders. This is the way Divine service is advanced and convents kept up at Rome. This will be introduced into Germany as well.

Thirdly, there are certain benefices that are said to be *incompatible;* that is, they may not be held together according to the canon law, such as two cures, two sees, and the like. Now the Holy See and avarice twists itself out of the canon law by making "glosses," or interpretations, called *Unio,* or *Incorporatio;* that is, several incom-

---

[11] Monks who forsook their order without any legal dispensation were called "apostates."

patible benefices are incorporated, so that one is a member of the other, and the whole is held to be one benefice: then they are no longer incompatible, and we have got rid of the holy canon law, so that it is no longer binding, except on those who do not buy those *glosses* of the Pope and his *Datarius*.[12] *Unio* is of the same kind: a number of benefices are tied together like a bundle of faggots, and on account of this coupling together they are held to be one benefice. Thus there may be found many a "courtling" at Rome who alone holds twenty-two cures, seven priories, and forty-four prebends, all which is done in virtue of this masterly *gloss,* so as not to be contrary to law. Any one can imagine what cardinals and other prelates may hold. In this way the Germans are to have their purses emptied and their conceit taken out of them.

There is another *gloss* called *Administratio;* that is, that besides his see a man holds an abbey or other high benefice, and possesses all the property of it, without any other title but *administrator.* For at Rome it is enough that words should change, and not deeds, just as if I said, a procuress was to be called a mayoress, yet may remain as good as she is now. Such Romish rule was foretold by St. Peter, when he said, "There shall be false teachers among you, . . . and through covetousness shall they with feigned words make merchandise of you" (2 Peter ii. 1, 3).

This precious Roman avarice has also invented the practice of selling and lending prebends and benefices on condition that the seller or lender has the reversion, so that if the incumbent dies, the benefice falls to him that has sold it, lent it, or abandoned it; in this way they have made benefices heritable property, so that none can come to hold them unless the seller sells them to him, or leaves them to him at his death. Then there are many that give a benefice to another in name only, and on condition that he shall not receive a farthing. It is now, too, an old practice for a man to give another a benefice and to receive a certain annual sum, which proceeding was formerly called simony. And there are many other such little things which I cannot recount; and so they deal worse with the benefices than the heathens by the cross dealt with Christ's clothes.

[12] The papal office for the issue and registration of certain documents was called Dataria, from the phrase appended to them, *Datum apud S. Petrum.* The chief of that office, usually a cardinal, bore the title of *Datarius,* or *Prodatarius.*

But all this that I have spoken of is old and common at Rome. Their avarice has invented other device, which I hope will be the last and choke it. The Pope has made a noble discovery, called *Pectoralis Reservatio,* that is, "mental reservation"—*et proprius motus,* that is, "and his own will and power." The matter is managed in this way: Suppose a man obtains a benefice at Rome, which is confirmed to him in due form; then comes another, who brings money, or who has done some other service of which the less said the better, and requests the Pope to give him the same benefice: then the Pope will take it from the first and give it him. If you say, that is wrong, the Most Holy Father must then excuse himself, that he may not be openly blamed for having violated justice; and he says "that in his heart and mind he reserved his authority over the said benefice," whilst he never had heard or thought of the same in all his life. Thus he has devised a *gloss* which allows him in his proper person to lie and cheat and fool us all, and all this impudently and in open daylight, and nevertheless he claims to be the head of Christendom, letting the evil spirit rule him with manifest lies.

This wantonness and lying reservation of the popes has brought about an unutterable state of things at Rome. There is a buying and a selling, a changing, blustering and bargaining, cheating and lying, robbing and stealing, debauchery and villainy, and all kinds of contempt of God, that antichrist himself could not rule worse. Venice, Antwerp, Cairo, are nothing to this fair and market at Rome, except that there things are done with some reason and justice, whilst here things are done as the devil himself could wish. And out of this ocean a like virtue overflows all the world. Is it not natural that such people should dread a reformation and a free council, and should rather embroil all kings and princes, than that their unity should bring about a council? Who would like his villainy to be exposed?

Finally, the Pope has built a special house for this fine traffic— that is, the house of the *Datarius* at Rome. Thither all must come that bargain in this way, for prebends and benefices; from him they must buy the *glosses* and obtain the right to practise such prime villainy. In former days it was fairly well at Rome, when justice had to be bought, or could only be put down by money; but now she has become so fastidious that she does not allow any one to commit villainies unless he has first bought the right to do it with great sums. If this is not a house of prostitution, worse than all houses of prostitution that can be conceived, I do not know what houses of prostitution really are.

If you bring money to this house, you can arrive at all that I have mentioned; and more than this, any sort of usury is made legitimate for money; property got by theft or robbery is here made legal. Here vows are annulled; here a monk obtains leave to quit his order; here priests can enter married life for money; here bastards can become legitimate; and dishonour and shame may arrive at high honours; all evil repute and disgrace is knighted and ennobled; here a marriage is suffered that is in a forbidden degree, or has some other defect. Oh, what a trafficking and plundering is there! one would think that the canon laws were only so many money-snares, from which he must free himself who would become a Christian man. Nay, here the devil becomes a saint, and a god besides. What heaven and earth might not do may be done by this house. Their ordinances are called *compositions*—compositions, forsooth! confusions rather.[13] Oh, what a poor treasury is the toll on the Rhine[14] compared with this holy house!

Let no one think that I say too much. It is all notorious, so that even at Rome they are forced to own that it is more terrible and worse than one can say. I have said and will say nothing of the infernal dregs of private vices. I only speak of well-known public matters, and yet my words do not suffice. Bishops, priests, and especially the doctors of the universities, who are paid to do it, ought to have unanimously written and exclaimed against it. Yea, if you will turn the leaf you will discover the truth.

I have still to give a farewell greeting. These treasures, that would have satisfied three mighty kings, were not enough for this unspeakable greed, and so they have made over and sold their traffic to Fugger[15] at Augsburg, so that the lending and buying and selling sees and benefices, and all this traffic in ecclesiastical property, has in the end come into the right hands, and spiritual and temporal

[13] Luther uses here the expressions *compositiones* and *confusiones* as a kind of pun.
[14] Tolls were levied at many places along the Rhine.
[15] The commercial house of Fugger was in those days the wealthiest in Europe.

matters have now become one business. Now I should like to know what the most cunning would devise for Romish greed to do that it has not done, except that Fugger might sell or pledge his two trades, that have now become one. I think they must have come to the end of their devices. For what they have stolen and yet steal in all countries by bulls of indulgences, letters of confession, letters of dispensation,[16] and other *confessionalia,* all this I think mere bungling work, and much like playing toss with a devil in hell. Not that they produce little, for a mighty king could support himself by them; but they are as nothing compared to the other streams of revenue mentioned above. I will not now consider what has become of that indulgence money; I shall inquire into this another time, for *Campofiore*[17] and *Belvedere*[18] and some other places probably know something about it.

Meanwhile, since this devilish state of things is not only an open robbery, deceit, and tyranny of the gates of hell, but also destroys Christianity body and soul, we are bound to use all our diligence to prevent this misery and destruction of Christendom. If we wish to fight the Turk, let us begin here, where they are worst. If we justly hang thieves and behead robbers, why do we leave the greed of Rome so unpunished, that is the greatest thief and robber that has appeared or can appear on earth, and does all this in the holy name of Christ and St. Peter? Who can suffer this and be silent about it? Almost everything that they possess has been stolen or got by robbery, as we learn from all histories. Why, the Pope never bought those great possessions, so as to be able to raise well-nigh ten hundred thousand ducats from his ecclesiastical offices, without counting his gold mines described above and his land. He did not inherit it from Christ and St. Peter; no one gave it or lent it him; he has not acquired it by prescription. Tell me, where can he have got it? You can learn from this what their object is when they send out legates to collect money to be used against the Turk.

[16] Luther uses the word *Butterbriefe, i. e.,* letters of indulgence allowing the enjoyment of butter, cheese, milk, etc., during Lent. They formed part only of the *confessionalia,* which granted various other indulgences.
[17] A public place at Rome.
[18] Part of the Vatican.

TWENTY-SEVEN ARTICLES RESPECTING THE REFORMATION OF THE CHRISTIAN ESTATE

Now though I am too lowly to submit articles that could serve for the reformation of these fearful evils, I will yet sing out my fool's song, and will show, as well as my wit will allow, what might and should be done by the temporal authorities or by a general council.

1. Princes, nobles, and cities should promptly forbid their subjects to pay the *annates* to Rome and should even abolish them altogether. For the Pope has broken the compact, and turned the *annates* into robbery for the harm and shame of the German nation; he gives them to his friends; he sells them for large sums of money and founds benefices on them. Therefore he has forfeited his right to them, and deserves punishment. In this way the temporal power should protect the innocent and prevent wrong-doing, as we are taught by St. Paul (Rom. xiii.) and by St. Peter (1 Peter ii.) and even by the canon law (16. q. 7. de Filiis). That is why we say to the Pope and his followers, *Tu ora!* "Thou shalt pray"; to the Emperor and his followers, *Tu protege!* "Thou shalt protect"; to the commons, *Tu labora!* "Thou shalt work." Not that each man should not pray, protect, and work; for if a man fulfils his duty, that is prayer, protection, and work; but every man must have his proper task.

2. Since by means of those Romish tricks, *commendams,* coadjutors, reservations, expectations, pope's months, incorporations, unions, Palls, rules of chancellery, and other such knaveries, the Pope takes unlawful possession of all German foundations, to give and sell them to strangers at Rome, that profit Germany in no way, so that the incumbents are robbed of their rights, and the bishops are made mere ciphers and anointed idols; and thus, besides natural justice and reason, the Pope's own canon law is violated; and things have come to such a pass that prebends and benefices are sold at Rome to vulgar, ignorant asses and knaves, out of sheer greed, while pious learned men have no profit by their merit and skill, whereby the unfortunate German people must needs lack good, learned prelates and suffer ruin—on account of these evils the Chris-

tian nobility should rise up against the Pope as a common enemy and destroyer of Christianity, for the sake of the salvation of the poor souls that such tyranny must ruin. They should ordain, order, and decree that henceforth no benefice shall be drawn away to Rome, and that no benefice shall be claimed there in any fashion whatsoever; and after having once got these benefices out of the hands of Romish tyranny, they must be kept from them, and their lawful incumbents must be reinstated in them to administer them as best they may within the German nation. And if a courtling came from Rome, he should receive the strict command to withdraw, or to leap into the Rhine, or whatever river be nearest, and to administer a cold bath to the Interdict, seal and letters and all. Thus those at Rome would learn that we Germans are not to remain drunken fools forever, but that we, too, are become Christians, and that as such we will no longer suffer this shameful mockery of Christ's holy name, that serves as a cloak for such knavery and destruction of souls, and that we shall respect God and the glory of God more than the power of men.

3. It should be decreed by an imperial law that no episcopal cloak and no confirmation of any appointment shall for the future be obtained from Rome. The order of the most holy and renowned Nicene Council must again be restored, namely that a bishop must be confirmed by the two nearest bishops or by the archbishop. If the Pope cancels the decrees of these and all other councils, what is the good of councils at all? Who has given him the right thus to despise councils and to cancel them? If this is allowed, we had better abolish all bishops, archbishops and primates, and make simple rectors of all of them, so that they would have the Pope alone over them as is indeed the case now; he deprives bishops, archbishops, and primates of all the authority of their office, taking everything to himself, and leaving them only the name and the empty title; more than this, by his exemption he has withdrawn convents, abbots, and prelates from the ordinary authority of the bishops, so that there remains no order in Christendom. The necessary result of this must be, and has been, laxity in punishing and such a liberty to do evil in all the world that I very much fear one might call the Pope "the man of sin" (2 Thess. ii. 3). Who but the

Pope is to blame for this absence of all order, of all punishment, of all government, of all discipline, in Christendom? By his own arbitrary power he ties the hands of all his prelates, and takes from them their rods, while all their subjects have their hands unloosed, and obtain licence by gift or purchase.

But, that he have no cause for complaint, as being deprived of his authority, it should be decreed that in cases where the primates and archbishops are unable to settle the matter, or where there is a dispute among them, the matters shall then be submitted to the Pope, but not every little matter, as was done formerly, and was ordered by the most renowned Nicene Council. His Holiness must not be troubled with small matters, that can be settled without his help; so that he may have leisure to devote himself to his prayers and study and to his care of all Christendom, as he professes to do, as indeed the Apostles did, saying, "It is not reason that we should leave the word of God, and serve tables. . . . But we will give ourselves continually to prayer, and to the ministry of the word" (Acts vi. 2, 4). But now we see at Rome nothing but contempt of the Gospel and of prayer, and the service of tables, that is the service of the goods of this world; and the government of the Pope agrees with the government of the Apostles as well as Lucifer with Christ, hell with heaven, night with day; and yet he calls himself Christ's vicar and the successor of the Apostles.

4. Let it be decreed that no temporal matter shall be submitted to Rome, but all shall be left to the jurisdiction of the temporal authorities. This is part of their own canon law, though they do not obey it. For this should be the Pope's office: that he, the most learned in the Scriptures and the most holy, not in name only, but in fact, should rule in matters concerning the faith and the holy life of Christians; he should make primates and bishops attend to this, and should work and take thought with them to this end, as St. Paul teaches (1 Cor. vi.), severely upbraiding those that occupy themselves with the things of this world. For all countries suffer unbearable damage by this practice of settling such matters at Rome, since it involves great expense; and besides this, the judges at Rome, not knowing the manners, laws, and customs of other countries, frequently pervert the matter according to their own laws and their

own opinions, thus causing injustice to all parties. Besides this, we should prohibit in all foundations the grievous extortion of the ecclesiastical judges; they should only be allowed to consider matters concerning faith and good morals; but matters concerning money, property, life, and honour should be left to temporal judges. Therefore, the temporal authorities should not permit excommunication or expulsion except in matters of faith and righteous living. It is only reasonable that spiritual authorities should have power in spiritual matters; spiritual matters, however, are not money or matters relating to the body, but faith and good works.

Still we might allow matters respecting benefices or prebends to be treated before bishops, archbishops, and primates. Therefore when it is necessary to decide quarrels and strifes let the Primate of Germany hold a general consistory, with assessors and chancellors, who would have the control over the *signaturas gratiæ* and *justitiæ* [19] and to whom matters arising in Germany might be submitted by appeal. The officers of such court should be paid out of the *annates,* or in some other way, and should not have to draw their salaries, as at Rome, from chance presents and offerings, whereby they grow accustomed to sell justice and injustice, as they must needs do at Rome, where the Pope gives them no salary, but allows them to fatten themselves on presents; for at Rome no one heeds what is right or what is wrong, but only what is money and what is not money. They might be paid out of the *annates,* or by some other means devised by men of higher understanding and of more experience in these things than I have. I am content with making these suggestions and giving some materials for consideration to those who may be able and willing to help the German nation to become a free people of Christians, after this wretched, heathen, unchristian misrule of the Pope.

5. Henceforth no reservations shall be valid, and no benefices shall be appropriated by Rome, whether the incumbent die there, or there be a dispute, or the incumbent be a servant of the Pope or of a cardinal; and all courtiers shall be strictly prohibited and prevented from causing a dispute about any benefice, so as to cite the pious

[19] At the time when the above was written the function of the *signatura gratiæ* was to superintend the conferring of grants, concessions, favours, etc., whilst the *signatura justitiæ* embraced the general administration of ecclesiastical matters.

priests, to trouble them, and to drive them to pay compensation. And if in consequence of this there comes an interdict from Rome, let it be despised, just as if a thief were to excommunicate any man because he would not allow him to steal in peace. Nay, they should be punished most severely for making such a blasphemous use of excommunication and of the name of God, to support their robberies, and for wishing by their false threats to drive us to suffer and approve this blasphemy of God's name and this abuse of Christian authority, and thus to become sharers before God in their wrong-doing, whereas it is our duty before God to punish it, as St. Paul (Rom. i.) upbraids the Romans for not only doing wrong, but allowing wrong to be done. But above all that lying mental reservation (*pectoralis reservatio*) is unbearable, by which Christendom is so openly mocked and insulted, in that its head notoriously deals with lies, and impudently cheats and fools every man for the sake of accursed wealth.

6. The cases reserved[20] (*casus reservati*) should be abolished, by which not only are the people cheated out of much money, but besides many poor consciences are confused and led into error by the ruthless tyrants, to the intolerable harm of their faith in God, especially those foolish and childish cases that are made important by the bull *In Cœna Domini*,[21] and which do not deserve the name of daily sins, not to mention those great cases for which the Pope gives no absolution, such as preventing a pilgrim from going to Rome, furnishing the Turks with arms, or forging the Pope's letters. They only fool us with these gross, mad, and clumsy matters: Sodom and Gomorrah, and all sins that are committed and that can be committed against God's commandments, are not reserved cases; but what God never commanded and they themselves have invented— these must be made reserved cases, solely in order that none may be prevented from bringing money to Rome, that they may live in their lust without fear of the Turk, and may keep the world in their bondage by their wicked useless bulls and briefs.

[20] "Reserved cases" refer to those great sins for which the Pope or the bishops only could give absolution.

[21] The celebrated papal bull known under the name of *In Cœna Domini*, containing anathemas and excommunications against all those who dissented in any way from the Roman Catholic creed, used until the year 1770 to be read publicly at Rome on Maundy Thursday.

Now all priests ought to know, or rather it should be a public ordinance, that no secret sin constitutes a reserved case, if there be no public accusation; and that every priest has power to absolve from all sin, whatever its name, if it be secret, and that no abbot, bishop, or pope has power to reserve any such case; and, lastly, that if they do this, it is null and void, and they should, moreover, be punished as interfering without authority in God's judgment and confusing and troubling without cause our poor witless consciences. But in respect to any great open sin, directly contrary to God's commandments, there is some reason for a "reserved case"; but there should not be too many, nor should they be reserved arbitrarily without due cause. For God has not ordained tyrants, but shepherds, in His Church, as St. Peter says (1 Peter v. 2).

7. The Roman See must abolish the papal offices, and diminish that crowd of crawling vermin at Rome, so that the Pope's servants may be supported out of the Pope's own pocket, and that his court may cease to surpass all royal courts in its pomp and extravagance; seeing that all this pomp has not only been of no service to the Christian faith, but has also kept them from study and prayer, so that they themselves know hardly anything concerning matters of faith, as they proved clumsily enough at the last Roman Council,[22] where, among many childishly trifling matters, they decided "that the soul is immortal," and that a priest is bound to pray once every month on pain of losing his benefice.[23] How are men to rule Christendom and to decide matters of faith who, callous and blinded by their greed, wealth, and worldly pomp, have only just decided that the soul is immortal? It is no slight shame to all Christendom that they should deal thus scandalously with the faith at Rome. If they had less wealth and lived in less pomp, they might be better able to study and pray that they might become able and worthy to treat matters of belief, as they were once, when they were content to be bishops, and not kings of kings.

8. The terrible oaths must be abolished which bishops are forced,

[22] The council alluded to above was held at Rome from 1512 to 1517.
[23] Luther's objection is not, of course, to the recognition of the immortality of the soul; what he objects to is (1) that it was thought necessary for a council to decree that the soul is immortal, and (2) that this question was put on a level with trivial matters of discipline.

without any right, to swear to the Pope, by which they are bound like servants, and which are arbitrarily and foolishly decreed in the absurd and shallow chapter *Significasti*.[24] Is it not enough that they oppress us in goods, body, and soul by all their mad laws, by which they have weakened faith and destroyed Christianity; but must they now take possession of the very persons of bishops, with their offices and functions, and also claim the *investiture*[25] which used formerly to be the right of the German emperors, and is still the right of the King in France and other kingdoms? This matter caused many wars and disputes with the emperors until the popes impudently took the power by force, since which time they have retained it, just as if it were only right for the Germans, above all Christians on earth, to be the fools of the Pope and the Holy See, and to do and suffer what no one beside would suffer or do. Seeing then that this is mere arbitrary power, robbery, and a hindrance to the exercise of the bishop's ordinary power, and to the injury of poor souls, therefore it is the duty of the Emperor and his nobles to prevent and punish this tyranny.

9. The Pope should have no power over the Emperor, except to anoint and crown him at the altar, as a bishop crowns a king; nor should that devilish pomp be allowed that the Emperor should kiss the Pope's feet or sit at his feet, or, as it is said, hold his stirrup or the reins of his mule, when he mounts to ride; much less should he pay homage to the Pope, or swear allegiance, as is impudently demanded by the popes, as if they had a right to it. The chapter *Solite*,[26] in which the papal authority is exalted above the imperial, is not worth a farthing, and so of all those that depend on it or fear it; for it does nothing but pervert God's holy words from their true meaning, according to their own imaginations, as I have proved in a Latin treatise.

All these excessive, over-presumptuous, and most wicked claims of the Pope are the invention of the devil, with the object of bringing in antichrist in due course and of raising the Pope above God, as indeed many have done and are now doing. It is not meet that the

[24] The above is the title of a chapter in the *Corpus Juris Canonici*.

[25] The right of investiture was the subject of the dispute between Gregory VII. and Henry IV., which led to the Emperor's submission at Canossa.

[26] The chapter *Solite* is also contained in the *Corpus Juris Canonici*.

Pope should exalt himself above temporal authority, except in spiritual matters, such as preaching and absolution; in other matters he should be subject to it, according to the teaching of St. Paul (Rom. xiii.) and St. Peter (1 Peter iii.), as I have said above. He is not the vicar of Christ in heaven, but only of Christ upon earth. For Christ in heaven, in the form of a ruler, requires no vicar, but there sits, sees, does, knows, and commands all things. But He requires him "in the form of a servant" to represent Him as He walked upon earth, working, preaching, suffering, and dying. But they reverse this: they take from Christ His power as a heavenly Ruler, and give it to the Pope, and allow "the form of a servant" to be entirely forgotten (Phil. ii. 7). He should properly be called the counter-Christ, whom the Scriptures call *antichrist;* for his whole existence, work, and proceedings are directed against Christ, to ruin and destroy the existence and will of Christ.

It is also absurd and puerile for the Pope to boast for such blind, foolish reasons, in his decretal *Pastoralis,* that he is the rightful heir to the empire, if the throne be vacant. Who gave it to him? Did Christ do so when He said, "The kings of the Gentiles exercise lordship over them, but ye shall not do so" (Luke xxii. 25, 26)? Did St. Peter bequeath it to him? It disgusts me that we have to read and teach such impudent, clumsy, foolish lies in the canon law, and, moreover, to take them for Christian doctrine, while in reality they are mere devilish lies. Of this kind also is the unheard-of lie touching the "donation of Constantine." [27] It must have been a plague sent by God that induced so many wise people to accept such lies, though they are so gross and clumsy that one would think a drunken boor could lie more skilfully. How could preaching, prayer, study, and the care of the poor consist with the government of the empire? These are the true offices of the Pope, which Christ imposed with such insistence that He forbade them to take either coat or scrip (Matt. x. 10), for he that has to govern a single house can hardly perform these duties. Yet the Pope wishes to rule an empire and to remain a pope. This is the invention of the knaves that would fain become lords of the world in the Pope's name, and set up again

[27] In order to legalize the secular power of the Pope, the fiction was invented during the latter part of the eighth century, that Constantine the Great had made over to the popes the dominion over Rome and over the whole of Italy.

the old Roman empire, as it was formerly, by means of the Pope and name of Christ, in its former condition.

10. The Pope must withdraw his hand from the dish, and on no pretence assume royal authority over Naples and Sicily. He has no more right to them than I, and yet claims to be the lord—their liege lord. They have been taken by force and robbery, like almost all his other possessions. Therefore the Emperor should grant him no such fief, nor any longer allow him those he has, but direct him instead to his Bibles and Prayer-books, so that he may leave the government of countries and peoples to the temporal power, especially of those that no one has given him. Let him rather preach and pray! The same should be done with Bologna, Imola, Vicenza, Ravenna, and whatever the Pope has taken by force and holds without right in the Ancontine territory, in the Romagna, and other parts of Italy, interfering in their affairs against all the commandments of Christ and St. Paul. For St. Paul says "that he that would be one of the soldiers of heaven must not entangle himself in the affairs of this life" (2 Tim. ii. 4). Now the Pope should be the head and the leader of the soldiers of heaven, and yet he engages more in worldly matters than any king or emperor. He should be relieved of his worldly cares and allowed to attend to his duties as a soldier of heaven. Christ also, whose vicar he claims to be, would have nothing to do with the things of this world, and even asked one that desired of Him a judgment concerning his brother, "Who made Me a judge over you?" (St.Luke xii. 14). But the Pope interferes in these matters unasked, and concerns himself with all matters, as though he were a god, until he himself has forgotten what this Christ is whose vicar he professes to be.

11. The custom of kissing the Pope's feet must cease. It is an unchristian, or rather an anti-Christian, example that a poor sinful man should suffer his feet to be kissed by one who is a hundred times better than he. If it is done in honour of his power, why does he not do it to others in honour of their holiness? Compare them together: Christ and the Pope. Christ washed His disciples' feet and dried them, and the disciples never washed His. The Pope, pretending to be higher than Christ, inverts this, and considers it a

great favour to let us kiss his feet; whereas, if any one wished to do so, he ought to do his utmost to prevent him, as St. Paul and Barnabas would not suffer themselves to be worshipped as gods by the men at Lystra, saying, "We also are men of like passions with you" (Acts xiv. 14 *seq*.). But our flatterers have brought things to such a pitch that they have set up an idol for us, until no one regards God with such fear or honours Him with such marks of reverence as he does the Pope. This they can suffer, but not that the Pope's glory should be diminished a single hair's-breadth. Now if they were Christians and preferred God's honour to their own, the Pope would never be pleased to have God's honour despised and his own exalted, nor would he allow any to honour him until he found that God's honour was again exalted above his own.

It is of a piece with this revolting pride that the Pope is not satisfied with riding on horseback or in a carriage, but though he be hale and strong, is carried by men, like an idol in unheard-of pomp. My friend, how does this Lucifer-like pride agree with the example of Christ, who went on foot, as did also all His Apostles? Where has there been a king who has ridden in such worldly pomp as he does, who professes to be the head of all whose duty it is to despise and flee from all worldly pomp—I mean, of all Christians? Not that this need concern us for his own sake, but that we have good reason to fear God's wrath, if we flatter such pride and do not show our discontent. It is enough that the Pope should be so mad and foolish; but it is too much that we should sanction and approve it.

For what Christian heart can be pleased at seeing the Pope when he communicates, sit still like a gracious lord and have the Sacrament handed to him on a golden reed by a cardinal bending on his knees before him? Just as if the Holy Sacrament were not worthy that a pope, a poor miserable sinner, should stand to do honour to his God, although all other Christians, who are much more holy than the Most Holy Father, receive it with all reverence! Could we be surprised if God visited us all with a plague for that we suffer such dishonour to be done to God by our prelates, and approve it, becoming partners of the Pope's damnable pride by our silence or flattery? It is the same when he carries the Sacrament in procession.

He must be carried, but the Sacrament stands before him like a cup of wine on a table. In short, at Rome Christ is nothing, the Pope is everything; yet they urge us and threaten us, to make us suffer and approve and honour this anti-Christian scandal, contrary to God and all Christian doctrine. Now may God so help a free council that it may teach the Pope that he too is a man, not above God, as he makes himself out to be.

12. Pilgrimages to Rome must be abolished, or at least no one must be allowed to go from his own wish or his own piety, unless his priest, his town magistrate, or his lord has found that there is sufficient reason for his pilgrimage. This I say, not because pilgrimages are bad in themselves, but because at the present time they lead to mischief; for at Rome a pilgrim sees no good examples, but only offence. They themselves have made a proverb, "The nearer to Rome, the farther from Christ," and accordingly men bring home contempt of God and of God's commandments. It is said, "The first time one goes to Rome, he goes to seek a rogue; the second time he finds him; the third time he brings him home with him." But now they have become so skilful that they can do their three journeys in one, and they have, in fact, brought home from Rome this saying: "It were better never to have seen or heard of Rome."

And even if this were not so, there is something of more importance to be considered; namely, that simple men are thus led into a false delusion and a wrong understanding of God's commandments. For they think that these pilgrimages are precious and good works; but this is not true. It is but a little good work, often a bad, misleading work, for God has not commanded it. But He has commanded that each man should care for his wife and children and whatever concerns the married state, and should, besides, serve and help his neighbour. Now it often happens that one goes on a pilgrimage to Rome, spends fifty or one hundred guilders more or less, which no one has commanded him, while his wife and children, or those dearest to him, are left at home in want and misery; and yet he thinks, poor foolish man, to atone for this disobedience and contempt of God's commandments by his self-willed pilgrimage, while he is in truth misled by idle curiosity or the wiles of the devil. This the popes have encouraged with their false and foolish invention of *Golden*

Years,[28] by which they have incited the people, have torn them away from God's commandments and turned them to their own delusive proceedings, and set up the very thing that they ought to have forbidden. But it brought them money and strengthened their false authority, and therefore it was allowed to continue, though against God's will and the salvation of souls.

That this false, misleading belief on the part of simple Christians may be destroyed, and a true opinion of good works may again be introduced, all pilgrimages should be done away with. For there is no good in them, no commandment, but countless causes of sin and of contempt of God's commandments. These pilgrimages are the reason for there being so many beggars, who commit numberless villainies, learn to beg without need and get accustomed to it. Hence arises a vagabond life, besides other miseries which I cannot dwell on now. If any one wishes to go on a pilgrimage or to make a vow for a pilgrimage, he should first inform his priest or the temporal authorities of the reason, and if it should turn out that he wishes to do it for the sake of good works, let this vow and work be just trampled upon by the priest or the temporal authority as an infernal delusion, and let them tell him to spend his money and the labour a pilgrimage would cost on God's commandments and on a thousandfold better work, namely, on his family and his poor neighbours. But if he does it out of curiosity, to see cities and countries, he may be allowed to do so. If he have vowed it in sickness, let such vows be prohibited, and let God's commandments be insisted upon in contrast to them; so that a man may be content with what he vowed in baptism, namely, to keep God's commandments. Yet for this once he may be suffered, for a quiet conscience' sake, to keep his silly vow. No one is content to walk on the broad high-road of God's commandments; every one makes for himself new roads and new vows, as if he had kept all God's commandments.

13. Now we come to the great crowd that promises much and performs little. Be not angry, my good sirs; I mean well. I have to

[28] The Jubilees, during which plenary indulgences were granted to those who visited the churches of St. Peter and St. Paul at Rome, were originally celebrated every hundred years and subsequently every twenty-five years. Those who were unable to go to Rome in person could obtain the plenary indulgences by paying the expenses of the journey to Rome into the papal treasury.

tell you this bitter and sweet truth: Let no more mendicant monasteries be built! God help us! there are too many as it is. Would to God they were all abolished, or at least made over to two or three orders! It has never done good, it will never do good, to go wandering about over the country. Therefore my advice is that ten, or as many as may be required, be put together and made into one, which one, sufficiently provided for, need not beg. Oh! it is of much more importance to consider what is necessary for the salvation of the common people, than what St. Francis, or St. Dominic, or St. Augustine,[29] or any other man, laid down, especially since things have not turned out as they expected. They should also be relieved from preaching and confession, unless specially required to do so by bishops, priests, the congregation, or other authority. For their preaching and confession has led to nought but mere hatred and envy between priests and monks, to the great offence and hindrance of the people, so that it well deserves to be put a stop to, since its place may very well be dispensed with. It does not look at all improbable that the Holy Roman See had its own reasons for encouraging all this crowd of monks: the Pope perhaps feared that priests and bishops, growing weary of his tyranny, might become too strong for him, and begin a reformation unendurable to his Holiness.

Besides this, one should also do away with the sections and the divisions in the same order which, caused for little reason and kept up for less, oppose each other with unspeakable hatred and malice, the result being that the Christian faith, which is very well able to stand without their divisions, is lost on both sides, and that a true Christian life is sought and judged only by outward rules, works, and practices, from which arise only hypocrisy and the destruction of souls, as every one can see for himself. Moreover, the Pope should be forbidden to institute or to confirm the institution of such new orders; nay, he should be commanded to abolish several and to lessen their number. For the faith of Christ, which alone is the important matter, and can stand without any particular order, incurs no little danger lest men should be led away by these diverse works and manners rather to live for such works and practices than to care

[29] The above-mentioned saints were the patrons of the well-known mendicant orders: Franciscans, Dominicans, and Augustines.

for faith; and unless there are wise prelates in the monasteries, who preach and urge faith rather than the rule of the order, it is inevitable that the order should be injurious and misleading to simple souls, who have regard to works alone.

Now, in our own time all the prelates are dead that had faith and founded orders, just as it was in old days with the children of Israel: when their fathers were dead, that had seen God's works and miracles, their children, out of ignorance of God's work and of faith, soon began to set up idolatry and their own human works. In the same way, alas! these orders, not understanding God's works and faith, grievously labour and torment themselves by their own laws and practices, and yet never arrive at a true understanding of a spiritual and good life, as was foretold by the Apostle, saying of them, "Having a form of godliness, but denying the power thereof, . . . ever learning, and never able to come to the knowledge" of what a true spiritual life is (2 Tim. iii. 2–7). Better to have no convents which are governed by a spiritual prelate, having no understanding of Christian faith to govern them; for such a prelate cannot but rule with injury and harm, and the greater the apparent holiness of his life in external works, the greater the harm.

It would be, I think, necessary, especially in these perilous times, that foundations and convents should again be organised as they were in the time of the Apostles and a long time after, namely when they were all free for every man to remain there as long as he wished. For what were they but Christian schools, in which the Scriptures and Christian life were taught, and where folk were trained to govern and to preach? as we read that St. Agnes went to school, and as we see even now in some nunneries, as at Quedlinburg and other places. Truly all foundations and convents ought to be free in this way: that they may serve God of a free will, and not as slaves. But now they have been bound round with vows and turned into eternal prisons, so that these vows are regarded even more than the vows of baptism. But what fruit has come of this we daily see, hear, read, and learn more and more.

I dare say that this my counsel will be thought very foolish, but I care not for this. I advise what I think best, reject it who will. I know how these vows are kept, especially that of chastity, which is so general in all these convents,[30] and yet was not ordered by Christ, and it is given to comparatively few to be able to keep it, as He says, and St. Paul also (Col. ii. 20). I wish all to be helped, and that Christian souls should not be held in bondage, through customs and laws invented by men.

14. We see also how the priesthood is fallen, and how many a poor priest is encumbered with a woman and children and burdened in his conscience, and no one does anything to help him, though he might very well be helped. Popes and bishops may let that be lost that is being lost, and that be destroyed which is being destroyed, I will save my conscience and open my mouth freely, let it vex popes and bishops or whoever it may be; therefore I say, According to the ordinances of Christ and His Apostles, every town should have a minister or bishop, as St. Paul plainly says (Titus i.), and this minister should not be forced to live without a lawful wife, but should be allowed to have one, as St. Paul writes, saying that "a bishop then must be blameless, the husband of one wife, . . . having his children in subjection with all gravity" (1 Tim. iii.). For with St. Paul a bishop and a presbyter are the same thing, as St. Jerome also confirms. But as for the bishops that we now have, of these the Scriptures know nothing; they were instituted by common Christian ordinance, so that one might rule over many ministers.

Therefore we learn from the Apostle clearly, that every town should elect a pious learned citizen from the congregation and charge him with the office of minister; the congregation should support him, and he should be left at liberty to marry or not. He should have as assistants several priests and deacons, married or not, as they please, who should help him to govern the people and the congregation with sermons and the ministration of the sacraments, as is still the case in the Greek Church. Then afterwards, when there were so many persecutions and contentions against heretics, there were many holy fathers who voluntarily abstained from the marriage state, that they might study more, and might be ready at all times for death and conflict. Now the Roman see has interfered of its own perversity, and has made a general law by which priests are

---

[30] Luther alludes here of course to the vow of celibacy, which was curiously styled the 'vow of chastity'; thus indirectly condemning marriage in general.

forbidden to marry. This must have been at the instigation of the devil, as was foretold by St. Paul, saying that "there shall come teachers giving heed to seducing spirits, . . . forbidding to marry," etc. (1 Tim. iv. 1, 2, *seq.*). This has been the cause of so much misery that it cannot be told, and has given occasion to the Greek Church to separate from us, and has caused infinite disunion, sin, shame, and scandal, like everything that the devil does or suggests. Now what are we to do?

My advice is to restore liberty, and to leave every man free to marry or not to marry. But if we did this we should have to introduce a very different rule and order for property; the whole canon law would be overthrown, and but few benefices would fall to Rome. I am afraid greed was a cause of this wretched, unchaste chastity, for the result of it was that every man wished to become a priest or to have his son brought up to the priesthood, not with the intention of living in chastity—for this could be done without the priestly state —but to obtain his worldly support without labour or trouble, contrary to God's command, "In the sweat of thy face shalt thou eat thy bread" (Gen. iii.); and they have given a colour to this commandment as though their work was praying and reading the mass. I am not here considering popes, bishops, canons, clergy, and monks who were not ordained by God; if they have laid burdens on themselves, they may bear them. I speak of the office of parish priest, which God ordained, who must rule a congregation with sermons and the ministration of the sacraments, and must live with them and lead a domestic life. These should have the liberty given them by a Christian council to marry and to avoid danger and sin. For as God has not bound them, no one may bind them, though he were an angel from heaven, let alone the Pope; and whatever is contrary to this in the canon law is mere idle talk and invention.

My advice further is, whoever henceforth is ordained priest, he should in no wise take the vow of chastity, but should protest to the bishop that he has no authority to demand this vow, and that it is a devilish tyranny to demand it. But if one is forced, or wishes to say, as some do, "so far as human frailty permits," let every man interpret that phrase as a plain negative, that is, "I do not promise chastity"; for "human frailty does not allow men to live an unmarried life," but only "angelic fortitude and celestial virtue." In this way he will have a clear conscience without any vow. I offer no opinion, one way or the other, whether those who have at present no wife should marry, or remain unmarried. This must be settled by the general order of the Church and by each man's discretion. But I will not conceal my honest counsel, nor withhold comfort from that unhappy crowd who now live in trouble with wife and children, and remain in shame, with a heavy conscience, hearing their wife called a priest's harlot, and the children bastards. And this I say frankly, in virtue of my good right.

There is many a poor priest free from blame in all other respects, except that he has succumbed to human frailty and come to shame with a woman, both minded in their hearts to live together always in conjugal fidelity, if only they could do so with a good conscience, though as it is they live in public shame. I say, these two are surely married before God. I say, moreover, that when two are so minded, and so come to live together, they should save their conscience; let the man take the woman as his lawful wife, and live with her faithfully as her husband, without considering whether the Pope approve or not, or whether it is forbidden by canon law, or temporal. The salvation of your soul is of more importance than their tyrannous, arbitrary, wicked laws, which are not necessary for salvation, nor ordained by God. You should do as the children of Israel did who stole from the Egyptians the wages they had earned, or as a servant steals his well-earned wages from a harsh master; in the same way do you also steal your wife and child from the Pope.

Let him who has faith enough to dare this only follow me courageously: I will not mislead him. I may not have the Pope's authority, yet I have the authority of a Christian to help my neighbour and to warn him against his sins and dangers. And here there is good reason for doing so.

(a) It is not every priest that can do without a woman, not only on account of human frailty, but still more for his household. If therefore he takes a woman, and the Pope allows this, but will not let them marry, what is this but expecting a man and a woman to live together and not to fall? Just as if one were to set fire to straw, and command it should neither smoke nor burn.

(*b*) The Pope having no authority for such a command, any more than to forbid a man to eat and drink, or to digest, or to grow fat, no one is bound to obey it, and the Pope is answerable for every sin against it, for all the souls that it has brought to destruction, and for all the consciences that have been troubled and tormented by it. He has long deserved to be driven out of the world, so many poor souls has he strangled with this devil's rope, though I hope that God has shown many more mercy at their death than the Pope did in their life. No good has ever come and can ever come from the papacy and its laws.

(*c*) Even though the Pope's laws forbid it, still, after the married state has been entered, the Pope's laws are superseded, and are valid no longer, for God has commanded that no man shall put asunder husband and wife, and this commandment is far above the Pope's laws, and God's command must not be cancelled or neglected for the papal commands. It is true that mad lawyers have helped the Pope to invent impediments, or hindrances to marriage, and thus troubled, divided, and perverted the married state, destroying the commandments of God. What need I say further? In the whole body of the Pope's canon law, there are not two lines that can instruct a pious Christian, and so many false and dangerous ones that it were better to burn it.

But if you object that this would give offence, and that one must first obtain the Pope's dispensation, I answer that if there is any offence in it, it is the fault of the see of Rome, which has made unjust and unholy laws. It is no offence to God and the Scriptures. Even where the Pope has power to grant dispensation for money by his covetous tyrannical laws, every Christian has power to grant dispensation in the same matter for the sake of Christ and the salvation of souls. For Christ has freed us from all human laws, especially when they are opposed to God and the salvation of souls, as St. Paul teaches (Gal. v. 1 and 1 Cor. viii. 9, 10).

15. I must not forget the poor convents. The evil spirit, who troubled all estates of life by human laws, and made them unendurable, has taken possession of some abbots, abbesses, and prelates, and led them so to rule their brothers and sisters that they do but go soon to hell, and live a wretched life even upon earth, as is the case

with all the devil's martyrs. For they have reserved in confession all, or at least some, deadly sins, which are secret, and from these no brother may on pain of excommunication and on his obedience absolve another. Now we do not always find angels everywhere, but men of flesh and blood, who would rather incur all excommunication and menace than confess their secret sins to a prelate or the confessor appointed for them; consequently they receive the Sacrament with these sins on their conscience, by which they become *irregular*[31] and suffer much misery. Oh blind shepherds! Oh foolish prelates! Oh ravenous wolves! Now I say that in cases where a sin is public and notorious it is only right that the prelate alone should punish it, and such sins, and no others, he may reserve and except for himself; over private sins he has no authority, even though they may be the worst that can be committed or imagined. And if the prelate excepts these, he becomes a tyrant and interferes with God's judgment.

Accordingly I advise these children, brothers and sisters: If your superiors will not allow you to confess your secret sins to whomsoever you will, then take them yourself, and confess them to your brother or sister, to whomsoever you will; be absolved and comforted, and then go or do what your wish or duty commands; only believe firmly that you have been absolved, and nothing more is necessary. And let not their threats of excommunication, or *irregularity,* or what not, trouble or disturb you; these only apply to public or notorious sins, if they are not confessed: you are not touched by them. How canst thou take upon thyself, thou blind prelate, to restrain private sins by thy threats? Give up what thou canst not keep publicly; let God's judgment and mercy also have its place with thy inferiors. He has not given them into thy hands so completely as to have let them go out of His own; nay, thou hast received the smaller portion. Consider thy statutes as nothing more than thy statutes, and do not make them equal to God's judgment in heaven.

16. It were also right to abolish annual festivals, processions, and masses for the dead, or at least to diminish their number; for we

---

[31] Luther uses the expression *irregulares,* which was applied to those monks who were guilty of heresy, apostasy, transgression of the vow of chastity, etc.

evidently see that they have become no better than a mockery, exciting the anger of God and having no object but money-getting, gluttony, and carousals. How should it please God to hear the poor vigils and masses mumbled in this wretched way, neither read nor prayed? Even when they are properly read, it is not done freely for the love of God, but for the love of money and as payment of a debt. Now it is impossible that anything should please God or win anything from Him that is not done freely, out of love for Him. Therefore, as true Christians, we ought to abolish or lessen a practice that we see is abused, and that angers God instead of appeasing Him. I should prefer, and it would be more agreeable to God's will, and far better for a foundation, church, or convent, to put all the yearly masses and vigils together into one mass, so that they would every year celebrate, on one day, a true vigil and mass with hearty sincerity, devotion, and faith for all their benefactors. This would be better than their thousand upon thousand masses said every year, each for a particular benefactor, without devotion and faith. My dear fellow-Christians, God cares not for much prayer, but for good prayer. Nay, He condemns long and frequent prayers, saying, "Verily I say unto you, they have their reward" (Matt. vi. 2, seq.). But it is the greed that cannot trust God by which such practices are set up; it is afraid it will die of starvation.

17. One should also abolish certain punishments inflicted by the canon law, especially the interdict, which is doubtless the invention of the evil one. Is it not the mark of the devil to wish to better one sin by more and worse sins? It is surely a greater sin to silence God's word, and service, than if we were to kill twenty popes at once, not to speak of a single priest or of keeping back the goods of the Church. This is one of those gentle virtues which are learnt in the spiritual law; for the canon or spiritual law is so called because it comes from a spirit, not, however, from the Holy Spirit, but from the evil spirit.

Excommunication should not be used except where the Scriptures command it, that is, against those that have not the right faith, or that live in open sin, and not in matters of temporal goods. But now the case has been inverted: each man believes and lives as he pleases, especially those that plunder and disgrace others with excommunications; and all excommunications are now only in matters of worldly goods, for which we have no one to thank but the holy canonical injustice. But of all this I have spoken previously in a sermon.

The other punishments and penalties—suspension, irregularity, aggravation, reaggravation, deposition,[32] thundering, lightning, cursing, damning, and what not—all these should be buried ten fathoms deep in the earth, that their very name and memory may no longer live upon earth. The evil spirit, who was let loose by the spiritual law, has brought all this terrible plague and misery into the heavenly kingdom of the holy Church, and has thereby brought about nothing but the harm and destruction of souls, that we may well apply to it the words of Christ, "But woe unto you, scribes and Pharisees, hypocrites! for you shut up the kingdom of heaven against men, for ye neither go in yourselves, neither suffer ye them that are entering to go in" (Matt. xxiii. 13).

18. One should abolish all saints' days, keeping only Sunday. But if it were desired to keep the festivals of Our Lady and the greater saints, they should all be held on Sundays, or only in the morning with the mass; the rest of the day being a working day. My reason is this: with our present abuses of drinking, gambling, idling, and all manner of sin, we vex God more on holy days than on others. And the matter is just reversed; we have made holy days unholy, and working days holy, and do no service, but great dishonour, to God and His saints with all our holy days. There are some foolish prelates that think they have done a good deed, if they establish a festival to St. Otilia or St. Barbara, and the like, each in his own blind fashion, whilst he would be doing a much better work to turn a saint's day into a working day in honour of a saint.

Besides these spiritual evils, these saints' days inflict bodily injury on the common man in two ways: he loses a day's work, and he spends more than usual, besides weakening his body and making himself unfit for labour, as we see every day, and yet no one tries to improve it. One should not consider whether the Pope instituted

---

[32] Luther enumerates here the various grades of punishment inflicted on priests. The *aggravation* consisted of a threat of excommunication after a thrice-repeated admonition, whilst the consequence of *reaggravation* was immediate excommunication.

these festivals, or whether we require his dispensation or permission. If anything is contrary to God's will and harmful to men in body and soul, not only has every community, council, or government authority to prevent and abolish such wrong without the knowledge or consent of pope or bishop, but it is their duty, as they value their soul's salvation, to prevent it, even though pope and bishop (that should be the first to do so) are unwilling to see it stopped. And first of all we should abolish church wakes, since they are nothing but taverns, fairs, and gaming places, to the greater dishonour of God and the damnation of souls. It is no good to make a talk about their having had a good origin and being good works. Did not God set aside His own law that He had given forth out of heaven when He saw that it was abused, and does He not now reverse every day what He has appointed, and destroy what He has made, on account of the same perverse misuse, as it is written in Psalm xviii. (ver. 26), "With the perverse Thou wilt show Thyself froward"?

19. The degrees of relationship in which marriage is forbidden must be altered, such as so-called spiritual relations[33] in the third and fourth degrees; and where the Pope at Rome can dispense in such matters for money, and make shameful bargains, every priest should have the power of granting the same dispensations freely for the salvation of souls. Would to God that all those things that have to be bought at Rome, for freedom from the golden snares of the canon law, might be given by any priest without payment, such as indulgences, letters of indulgences, letters of dispensation, mass letters, and all the other religious licences and knaveries at Rome by which the poor people are deceived and robbed! For if the Pope has the power to sell for money his golden snares, or canon nets (laws, I should say), much more has a priest the power to cancel them and to trample on them for God's sake. But if he has no such power, then the Pope can have no authority to sell them in his shameful fair.

Besides this, fasts must be made optional, and every kind of food made free, as is commanded in the Gospels (Matt. xv. 11). For whilst at Rome they laugh at fasts, they let us abroad consume oil which

[33] Those, namely, between sponsors at baptism and their god-children.

they would not think fit for greasing their boots, and then sell us the liberty of eating butter and other things, whereas the Apostle says that the Gospel has given us freedom in all such matters (1 Cor. x. 25, *seq.*). But they have caught us in their canon law and have robbed us of this right, so that we have to buy it back from them; they have so terrified the consciences of the people that one cannot preach this liberty without rousing the anger of the people, who think the eating of butter to be a worse sin than lying, swearing, and unchastity. We may make of it what we will; it is but the work of man, and no good can ever come of it.

20. The country chapels and churches must be destroyed, such as those to which the new pilgrimages have been set on foot: Wilsnack, Sternberg, Treves, the Grimmenthal, and now Ratisbon, and many others. Oh, what a reckoning there will be for those bishops that allow these inventions of the devil and make a profit out of them! They should be the first to stop it; they think that it is a godly, holy thing, and do not see that the devil does this to strengthen covetousness, to teach false beliefs, to weaken parish churches, to increase drunkenness and debauchery, to waste money and labour, and simply to lead the poor people by the nose. If they had only studied the Scriptures as much as their accursed canon law, they would know well how to deal with the matter.

The miracles performed there prove nothing, for the evil one can show also wonders, as Christ has taught us (Matt. xxiv. 24). If they took up the matter earnestly and forbade such doings, the miracles would soon cease: or if they were done by God, they would not be prevented by their commands. And if there were nothing else to prove that these are not works of God, it would be enough that people go about turbulently and irrationally like herds of cattle, which could not possibly come from God. God has not commanded it; there is no obedience, and no merit in it; and therefore it should be vigorously interfered with, and the people warned against it. For what is not commanded by God and goes beyond God's commandments is surely the devil's own work. In this way also the parish churches suffer: in that they are less venerated. In fine, these pilgrimages are signs of great want of faith in the people; for if they truly believed, they would find all things in their own churches, where they are commanded to go.

But what is the use of my speaking. Every man thinks only how he may get up such a pilgrimage in his own district, not caring whether the people believe and live rightly. The rulers are like the people: blind leaders of the blind. Where pilgrimages are a failure, they begin to glorify their saints, not to honour the saints, who are sufficiently honoured without them, but to cause a concourse, and to bring in money. Herein pope and bishops help them; it rains indulgences, and every one can afford to buy them: but what God has commanded no one cares for; no one runs after it, no one can afford any money for it. Alas for our blindness, that we not only suffer the devil to have his way with his phantoms, but support him! I wish one would leave the good saints alone, and not lead the poor people astray. What spirit gave the Pope authority to "glorify" the saints? Who tells him whether they are holy or not holy? Are there not enough sins on earth as it is but we must tempt God, interfere in His judgment, and make money-bags of His saints? Therefore my advice is to let the saints glorify themselves. Nay, God alone should be glorified, and every man should keep to his own parish, where he will profit more than in all these shrines, even if they were all put together into one shrine. Here a man finds baptism, the Sacrament, preaching, and his neighbour, and these are more than all the saints in heaven, for it is by God's word and sacrament that they have all been hallowed.

Our contempt for these great matters justifies God's anger in giving us over to the devil to lead us astray, to get up pilgrimages, to found churches and chapels, to glorify the saints, and to commit other like follies, by which we are led astray from the true faith into new false beliefs, just as He did in old time with the people of Israel, whom He led away from the Temple to countless other places, all the while in God's name, and with the appearance of holiness, against which all the prophets preached, suffering martyrdom for their words. But now no one preaches against it; for if he did, bishops, popes, priests, and monks would perchance combine to martyr him. In this way Antonius of Florence and many others are made saints, so that their holiness may serve to produce glory and wealth, which served before to the honour of God and as a good example alone.

Even if this glorification of the saints had been good once, it is not good now, just as many other things were good once and are now occasion of offence and injurious, such as holidays, ecclesiastical treasures and ornaments. For it is evident that what is aimed at in the glorification of saints is not the glory of God nor the bettering of Christendom, but money and fame alone; one Church wishes to have an advantage over another, and would be sorry to see another Church enjoying the same advantages. In this way they have in these latter days abused the goods of the Church so as to gain the goods of the world; so that everything, and even God Himself, must serve their avarice. Moreover, these privileges cause nothing but dissensions and worldly pride; one Church being different from the rest, they despise or magnify one another, whereas all goods that are of God should be common to all, and should serve to produce unity. This, too, is much liked by the Pope, who would be sorry to see all Christians equal and at one with one another.

Here must be added that one should abolish, or treat as of no account, or give to all Churches alike, the licences, bulls, and whatever the Pope sells at his flaying-ground at Rome. For if he sells or gives to Wittenberg, to Halle, to Venice, and above all, to his own city of Rome, permissions, privileges, indulgences, graces, advantages, faculties, why does he not give them to all Churches alike? Is it not his duty to do all that he can for all Christians without reward, solely for God's sake, nay, even to shed his blood for them? Why then, I should like to know, does he give or sell these things to one Church and not to another? Or does this accursed gold make a difference in his Holiness's eyes between Christians who all alike have baptism, Gospel, faith, Christ, God, and all things? Do they wish us to be blind, when our eyes can see, to be fools, when we have reason, that we should worship this greed knavery, and delusion? He is a shepherd, forsooth—so long as you have money, no further; and yet they are not ashamed to practise all this knavery right and left with their bulls. They care only for that accursed gold, and for nought besides.

Therefore my advice is this: If this folly is not done away with, let all pious Christians open their eyes, and not be deceived by these Romish bulls and seals and all their specious pretences; let them stop at home in their own churches, and be satisfied with their baptism, Gospel, faith, Christ, and God (who is everywhere the same), and let the Pope continue to be a blind leader of the blind. Neither pope nor angel can give you as much as God gives you in your own parish; nay, he only leads you away from God's gifts, which you have for nothing, to his own gifts, which you must buy, giving you lead for gold, skin for meat, strings for a purse, wax for honey, words for goods, the letter for the spirit, as you can see for yourselves though you will not perceive it. If you try to ride to heaven on the Pope's wax and parchment, your carriage will soon break down, and you will fall into hell, not in God's name.

Let this be a fixed rule for you: Whatever has to be bought of the Pope is neither good, nor of God. For whatever comes from God is not only given freely, but all the world is punished and condemned for not accepting it freely. So is it with the Gospel and the works of God. We have deserved to be led into these errors, because we have despised God's holy word and the grace of baptism; as St. Paul says, "And for this cause God shall send them strong delusion, that they should believe a lie, that they all might be damned who believed not the truth, but had pleasure in unrighteousness" (2 Thess. ii. 11, 12).

21. It is one of the most urgent necessities to abolish all begging in Christendom. No one should go about begging among Christians. It would not be hard to do this, if we attempted it with good heart and courage: each town should support its own poor and should not allow strange beggars to come in, whatever they may call themselves, pilgrims or mendicant monks. Every town could feed its own poor; and if it were too small, the people in the neighbouring villages should be called upon to contribute. As it is, they have to support many knaves and vagabonds under the name of beggars. If they did what I propose, they would at least know who were really poor or not.

There should also be an overseer or guardian who should know all the poor, and should inform the town-council, or the priest, of their requirements; or some other similar provision might be made. There is no occupation, in my opinion, in which there is so much knavery and cheating as among beggars; which could easily be done away with. This general, unrestricted begging is, besides, injurious for the common people. I estimate that of the five or six orders of mendicant monks each one visits every place more than six or seven times in the year; then there are the common beggars, emissaries, and pilgrims; in this way I calculate every city has a blackmail levied on it about sixty times a year, not counting rates and taxes paid to the civil government and the useless robberies of the Roman see; so that it is to my mind one of the greatest of God's miracles how we manage to live and support ourselves.

Some may think that in this way the poor would not be well cared for, and that such great stone houses and convents would not be built, and not so plentifully, and I think so too. Nor is it necessary. If a man will be poor, he should not be rich; if he will be rich, let him put his hand to the plough, and get wealth himself out of the earth. It is enough to provide decently for the poor, that they may not die of cold and hunger. It is not right that one should work that another may be idle, and live ill that another may live well, as is now the perverse abuse, for St. Paul says, "If any would not work, neither should he eat" (2 Thess. iii. 10). God has not ordained that any one should live of the goods of others, except priests and ministers alone, as St. Paul says (1 Cor. ix. 14), for their spiritual work's sake, as also Christ says to the Apostles, "The labourer is worthy of his hire" (Luke x. 7).

22. It is also to be feared that the *many masses* that have been founded in convents and foundations, instead of doing any good, arouse God's anger; wherefore it would be well to endow no more masses and to abolish many of those that have been endowed; for we see that they are only looked upon as sacrifices and good works, though in truth they are sacraments like baptism and confession, and as such profit him only that receives them. But now the custom obtains of saying masses for the living and the dead, and everything is based upon them. This is the reason why there are so many, and that they have come to be what we see.

But perhaps all this is a new and unheard-of doctrine, especially in the eyes of those that fear to lose their livelihood, if these masses were abolished. I must therefore reserve what I have to say on this subject until men have arrived at a truer understanding of the mass, its nature and use. The mass has, alas! for so many years been turned into means of gaining a livelihood, that I should advise a man to become a shepherd, a labourer, rather than a priest or monk, unless he knows what the mass is.

All this, however, does not apply to the old foundations and chapters, which were doubtless founded in order that since, according to the custom of Germany, all the children of nobles cannot be landowners and rulers, they should be provided for in these foundations, and these serve God freely, study, and become learned themselves, and help others to acquire learning. I am speaking only of the new foundations, endowed for prayers and masses, by the example of which the old foundations have become burdened with the like prayers and masses, making them of very little, if of any, use. Through God's righteous punishment, they have at last come down to the dregs, as they deserve—that is, to the noise of singers and organs, and cold, spiritless masses, with no end but to gain and spend the money due to them. Popes, bishops, and doctors should examine and report on such things; as it is they are the guiltiest, allowing anything that brings them money; the blind ever leading the blind. This comes of covetousness and the canon law.

It must, moreover, not be allowed in future that one man should have more than one endowment or prebend. He should be content with a moderate position in life, so that others may have something besides himself; and thus we must put a stop to the excuses of those that say that they must have more than one office to enable them to live in their proper station. It is possible to estimate one's "proper station" in such a way that a whole kingdom would not suffice to maintain it. So it is that covetousness and want of faith in God go hand in hand, and often men take for the requirements of their "proper station" what is mere covetousness and want of faith.

23. As for the fraternities, together with indulgences, letters of indulgence, dispensations for Lent, and masses, and all the rest of such things, let them all be drowned and abolished; there is no good

in them at all. If the Pope has the authority to grant dispensation in the matter of eating butter and hearing masses, let him allow priests to do the same; he has no right to take the power from them. I speak also of the fraternities in which indulgences, masses, and good works are distributed. My friend, in baptism you joined a fraternity of which Christ, the angels, and saints, and all Christians are members; be true to this, and satisfy it, and you will have fraternities enough. Let others make what show they wish; they are as counters compared to coins. But if there were a fraternity that subscribed money to feed the poor or to help others in any way, this would be good, and it would have its indulgence and its deserts in heaven. But now they are good for nothing but gluttony and drunkenness.

First of all we should expel from all German lands the Pope's legates, with their faculties, which they sell to us for much money, though it is all knavery—as, for instance, their taking money for making goods unlawfully acquired to be good, for freeing from oaths, vows, and bonds, thus destroying and teaching others to destroy truth and faith mutually pledged, saying the Pope has authority to do so. It is the evil spirit that bids them talk thus, and so they sell us the devil's teaching, and take money for teaching us sins and leading us to hell.

If there were nothing else to show that the Pope is antichrist, this would be enough. Dost thou hear this, O Pope! not the most holy, but the most sinful? Would that God would hurl thy chair headlong from heaven, and cast it down into the abyss of hell! Who gave you the power to exalt yourself above your God; to break and to loose what He has commanded; to teach Christians, more especially Germans, who are of noble nature, and are famed in all histories for uprightness and truth, to be false, unfaithful, perjured, treacherous, and wicked? God has commanded to keep faith and observe oaths even with enemies; you dare to cancel this command, laying it down in your heretical, anti-Christian decretals that you have power to do so; and through your mouth and your pen Satan lies as he never lied before, teaching you to twist and pervert the Scriptures according to your own arbitrary will. O Lord Christ, look down upon this; let Thy day of judgment come and destroy the devil's lair at Rome. Behold him of whom St. Paul spoke (2 Thess. ii, 3, 4) that he should exalt himself above Thee and sit in Thy Church, showing himself as God—the man of sin and the child of damnation. What else does the Pope's power do but teach and strengthen sin and wickedness, leading souls to damnation in Thy name?

The children of Israel in old times were obliged to keep the oath that they had sworn, in ignorance and error, to the Gibeonites, their enemies; and King Zedekiah was destroyed utterly, with his people, because he broke the oath that he had sworn to the King of Babylon; and among us, a hundred years ago, the noble King Ladislaus V. of Poland and Hungary, was slain by the Turk, with so many of his people, because he allowed himself to be misled by papal legates and cardinals and broke the good and useful treaty that he had made with the Turk. The pious Emperor Sigismond had no good fortune after the Council of Constance, in which he allowed the knaves to violate the safe-conduct that he had promised to John Huss and Jerome; from this has followed all the miserable strife between Bohemia and ourselves. And in our own time, God help us! how much Christian blood has been shed on account of the oath and bond which Pope Julius made and unmade between the Emperor Maximilian and King Louis of France! How can I tell all the misery the popes have caused by such devilish insolence, claiming the power of breaking oaths between great lords, causing a shameful scandal for the sake of money? I hope the day of judgment is at hand; things cannot and will not become worse than the dealings of the Roman chair. The Pope treads God's commandments under foot and exalts his own; if this is not antichrist, I do not know what is. But of this, and to more purpose, another time.

24. It is high time to take up earnestly and truthfully the cause of the Bohemians, to unite them with ourselves and ourselves with them, so that all mutual accusations, envy, and hatred may cease. I will be the first, in my folly, to give my opinion, with all due deference to those of better understanding.

First of all, we must honestly confess the truth, without attempting self-justification, and own one thing to the Bohemians, namely that John Huss and Jerome of Prague were burnt at Constance in violation of the papal, Christian, and imperial oath and safe-conduct, and that thus God's commandment was broken and the Bohemians excited to great anger. And though they may have deserved such great wrong and disobedience to God on our part, they were not obliged to approve it and think it right. Nay, even now they should run any danger of life and limb rather than own that it is right to break an imperial, papal, Christian safe-conduct and act faithlessly in opposition to it. Therefore, though the Bohemians may be to blame for their impatience, yet the Pope and his followers are most to blame for all the misery, all the error and destruction of souls, that followed this council of Constance.

It is not my intention here to judge John Huss's belief and to defend his errors, although my understanding has not been able to find any error in him, and I would willingly believe that men who violated a safe-conduct and God's commandment (doubtless possessed rather by the evil spirit than by the Spirit of God) were unable to judge well or to condemn with truth. No one can imagine that the Holy Ghost can break God's commandments; no one can deny that it is breaking God's commandments to violate faith and a safe-conduct, even though it were promised to the devil himself, much more then in the case of a heretic; it is also notorious that a safe-conduct was promised to John Huss and the Bohemians, and that the promise was broken and Huss was burnt. I have no wish to make a saint or a martyr of John Huss (as some Bohemians do), though I own that he was treated unjustly, and that his books and his doctrines were wrongfully condemned; for God's judgments are inscrutable and terrible, and none but Himself may reveal or explain them.

All I say is this: Granting he was a heretic, however bad he may have been, yet he was burnt unjustly and in violation of God's commandments, and we must not force the Bohemians to approve this, if we wish ever to be at one with them. Plain truth must unite us, not obstinacy. It is no use to say, as they said at the time, that a safe-conduct need not be kept, if promised to a heretic; that is as much as to say, one may break God's commandments in order to keep God's commandments. They were infatuated and blinded by the devil, that they could not see what they said or did. God has commanded us to observe a safe-conduct; and this we must do though the world should perish: much more then where it is only a question of a heretic being set free. We should overcome heretics with books, not with fire, as the old Fathers did. If there were any skill in overcoming heretics with fire, the executioner would be the most learned doctor in the world; and there would be no need to study, but he that could get another into his power could burn him.

Besides this, the Emperor and the princes should send to Bohemia several pious, learned bishops and doctors, but, for their life, no cardinal or legate or inquisitor, for such people are far too unlearned in all Christian matters, and do not seek the salvation of souls; but, like all the papal hypocrites, they seek only their own glory, profit, and honour; they were also the leaders in that calamitous affair at Constance. But those envoys should inquire into the faith of the Bohemians, to ascertain whether it would be possible to unite all their sects into one. Moreover, the Pope should (for their souls' sake) for a time abandon his supremacy and, in accordance with the statutes of the Nicene Council, allow the Bohemians to choose for themselves an archbishop of Prague, this choice to be confirmed by the Bishops of Olmütz in Moravia or of Gran in Hungary, or the Bishop of Gnesen in Poland, or the Bishop of Magdeburg in Germany. It is enough that it be confirmed by one or two of these bishops, as in the time of St. Cyprian. And the Pope has no authority to forbid it; if he forbids it, he acts as a wolf and a tyrant, and no one should obey him, but answer his excommunication by excommunicating him.

Yet if, for the honour of the chair of St. Peter, any one prefers to do this with the Pope's knowledge, I do not object, provided that the Bohemians do not pay a farthing for it, and that the Pope do not bind them a single hair's-breadth, or subject them to his tyranny by oath, as he does all other bishops, against God and justice. If he is not satisfied with the honour of his assent being asked, leave him alone, by all means, with his own rights, laws, and tyrannies; be content with the election, and let the blood of all the souls that are in danger be upon his head. For no man may countenance wrong, and it is enough to show respect to tyranny. If we cannot do otherwise, we may consider the popular election and consent as equal to a tyrannical confirmation; but I hope this will not be necessary. Sooner or later some Romans, or pious bishops and learned men, must perceive and avert the Pope's tyranny.

I do not advise that they be forced to abandon the Sacrament in both kinds, for it is neither unchristian nor heretical. They should be allowed to continue in their present way; but the new bishop must see that there be no dissensions about this matter, and they must learn that neither practice is actually wrong, just as there need be no disputes about the priests not wearing the same dress as the laity. In the same way, if they do not wish to submit to the canon laws of the Roman Church, we must not force them, but we must content ourselves with seeing that they live in faith and according to the Scriptures. For Christian life and Christian faith may very well exist without the Pope's unbearable laws; nay, they cannot well exist until there are fewer of those laws or none. Our baptism has freed us and made us subject to God's word alone; why then should we suffer a man to make us the slaves of his words? As St. Paul says, "Stand fast therefore in the liberty wherewith Christ hath made us free, and be not entangled again with the yoke of bondage" (Gal. v. 1).

If I knew that the only error of the Hussites[34] was that they believe that in the Sacrament of the altar there is true bread and wine, though under it the body and the blood of Christ—if, I say, this were their only error, I should not condemn them; but let the Bishop of Prague see to this. For it is not an article of faith that in the Sacrament there is no bread and wine in substance and nature, which is a delusion of St. Thomas and the Pope; but it is an article of faith that in the natural bread and wine there is Christ's true flesh and blood. We should accordingly tolerate the views of both parties until they are at one; for there is not much danger whether you believe there is or there is not bread in the Sacrament. For we have to suffer many forms of belief and order that do not injure the faith; but if they believe otherwise, it would be better not to unite with them, and yet to instruct them in the truth.

All other errors and dissensions to be found in Bohemia should be

[34] Luther uses here the word *Pikarden*, which is a corruption of *Begharden, i. e.* "Beghards," a nickname frequently applied in those days to the Hussites.

tolerated until the Archbishop has been reinstated, and has succeeded in time in uniting the whole people in one harmonious doctrine. We shall never unite them by force, by driving or hurrying them. We must be patient, and use gentleness. Did not Christ have to walk with His disciples, suffering their unbelief, until they believed in His resurrection? If they had but once more a regular bishop and good government without Romish tyranny, I think matters would mend.

The temporal possessions of the Church should not be too strictly claimed; but since we are Christians and bound to help one another, we have the right to give them these things for the sake of unity, and to let them keep them, before God and the world; for Christ says, "Where two or three are gathered together in My name, there am I in the midst of them." Would to God we helped on both sides to bring about this unity, giving our hands one to the other in brotherly humility, not insisting on our authority or our rights! Love is more, and more necessary, than the papacy at Rome, which is without love, and love can exist without the papacy. I hope I have done my best for this end. If the Pope or his followers hinder this good work, they will have to give an account of their actions for having, against the love of God, sought their own advantage more than their neighbours'. The Pope should abandon his papacy, all his possessions and honours, if he could save a soul by so doing. But he would rather see the world go to ruin than give up a hair's-breadth of the power he has usurped; and yet he would be our most holy father. Herewith I am excused.

25. The universities also require a good, sound reformation. I must say this, let it vex whom it may. The fact is that whatever the papacy has ordered or instituted is only designed for the propagation of sin and error. What are the universities, as at present ordered, but, as the book of Maccabees says, "schools of 'Greek fashion' and 'heathenish manners'" (2 Macc. iv. 12, 13), full of dissolute living, where very little is taught of the Holy Scriptures and of the Christian faith, and the blind heathen teacher, Aristotle, rules even further than Christ? Now, my advice would be that the books of Aristotle, the *Physics,* the *Metaphysics, Of the Soul, Ethics,* which have hitherto been considered the best, be altogether abolished, with all others

that profess to treat of nature, though nothing can be learned from them, either of natural or of spiritual things. Besides, no one has been able to understand his meaning, and much time has been wasted and many noble souls vexed with much useless labour, study, and expense. I venture to say that any potter has more knowledge of natural things than is to be found in these books. My heart is grieved to see how many of the best Christians this accursed, proud, knavish heathen has fooled and led astray with his false words. God sent him as a plague for our sins.

Does not the wretched man in his best book, *Of the Soul,* teach that the soul dies with the body, though many have tried to save him with vain words, as if we had not the Holy Scriptures to teach us fully of all things of which Aristotle had not the slightest perception? Yet this dead heathen has conquered, and has hindered and almost suppressed the books of the living God; so that, when I see all this misery I cannot but think that the evil spirit has introduced this study.

Then there is the *Ethics,* which is accounted one of the best, though no book is more directly contrary to God's will and the Christian virtues. Oh that such books could be kept out of the reach of all Christians! Let no one object that I say too much, or speak without knowledge. My friend, I know of what I speak. I know Aristotle as well as you or men like you. I have read him with more understanding than St. Thomas or Scotus, which I may say without arrogance, and can prove if need be. It matters not that so many great minds have exercised themselves in these matters for many hundred years. Such objections do not affect me as they might have done once, since it is plain as day that many more errors have existed for many hundred years in the world and the universities.

I would, however, gladly consent that Aristotle's books of Logic, Rhetoric, and Poetry, should be retained, or they might be usefully studied in a condensed form, to practise young people in speaking and preaching; but the notes and comments should be abolished, and, just as Cicero's Rhetoric is read without note or comment, Aristotle's Logic should be read without such long commentaries. But now neither speaking nor preaching is taught out of them, and they are used only for disputation and toilsomeness. Besides this, there are languages—Latin, Greek, and Hebrew—the mathematics, history; which I recommend to men of higher understanding: and other matters, which will come of themselves, if they seriously strive after reform. And truly it is an important matter, for it concerns the teaching and training of Christian youths and of our noble people, in whom Christianity still abides. Therefore I think that pope and emperor could have no better task than the reformation of the universities, just as there is nothing more devilishly mischievous than an unreformed university.

Physicians I would leave to reform their own faculty; lawyers and theologians I take under my charge, and say firstly that it would be right to abolish the canon law entirely, from beginning to end, more especially the decretals. We are taught quite sufficiently in the Bible how we ought to act; all this study only prevents the study of the Scriptures, and for the most part it is tainted with covetousness and pride. And even though there were some good in it, it should nevertheless be destroyed, for the Pope, having the canon law *in scrinio pectoris,*[35] all further study is useless and deceitful. At the present time the canon law is not to be found in the books, but in the whims of the Pope and his sycophants. You may have settled a matter in the best possible way according to the canon law, but the Pope has his *scrinium pectoris,* to which all law must bow in all the world. Now this *scrinium* is oftentimes directed by some knave and the devil himself, whilst it boasts that it is directed by the Holy Ghost. This is the way they treat Christ's poor people, imposing many laws and keeping none, forcing others to keep them or to free themselves by money.

Therefore, since the Pope and his followers have cancelled the whole canon law, despising it and setting their own will above all the world, we should follow them and reject the books. Why should we study them to no purpose? We should never be able to know the Pope's caprice, which has now become the canon law. Let it fall then in God's name, after having risen in the devil's name. Let there be henceforth no *doctor decretorum,* but let them all be *doctores scrinii papalis,* that is, the Pope's sycophants. They say that there is no better temporal government than among the Turks,

[35] In the shrine of his heart.

though they have no canon nor civil law, but only their Koran; we must at least own that there is no worse government than ours, with its canon and civil law, for no estate lives according to the Scriptures, or even according to natural reason.

The civil law, too, good God! what a wilderness it is become! It is, indeed, much better, more skilful, and more honest than the canon law, of which nothing is good but the name. Still there is far too much of it. Surely good governors, in addition to the Holy Scriptures, would be law enough; as St. Paul says, "Is it so that there is not a wise man among you, no, not one that shall be able to judge between his brethren?" (1 Cor. vi. 5). I think also that the common law and the usage of the country should be preferred to the law of the empire, and that the law of the empire should only be used in cases of necessity. And would to God, that, as each land has its own peculiar character and nature, they could all be governed by their own simple laws, just as they were governed before the law of the empire was devised, and as many are governed even now! Elaborate and far-fetched laws are only burdensome to the people, and a hindrance rather than a help to business. But I hope that others have thought of this, and considered it to more purpose than I could.

Our worthy theologians have saved themselves much trouble and labour by leaving the Bible alone and only reading the Sentences.[36] I should have thought that young theologians might begin by studying the Sentences, and that doctors should study the Bible. Now they invert this: the Bible is the first thing they study; this ceases with the Bachelor's degree; the Sentences are the last, and these they keep forever with the Doctor's degree, and this, too, under such sacred obligation that one that is not a priest may read the Bible, but a priest must read the Sentences; so that, as far as I can see, a married man might be a doctor in the Bible, but not in the Sentences. How should we prosper so long as we act so perversely, and degrade the Bible, the holy word of God? Besides this, the Pope orders with many stringent words that his laws be read and used in schools and courts; while the law of the Gospel is but little considered. The result is that in schools and courts the Gospel lies dusty underneath

---

[36] Luther refers here to the "Sentences" of *Petrus Lombardus,* the so-called *magister sententiarum,* which formed the basis of all dogmatic interpretation from about the middle of the twelfth century down to the Reformation.

the benches, so that the Pope's mischievous laws may alone be in force.

Since then we hold the name and title of teachers of the Holy Scriptures, we should verily be forced to act according to our title, and to teach the Holy Scriptures and nothing else. Although, indeed, it is a proud, presumptuous title for a man to proclaim himself teacher of the Scriptures, still it could be suffered, if the works confirmed the title. But as it is, under the rule of the Sentences, we find among theologians more human and heathenish fallacies than true holy knowledge of the Scriptures. What then are we to do? I know not, except to pray humbly to God to give us Doctors of Theology. Doctors of Arts, of Medicine, of Law, of the Sentences, may be made by popes, emperors, and the universities; but of this we may be certain: a Doctor of the Holy Scriptures can be made by none but the Holy Ghost, as Christ says, "They shall all be taught of God" (John vi. 45). Now the Holy Ghost does not consider red caps or brown, or any other pomp, nor whether we are young or old, layman or priest, monk or secular, virgin or married; nay, He once spoke by an ass against the prophet that rode on it. Would to God we were worthy of having such doctors given us, be they laymen or priests, married or unmarried! But now they try to force the Holy Ghost to enter into popes, bishops, or doctors, though there is no sign to show that He is in them.

We must also lessen the number of theological books, and choose the best, for it is not the number of books that makes the learned man, nor much reading, but good books often read, however few, makes a man learned in the Scriptures and pious. Even the Fathers should only be read for a short time as an introduction to the Scriptures. As it is we read nothing else, and never get from them into the Scriptures, as if one should be gazing at the signposts and never follow the road. These good Fathers wished to lead us into the Scriptures by their writings, whereas we lead ourselves out by them, though the Scriptures are our vineyard, in which we should all work and exercise ourselves.

Above all, in schools of all kinds the chief and most common lesson should be the Scriptures, and for young boys the Gospel; and would to God each town had also a girls' school, in which girls might be taught the Gospel for an hour daily, either in German or Latin! In truth, schools, monasteries, and convents were founded for this purpose, and with good Christian intentions, as we read concerning St. Agnes and other saints [37]; then were there holy virgins and martyrs; and in those times it was well with Christendom; but now it has been turned into nothing but praying and singing. Should not every Christian be expected by his ninth or tenth year to know all the holy Gospels, containing as they do his very name and life? A spinner or a seamstress teaches her daughter her trade while she is young, but now even the most learned prelates and bishops do not know the Gospel.

Oh, how badly we treat all these poor young people that are entrusted to us for discipline and instruction! and a heavy reckoning shall we have to give for it that we keep them from the word of God; their fate is that described by Jeremiah: "Mine eyes do fail with tears, my bowels are troubled, my liver is poured upon the earth, for the destruction of the daughter of my people, because the children and the sucklings swoon in the streets of the city. They say to their mothers, Where is corn and wine? when they swooned as the wounded in the streets of the city, when their soul was poured out into their mothers' bosom" (Lam. ii. 11, 12). We do not perceive all this misery, how the young folk are being pitifully corrupted in the midst of Christendom, all for want of the Gospel, which we should always read and study with them.

However, even if the high schools studied the Scriptures diligently we should not send every one to them, as we do now, when nothing is considered but numbers, and every man wishes to have a Doctor's title; we should only send the aptest pupils, well prepared in the lower schools. This should be seen to by princes or the magistrates of the towns, and they should take care none but apt pupils be sent. But where the Holy Scriptures are not the rule, I advise no one to send his child. Everything must perish where God's word is not studied unceasingly; and so we see what manner of men there are now in the high schools, and all this is the fault of no one but of the Pope, the bishops, and the prelates, to whom the welfare of the young has been entrusted. For the high schools should only train men of

[37] See above, pp. 301, *seq.*

good understanding in the Scriptures, who wish to become bishops and priests, and to stand at our head against heretics and the devil and all the world. But where do we find this? I greatly fear the high schools are nothing but great gates of hell, unless they diligently study the Holy Scriptures and teach them to the young people.

26. I know well the Romish mob will object and loudly pretend that the Pope took the holy Roman empire from the Greek emperor and gave it to Germany, for which honour and favour he is supposed to deserve submission and thanks and all other kinds of returns from the Germans. For this reason they will perhaps assume to oppose all attempts to reform them, and will let no regard be paid to anything but those donations of the Roman empire. This is also the reason why they have so arbitrarily and proudly persecuted and oppressed many good emperors, so that it were pity to tell, and with the same cleverness have they made themselves lords of all the temporal power and authority, in violation of the holy Gospel; and accordingly I must speak of this matter also.

There is no doubt that the true Roman empire, of which the prophets (Num. xxiv. 24 and Daniel ii. 44) spoke, was long ago destroyed, as Balaam clearly foretold, saying, "And ships shall come from the coast of Chittim, and shall afflict Asshur, and shall afflict Eber, and he also shall perish for ever" (Num. xxiv. 24).[38] And this was done by the Goths, and more especially since the empire of the Turks was formed, about one thousand years ago, and so gradually Asia and Africa were lost, and subsequently France, Spain, and finally Venice arose, so that Rome retains no part of its former power.

Since then the Pope could not force the Greeks and the emperor at Constantinople, who is the hereditary Roman emperor, to obey his will, he invented this device to rob him of his empire and title, and to give it to the Germans, who were at that time strong and of good repute, in order that they might take the power of the Roman empire and hold it of the Pope; and this is what actually has happened. It was taken from the emperor at Constantinople, and the name and title were given to us Germans, and therewith we became

---

[38] Luther here follows the Vulgate, translating the above verse: "Es werden die Römer kommen und die Juden verstören: und hernach werden sie auch untergehen."

subject to the Pope, and he has built up a new Roman empire on the Germans. For the other empire, the original, came to an end long ago, as was said above.

Thus the Roman see has got what it wished: Rome has been taken possession of, and the German emperor driven out and bound by oaths not to dwell in Rome. He is to be Roman emperor and nevertheless not to dwell in Rome, and, moreover, always to depend on the Pope and his followers, and to do their will. We are to have the title, and they are to have the lands and the cities. For they have always made our simplicity the tool of their pride and tyranny, and they consider us as stupid Germans, to be deceived and fooled by them as they choose.

Well, for our Lord God it is a small thing to toss kingdoms and principalities hither and thither; He is so free with them that He will sometimes take a kingdom from a good man and give it to a knave, sometimes through the treachery of false, wicked men, sometimes by inheritance, as we read concerning Persia, Greece, and nearly all kingdoms; and Daniel says, "Wisdom and might are His; and He changes the times and the seasons, and He removeth kings and setteth up kings" (Dan. ii. 20, 21). Therefore no one need think it a grand matter if he has a kingdom given to him, especially if he be a Christian; and so we Germans need not be proud of having had a new Roman empire given us. For in His eyes it is a poor gift, that He sometimes gives to the least deserving, as Daniel says, "And all the inhabitants of the earth are reputed as nothing; and He does according to His will in the army of heaven, and among the inhabitants of the earth" (Dan. iv. 35).

Now, although the Pope has violently and unjustly robbed the true emperor of the Roman empire, or its name, and has given it to us Germans, yet it is certain that God has used the Pope's wickedness to give the German nation this empire and to raise up a new Roman empire, that exists now, after the fall of the old empire. We gave the Pope no cause for this action, nor did we understand his false aims and schemes; but still, through the craft and knavery of the popes, we have, alas! all too dearly, paid the price of this empire with incalculable bloodshed, with the loss of our liberty, with the robbery of our wealth, especially of our churches and benefices, and with unspeakable treachery and insult. We have the empire in name, but the Pope has our wealth, our honour, our bodies, lives, and souls and all that we have. This was the way to deceive the Germans, and to deceive them by shuffling. What the popes wished was to become emperors; and as they could not do this, they put themselves above the emperors.

Since, then, we have received this empire through God's providence and the schemes of evil men, without our fault, I would not advise that we should give it up, but that we should govern it honestly, in the fear of God, so long as He is pleased to let us hold it. For, as I have said, it is no matter to Him how a kingdom is come by, but He will have it duly governed. If the popes took it from others dishonestly, we at least did not come by it dishonestly. It was given to us through evil men, under the will of God, to whom we have more regard than the false intentions of the popes, who wished to be emperors and more than emperors and to fool and mock us with the name.

The King of Babylon obtained his kingdom by force and robbery; yet God would have it governed by the holy princes Daniel, Ananias, Asarias, and Misael. Much more then does He require this empire to be governed by the Christian princes of Germany, though the Pope may have stolen, or robbed, or newly fashioned it. It is all God's ordering, which came to pass before we knew of it.

Therefore the Pope and his followers have no reason to boast that they did a great kindness to the German nation in giving them this Roman empire; firstly, because they intended no good to us, in the matter, but only abused our simplicity to strengthen their own power against the Roman emperor at Constantinople, from whom, against God and justice, the Pope has taken what he had no right to.

Secondly, the Pope sought to give the empire, not to us, but to himself, and to become lord over all our power, liberty, wealth, body and soul, and through us over all the world, if God had not prevented it, as he plainly says in his decretals, and has tried with many mischievous tricks in the case of many German emperors. Thus we Germans have been taught in plain German: whilst we expected to become lords, we have become the servants of the most crafty tyrants; we have the name, title, and arms of the empire, but the

Pope has the treasure, authority, law, and freedom; thus, whilst the Pope eats the kernel, he leaves us the empty shells to play with.

Now may God help us (who, as I have said, assigned us this kingdom through crafty tyrants, and charged us to govern it) to act according to our name, title, and arms, and to secure our freedom, and thus let the Romans see at last what we have received of God through them. If they boast that they have given us an empire, well, be it so, by all means; then let the Pope give up Rome, all he has of the empire, and free our country from his unbearable taxes and robberies, and give back to us our liberty, authority, wealth, honour, body, and soul, rendering to the empire those things that are the empire's, so as to act in accordance with his words and pretences.

But if he will not do this, what game is he playing with all his falsehoods and pretences? Was it not enough to lead this great people by the nose for so many hundred years? Because the Pope crowns or makes the Emperor, it does not follow that he is above him; for the prophet, St. Samuel, anointed and crowned King Saul and David, at God's command, and was yet subject to them. And the prophet Nathan anointed King Solomon, and yet was not placed over him; moreover, St. Elisha let one of his servants anoint King Jehu of Israel, yet they obeyed him. And it has never yet happened in the whole world that any one was above the king because he consecrated or crowned him, except in the case of the Pope.

Now he is himself crowned pope by three cardinals; yet they are subject to him, and he is above them. Why, then, contrary to his own example and to the doctrine and practice of the whole world and the Scriptures, should he exalt himself above the temporal authorities, and the empire, for no other reason than that he crowns, and consecrates the Emperor? It suffices that he is above him in all divine matters—that is, in preaching, teaching, and the ministration of the Sacrament—in which matters, however, every priest or bishop is above all other men, just as St. Ambrose in his chair was above the Emperor Theodosius, and the prophet Nathan above David, and Samuel above Saul. Therefore let the German emperor be a true free emperor, and let not his authority or his sword be overborne by these blind pretences of the Pope's sycophants, as if they were to be exceptions, and be above the temporal sword in all things.

27. Let this be enough about the faults of the spiritual estate, though many more might be found, if the matter were properly considered; we must now consider the defects of the temporal estates. In the first place, we require a general law and consent of the German nation against profusion and extravagance in dress, which is the cause of so much poverty among the nobles and the people. Surely God has given to us, as to other nations, enough wool, fur, flax, and whatever else is required for the decent clothing of every class; and it cannot be necessary to spend such enormous sums for silk, velvet, cloth of gold, and all other kinds of outlandish stuff. I think that even if the Pope did not rob us Germans with his unbearable taxes, we should be robbed more than enough by these secret thieves, the dealers in silk and velvet. As it is, we see that every man wishes to be every other man's equal, and that this causes and increases pride and envy among us, as we deserve, all which would cease, with many other misfortunes, if our self-will would but let us be gratefully content with what God has given us.

It is similarly necessary to diminish the use of spices, which is one of the ships in which our gold is sent away from Germany. God's mercy has given us more food, and that both precious and good, than is to be found in other countries. I shall probably be accused of making foolish and impossible suggestions, as if I wished to destroy the great business of commerce. But I am only doing my part; if the community does not mend matters, every man should do it himself. I do not see many good manners that have ever come into a land through commerce, and therefore God let the people of Israel dwell far from the sea and not carry on much trade.

But without doubt the greatest misfortune of the Germans is buying on usury. But for this, many a man would have to leave unbought his silk, velvet, cloth of gold, spices, and all other luxuries. The system has not been in force for more than one hundred years, and has already brought poverty, misery, and destruction on almost all princes, foundations, cities, nobles, and heirs. If it continues for another hundred years Germany will be left without a farthing, and we shall be reduced to eating one another. The devil invented this system, and the Pope has done an injury to the whole world by sanctioning it.

My request and my cry therefore is this: Let each man consider the destruction of himself and his family, which is no longer at the door, but has entered the house; and let emperors, princes, lords, and corporations see to the condemnation and prohibition of this kind of trade, without considering the opposition of the Pope and all his justice and injustice, nor whether livings or endowments depend upon it. Better a single fief in a city based on a freehold estate or honest interest, than a hundred based on usury; yea, a single endowment on usury is worse and more grievous than twenty based on freehold estate. Truly this usury is a sign and warning that the world has been given over to the devil for its sins, and that we are losing our spiritual and temporal welfare alike; yet we heed it not.

Doubtless we should also find some bridle for the *Fuggers* and similar companies. Is it possible that in a single man's lifetime such great wealth should be collected together, if all were done rightly and according to God's will? I am not skilled in accounts, but I do not understand how it is possible for one hundred guilders to gain twenty in a year, or how one guilder can gain another, and that not out of the soil, or by cattle, seeing that possessions depend not on the wit of men, but on the blessing of God. I commend this to those that are skilled in worldly affairs. I as a theologian blame nothing but the evil appearance, of which St. Paul says, "Abstain from all appearance of evil" (I Thess. v. 22). All I know is that it were much more godly to encourage agriculture and lessen commerce; and that they do the best who, according to the Scriptures, till the ground to get their living, as we are all commanded in Adam: "Cursed is the ground for thy sake. . . . Thorns also and thistles shall it bring forth to thee. . . . In the sweat of thy face shalt thou eat bread" (Gen. iii. 17–19). There is still much ground that is not ploughed or tilled.

Then there is the excess in eating and drinking, for which we Germans have an ill reputation in foreign countries, as our special vice, and which has become so common, and gained so much the upper hand, that sermons avail nothing. The loss of money caused by it is not the worst; but in its train come murder, adultery, theft, blasphemy, and all vices. The temporal power should do something to prevent it; otherwise it will come to pass, as Christ foretold, that the last day shall come as a thief in the night, and shall find them eating and drinking, marrying and giving in marriage, planting and building, buying and selling (Matt. xxiv. 38; Luke xvii. 26), just as things go on now, and that so strongly that I apprehend lest the day of judgment be at hand, even now when we least expect it.

Lastly, is it not a terrible thing that we Christians should maintain public brothels, though we all vow chastity in our baptism? I well know all that can be said on this matter: that it is not peculiar to one nation, that it would be difficult to demolish it, and that it is better thus than that virgins, or married women, or honourable women should be dishonoured. But should not the spiritual and temporal powers combine to find some means of meeting these difficulties without any such heathen practice? If the people of Israel existed without this scandal, why should not a Christian nation be able to do so? How do so many towns and villages manage to exist without these houses? Why should not great cities be able to do so?

In all, however, that I have said above, my object has been to show how much good temporal authority might do, and what should be the duty of all authorities, so that every man might learn what a terrible thing it is to rule and to have the chief place. What boots it though a ruler be in his own person as holy as St. Peter, if he be not diligent to help his subjects in these matters? His very authority will be his condemnation; for it is the duty of those in authority to seek the good of their subjects. But if those in authority considered how young people might be brought together in marriage, the prospect of marriage would help every man and protect him from temptations.

But as it is every man is induced to become a priest or a monk; and of all these I am afraid not one in a hundred has any other motive but the wish of getting a livelihood and the uncertainty of maintaining a family. Therefore they begin by a dissolute life and sow their wild oats, (as they say), but I fear they rather gather in a store of wild oats.[39] I hold the proverb to be true, "Most men become monks and priests in desperation." That is why things are as we see them.

[39] Luther uses the expression *ausbuben* in the sense of *sich austoben*, viz., "to storm *out* one's passions," and then coins the word *sich einbuben*, viz., "to storm *in* one's passions."

But in order that many sins may be prevented that are becoming too common, I would honestly advise that no boy or girl be allowed to take the vow of chastity or to enter a religious life before the age of thirty years. For this requires a special grace, as St. Paul says. Therefore, unless God specially urge any one to a religious life, he will do well to leave all vows and devotions alone. I say further, If a man has so little faith in God as to fear that he will be unable to maintain himself in the married state, and if this fear is the only thing that makes him become a priest, then I implore him, for his own soul's sake, not to become a priest, but rather to become a peasant, or what he will. For if simple trust in God be necessary to ensure temporal support, tenfold trust in God is necessary to live a religious life. If you do not trust to God for your worldly food, how can you trust to Him for your spiritual food? Alas! this unbelief and want of faith destroys all things, and leads us into all misery, as we see among all conditions of men.

Much might be said concerning all this misery. Young people have no one to look after them, they are left to go on just as they like, and those in authority are of no more use to them than if they did not exist, though this should be the chief care of the Pope, of bishops, lords, and councils. They wish to rule over everything, everywhere, and yet they are of no use. Oh, what a rare sight, for these reasons, will a lord or ruler be in heaven, though he might build a hundred churches to God and raise all the dead!

But this may suffice for the present. For of what concerns the temporal authority and the nobles I have, I think, said enough in my tract on *Good Works*. For their lives and governments leave room enough for improvement; but there is no comparison between spiritual and temporal abuses, as I have there shown. I daresay I have sung a lofty strain, that I have proposed many things that will be thought impossible, and attacked many points too sharply. But what was I to do? I was bound to say this: if I had the power, this is what I would do. I had rather incur the world's anger than God's; they cannot take from me more than my life. I have hitherto made many offers of peace to my adversaries; but, as I see, God has forced me through them to open my mouth wider and wider, and, because they do not keep quiet, to give them enough cause for speaking, barking, shouting, and writing. Well, then, I have another song still to sing concerning them and Rome; if they wish to hear it, I will sing it to them, and sing with all my might. Do you understand, my friend Rome, what I mean?

I have frequently offered to submit my writings for inquiry and examination, but in vain, though I know, if I am in the right, I must be condemned upon earth and justified by Christ alone in heaven. For all the Scriptures teach us that the affairs of Christians and Christendom must be judged by God alone; they have never yet been justified by men in this world, but the opposition has always been too strong. My greatest care and fear is lest my cause be not condemned by men, by which I should know for certain that it does not please God. Therefore let them go freely to work, pope, bishop, priest, monk, or doctor; they are the true people to persecute the truth, as they have always done. May God grant us all a Christian understanding, and especially to the Christian nobility of the German nation true spiritual courage, to do what is best for our unhappy Church. Amen!

At Wittenberg, in the year 1520.

CONCERNING
CHRISTIAN LIBERTY

LETTER OF MARTIN LUTHER TO POPE LEO X

AMONG those monstrous evils of this age with which I have
now for three years been waging war, I am sometimes compelled to look to you and to call you to mind, most blessed
father Leo. In truth, since you alone are everywhere considered as
being the cause of my engaging in war, I cannot at any time fail
to remember you; and although I have been compelled by the causeless raging of your impious flatterers against me to appeal from your
seat to a future council—fearless of the futile decrees of your predecessors Pius and Julius, who in their foolish tyranny prohibited such
an action—yet I have never been so alienated in feeling from your
Blessedness as not to have sought with all my might, in diligent
prayer and crying to God, all the best gifts for you and for your see.
But those who have hitherto endeavoured to terrify me with the
majesty of your name and authority, I have begun quite to despise
and triumph over. One thing I see remaining which I cannot despise,
and this has been the reason of my writing anew to your Blessedness: namely, that I find that blame is cast on me, and that it is
imputed to me as a great offence, that in my rashness I am judged
to have spared not even your person.

Now, to confess the truth openly, I am conscious that, whenever
I have had to mention your person, I have said nothing of you but
what was honourable and good. If I had done otherwise, I could
by no means have approved my own conduct, but should have supported with all my power the judgment of those men concerning me,
nor would anything have pleased me better, than to recant such rashness and impiety. I have called you Daniel in Babylon; and every
reader thoroughly knows with what distinguished zeal I defended

your conspicuous innocence against Silvester, who tried to stain it. Indeed, the published opinion of so many great men and the repute of your blameless life are too widely famed and too much reverenced throughout the world to be assailable by any man, of however great name, or by any arts. I am not so foolish as to attack one whom everybody praises; nay, it has been and always will be my desire not to attack even those whom public repute disgraces. I am not delighted at the faults of any man, since I am very conscious myself of the great beam in my own eye, nor can I be the first to cast a stone at the adulteress.

I have indeed inveighed sharply against impious doctrines, and I have not been slack to censure my adversaries on account, not of their bad morals, but of their impiety. And for this I am so far from being sorry that I have brought my mind to despise the judgments of men and to persevere in this vehement zeal, according to the example of Christ, who, in His zeal, calls His adversaries a generation of vipers, blind, hypocrites, and children of the devil. Paul, too, charges the sorcerer with being a child of the devil, full of all subtlety and all malice; and defames certain persons as evil workers, dogs, and deceivers. In the opinion of those delicate-eared persons, nothing could be more bitter or intemperate than Paul's language. What can be more bitter than the words of the prophets? The ears of our generation have been made so delicate by the senseless multitude of flatterers that, as soon as we perceive that anything of ours is not approved of, we cry out that we are being bitterly assailed; and when we can repel the truth by no other pretence, we escape by attributing bitterness, impatience, intemperance, to our adversaries. What would be the use of salt if it were not pungent, or of the edge of the sword if it did not slay? Accursed is the man who does the work of the Lord deceitfully.

Wherefore, most excellent Leo, I beseech you to accept my vindication, made in this letter, and to persuade yourself that I have never thought any evil concerning your person; further, that I am one who desires that eternal blessing may fall to your lot, and that I have no dispute with any man concerning morals, but only concerning the word of truth. In all other things I will yield to any one, but I

neither can nor will forsake and deny the word. He who thinks
otherwise of me, or has taken in my words in another sense, does
not think rightly, and has not taken in the truth.

Your see, however, which is called the Court of Rome, and which
neither you nor any man can deny to be more corrupt than any
Babylon or Sodom, and quite, as I believe, of a lost, desperate, and
hopeless impiety, this I have verily abominated, and have felt indig-
nant that the people of Christ should be cheated under your name
and the pretext of the Church of Rome; and so I have resisted, and
will resist, as long as the spirit of faith shall live in me. Not that I am
striving after impossibilities, or hoping that by my labours alone,
against the furious opposition of so many flatterers, any good can
be done in that most disordered Babylon; but that I feel myself a
debtor to my brethren, and am bound to take thought for them,
that fewer of them may be ruined, or that their ruin may be less
complete, by the plagues of Rome. For many years now, nothing
else has overflowed from Rome into the world—as you are not ignorant—than the laying waste of goods, of bodies, and of souls, and the
worst examples of all the worst things. These things are clearer than
the light to all men; and the Church of Rome, formerly the most
holy of all Churches, has become the most lawless den of thieves,
the most shameless of all brothels, the very kingdom of sin, death,
and hell; so that not even antichrist, if he were to come, could devise
any addition to its wickedness.

Meanwhile you, Leo, are sitting like a lamb in the midst of wolves,
like Daniel in the midst of lions, and, with Ezekiel, you dwell
among scorpions. What opposition can you alone make to these
monstrous evils? Take to yourself three or four of the most learned
and best of the cardinals. What are these among so many? You
would all perish by poison before you could undertake to decide on
a remedy. It is all over with the Court of Rome; the wrath of God
has come upon her to the uttermost. She hates councils; she dreads
to be reformed; she cannot restrain the madness of her impiety; she
fills up the sentence passed on her mother, of whom it is said, "We
would have healed Babylon, but she is not healed; let us forsake her."
It had been your duty and that of your cardinals to apply a remedy
to these evils, but this gout laughs at the physician's hand, and the

chariot does not obey the reins. Under the influence of these feelings, I have always grieved that you, most excellent Leo, who were worthy of a better age, have been made pontiff in this. For the Roman Court is not worthy of you and those like you, but of Satan himself, who in truth is more the ruler in that Babylon than you are.

Oh, would that, having laid aside that glory which your most abandoned enemies declare to be yours, you were living rather in the office of a private priest or on your paternal inheritance! In that glory none are worthy to glory, except the race of Iscariot, the children of perdition. For what happens in your court, Leo, except that, the more wicked and execrable any man is, the more prosperously he can use your name and authority for the ruin of the property and souls of men, for the multiplication of crimes, for the oppression of faith and truth and of the whole Church of God? Oh, Leo! in reality most unfortunate, and sitting on a most perilous throne, I tell you the truth, because I wish you well; for if Bernard felt compassion for his Anastasius at a time when the Roman see, though even then most corrupt, was as yet ruling with better hope than now, why should not we lament, to whom so much further corruption and ruin has been added in three hundred years?

Is it not true that there is nothing under the vast heavens more corrupt, more pestilential, more hateful, than the Court of Rome? She incomparably surpasses the impiety of the Turks, so that in very truth she, who was formerly the gate of heaven, is now a sort of open mouth of hell, and such a mouth as, under the urgent wrath of God, cannot be blocked up; one course alone being left to us wretched men: to call back and save some few, if we can, from that Roman gulf.

Behold, Leo, my father, with what purpose and on what principle it is that I have stormed against that seat of pestilence. I am so far from having felt any rage against your person that I even hoped to gain favour with you and to aid you in your welfare by striking actively and vigorously at that your prison, nay, your hell. For whatever the efforts of all minds can contrive against the confusion of that impious Court will be advantageous to you and to your welfare, and to many others with you. Those who do harm to her are doing your office; those who in every way abhor her are glorifying Christ; in short, those are Christians who are not Romans.

But, to say yet more, even this never entered my heart: to inveigh against the Court of Rome or to dispute at all about her. For, seeing all remedies for her health to be desperate, I looked on her with contempt, and, giving her a bill of divorcement, said to her, "He that is unjust, let him be unjust still; and he that is filthy, let him be filthy still," giving myself up to the peaceful and quiet study of sacred literature, that by this I might be of use to the brethren living about me.

While I was making some advance in these studies, Satan opened his eyes and goaded on his servant John Eccius, that notorious adversary of Christ, by the unchecked lust for fame, to drag me unexpectedly into the arena, trying to catch me in one little word concerning the primacy of the Church of Rome, which had fallen from me in passing. That boastful Thraso, foaming and gnashing his teeth, proclaimed that he would dare all things for the glory of God and for the honour of the holy apostolic seat; and, being puffed up respecting your power, which he was about to misuse, he looked forward with all certainty to victory; seeking to promote, not so much the primacy of Peter, as his own pre-eminence among the theologians of this age; for he thought it would contribute in no slight degree to this, if he were to lead Luther in triumph. The result having proved unfortunate for the sophist, an incredible rage torments him; for he feels that whatever discredit to Rome has arisen through me has been caused by the fault of himself alone.

Suffer me, I pray you, most excellent Leo, both to plead my own cause, and to accuse your true enemies. I believe it is known to you in what way Cardinal Cajetan, your imprudent and unfortunate, nay unfaithful, legate, acted towards me. When, on account of my reverence for your name, I had placed myself and all that was mine in his hands, he did not so act as to establish peace, which he could easily have established by one little word, since I, at that time, promised to be silent and to make an end of my case, if he would command my adversaries to do the same. But that man of pride, not content with this agreement, began to justify my adversaries, to give them free licence, and to order me to recant, a thing which was certainly not in his commission. Thus indeed, when the case was in the best position, it came through his vexatious tyranny into a much worse one. Therefore, whatever has followed upon this is the fault not of Luther, but entirely of Cajetan, since he did not suffer me to be silent and remain quiet, which at that time I was entreating for with all my might. What more was it my duty to do?

Next came Charles Miltitz, also a nuncio from your Blessedness. He, though he went up and down with much and varied exertion, and omitted nothing which could tend to restore the position of the cause thrown into confusion by the rashness and pride of Cajetan, had difficulty, even with the help of that very illustrious prince the Elector Frederick, in at last bringing about more than one familiar conference with me. In these I again yielded to your great name, and was prepared to keep silence, and to accept as my judge either the Archbishop of Treves, or the Bishop of Naumburg; and thus it was done and concluded. While this was being done with good hope of success, lo! that other and greater enemy of yours, Eccius, rushed in with his Leipsic disputation, which he had undertaken against Carlstadt, and, having taken up a new question concerning the primacy of the Pope, turned his arms unexpectedly against me, and completely overthrew the plan for peace. Meanwhile Charles Miltitz was waiting, disputations were held, judges were being chosen, but no decision was arrived at. And no wonder! for by the falsehoods, pretences, and arts of Eccius the whole business was brought into such thorough disorder, confusion, and festering soreness, that, whichever way the sentence might lean, a greater conflagration was sure to arise; for he was seeking, not after truth, but after his own credit. In this case too, I omitted nothing which it was right that I should do.

I confess that on this occasion no small part of the corruptions of Rome came to light; but, if there was any offence in this, it was the fault of Eccius, who, in taking on him a burden beyond his strength, and in furiously aiming at credit for himself, unveiled to the whole world the disgrace of Rome.

Here is that enemy of yours, Leo, or rather of your Court; by his example alone we may learn that an enemy is not more baneful than a flatterer. For what did he bring about by his flattery, except evils which no king could have brought about? At this day, the name of the Court of Rome stinks in the nostrils of the world, the papal authority is growing weak, and its notorious ignorance is evil spoken of. We should hear none of these things, if Eccius had not disturbed the plans of Miltitz and myself for peace. He feels this clearly enough himself in the indignation he shows, too late and in vain, against the publication of my books. He ought to have reflected on this at the time when he was all mad for renown, and was seeking in your cause nothing but his own objects, and that with the greatest peril to you. The foolish man hoped that, from fear of your name, I should yield and keep silence; for I do not think he presumed on his talents and learning. Now, when he sees that I am very confident and speak aloud, he repents too late of his rashness, and sees—if indeed he does see it—that there is One in heaven who resists the proud, and humbles the presumptuous.

Since then we were bringing about by this disputation nothing but the greater confusion of the cause of Rome, Charles Miltitz for the third time addressed the Fathers of the Order, assembled in chapter, and sought their advice for the settlement of the case, as being now in a most troubled and perilous state. Since, by the favour of God, there was no hope of proceeding against me by force, some of the more noted of their number were sent to me, and begged me at least to show respect to your person and to vindicate in a humble letter both your innocence and my own. They said that the affair was not as yet in a position of extreme hopelessness, if Leo X., in his inborn kindliness, would put his hand to it. On this I, who have always offered and wished for peace, in order that I might devote myself to calmer and more useful pursuits, and who for this very purpose have acted with so much spirit and vehemence, in order to put down by the strength and impetuosity of my words, as well as of my feelings, men whom I saw to be very far from equal to myself —I, I say, not only gladly yielded, but even accepted it with joy and gratitude, as the greatest kindness and benefit, if you should think it right to satisfy my hopes.

Thus I come, most blessed Father, and in all abasement beseech you to put your hand, if it is possible, and impose a curb to those flatterers who are enemies of peace, while they pretend peace. But there is no reason, most blessed Father, why any one should assume that I am to utter a recantation, unless he prefers to involve the case in still greater confusion. Moreover, I cannot bear with laws for the interpretation of the word of God, since the word of God, which teaches liberty in all other things, ought not to be bound. Saving these two things, there is nothing which I am not able, and most heartily willing, to do or to suffer. I hate contention; I will challenge no one; in return I wish not to be challenged; but, being challenged, I will not be dumb in the cause of Christ, my Master. For your Blessedness will be able by one short and easy word to call these controversies before you and suppress them, and to impose silence and peace on both sides——a word which I have ever longed to hear.

Therefore, Leo, my Father, beware of listening to those sirens who make you out to be not simply a man, but partly a god, so that you can command and require whatever you will. It will not happen so, nor will you prevail. You are the servant of servants, and more than any other man, in a most pitiable and perilous position. Let not those men deceive you who pretend that you are lord of the world; who will not allow any one to be a Christian without your authority; who babble of your having power over heaven, hell, and purgatory. These men are your enemies and are seeking your soul to destroy it, as Isaiah says, "My people, they that call thee blessed are themselves deceiving thee." They are in error who raise you above councils and the universal Church; they are in error who attribute to you alone the right of interpreting Scripture. All these men are seeking to set up their own impieties in the Church under your name, and alas! Satan has gained much through them in the time of your predecessors.

In brief, trust not in any who exalt you, but in those who humiliate you. For this is the judgment of God: "He hath cast down the mighty from their seat, and hath exalted the humble." See how unlike Christ was to His successors, though all will have it that they are His vicars. I fear that in truth very many of them have been in too serious a sense His vicars, for a vicar represents a prince who is absent. Now if a pontiff rules while Christ is absent and does not dwell in his heart, what else is he but a vicar of Christ? And then what is that Church but a multitude without Christ? What indeed is such a vicar but antichrist and an idol? How much more rightly did the Apostles speak, who call themselves servants of a present Christ, not the vicars of an absent one!

Perhaps I am shamelessly bold in seeming to teach so great a head, by whom all men ought to be taught, and from whom, as those plagues of yours boast, the thrones of judges receive their sentence; but I imitate St. Bernard in his book concerning *Considerations* addressed to Eugenius, a book which ought to be known by heart by every pontiff. I do this, not from any desire to teach, but as a duty, from that simple and faithful solicitude which teaches us to be anxious for all that is safe for our neighbours, and does not allow considerations of worthiness or unworthiness to be entertained, being intent only on the dangers or advantage of others. For since I know that your Blessedness is driven and tossed by the waves at Rome, so that the depths of the sea press on you with infinite perils, and that you are labouring under such a condition of misery that you need even the least help from any the least brother, I do not seem to myself to be acting unsuitably if I forget your majesty till I shall have fulfilled the office of charity. I will not flatter in so serious and perilous a matter; and if in this you do not see that I am your friend and most thoroughly your subject, there is One to see and judge.

In fine, that I may not approach you empty-handed, blessed Father, I bring with me this little treatise, published under your name, as a good omen of the establishment of peace and of good hope. By this you may perceive in what pursuits I should prefer and be able to occupy myself to more profit, if I were allowed, or had been hitherto allowed, by your impious flatterers. It is a small matter, if you look to its exterior, but, unless I mistake, it is a summary of the Christian life put together in small compass, if you apprehend its meaning. I, in my poverty, have no other present to make you, nor do you need anything else than to be enriched by a spiritual gift. I commend myself to your Paternity and Blessedness, whom may the Lord Jesus preserve for ever. Amen.

Wittenberg, 6th September, 1520.

CONCERNING CHRISTIAN LIBERTY

CHRISTIAN faith has appeared to many an easy thing; nay, not a few even reckon it among the social virtues, as it were; and this they do because they have not made proof of it experimentally, and have never tasted of what efficacy it is. For it is not possible for any man to write well about it, or to understand well what is rightly written, who has not at some time tasted of its spirit, under the pressure of tribulation; while he who has tasted of it, even to a very small extent, can never write, speak, think, or hear about it sufficiently. For it is a living fountain, springing up into eternal life, as Christ calls it in John iv.

Now, though I cannot boast of my abundance, and though I know how poorly I am furnished, yet I hope that, after having been vexed by various temptations, I have attained some little drop of faith, and that I can speak of this matter, if not with more elegance, certainly with more solidity, than those literal and too subtle disputants who have hitherto discoursed upon it without understanding their own words. That I may open then an easier way for the ignorant—for these alone I am trying to serve—I first lay down these two propositions, concerning spiritual liberty and servitude:—

A Christian man is the most free lord of all, and subject to none; a Christian man is the most dutiful servant of all, and subject to every one.

Although these statements appear contradictory, yet, when they are found to agree together, they will make excellently for my purpose. They are both the statements of Paul himself, who says, "Though I be free from all men, yet have I made myself servant unto all" (1 Cor. ix. 19), and "Owe no man anything, but to love one another" (Rom. xiii. 8). Now love is by its own nature dutiful and obedient to the beloved object. Thus even Christ, though Lord of all things, was yet made of a woman; made under the law; at once free and a servant; at once in the form of God and in the form of a servant.

Let us examine the subject on a deeper and less simple principle. Man is composed of a twofold nature, a spiritual and a bodily. As regards the spiritual nature, which they name the soul, he is called the spiritual, inward, new man; as regards the bodily nature, which they name the flesh, he is called the fleshly, outward, old man. The Apostle speaks of this: "Though our outward man perish, yet the inward man is renewed day by day" (2 Cor. iv. 16). The result of this diversity is that in the Scriptures opposing statements are made concerning the same man, the fact being that in the same man these two men are opposed to one another; the flesh lusting against the spirit, and the spirit against the flesh (Gal. v. 17).

We first approach the subject of the inward man, that we may see by what means a man becomes justified, free, and a true Christian; that is, a spiritual, new, and inward man. It is certain that absolutely none among outward things, under whatever name they may be reckoned, has any influence in producing Christian righteousness or liberty, nor, on the other hand, unrighteousness or slavery. This can be shown by an easy argument.

What can it profit the soul that the body should be in good condition, free, and full of life; that it should eat, drink, and act according to its pleasure; when even the most impious slaves of every kind of vice are prosperous in these matters? Again, what harm can ill-health, bondage, hunger, thirst, or any other outward evil, do to the soul, when even the most pious of men and the freest in the purity of their conscience, are harassed by these things? Neither of these states of things has to do with the liberty or the slavery of the soul.

And so it will profit nothing that the body should be adorned with sacred vestments, or dwell in holy places, or be occupied in sacred offices, or pray, fast, and abstain from certain meats, or do whatever works can be done through the body and in the body. Something widely different will be necessary for the justification and liberty of the soul, since the things I have spoken of can be done by any impious person, and only hypocrites are produced by devotion to these things. On the other hand, it will not at all injure the soul that the body should be clothed in profane raiment, should dwell in profane places, should eat and drink in the ordinary fashion, should not pray aloud, and should leave undone all the things above mentioned, which may be done by hypocrites.

And, to cast everything aside, even speculation, meditations, and whatever things can be performed by the exertions of the soul itself, are of no profit. One thing, and one alone, is necessary for life, justification, and Christian liberty; and that is the most holy word of God, the Gospel of Christ, as He says, "I am the resurrection and

the life; he that believeth in Me shall not die eternally" (John xi.
25), and also, "If the Son shall make you free, ye shall be free indeed"
(John viii. 36), and, "Man shall not live by bread alone, but by every
word that proceedeth out of the mouth of God" (Matt. iv. 4).

Let us therefore hold it for certain and firmly established that the
soul can do without everything except the word of God, without
which none at all of its wants are provided for. But, having the
word, it is rich and wants for nothing, since that is the word of life,
of truth, of light, of peace, of justification, of salvation, of joy, of
liberty, of wisdom, of virtue, of grace, of glory, and of every good
thing. It is on this account that the prophet in a whole Psalm
(Psalm cxix.) and in many other places, sighs for and calls upon the
word of God with so many groanings and words.

Again, there is no more cruel stroke of the wrath of God than
when He sends a famine of hearing His words (Amos viii. 11), just
as there is no greater favour from Him than the sending forth of
His word, as it is said, "He sent His word and healed them, and
delivered them from their destructions" (Psalm cvii. 20). Christ was
sent for no other office than that of the word; and the order of
Apostles, that of bishops, and that of the whole body of the clergy,
have been called and instituted for no object but the ministry of
the word.

But you will ask, What is this word, and by what means is it to
be used, since there are so many words of God? I answer, The
Apostle Paul (Rom. i.) explains what it is, namely the Gospel of
God, concerning His Son, incarnate, suffering, risen, and glorified,
through the Spirit, the Sanctifier. To preach Christ is to feed the
soul, to justify it, to set it free, and to save it, if it believes the preaching. For faith alone and the efficacious use of the word of God, bring
salvation. "If thou shalt confess with thy mouth the Lord Jesus, and
shalt believe in thine heart that God hath raised Him from the dead,
thou shalt be saved" (Rom. x. 9); and again, "Christ is the end of
the law for righteousness to every one that believeth" (Rom. x. 4),
and "The just shall live by faith" (Rom. i. 17). For the word of
God cannot be received and honoured by any works, but by faith
alone. Hence it is clear that as the soul needs the word alone for
life and justification, so it is justified by faith alone, and not by any

works. For if it could be justified by any other means, it would have no need of the word, nor consequently of faith.

But this faith cannot consist at all with works; that is, if you imagine that you can be justified by those works, whatever they are, along with it. For this would be to halt between two opinions, to worship Baal, and to kiss the hand to him, which is a very great iniquity, as Job says. Therefore, when you begin to believe, you learn at the same time that all that is in you is utterly guilty, sinful, and damnable, according to that saying, "All have sinned, and come short of the glory of God" (Rom. iii. 23), and also: "There is none righteous, no, not one; they are all gone out of the way; they are together become unprofitable: there is none that doeth good, no, not one" (Rom. iii. 10–12). When you have learnt this, you will know that Christ is necessary for you, since He has suffered and risen again for you, that, believing on Him, you might by this faith become another man, all your sins being remitted, and you being justified by the merits of another, namely of Christ alone.

Since then this faith can reign only in the inward man, as it is said, "With the heart man believeth unto righteousness" (Rom. x. 10); and since it alone justifies, it is evident that by no outward work or labour can the inward man be at all justified, made free, and saved; and that no works whatever have any relation to him. And so, on the other hand, it is solely by impiety and incredulity of heart that he becomes guilty and a slave of sin, deserving condemnation, not by any outward sin or work. Therefore, the first care of every Christian ought to be to lay aside all reliance on works, and strengthen his faith alone more and more, and by it grow in the knowledge, not of works, but of Christ Jesus, who has suffered and risen again for him, as Peter teaches (1 Peter v.) when he makes no other work to be a Christian one. Thus Christ, when the Jews asked Him what they should do that they might work the works of God, rejected the multitude of works, with which He saw that they were puffed up, and commanded them one thing only, saying, "This is the work of God: that ye believe on Him whom He hath sent, for Him hath God the Father sealed" (John vi. 27, 29).

Hence a right faith in Christ is an incomparable treasure, carrying with it universal salvation and preserving from all evil, as it is said,

"He that believeth and is baptised shall be saved; but he that believeth not shall be damned" (Mark xvi. 16). Isaiah, looking to this treasure, predicted, "The consumption decreed shall overflow with righteousness. For the Lord God of hosts shall make a consumption, even determined (*verbum abbreviatum et consummans*), in the midst of the land" (Isa. x. 22, 23). As if he said, "Faith, which is the brief and complete fulfilling of the law, will fill those who believe with such righteousness that they will need nothing else for justification." Thus, too, Paul says, "For with the heart man believeth unto righteousness" (Rom. x. 10).

But you ask how it can be the fact that faith alone justifies, and affords without works so great a treasure of good things, when so many works, ceremonies, and laws are prescribed to us in the Scriptures? I answer: Before all things bear in mind what I have said: that faith alone without works justifies, sets free, and saves, as I shall show more clearly below.

Meanwhile it is to be noted that the whole Scripture of God is divided into two parts: precepts and promises. The precepts certainly teach us what is good, but what they teach is not forthwith done. For they show us what we ought to do, but do not give us the power to do it. They were ordained, however, for the purpose of showing man to himself, that through them he may learn his own impotence for good and may despair of his own strength. For this reason they are called the Old Testament, and are so.

For example, "Thou shalt not covet," is a precept by which we are all convicted of sin, since no man can help coveting, whatever efforts to the contrary he may make. In order therefore that he may fulfil the precept, and not covet, he is constrained to despair of himself and to seek elsewhere and through another the help which he cannot find in himself; as it is said, "O Israel, thou hast destroyed thyself; but in Me is thine help" (Hosea xiii. 9). Now what is done by this one precept is done by all; for all are equally impossible of fulfilment by us.

Now when a man has through the precepts been taught his own impotence, and become anxious by what means he may satisfy the law—for the law must be satisfied, so that no jot or tittle of it may pass away, otherwise he must be hopelessly condemned—then, being truly humbled and brought to nothing in his own eyes, he finds in himself no resource for justification and salvation.

Then comes in that other part of Scripture, the promises of God, which declare the glory of God, and say, "If you wish to fulfil the law, and, as the law requires, not to covet, lo! believe in Christ, in whom are promised to you grace, justification, peace and liberty." All these things you shall have, if you believe, and shall be without them if you do not believe. For what is impossible for you by all the works of the law, which are many and yet useless, you shall fulfil in an easy and summary way through faith, because God the Father has made everything to depend on faith, so that whosoever has it has all things, and he who has it not has nothing. "For God hath concluded them all in unbelief, that He might have mercy upon all" (Rom. xi. 32). Thus the promises of God give that which the precepts exact, and fulfil what the law commands; so that all is of God alone, both the precepts and their fulfilment. He alone commands; He alone also fulfils. Hence the promises of God belong to the New Testament; nay, are the New Testament.

Now, since these promises of God are words of holiness, truth, righteousness, liberty, and peace, and are full of universal goodness, the soul, which cleaves to them with a firm faith, is so united to them, nay, thoroughly absorbed by them, that it not only partakes in, but is penetrated and saturated by, all their virtues. For if the touch of Christ was healing, how much more does that most tender spiritual touch, nay, absorption of the word, communicate to the soul all that belongs to the word! In this way therefore the soul, through faith alone, without works, is from the word of God justified, sanctified, endued with truth, peace, and liberty, and filled full with every good thing, and is truly made the child of God, as it is said, "To them gave He power to become the sons of God, even to them that believe on His name" (John i. 12).

From all this it is easy to understand why faith has such great power, and why no good works, nor even all good works put together, can compare with it, since no work can cleave to the word of God or be in the soul. Faith alone and the word reign in it; and such as is the word, such is the soul made by it, just as iron exposed to fire glows like fire, on account of its union with the fire. It is clear then that to a Christian man his faith suffices for everything, and that he has no need of works for justification. But if he has no need of works, neither has he need of the law; and if he has no need of the law, he is certainly free from the law, and the saying is true, "The law is not made for a righteous man" (1 Tim. i. 9). This is that Christian liberty, our faith, the effect of which is, not that we should be careless or lead a bad life, but that no one should need the law or works for justification and salvation.

Let us consider this as the first virtue of faith; and let us look also to the second. This also is an office of faith: that it honours with the utmost veneration and the highest reputation Him in whom it believes, inasmuch as it holds Him to be truthful and worthy of belief. For there is no honour like that reputation of truth and righteousness with which we honour Him in whom we believe. What higher credit can we attribute to any one than truth and righteousness, and absolute goodness? On the other hand, it is the greatest insult to brand any one with the reputation of falsehood and unrighteousness, or to suspect him of these, as we do when we disbelieve him.

Thus the soul, in firmly believing the promises of God, holds Him to be true and righteous; and it can attribute to God no higher glory than the credit of being so. The highest worship of God is to ascribe to Him, truth, righteousness, and whatever qualities we must ascribe to one in whom we believe. In doing this, the soul shows itself prepared to do His whole will; in doing this it hallows His name, and gives itself up to be dealt with as it may please God. For it cleaves to His promises, and never doubts that He is true, just, and wise, and will do, dispose, and provide for all things in the best way. Is not such a soul, in this its faith, most obedient to God in all things? What commandment does there remain which has not been amply fulfilled by such an obedience? What fulfilment can be more full than universal obedience? Now this is not accomplished by works, but by faith alone.

On the other hand, what greater rebellion, impiety, or insult to God can there be, than not to believe His promises? What else is this, than either to make God a liar, or to doubt His truth—that is, to attribute truth to ourselves, but to God falsehood and levity? In doing this, is not a man denying God and setting himself up as an idol in his own heart? What then can works, done in such a state of impiety, profit us, were they even angelic or apostolic works? Rightly hath God shut up all, not in wrath nor in lust, but in unbelief, in order that those who pretend that they are fulfilling the law by works of purity and benevolence (which are social and human virtues) may not presume that they will therefore be saved, but, being included in the sin of unbelief, may either seek mercy, or be justly condemned.

But when God sees that truth is ascribed to Him, and that in the faith of our hearts He is honoured with all the honour of which He is worthy, then in return He honours us on account of that faith, attributing to us truth and righteousness. For faith does truth and righteousness in rendering to God what is His; and therefore in return, God gives glory to our righteousness. It is true and righteous that God is true and righteous; and to confess this and ascribe these attributes to Him, this it is to be true and righteous. Thus He says, "Them that honour Me I will honour, and they that despise Me shall be lightly esteemed" (1 Sam. ii. 30). And so Paul says that Abraham's faith was imputed to him for righteousness, because by it he gave glory to God; and that to us also, for the same reason, it shall be imputed for righteousness, if we believe (Rom. iv.).

The third incomparable grace of faith is this: that it unites the soul to Christ, as the wife to the husband, by which mystery, as the Apostle teaches, Christ and the soul are made one flesh. Now if they are one flesh, and if a true marriage—nay, by far the most perfect of all marriages—is accomplished between them (for human marriages are but feeble types of this one great marriage), then it follows that all they have becomes theirs in common, as well good things as evil things; so that whatsoever Christ possesses, that the believing soul may take to itself and boast of as its own, and whatever belongs to the soul, that Christ claims as His.

If we compare these possessions, we shall see how inestimable is the gain. Christ is full of grace, life, and salvation; the soul is full of sin, death, and condemnation. Let faith step in, and then sin, death, and hell will belong to Christ, and grace, life, and salvation to the soul. For, if He is a Husband, He must needs take to Him-

self that which is His wife's and at the same time, impart to His
wife that which is His. For, in giving her His own body and Himself, how can He but give her all that is His? And, in taking to
Himself the body of His wife, how can He but take to Himself all
that is hers?

In this is displayed the delightful sight, not only of communion,
but of a prosperous warfare, of victory, salvation, and redemption.
For, since Christ is God and man, and is such a Person as neither
has sinned, nor dies, nor is condemned, nay, cannot sin, die, or be
condemned, and since IIis righteousness, life, and salvation are
invincible, eternal, and almighty,—when I say, such a Person, by the
wedding-ring of faith, takes a share in the sins, death, and hell of
His wife, nay, makes them His own, and deals with them no otherwise than as if they were His, and as if He himself had sinned;
and when He suffers, dies, and descends to hell, that He may overcome all things, and since sin, death, and hell cannot swallow Him
up, they must needs be swallowed up by Him in stupendous conflict. For His righteousness rises above the sins of all men; His life
is more powerful than all death; His salvation is more unconquer-
able than all hell.

Thus the believing soul, by the pledge of its faith in Christ,
becomes free from all sin, fearless of death, safe from hell, and
endowed with the eternal righteousness, life, and salvation of its
Husband Christ. Thus He presents to Himself a glorious bride,
without spot or wrinkle, cleansing her with the washing of water
by the word; that is, by faith in the word of life, righteousness, and
salvation. Thus He betrothes her unto Himself "in faithfulness, in
righteousness, and in judgment, and in loving kindness, and in
mercies" (Hosea ii. 19, 20).

Who then can value highly enough these royal nuptials? Who
can comprehend the riches of the glory of this grace? Christ, that
rich and pious Husband, takes as a wife a needy and impious harlot,
redeeming her from all her evils and supplying her with all His
good things. It is impossible now that her sins should destroy her,
since they have been laid upon Christ and swallowed up in Him,
and since she has in her Husband Christ, a righteousness which she
may claim as her own, and which she can set up with confidence

against all her sins, against death and hell, saying, "If I have sinned, my Christ, in whom I believe, has not sinned; all mine is His, and all His is mine," as it is written, "My beloved is mine, and I am His" (Cant. ii. 16). This is what Paul says: "Thanks be to God, which giveth us the victory through our Lord Jesus Christ," victory over sin and death, as he says, "The sting of death is sin, and the strength of sin is the law" (1 Cor. xv. 56, 57).

From all this you will again understand why so much importance is attributed to faith, so that it alone can fulfil the law and justify without any works. For you see that the First Commandment, which says, "Thou shalt worship one God only," is fulfilled by faith alone. If you were nothing but good works from the soles of your feet to the crown of your head, you would not be worshipping God, nor fulfilling the First Commandment, since it is impossible to worship God without ascribing to Him the glory of truth and of universal goodness, as it ought in truth to be ascribed. Now this is not done by works, but only by faith of heart. It is not by working, but by believing, that we glorify God, and confess Him to be true. On this ground, faith alone is the righteousness of a Christian man, and the fulfilling of all the commandments. For to him who fulfils the first, the task of fulfilling all the rest is easy.

Works, since they are irrational things, cannot glorify God, although they may be done to the glory of God, if faith be present. But at present we are inquiring, not into the quality of the works done, but into him who does them, who glorifies God, and brings forth good works. This is faith of heart, the head and the substance of all our righteousness. Hence that is a blind and perilous doctrine which teaches that the commandments are fulfilled by works. The commandments must have been fulfilled previous to any good works, and good works follow their fulfillment, as we shall see.

But, that we may have a wider view of that grace which our inner man has in Christ, we must know that in the Old Testament, God sanctified to Himself every first-born male. The birthright was of great value, giving a superiority over the rest by the double honour of priesthood and kingship. For the first-born brother was priest and lord of all the rest.

Under this figure was foreshown Christ, the true and only First-born of God the Father and of the Virgin Mary, and a true King and Priest, not in a fleshly and earthly sense. For His kingdom is not of this world; it is in heavenly and spiritual things that He reigns and acts as Priest; and these are righteousness, truth, wisdom, peace, salvation, etc. Not but that all things, even those of earth and hell, are subject to Him—for otherwise how could He defend and save us from them?—but it is not in these, nor by these, that His kingdom stands.

So, too, His priesthood does not consist in the outward display of vestments and gestures, as did the human priesthood of Aaron and our ecclesiastical priesthood at this day, but in spiritual things, wherein, in His invisible office, He intercedes for us with God in heaven, and there offers Himself, and performs all the duties of a priest, as Paul describes Him to the Hebrews under the figure of Melchizedek. Nor does He only pray and intercede for us; He also teaches us inwardly in the spirit with the living teachings of His Spirit. Now these are the two special offices of a priest, as is figured to us in the case of fleshly priests by visible prayers and sermons.

As Christ by His birthright has obtained these two dignities, so He imparts and communicates them to every believer in Him, under that law of matrimony of which we have spoken above, by which all that is the husband's is also the wife's. Hence all we who believe on Christ are kings and priests in Christ, as it is said, "Ye are a chosen generation, a royal priesthood, a holy nation, a peculiar people, that ye should show forth the praises of Him who hath called you out of darkness into His marvellous light" (1 Peter ii. 9).

These two things stand thus. First, as regards kingship, every Christian is by faith so exalted above all things that, in spiritual power, he is completely lord of all things, so that nothing whatever can do him any hurt; yea, all things are subject to him, and are compelled to be subservient to his salvation. Thus Paul says, "All things work together for good to them who are called" (Rom. viii. 28), and also, "Whether life, or death, or things present, or things to come, all are yours; and ye are Christ's" (1 Cor. iii. 22, 23).

Not that in the sense of corporeal power any one among Christians has been appointed to possess and rule all things, according to the mad and senseless idea of certain ecclesiastics. That is the office of kings, princes, and men upon earth. In the experience of life we see that we are subjected to all things, and suffer many things, even death. Yea, the more of a Christian any man is, to so many the more evils, sufferings, and deaths is he subject, as we see in the first place in Christ the First-born, and in all His holy brethren.

This is a spiritual power, which rules in the midst of enemies, and is powerful in the midst of distresses. And this is nothing else than that strength is made perfect in my weakness, and that I can turn all things to the profit of my salvation; so that even the cross and death are compelled to serve me and to work together for my salvation. This is a lofty and eminent dignity, a true and almighty dominion, a spiritual empire, in which there is nothing so good, nothing so bad, as not to work together for my good, if only I believe. And yet there is nothing of which I have need—for faith alone suffices for my salvation—unless that in it faith may exercise the power and empire of its liberty. This is the inestimable power and liberty of Christians.

Nor are we only kings and the freest of all men, but also priests for ever, a dignity far higher than kingship, because by that priesthood we are worthy to appear before God, to pray for others, and to teach one another mutually the things which are of God. For these are the duties of priests, and they cannot possibly be permitted to any unbeliever. Christ has obtained for us this favour, if we believe in Him: that just as we are His brethren and co-heirs and fellow-kings with Him, so we should be also fellow-priests with Him, and venture with confidence, through the spirit of faith, to come into the presence of God, and cry, "Abba, Father!" and to pray for one another, and to do all things which we see done and figured in the visible and corporeal office of priesthood. But to an unbelieving person nothing renders service or work for good. He himself is in servitude to all things, and all things turn out for evil to him, because he uses all things in an impious way for his own advantage, and not for the glory of God. And thus he is not a priest, but a profane person, whose prayers are turned into sin, nor does he ever appear in the presence of God, because God does not hear sinners.

Who then can comprehend the loftiness of that Christian dignity which, by its royal power, rules over all things, even over death, life, and sin, and, by its priestly glory, is all-powerful with God, since God does what He Himself seeks and wishes, as it is written, "He will fulfil the desire of them that fear Him; He also will hear their cry, and will save them"? (Psalm cxlv. 19). This glory certainly cannot be attained by any works, but by faith only.

From these considerations any one may clearly see how a Christian man is free from all things; so that he needs no works in order to be justified and saved, but receives these gifts in abundance from faith alone. Nay, were he so foolish as to pretend to be justified, set free, saved, and made a Christian, by means of any good work, he would immediately lose faith, with all its benefits. Such folly is prettily represented in the fable where a dog, running along in the water and carrying in his mouth a real piece of meat, is deceived by the reflection of the meat in the water, and, in trying with open mouth to seize it, loses the meat and its image at the same time.

Here you will ask, "If all who are in the Church are priests, by what character are those whom we now call priests to be distinguished from the laity?" I reply, By the use of these words, "priest," "clergy," "spiritual person," "ecclesiastic," an injustice has been done, since they have been transferred from the remaining body of Christians to those few who are now, by hurtful custom, called ecclesiastics. For Holy Scripture makes no distinction between them, except that those who are now boastfully called popes, bishops, and lords, it calls ministers, servants, and stewards, who are to serve the rest in the ministry of the word, for teaching the faith of Christ and the liberty of believers. For though it is true that we are all equally priests, yet we cannot, nor, if we could, ought we all to, minister and teach publicly. Thus Paul says, "Let a man so account of us as of the ministers of Christ and stewards of the mysteries of God" (1 Cor. iv. 1).

This bad system has now issued in such a pompous display of power and such a terrible tyranny that no earthly government can be compared to it, as if the laity were something else than Christians. Through this perversion of things it has happened that the knowledge of Christian grace, of faith, of liberty, and altogether of Christ, has utterly perished, and has been succeeded by an intolerable bondage to human works and laws; and, according to the Lamentations of Jeremiah, we have become the slaves of the vilest men on earth, who abuse our misery to all the disgraceful and ignominious purposes of their own will.

Returning to the subject which we had begun, I think it is made clear by these considerations that it is not sufficient, nor a Christian course, to preach the works, life, and words of Christ in a historic manner, as facts which it suffices to know as an example how to frame our life, as do those who are now held the best preachers, and much less so to keep silence altogether on these things and to teach in their stead the laws of men and the decrees of the Fathers. There are now not a few persons who preach and read about Christ with the object of moving the human affections to sympathize with Christ, to indignation against the Jews, and other childish and womanish absurdities of that kind.

Now preaching ought to have the object of promoting faith in Him, so that He may not only be Christ, but a Christ for you and for me, and that what is said of Him, and what He is called, may work in us. And this faith is produced and is maintained by preaching why Christ came, what He has brought us and given to us, and to what profit and advantage He is to be received. This is done when the Christian liberty which we have from Christ Himself is rightly taught, and we are shown in what manner all we Christians are kings and priests, and how we are lords of all things, and may be confident that whatever we do in the presence of God is pleasing and acceptable to Him.

Whose heart would not rejoice in its inmost core at hearing these things? Whose heart, on receiving so great a consolation, would not become sweet with the love of Christ, a love to which it can never attain by any laws or works? Who can injure such a heart, or make it afraid? If the consciousness of sin or the horror of death rush in upon it, it is prepared to hope in the Lord, and is fearless of such evils, and undisturbed, until it shall look down upon its enemies. For it believes that the righteousness of Christ is its own, and that its sin is no longer its own, but that of Christ; but, on account of its faith in Christ, all its sin must needs be swallowed up from before the face of the righteousness of Christ, as I have said above. It learns, too, with the Apostle, to scoff at death and sin, and to say, "O death, where is thy sting? O grave, where is thy victory? The sting of death is sin, and the strength of sin is the law. But thanks be to God, which giveth us the victory through our Lord Jesus Christ" (1 Cor. xv. 55–57). For death is swallowed up in victory, not only the victory of Christ, but ours also, since by faith it becomes ours, and in it we too conquer.

Let it suffice to say this concerning the inner man and its liberty, and concerning that righteousness of faith which needs neither laws nor good works; nay, they are even hurtful to it, if any one pretends to be justified by them.

And now let us turn to the other part: to the outward man. Here we shall give an answer to all those who, taking offence at the word of faith and at what I have asserted, say, "If faith does everything, and by itself suffices for justification, why then are good works commanded? Are we then to take our ease and do no works, content with faith?" Not so, impious men, I reply; not so. That would indeed really be the case, if we were thoroughly and completely inner and spiritual persons; but that will not happen until the last day, when the dead shall be raised. As long as we live in the flesh, we are but beginning and making advances in that which shall be completed in a future life. On this account the Apostle calls that which we have in this life the first-fruits of the Spirit (Rom. viii. 23). In future we shall have the tenths, and the fullness of the Spirit. To this part belongs the fact I have stated before: that the Christian is the servant of all and subject to all. For in that part in which he is free he does no works, but in that in which he is a servant he does all works. Let us see on what principle this is so.

Although, as I have said, inwardly, and according to the spirit, a man is amply enough justified by faith, having all that he requires to have, except that this very faith and abundance ought to increase from day to day, even till the future life, still he remains in this mortal life upon earth, in which it is necessary that he should rule his own body and have intercourse with men. Here then works begin; here he must not take his ease; here he must give heed to exercise his body by fastings, watchings, labour, and other regular discipline, so that it may be subdued to the spirit, and obey and conform itself to the inner man and faith, and not rebel against them nor hinder them, as is its nature to do if it is not kept under. For the inner man, being conformed to God and created after the image of God through faith, rejoices and delights itself in Christ, in whom such blessings have been conferred on it, and hence has only this task before it: to serve God with joy and for nought in free love.

But in doing this he comes into collision with that contrary will in his own flesh, which is striving to serve the world and to seek its own gratification. This the spirit of faith cannot and will not bear, but applies itself with cheerfulness and zeal to keep it down and restrain it, as Paul says, "I delight in the law of God after the inward man; but I see another law in my members, warring against the law of my mind and bringing me into captivity to the law of sin" (Rom. vii. 22, 23), and again, "I keep under my body, and bring it unto subjection, lest that by any means, when I have preached to others, I myself should be a castaway" (1 Cor. ix. 27), and "They that are Christ's have crucified the flesh, with the affections and lusts" (Gal. v. 24).

These works, however, must not be done with any notion that by them a man can be justified before God—for faith, which alone is righteousness before God, will not bear with this false notion—but solely with this purpose: that the body may be brought into subjection, and be purified from its evil lusts, so that our eyes may be turned only to purging away those lusts. For when the soul has been cleansed by faith and made to love God, it would have all things to be cleansed in like manner, and especially its own body, so that all things might unite with it in the love and praise of God. Thus it comes that, from the requirements of his own body, a man cannot take his ease, but is compelled on its account to do many good works, that he may bring it into subjection. Yet these works are not the means of his justification before God; he does them out of disinterested love to the service of God; looking to no other end than to do what is well-pleasing to Him whom he desires to obey most dutifully in all things.

On this principle every man may easily instruct himself in what measure, and with what distinctions, he ought to chasten his own body. He will fast, watch, and labour, just as much as he sees to suffice for keeping down the wantonness and concupiscence of the body. But those who pretend to be justified by works are looking, not to the mortification of their lusts, but only to the works themselves; thinking that, if they can accomplish as many works and as great ones as possible, all is well with them, and they are justified. Sometimes they even injure their brain, and extinguish nature, or at least make it useless. This is enormous folly, and ignorance of Christian life and faith, when a man seeks, without faith, to be justified and saved by works.

To make what we have said more easily understood, let us set it forth under a figure. The works of a Christian man, who is justified and saved by his faith out of the pure and unbought mercy of God, ought to be regarded in the same light as would have been those of Adam and Eve in paradise and of all their posterity if they had not sinned. Of them it is said, "The Lord God took the man and put him into the garden of Eden to dress it and to keep it" (Gen. ii. 15). Now Adam had been created by God just and righteous, so that he could not have needed to be justified and made righteous by keeping the garden and working in it; but, that he might not be unemployed, God gave him the business of keeping and cultivating paradise. These would have indeed been works of perfect freedom, being done for no object but that of pleasing God, and not in order to obtain justification, which he already had to the full, and which would have been innate in us all.

So it is with the works of a believer. Being by his faith replaced afresh in paradise and created anew, he does not need works for his justification, but that he may not be idle, but may exercise his own body and preserve it. His works are to be done freely, with the sole object of pleasing God. Only we are not yet fully created anew in perfect faith and love; these require to be increased, not, however, through works, but through themselves.

A bishop, when he consecrates a church, confirms children, or performs any other duty of his office, is not consecrated as bishop by these works; nay, unless he had been previously consecrated as bishop, not one of those works would have any validity; they would be foolish, childish, and ridiculous. Thus a Christian, being consecrated by his faith, does good works; but he is not by these works made a more sacred person, or more a Christian. That is the effect of faith alone; nay, unless he were previously a believer and a Christian, none of his works would have any value at all; they would really be impious and damnable sins.

True, then, are these two sayings: "Good works do not make a good man, but a good man does good works"; "Bad works do not make a bad man, but a bad man does bad works." Thus it is always necessary that the substance or person should be good before any good works can be done, and that good works should follow and proceed from a good person. As Christ says, "A good tree cannot bring forth evil fruit, neither can a corrupt tree bring forth good fruit" (Matt. vii. 18). Now it is clear that the fruit does not bear the tree, nor does the tree grow on the fruit; but, on the contrary, the trees bear the fruit, and the fruit grows on the trees.

As then trees must exist before their fruit, and as the fruit does not make the tree either good or bad, but on the contrary, a tree of either kind produces fruit of the same kind, so must first the person of the man be good or bad before he can do either a good or a bad work; and his works do not make him bad or good, but he himself makes his works either bad or good.

We may see the same thing in all handicrafts. A bad or good house does not make a bad or good builder, but a good or bad builder makes a good or bad house. And in general no work makes the workman such as it is itself; but the workman makes the work such as he is himself. Such is the case, too, with the works of men. Such as the man himself is, whether in faith or in unbelief, such is his work: good if it be done in faith; bad if in unbelief. But the converse is not true that, such as the work is, such the man becomes in faith or in unbelief. For as works do not make a believing man, so neither do they make a justified man; but faith, as it makes a man a believer and justified, so also it makes his works good.

Since then works justify no man, but a man must be justified before he can do any good work, it is most evident that it is faith alone which, by the mere mercy of God through Christ, and by means of His word, can worthily and sufficiently justify and save the person; and that a Christian man needs no work, no law, for his salvation; for by faith he is free from all law, and in perfect freedom does gratuitously all that he does, seeking nothing either of profit or of salvation—since by the grace of God he is already saved and rich in all things through his faith—but solely that which is well-pleasing to God.

So, too, no good work can profit an unbeliever to justification and salvation; and, on the other hand, no evil work makes him an evil and condemned person, but that unbelief, which makes the person and the tree bad, makes his works evil and condemned. Wherefore, when any man is made good or bad, this does not arise from his works, but from his faith or unbelief, as the wise man says, "The beginning of sin is to fall away from God"; that is, not to believe. Paul says, "He that cometh to God must believe" (Heb. xi. 6); and Christ says the same thing: "Either make the tree good and his fruit good; or else make the tree corrupt and his fruit corrupt" (Matt. xii. 33),—as much as to say, He who wishes to have good fruit will begin with the tree, and plant a good one; even so he who wishes to do good works must begin, not by working, but by believing, since it is this which makes the person good. For nothing makes the person good but faith, nor bad but unbelief.

It is certainly true that, in the sight of men, a man becomes good or evil by his works; but here "becoming" means that it is thus shown and recognised who is good or evil, as Christ says, "By their fruits ye shall know them" (Matt. vii. 20). But all this stops at appearances and externals; and in this matter very many deceive themselves, when they presume to write and teach that we are to be justified by good works, and meanwhile make no mention even of faith, walking in their own ways, ever deceived and deceiving, going from bad to worse, blind leaders of the blind, wearying themselves with many works, and yet never attaining to true righteousness, of whom Paul says, "Having a form of godliness, but denying the power thereof, ever learning and never able to come to the knowledge of the truth" (2 Tim. iii. 5, 7).

He then who does not wish to go astray, with these blind ones, must look further than to the works of the law or the doctrine of works; nay, must turn away his sight from works, and look to the person, and to the manner in which it may be justified. Now it is justified and saved, not by works or laws, but by the word of God—

that is, by the promise of His grace—so that the glory may be to the Divine majesty, which has saved us who believe, not by works of righteousness which we have done, but according to His mercy, by the word of His grace.

From all this it is easy to perceive on what principle good works are to be cast aside or embraced, and by what rule all teachings put forth concerning works are to be understood. For if works are brought forward as grounds of justification, and are done under the false persuasion that we can pretend to be justified by them, they lay on us the yoke of necessity, and extinguish liberty along with faith, and by this very addition to their use they become no longer good, but really worthy of condemnation. For such works are not free, but blaspheme the grace of God, to which alone it belongs to justify and save through faith. Works cannot accomplish this, and yet, with impious presumption, through our folly, they take it on themselves to do so; and thus break in with violence upon the office and glory of grace.

We do not then reject good works; nay, we embrace them and teach them in the highest degree. It is not on their own account that we condemn them, but on account of this impious addition to them and the perverse notion of seeking justification by them. These things cause them to be only good in outward show, but in reality not good, since by them men are deceived and deceive others, like ravening wolves in sheep's clothing.

Now this leviathan, this perverted notion about works, is invincible when sincere faith is wanting. For those sanctified doers of works cannot but hold it till faith, which destroys it, comes and reigns in the heart. Nature cannot expel it by her own power; nay, cannot even see it for what it is, but considers it as a most holy will. And when custom steps in besides, and strengthens this pravity of nature, as has happened by means of impious teachers, then the evil is incurable, and leads astray multitudes to irreparable ruin. Therefore, though it is good to preach and write about penitence, confession, and satisfaction, yet if we stop there, and do not go on to teach faith, such teaching is without doubt deceitful and devilish. For Christ, speaking by His servant John, not only said, "Repent ye," but added, "for the kingdom of heaven is at hand" (Matt. iii. 2).

For not one word of God only, but both, should be preached; new and old things should be brought out of the treasury, as well the voice of the law as the word of grace. The voice of the law should be brought forward, that men may be terrified and brought to a knowledge of their sins, and thence be converted to penitence and to a better manner of life. But we must not stop here; that would be to wound only and not to bind up, to strike and not to heal, to kill and not to make alive, to bring down to hell and not to bring back, to humble and not to exalt. Therefore, the word of grace and of the promised remission of sin must also be preached, in order to teach and set up faith, since without that word contrition, penitence, and all other duties, are performed and taught in vain.

There still remain, it is true, preachers of repentance and grace, but they do not explain the law and the promises of God to such an end, and in such a spirit, that men may learn whence repentance and grace are to come. For repentance comes from the law of God, but faith or grace from the promises of God, as it is said, "Faith cometh by hearing, and hearing by the word of God" (Rom. x. 17), whence it comes that a man, when humbled and brought to the knowledge of himself by the threatenings and terrors of the law, is consoled and raised up by faith in the Divine promise. Thus "weeping may endure for a night, but joy cometh in the morning" (Psalm xxx. 5). Thus much we say concerning works in general, and also concerning those which the Christian practises with regard to his own body.

Lastly, we will speak also of those works which he performs towards his neighbour. For man does not live for himself alone in this mortal body, in order to work on its account, but also for all men on earth; nay, he lives only for others, and not for himself. For it is to this end that he brings his own body into subjection, that he may be able to serve others more sincerely and more freely, as Paul says, "None of us liveth to himself, and no man dieth to himself. For whether we live, we live unto the Lord; and whether we die, we die unto the Lord" (Rom. xiv. 7, 8). Thus it is impossible that he should take his ease in this life, and not work for the good of his neighbours, since he must needs speak, act, and converse among men, just as Christ was made in the likeness of men and found in fashion as a man, and had His conversation among men.

Yet a Christian has need of none of these things for justification and salvation, but in all his works he ought to entertain this view and look only to this object—that he may serve and be useful to others in all that he does; having nothing before his eyes but the necessities and the advantage of his neighbour. Thus the Apostle commands us to work with our own hands, that we may have to give to those that need. He might have said, that we may support ourselves; but he tells us to give to those that need. It is the part of a Christian to take care of his own body for the very purpose that, by its soundness and well-being, he may be enabled to labour, and to acquire and preserve property, for the aid of those who are in want, that thus the stronger member may serve the weaker member, and we may be children of God, thoughtful and busy one for another, bearing one another's burdens, and so fulfilling the law of Christ.

Here is the truly Christian life, here is faith really working by love, when a man applies himself with joy and love to the works of that freest servitude in which he serves others voluntarily and for nought, himself abundantly satisfied in the fulness and riches of his own faith.

Thus, when Paul had taught the Philippians how they had been made rich by that faith in Christ in which they had obtained all things, he teaches them further in these words: "If there be therefore any consolation in Christ, if any comfort of love, if any fellowship of the Spirit, if any bowels and mercies, fulfil ye my joy, that ye be like-minded, having the same love, being of one accord, of one mind. Let nothing be done through strife or vain-glory; but in lowliness of mind let each esteem other better than themselves. Look not every man on his own things, but every man also on the things of others" (Phil. ii. 1–4).

In this we see clearly that the Apostle lays down this rule for a Christian life: that all our works should be directed to the advantage of others, since every Christian has such abundance through his faith that all his other works and his whole life remain over and above wherewith to serve and benefit his neighbour of spontaneous goodwill.

To this end he brings forward Christ as an example, saying, "Let this mind be in you, which was also in Christ Jesus, who, being in the form of God, thought it not robbery to be equal with God, but made Himself of no reputation, and took upon Him the form of a servant, and was made in the likeness of men; and being found in fashion as a man, He humbled Himself, and became obedient unto death" (Phil. ii. 5-8). This most wholesome saying of the Apostle has been darkened to us by men who, totally misunderstanding the expressions "form of God," "form of a servant," "fashion," "likeness of men," have transferred them to the natures of Godhead and manhood. Paul's meaning is this: Christ, when He was full of the form of God and abounded in all good things, so that He had no need of works or sufferings to be just and saved—for all these things He had from the very beginning—yet was not puffed up with these things, and did not raise Himself above us and arrogate to Himself power over us, though He might lawfully have done so, but, on the contrary, so acted in labouring, working, suffering, and dying, as to be like the rest of men, and no otherwise than a man in fashion and in conduct, as if He were in want of all things and had nothing of the form of God; and yet all this He did for our sakes, that He might serve us, and that all the works He should do under that form of a servant might become ours.

Thus a Christian, like Christ his Head, being full and in abundance through his faith, ought to be content with this form of God, obtained by faith; except that, as I have said, he ought to increase this faith till it be perfected. For this faith is his life, justification, and salvation, preserving his person itself and making it pleasing to God, and bestowing on him all that Christ has, as I have said above, and as Paul affirms: "The life which I now live in the flesh I live by the faith of the Son of God" (Gal. ii. 20). Though he is thus free from all works, yet he ought to empty himself of this liberty, take on him the form of a servant, be made in the likeness of men, be found in fashion as a man, serve, help, and in every way act towards his neighbour as he sees that God through Christ has acted and is acting towards him. All this he should do freely, and with regard to nothing but the good pleasure of God, and he should reason thus:—

Lo! my God, without merit on my part, of His pure and free mercy, has given to me, an unworthy, condemned, and contemptible creature all the riches of justification and salvation in Christ, so that I no longer am in want of anything, except of faith to believe that this is so. For such a Father, then, who has overwhelmed me with these inestimable riches of His, why should I not freely, cheerfully, and with my whole heart, and from voluntary zeal, do all that I know will be pleasing to Him and acceptable in His sight? I will therefore give myself as a sort of Christ, to my neighbour, as Christ has given Himself to me; and will do nothing in this life except what I see will be needful, advantageous, and wholesome for my neighbour, since by faith I abound in all good things in Christ.

Thus from faith flow forth love and joy in the Lord, and from love a cheerful, willing, free spirit, disposed to serve our neighbour voluntarily, without taking any account of gratitude or ingratitude, praise or blame, gain or loss. Its object is not to lay men under obligations, nor does it distinguish between friends and enemies, or look to gratitude or ingratitude, but most freely and willingly spends itself and its goods, whether it loses them through ingratitude, or gains goodwill. For thus did its Father, distributing all things to all men abundantly and freely, making His sun to rise upon the just and the unjust. Thus, too, the child does and endures nothing except from the free joy with which it delights through Christ in God, the Giver of such great gifts.

You see, then, that, if we recognize those great and precious gifts, as Peter says, which have been given to us, love is quickly diffused in our hearts through the Spirit, and by love we are made free, joyful, all-powerful, active workers, victors over all our tribulations, servants to our neighbour, and nevertheless lords of all things. But, for those who do not recognize the good things given to them through Christ, Christ has been born in vain; such persons walk by works, and will never attain the taste and feeling of these great things. Therefore just as our neighbour is in want, and has need of our abundance, so we too in the sight of God were in want and had need of His mercy. And as our heavenly Father has freely helped us in Christ, so ought we freely to help our neighbour by our body and works, and each should become to other a sort of Christ, so that we may be mutually Christs, and that the same Christ may be in all of us; that is, that we may be truly Christians.

Who then can comprehend the riches and glory of the Christian life? It can do all things, has all things, and is in want of nothing; is lord over sin, death, and hell, and at the same time is the obedient and useful servant of all. But alas! it is at this day unknown throughout the world; it is neither preached nor sought after, so that we are quite ignorant about our own name, why we are and are called Christians. We are certainly called so from Christ, who is not absent, but dwells among us—provided, that is, that we believe in Him and are reciprocally and mutually one the Christ of the other, doing to our neighbour as Christ does to us. But now, in the doctrine of men, we are taught only to seek after merits, rewards, and things which are already ours, and we have made of Christ a taskmaster far more severe than Moses.

The Blessed Virgin beyond all others, affords us an example of the same faith, in that she was purified according to the law of Moses, and like all other women, though she was bound by no such law and had no need of purification. Still she submitted to the law voluntarily and of free love, making herself like the rest of women, that she might not offend or throw contempt on them. She was not justified by doing this; but, being already justified, she did it freely and gratuitously. Thus ought our works too to be done, and not in order to be justified by them; for, being first justified by faith, we ought to do all our works freely and cheerfully for the sake of others.

St. Paul circumcised his disciple Timothy, not because he needed circumcision for his justification, but that he might not offend or contemn those Jews, weak in the faith, who had not yet been able to comprehend the liberty of faith. On the other hand, when they contemned liberty and urged that circumcision was necessary for justification, he resisted them, and would not allow Titus to be circumcised. For, as he would not offend or contemn any one's weakness in faith, but yielded for the time to their will, so, again, he would not have the liberty of faith offended or contemned by hardened self-justifiers, but walked in a middle path, sparing the weak for the time, and always resisting the hardened, that he might convert all to the liberty of faith. On the same principle we ought to act, receiving those that are weak in the faith, but boldly resisting these hardened teachers of works, of whom we shall hereafter speak at more length.

Christ also, when His disciples were asked for the tribute money, asked of Peter whether the children of a king were not free from taxes. Peter agreed to this; yet Jesus commanded him to go to the sea, saying, "Lest we should offend them, go thou to the sea, and cast a hook, and take up the fish that first cometh up; and when thou hast opened his mouth thou shalt find a piece of money; that take, and give unto them for Me and thee" (Matt. xvii. 27).

This example is very much to our purpose; for here Christ calls Himself and His disciples free men and children of a King, in want of nothing; and yet He voluntarily submits and pays the tax. Just as far, then, as this work was necessary or useful to Christ for justification or salvation, so far do all His other works or those of His disciples avail for justification. They are really free and subsequent to justification, and only done to serve others and set them an example.

Such are the works which Paul inculcated, that Christians should be subject to principalities and powers and ready to every good work (Titus iii. 1), not that they may be justified by these things—for they are already justified by faith—but that in liberty of spirit they may thus be the servants of others and subject to powers, obeying their will out of gratuitous love.

Such, too, ought to have been the works of all colleges, monasteries, and priests; every one doing the works of his own profession and state of life, not in order to be justified by them, but in order to bring his own body into subjection, as an example to others, who themselves also need to keep under their bodies, and also in order to accommodate himself to the will of others, out of free love. But we must always guard most carefully against any vain confidence or presumption of being justified, gaining merit, or being saved by these works, this being the part of faith alone, as I have so often said.

Any man possessing this knowledge may easily keep clear of danger among those innumerable commands and precepts of the Pope, of bishops, of monasteries, of churches, of princes, and of magistrates, which some foolish pastors urge on us as being necessary for justification and salvation, calling them precepts of the Church, when they are not so at all. For the Christian freeman will speak thus: I will fast, I will pray, I will do this or that which is commanded me by men, not as having any need of these things for justification or salvation, but that I may thus comply with the will of the Pope, of the bishop, of such a community or such a magistrate, or of my neighbour as an example to him; for this cause I will do and suffer all things, just as Christ did and suffered much more for me, though He needed not at all to do so on His own account, and made Himself for my sake under the law, when He was not under the law. And although tyrants may do me violence or wrong in requiring obedience to these things, yet it will not hurt me to do them, so long as they are not done against God.

From all this every man will be able to attain a sure judgment and faithful discrimination between all works and laws, and to know who are blind and foolish pastors, and who are true and good ones. For whatsoever work is not directed to the sole end either of keeping under the body, or of doing service to our neighbour—provided he require nothing contrary to the will of God—is no good or Christian work. Hence I greatly fear that at this day few or no colleges, monasteries, altars, or ecclesiastical functions are Christian ones; and the same may be said of fasts and special prayers to certain saints. I fear that in all these, nothing is being sought but what is already ours; while we fancy that by these things our sins are purged away and salvation is attained, and thus utterly do away with Christian liberty. This comes from ignorance of Christian faith and liberty.

This ignorance and this crushing of liberty are diligently promoted by the teaching of very many blind pastors, who stir up and urge the people to a zeal for these things, praising them and puffing them up with their indulgences, but never teaching faith. Now I would advise you, if you have any wish to pray, to fast, or to make foundations in churches, as they call it, to take care not to do so with the object of gaining any advantage, either temporal or eternal. You will thus wrong your faith, which alone bestows all things on you, and the increase of which, either by working or by suffering, is alone to be cared for. What you give, give freely and without price, that others may prosper and have increase from you and your goodness. Thus you will be a truly good man and a Christian. For what to you are your goods and your works, which are done over and above for the subjection of the body, since you have abundance for yourself through your faith, in which God has given you all things?

We give this rule: the good things which we have from God ought to flow from one to another and become common to all, so that every one of us may, as it were, put on his neighbour, and so behave towards him as if he were himself in his place. They flowed and do flow from Christ to us; He put us on, and acted for us as if He Himself were what we are. From us they flow to those who have need of them; so that my faith and righteousness ought to be laid down before God as a covering and intercession for the sins of my neighbour, which I am to take on myself, and so labour and endure servitude in them, as if they were my own; for thus has Christ done for us. This is true love and the genuine truth of Christian life. But only there is it true and genuine where there is true and genuine faith. Hence the Apostle attributes to charity this quality: that she seeketh not her own.

We conclude therefore that a Christian man does not live in himself, but in Christ and in his neighbour, or else is no Christian: in Christ by faith; in his neighbour by love. By faith he is carried upwards above himself to God, and by love he sinks back below himself to his neighbour, still always abiding in God and His love, as Christ says, "Verily I say unto you, Hereafter ye shall see heaven open, and the angels of God ascending and descending upon the Son of man" (John i. 51).

Thus much concerning liberty, which, as you see, is a true and spiritual liberty, making our hearts free from all sins, laws, and commandments, as Paul says, "The law is not made for a righteous man" (1 Tim. i. 9), and one which surpasses all other external liberties, as far as heaven is above earth. May Christ make us to understand and preserve this liberty. Amen.

Finally, for the sake of those to whom nothing can be stated so well but that they misunderstand and distort it, we must add a word, in case they can understand even that. There are very many persons who, when they hear of this liberty of faith, straightway turn it into an occasion of licence. They think that everything is now lawful for them, and do not choose to show themselves free men and

Christians in any other way than by their contempt and reprehension of ceremonies, of traditions, of human laws; as if they were Christians merely because they refuse to fast on stated days, or eat flesh when others fast, or omit the customary prayers; scoffing at the precepts of men, but utterly passing over all the rest that belongs to the Christian religion. On the other hand, they are most pertinaciously resisted by those who strive after salvation solely by their observance of and reverence for ceremonies, as if they would be saved merely because they fast on stated days, or abstain from flesh, or make formal prayers; talking loudly of the precepts of the Church and of the Fathers, and not caring a straw about those things which belong to our genuine faith. Both these parties are plainly culpable, in that, while they neglect matters which are of weight and necessary for salvation, they contend noisily about such as are without weight and not necessary.

How much more rightly does the Apostle Paul teach us to walk in the middle path, condemning either extreme and saying, "Let not him that eateth despise him that eateth not; and let not him which eateth not judge him that eateth" (Rom. xiv. 3)! You see here how the Apostle blames those who, not from religious feeling, but in mere contempt, neglect and rail at ceremonial observances, and teaches them not to despise, since this "knowledge puffeth up." Again, he teaches the pertinacious upholders of these things not to judge their opponents. For neither party observes towards the other that charity which edifieth. In this matter we must listen to Scripture, which teaches us to turn aside neither to the right hand nor to the left, but to follow those right precepts of the Lord which rejoice the heart. For just as a man is not righteous merely because he serves and is devoted to works and ceremonial rites, so neither will he be accounted righteous merely because he neglects and despises them.

It is not from works that we are set free by the faith of Christ, but from the belief in works, that is from foolishly presuming to seek justification through works. Faith redeems our consciences, makes them upright, and preserves them, since by it we recognize the truth that justification does not depend on our works, although good works neither can nor ought to be absent, just as we cannot exist without food and drink and all the functions of this mortal body. Still it is not on them that our justification is based, but on faith; and yet they ought not on that account to be despised or neglected. Thus in this world we are compelled by the needs of this bodily life; but we are not hereby justified. "My kingdom is not hence, nor of this world," says Christ; but He does not say, "My kingdom is not here, nor in this world." Paul, too, says, "Though we walk in the flesh, we do not war after the flesh" (2 Cor. x. 3), and "The life which I now live in the flesh I live by the faith of the Son of God" (Gal. ii. 20). Thus our doings, life, and being, in works and ceremonies, are done from the necessities of this life, and with the motive of governing our bodies; but yet we are not justified by these things, but by the faith of the Son of God.

The Christian must therefore walk in the middle path, and set these two classes of men before his eyes. He may meet with hardened and obstinate ceremonialists, who, like deaf adders, refuse to listen to the truth of liberty, and cry up, enjoin, and urge on us their ceremonies, as if they could justify us without faith. Such were the Jews of old, who would not understand, that they might act well. These men we must resist, do just the contrary to what they do, and be bold to give them offence, lest by this impious notion of theirs they should deceive many along with themselves. Before the eyes of these men it is expedient to eat flesh, to break fasts, and to do in behalf of the liberty of faith things which they hold to be the greatest sins. We must say of them, "Let them alone; they be blind leaders of the blind" (Matt. xv. 14). In this way Paul also would not have Titus circumcised, though these men urged it; and Christ defended the Apostles, who had plucked ears of corn on the Sabbath day; and many like instances.

Or else we may meet with simple-minded and ignorant persons, weak in the faith, as the Apostle calls them, who are as yet unable to apprehend that liberty of faith, even if willing to do so. These we must spare, lest they should be offended. We must bear with their infirmity, till they shall be more fully instructed. For since these men do not act thus from hardened malice, but only from weakness of faith, therefore, in order to avoid giving them offence, we must keep fasts and do other things which they consider necessary.

This is required of us by charity, which injures no one, but serves all men. It is not the fault of these persons that they are weak, but that of their pastors, who by the snares and weapons of their own traditions have brought them into bondage and wounded their souls when they ought to have been set free and healed by the teaching of faith and liberty. Thus the Apostle says, "If meat make my brother to offend, I will eat no flesh while the world standeth" (1 Cor. viii. 13); and again, "I know, and am persuaded by the Lord Jesus, that there is nothing unclean of itself; but to him that esteemeth anything to be unclean, to him it is unclean. It is evil for that man who eateth with offence" (Rom. xiv. 14, 20).

Thus, though we ought boldly to resist those teachers of tradition, and though the laws of the pontiffs, by which they make aggressions on the people of God, deserve sharp reproof, yet we must spare the timid crowd, who are held captive by the laws of those impious tyrants, till they are set free. Fight vigorously against the wolves, but on behalf of the sheep, not against the sheep. And this you may do by inveighing against the laws and lawgivers, and yet at the same time observing these laws with the weak, lest they be offended, until they shall themselves recognize the tyranny, and understand their own liberty. If you wish to use your liberty, do it secretly, as Paul says, "Hast thou faith? have it to thyself before God" (Rom. xiv. 22). But take care not to use it in the presence of the weak. On the other hand, in the presence of tyrants and obstinate opposers, use your liberty in their despite, and with the utmost pertinacity, that they too may understand that they are tyrants, and their laws useless for justification, nay that they had no right to establish such laws.

Since then we cannot live in this world without ceremonies and works, since the hot and inexperienced period of youth has need of being restrained and protected by such bonds, and since every one is bound to keep under his own body by attention to these things, therefore the minister of Christ must be prudent and faithful in so ruling and teaching the people of Christ, in all these matters, that no root of bitterness may spring up among them, and so many be defiled, as Paul warned the Hebrews; that is, that they may not lose the faith, and begin to be defiled by a belief in works as the means of justification. This is a thing which easily happens, and defiles very many, unless faith be constantly inculcated along with works. It is impossible to avoid this evil, when faith is passed over in silence, and only the ordinances of men are taught, as has been done hitherto by the pestilent, impious, and soul-destroying traditions of our pontiffs and opinions of our theologians. An infinite number of souls have been drawn down to hell by these snares, so that you may recognize the work of antichrist.

In brief, as poverty is imperilled amid riches, honesty amid business, humility amid honours, abstinence amid feasting, purity amid pleasures, so is justification by faith imperilled among ceremonies. Solomon says, "Can a man take fire in his bosom, and his clothes not be burned?" (Prov. vi. 27). And yet as we must live among riches, business, honours, pleasures, feastings, so must we among ceremonies, that is among perils. Just as infant boys have the greatest need of being cherished in the bosoms and by the care of girls, that they may not die, and yet, when they are grown, there is peril to their salvation in living among girls, so inexperienced and fervid young men require to be kept in and restrained by the barriers of ceremonies, even were they of iron, lest their weak minds should rush headlong into vice. And yet it would be death to them to persevere in believing that they can be justified by these things. They must rather be taught that they have been thus imprisoned, not with the purpose of their being justified or gaining merit in this way, but in order that they might avoid wrong-doing, and be more easily instructed in that righteousness which is by faith, a thing which the headlong character of youth would not bear unless it were put under restraint.

Hence in the Christian life ceremonies are to be no otherwise looked upon than as builders and workmen look upon those preparations for building or working which are not made with any view of being permanent or anything in themselves, but only because without them there could be no building and no work. When the structure is completed, they are laid aside. Here you see that we do not contemn these preparations, but set the highest value on them; a belief in them we do contemn, because no one thinks that they constitute a real and permanent structure. If any one were so manifestly out of his senses as to have no other object in life but that of setting up these preparations with all possible expense, diligence, and perseverance, while he never thought of the structure itself, but pleased himself and made his boast of these useless preparations and props, should we not all pity his madness and think that, at the cost thus thrown away, some great building might have been raised?

Thus, too, we do not contemn works and ceremonies—nay, we set the highest value on them; but we contemn the belief in works, which no one should consider to constitute true righteousness, as do those hypocrites who employ and throw away their whole life in the pursuit of works, and yet never attain to that for the sake of which the works are done. As the Apostle says, they are "ever learning and never able to come to the knowledge of the truth" (2 Tim. iii. 7). They appear to wish to build, they make preparations, and yet they never do build; and thus they continue in a show of godliness, but never attain to its power.

Meanwhile they please themselves with this zealous pursuit, and even dare to judge all others, whom they do not see adorned with such a glittering display of works; while, if they had been imbued with faith, they might have done great things for their own and others' salvation, at the came cost which they now waste in abuse of the gifts of God. But since human nature and natural reason, as they call it, are naturally superstitious, and quick to believe that justification can be attained by any laws or works proposed to them, and since nature is also exercised and confirmed in the same view by the practice of all earthly lawgivers, she can never of her own power free herself from this bondage to works, and come to a recognition of the liberty of faith.

We have therefore need to pray that God will lead us and make us taught of God, that is, ready to learn from God; and will Himself, as He has promised, write His law in our hearts; otherwise there is no hope for us. For unless He himself teach us inwardly this wisdom hidden in a mystery, nature cannot but condemn it and judge it to be heretical. She takes offence at it, and it seems folly to her, just as we see that it happened of old in the case of the prophets and Apostles, and just as blind and impious pontiffs, with their flatterers, do now in my case and that of those who are like me, upon whom, together with ourselves, may God at length have mercy, and lift up the light of His countenance upon them, that we may know His way upon earth and His saving health among all nations, who is blessed for evermore. Amen. In the year of the Lord MDXX.

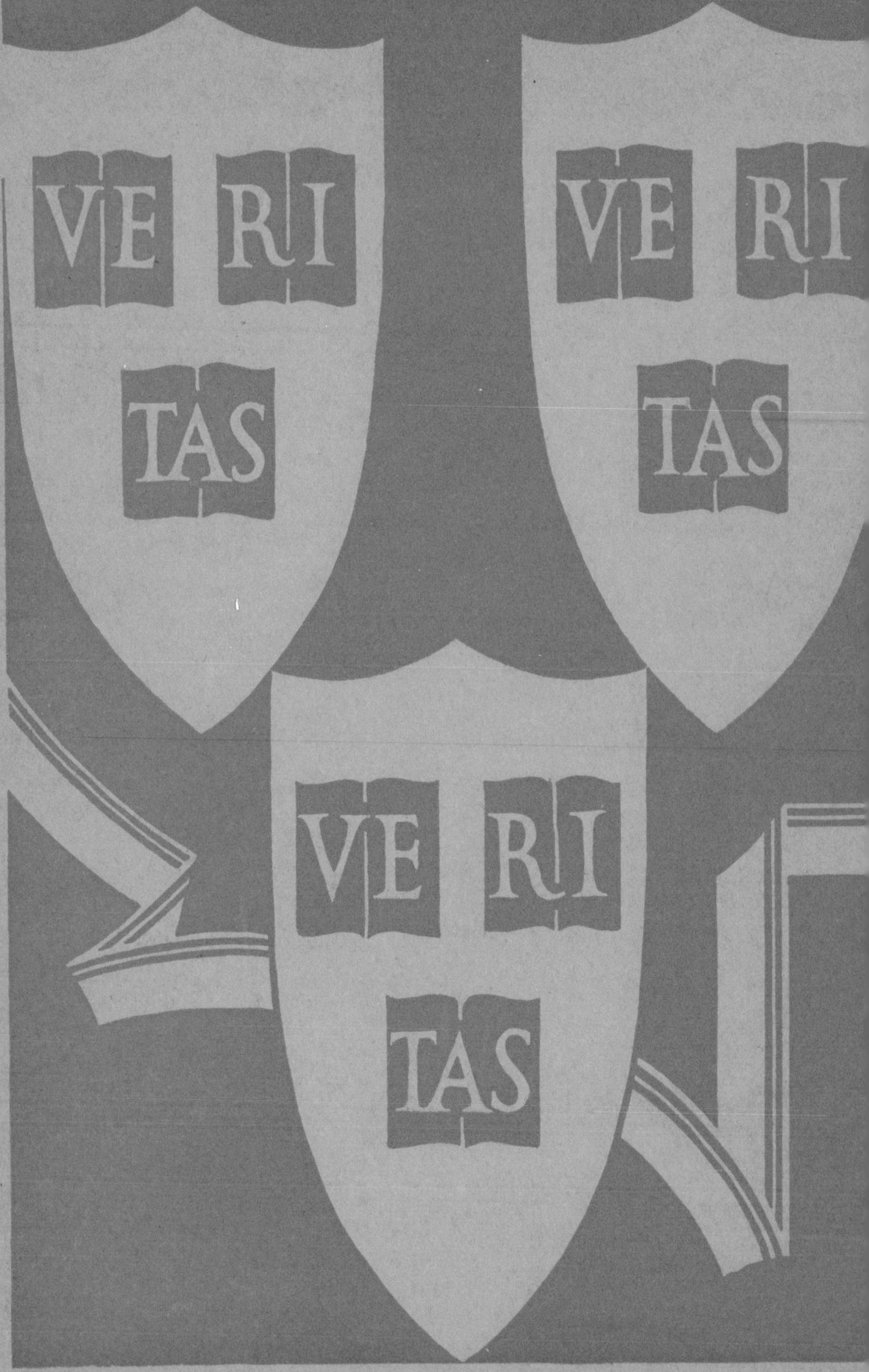
VE RI
TAS
VE RI
TAS
VE RI
TAS